MULTIMEDIA TECHNOLOGIES
AND APPLICATIONS FOR
THE 21st CENTURY
Visions of World Experts

THE KLUWER INTERNATIONAL SERIES IN ENGINEERING AND COMPUTER SCIENCE

MULTIMEDIA SYSTEMS AND APPLICATIONS

Consulting Editor

Borko Furht
Florida Atlantic University

Recently Published Titles:

BUFFERING TECHNIQUES FOR DELIVERY OF COMPRESSED VIDEO IN VIDEO-ON-DEMAND SYSTEMS, by Wu-chi Feng
ISBN: 0-7923-9998-6
HUMAN FACE RECOGNITION USING THIRD-ORDER SYNTHETIC NEURAL NETWORKS, by Okechukwu A. Uwechue, and Abhijit S. Pandya
ISBN: 0-7923-9957-9
MULTIMEDIA INFORMATION SYSTEMS, by Marios C. Angelides and Schahram Dustdar
ISBN: 0-7923-9915-3
MOTION ESTIMATION ALGORITHMS FOR VIDEO COMPRESSION, by Borko Furht, Joshua Greenberg and Raymond Westwater
ISBN: 0-7923-9793-2
VIDEO DATA COMPRESSION FOR MULTIMEDIA COMPUTING, edited by Hua Harry Li, Shan Sun, Haluk Derin
ISBN: 0-7923-9790-8
REAL-TIME VIDEO COMPRESSION: Techniques and Algorithms, by Raymond Westwater and Borko Furht
ISBN: 0-7923-9787-8
MULTIMEDIA DATABASE MANAGEMENT SYSTEMS, by B. Prabhakaran
ISBN: 0-7923-9784-3
MULTIMEDIA TOOLS AND APPLICATIONS, edited by Borko Furht
ISBN: 0-7923-9721-5
MULTIMEDIA SYSTEMS AND TECHNIQUES, edited by Borko Furht
ISBN: 0-7923-9683-9
VIDEO AND IMAGE PROCESSING IN MULTIMEDIA SYSTEMS, by Borko Furht, Stephen W. Smoliar, HongJiang Zhang
ISBN: 0-7923-9604-9

MULTIMEDIA TECHNOLOGIES AND APPLICATIONS FOR THE 21st CENTURY
Visions of World Experts

edited by

Borko Furht
Florida Atlantic University

KLUWER ACADEMIC PUBLISHERS
Boston / Dordrecht / London

Distributors for North America:
Kluwer Academic Publishers
101 Philip Drive
Assinippi Park
Norwell, Massachusetts 02061 USA

Distributors for all other countries:
Kluwer Academic Publishers Group
Distribution Centre
Post Office Box 322
3300 AH Dordrecht, THE NETHERLANDS

Library of Congress Cataloging-in-Publication Data
Multimedia technologies and applications for the 21st century :
  visions of world experts / edited by Borko Furht.
    p.   cm. -- (The Kluwer international series in engineering and
  computer science ; SECS 431)
    Includes bibliographical references and index.
    ISBN 0-7923-8074-6 (alk. paper)
    1. Multimedia systems.   I. Furht, Borivoje.   II. Series.
  QA76.575.M8522   1998
  006.7--dc21   97-32126
                                                                    CIP

Printed on acid-free paper.

Printed in the United States of America

CONTENTS

PREFACE

The main objective of this book is to excite the curiosity of its readers and inspire new technological breakthroughs in this exciting field.

Only a few years ago multimedia seemed like a brand new research field and an emerging new industry. Today, at the edge of 21st century, multimedia research is coming of age, and the multimedia industry has significantly grown with the total market estimated to be about $50 billion. Several years ago it was taught that the digital media revolution had just started; however, the seeds had been sown long before. The historical road map of digital media, illustrated in Figure 1, shows that fundamental technologies, such as interactive laser disks, video games, and electronic encyclopedias were invented in 1970s and 80s. They represented the seeds for presently "hot" applications, such as digital libraries, video-on-demand, interactive television, and videoconferencing.

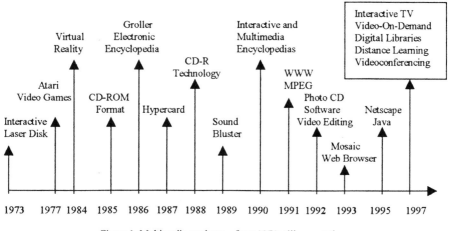

Figure 1. Multimedia roadmap – from 1970s till present time.

Another aspect of the digital media revolution is the forming of a new media industry comprised of computer, entertainment, communication, and consumer electronics companies. Many industry segments are currently involved in creating new products and services, positioning themselves for the 21st century. They include telephone, cable, and satellite TV companies, communication equipment companies, TV and radio broadcasters, on-line Internet service providers, cable channels, movie studios, record companies, book publishers, CD-ROM title creators, Internet tool vendors, multimedia software tools companies, computer companies, general software tools companies, computer add-on vendors, semiconductor vendors, and consumer electronics vendors.

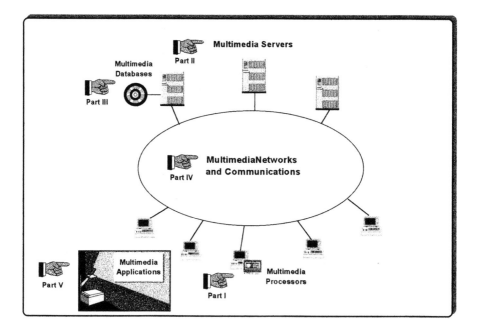

Figure 2. Issues in distributed multimedia systems covered in this book.

We invited a group of leading researchers and experts in the field to contribute to this book with their visionary articles, describing their current research and their views of the future trends in the field. The book consists of 13 chapters divided into five parts. These chapters tackle a number of critical issues in distributed multimedia systems and applications – from VLSI processors that support multimedia and multimedia servers, to multimedia databases and multimedia

Networks and communications, to merging multimedia applications, as illustrated in Figure 2.

This book is intended to serve as a valuable reference for system designers, engineers, programmers, and managers who are involved in multimedia systems, the Internet, and their applications. This book can also be used as a textbook for advanced courses on multimedia in engineering curricula.

Borko Furht
Boca Raton, Florida

PART I

MULTIMEDIA PROCESSORS

1

Processor Architectures
for Multimedia

BORKO FURHT
Department of Computer Science and Engineering
Florida Atlantic University
Boca Raton, Florida 33431

Abstract. In this chapter, we present contemporary VLSI processor architectures that support multimedia applications. We classified these processors into two groups: dedicated multimedia processors, which perform dedicated multimedia functions, such as MPEG encoding or decoding, and general-purpose processors that provide support for multimedia. Dedicated multimedia processors use either function-specific architectures with limited flexibility but higher speed and efficiency, or programmable architectures with increased flexibility. Both architectures are exploring parallelism inherent in video and image applications by applying single-instruction, multiple-data (SIMD) or/and very-large-instruction-word (VLIW) concepts. Advanced general-purpose processors provide the support for multimedia by incorporating new multimedia instructions and executing them in parallel by using the SIMD coprocessor approach. A survey of these processor architectures and their performance is presented in this chapter.

Keywords: multimedia processors, function-oriented architectures, complexity

1. Introduction and Classification

During the last few years we have been witnessing the process of "posing" for multimedia: from PC and workstation manufacturers (multimedia PCs and workstations), and add-in-board vendors (video and audio capture and playback cards), and silicon vendors (compression and graphics chips), to operating systems designers (OS support for multimedia) and software creators (authoring tools and a variety of multimedia applications). The last players to enter this poising game have been microprocessor designers.

In this chapter, we present a survey of processor architectures designed to support multimedia applications. Designs of these architectures ranges from fully custom to fully programmable dedicated architectures, and to general-purpose processor architectures with an extensive support for multimedia. The classification of these architectures is shown in Figure 1.

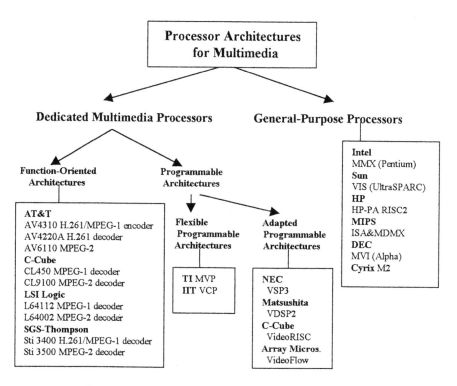

Figure 1. Classification of processor architectures that support multimedia.

Dedicated multimedia processors are typically custom designed architectures intended to perform specific multimedia functions. These functions usually include video and audio compression and decompression, and in this case these processors are referred to as video codecs. Besides the support for compression, some advanced multimedia processors provide also support for 2D and 3D graphics applications. Designs of dedicated multimedia processors ranges from fully custom architectures, referred to as function specific architectures, with minimal programmability, to fully programmable architectures. Furthermore, programmable architectures can be classified to flexible programmable architectures, which provide moderate to high flexibility, and adapted programmable architectures, which provide an increased efficiency and less flexibility [1]. The dedicated multimedia processors use a variety of architectural schemes: from multiple functional units and a RISC or DSP (digital signal processor) core processors to multiple processor schemes. Furthermore, the latest dedicated processors use single-instruction-multiple-data (SIMD) and very-long-instruction-word (VLIW) architectures, as well as some hybrid schemes. These architectures are presented in Section 3.

General-purpose (GP) processors provide support for multimedia by including multimedia instructions into the instruction set. Instead performing specific multimedia functions (such as compression and 2D/3D graphics), GP processors provide instructions specifically created to support generic operations in video processing. For example, these instructions include support for 8-bit data types (pixels), efficient data addressing and I/O instructions, and even instructions to support motion estimation. The latest processors, such as MMX (Intel), VIS (Sun) and MAX-2 (HP), incorporate some types of SIMD architectures, which perform the same operation on multiple data elements in parallel.

2.   Complexity of Multimedia Functions

In video and signal processing applications, a measure of algorithmic complexity is the total number of operations per second, expressed in MOPS (million operations per second), or GOPS (giga operations per second). This measure incorporates the total number of primitive operations needed to perform specific functions, and includes data load and store operations as well as arithmetic and logic operations on data elements.

For illustration purposes, we present the calculation of the complexity, adapted from [2], for an MPEG-2 decoder, shown in Figure 2. We assume that encoded bit rate for the input bit sequence is 4 Mbps. Assuming that the average symbol size is 4 bits, the average rate is then 1 million symbols/second.

The input video is 720x480 at 30 fps, encoded in 4:2:0 YUV format. In 4:2:0 format, Y component contains 720x480 pixels, while U and V components have 320x240 pixels. Total number of 8x8 blocks in each frame is 90x60=5,400 (in Y) and 45x30=1,350 (in U and V). This gives 8,100 blocks in each frame, and total of 8,100 x 30 sec=243,000 blocks per second. The MPEG sequence used for this calculation includes group of pictures (GOP) consisting of 1 I-, 4 P-, and 10 B-frames.

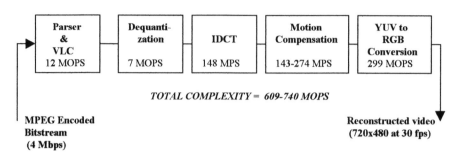

Figure 2. MPEG decoder and the complexity of its blocks.

Block 1: Bit stream parser and variable length (Huffman) decoder
The decoding of 1 symbols requires the following operations:

- 1 compare, 1 subtract, and 1 shift for grabbing a variable number of bits from data buffer (total 3 operations),
- 1 load, 2 shifts, and 1 mask for searching for a code in a code table (total 4 operations), and
- 1 compare, 1 subtract,1 shift, 1 add, and 1 mask for updating the data buffer (total 5 operations).

This gives total of 12 operations per symbol, and total of 12 x 1million symbols = 12 MOPS for this block.

Block 2: Dequantization
The dequantization, applied to each non-zero DCT coefficient, requires the following operations:

- 1 load for reading the quantizer scale matrix (total 1 operation),
- 2 integer multiplications and 1 division (by a constant of 8 or 16) for dequantization (total 3 operations), and
- 2 logical, 1 compare, 1 shift, and 1 add for the oddification (total 5 operations).

The total operation count for one DCT coefficient is 9 operations. Among 1 millions symbols we assume that 80% are coded DCT coefficients. This gives the total complexity of the quantization block: 9 x 800,000 = 7.2 MOPS.

Block 3: Inverse Discrete Cosine Transform (IDCT)
There are many different implementations for the inverse DCT. For illustration purpose, we assume the fast inverse DCT algorithm, described in [3] that requires the following operations:

- 464 additions, 80 integer multiplications, and 64 stores for each 8x8 block (total 608 operations per block).

Then, the total complexity of the IDCT block becomes: 243,000 blocks x 608 = 147.7 MOPS. Since not every block is coded in a P- or B-frame, this is the maximum complexity for using the fast IDCT.

Block 4: Motion compensation
The worst case scenario is that all blocks in a P-frame are motion compensated with 4-pixel interpolation and all blocks in a B-frame are motion compensated with 8-pixel interpolation from two predictor frames. For an 8x8 block in a P-frame, the following operations are required:

- 8x9x2=144 load operations for reading blocks with both horizontal and vertical overlapping (total 144 operations),
- 3 additions and 1 shift for interpolating one predictor pixel (total 4x64=256 operations), and
- 1 load, 1 addition, 2 compares, 1 assignment, and 1 store for reconstructing the pixel (total 6x64=384 operations).

The total number of operations for each block is 784. Because there are 8 P-frames in one-second sequence, the total complexity for P-frames is: 8 x 8,100 blocks x 784 = 50.8 MOPS.

For each 8x8 block in a B-frame, the following operations are required:

- 2x(8x9x2)=288 operations for reading blocks from two predictor frames (total 288 operations),
- 3 additions and 1 shift for interpolating one predictor pixel from the first frame (total 4x64=256 operations),
- 3 additions and 1 shift for interpolating one predictor pixel from the second frame (total 4x64=256 operations),
- 2 additions and 1 shift for forming the final pixel predictors (total 3x64=192 operations), and
- 1 load, 1 addition, 2 compares, 1 assignment, and 1 store for reconstructing the pixel with clipping (total 6x64=384 operations).

The total number of operations for each block is 1,376. There are total of 20 B-frames in one-second sequence, and therefore the total complexity for B frames is: 20 x 8,100 blocks x 1,376 = 222.9 MOPS. Adding complexities for P and B frames, the complexity for motion compensation becomes 273.7 MOPS.

The best case scenario for motion compensation is when all P and B frame blocks have no pixel interpolation. Then, the total number of operations is 143.1 MOPS.

Block 5: YUV to RGB color conversion

The conversion from YUV to RGB color format, based on CCIR-601 standard, can be done using the following formula:

$$\begin{bmatrix} R \\ G \\ B \end{bmatrix} = \begin{bmatrix} 1.1644 & 0 & 1.5966 \\ 1.1644 & -0.3920 & -0.8132 \\ 1.1644 & 2.0184 & 0 \end{bmatrix} \begin{bmatrix} Y - 16 \\ U - 128 \\ V - 128 \end{bmatrix}$$

(1)

where Y, U/V are clipped prior to transform to the ranges [16,240], and [16,235], respectively.

The following operations are required for each pixel:

- 1.5 loads for reading YUV (total 1.5 operation per pixel),
- 1.5 subtractions, 2.5 compares, and 3 assignments for YUV clipping (total 7 operations per pixel),
- 2 integer multiplications, 3.25 additions, and 3 shifts for the transformation (total 8.25 operations per pixel),
- 6 compares and 3 assignments for RGB clipping (total 9 operations per pixel), and
- 3 stores for writing RGB (total 3 operations per pixel).

The total number of operations per each pixel is 28.75. In the 4:2:0 YUV format, there are 4 Ys, 1 U and 1 V for each pixel. The total number of pixels in one second becomes 10.4 millions, which gives the total complexity for YUV to RGB color conversation: 28.5 x 10.4 millions = 299 MOPS.

In summary the complexity of the analyzed MPEG decoder is in the range from 609.0 to 739.6 MOPS, as indicated in Figure 2.

Table 1 shows complexities of various H.261 and MPEG encoders and decoders, reported in the literature. They differ from one to another implementation due to different implementations of DCT and IDCT algorithms, search algorithms for motion estimation, and formulas used for RGB to YUV transformations.

H.261 CODECS	Complexity of Encoders [MOPS]	Complexity of Decoders [MOPS]
CIF format at 30 fps Fast implementation of DCT Logarithmic search for motion estimation [5]	968	198
CIF at 15 fps Exhaustive motion estimation algorithm [4]	1,240-1,320	220-315
CIF at 30 fps Exhaustive motion estimation algorithm [4]	2,480-2,640	440-630
CIF at 30 fps Logarithmic search for motion estimation [6]	Total Encoder/Decoder 1,193	Total Encoder/Decoder 1,193

	Complexity of Encoders [MOPS]			Complexity of Decoders [MOPS]		
MPEG CODECS [5]	SIF 352x240	CCIR 601 720x486	HDTV 1440x1152	SIF 352x240	CCIR 601 720x486	HDTV 1440x1152
No B-frames	738	3,020	14,498	96	395	1,898
20% B-frames	847	3,467	16,645	101	415	1,996
50% B-frames	1,011	4,138	19,865	108	446	2,143
70% B-frames	1,120	4,585	22,012	113	466	2,241

Table 1. MOPS requirements for (a) various H.261 and (b) MPEG encoders and decoders, reported in the literature [4], [5], [6].

MOPS requirements for a variety of multimedia functions are estimated and presented in Figure 3. In the same figure, the current trends in computing power of GP processors, programmable digital signal processors and programmable video processors is plotted [5],[7]. It can be concluded that today is achievable to implement MPEG-1 or MPEG-2 decoders using GP or DSP processors. However, the encoder requirements, which are more than 1000 MOPS, are still outside of the complexity of GP processors, and therefore dedicated multimedia processors must be designed.

3.   Dedicated Multimedia Processors

In designing dedicated multimedia processors, the selection of architectures depends on the speed requirements of the target function, and the constraints on circuit integration, performance, power requirements, and cost. In order to assess and

$$E = \frac{1}{Asi \times Tp} \tag{2}$$

where:
Asi is the required silicon area for a specific architecture under evaluation, and
Tp is the effective processing time for one sample.

A comprehensive evaluation of dedicated multimedia processors can be found in
[1]. Dedicated multimedia processors, presented in this section, are based on
function specific architectures and programmable architectures.

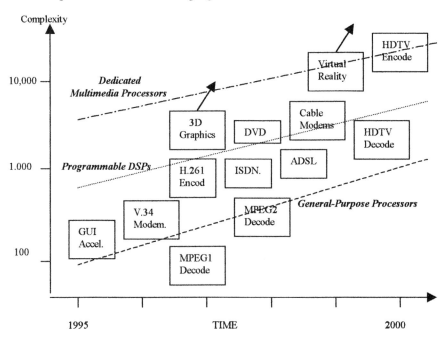

Figure 3. MOPS requirements for various multimedia functions and current trends in computing power.

3.1 Function Specific Architectures

Function specific dedicated multimedia architectures provide limited, if any,
programmability, because they use dedicated architectures for a specific encoding or
decoding standard. However, their efficiency and speed are typically better
compared to programmable architectures. The silicon area optimization achieved by
function specific architectures allows lower production cost.

Regardless of implementation details, the general design theme for dedicated multimedia processors consists of using:

- DSP or RISC core processor for main control, and
- special hardware accelerators for the DCT, quantization, entropy encoding, and motion estimation.

Block diagram of a typical function specific architecture for a video encoder is shown in Figure 4. In the first generation of function specific video processors, each of these functions was implemented in one chip, and a chipset was necessary to create the system for encoding or decoding. However, the next generations of function specific architectures integrate all these functions in a single VLSI chip.

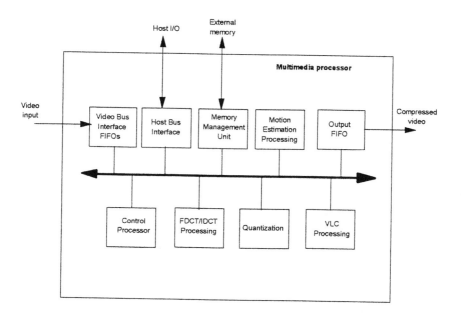

Figure 4. Block diagram of a typical function specific architecture for a video encoder. The dedicated processors (or functional units) are used for various operations, such as DCT, quantization, variable length coding (VLC), motion estimation, etc.

Some popular commercially available dedicated function specific video processors are listed in Figure 1.

3.2 Programmable Dedicated Architectures

In contrast to function oriented approach with limited flexibility, programmable architectures enable the processing of different tasks under software control. The main advantage of programmable architectures is the increased flexibility. Changes of architectural requirements, such as changes of algorithms or an extension of the application domain, can be handled by software changes.

On the other hand, programmable architectures require a higher cost for design and manufacturing, since additional hardware for program control is required. In addition, programmable architectures require software development for the application. Video coding applications require a real-time processing of the image data, and therefore parallelization strategies have to be applied.

Two alternative programmable architectures include:

Flexible programmable architectures, with moderate to high flexibility, are based on coprocessor concept as well as parallel datapaths and deeply pipelined designs. An example of a commercially available video processor, based on flexible programmable architecture, is TI's Multimedia Video Processor (MVP) TMS320C80 [6]. The MVP combines a RISC master processor and four DSP processors in a crossbar-based SIMD shared-memory architecture, as shown in Figure 5.

The master processor can be used for control, floating-point operations, audio processing, or 3D graphics transformations. Each DSP performs all the typical operations of a general-purpose DSP and can also perform bit-field and multiple-pixel operations. Each DSP has multiple functional elements (multiplier, ALU, local registers, a barrel shifter, address generators, and a program-control flow unit), all controlled by very long 64-bit instruction words (VLIW concept). The RISC processor, DSP processors, and the memory modules are fully interconnected through the global crossbar network that can be switched at the instruction clock rate of 20 ns. A 50 MHz MVP executes more than 2 GOPS.

The MVP has been integrated into the MediaStation 5000, programmable multimedia system [8]. Its key function in this system is MPEG compression. The data flow in the system during MPEG compression is shown in Figure 6. Video data is captured into the video buffer at a resolution of 320x240. The MVP reads the data from the video buffer and stores it in the main (DRAM) memory. The MVP performs all MPEG compression functions on the data stored in the main memory. Similar operations are performed on the digitized audio samples. Once when the MVP completes the compression of a video or audio frame, the compressed bit stream is sent to the host computer, where the audio and video streams are multiplexed together, synchronized, and stored on a disk or transferred to a network.

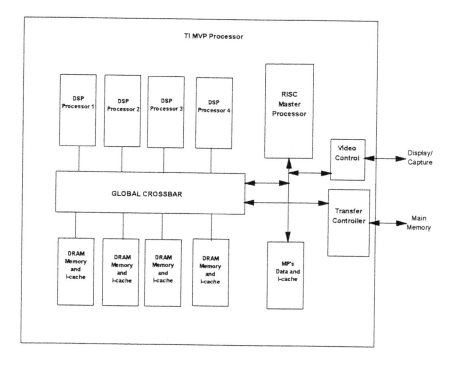

Figure 5. Block diagram of the TI's Multimedia Video Processor

Performance results, reported in [8], show that the MediaStation 5000 system can achieve a real-time compression (30 fps) of MPEG-1 video sequences with resolutions of 320x240 (SIF format). The reported compression times for I frames is 17.7 ms, for P frames 27.3 ms, and for B frames 30.5 ms; for all frame types less than the video frame period of 33 ms. Multiple MVPs are needed for real-time MPEG-2 encoding.

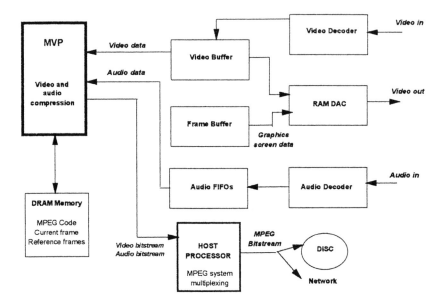

Figure 6. Data flow in the MVP during the MPEG compression [8].

Adapted programmable architectures provide increased efficiency by adapting the architecture to the specific requirements of video coding applications. These architectures provide dedicated modules for several tasks of the video codec algorithm, such as DCT module, or variable length coding [9],[10].

Examples of a commercially available multimedia processor based on adapted programmable architecture are VideoRISC processors (VRP and VRP2) from C-Cube Microsystems. The VRP2 processor consists of a 32-bit RISC processor and two special functional units for variable-length coding and motion estimation, as shown in the block diagram in Figure 7. Specially designed instructions in the RISC processor provide an efficient implementation of the DCT and other video-related operations. The VRP can perform real-time MPEG-1 encoding and decoding. However, the real-time MPEG-2 encoding requires the design consisting of 8 to 13 VRP2 processors.

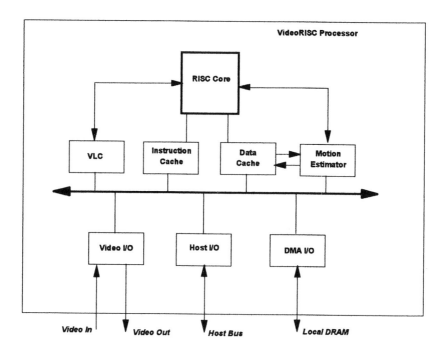

Figure 7. Block diagram of the C-Cube's VideoRISC processor, which applies an adapted programmable architecture.

Table 2, adapted from [5], shows commercially available programmable processors and their features.

Comparison of these two programmable architectures in terms of silicon area and frame rate, for a variety of codec implementations reported in the literature, is performed in [1]. Adapted processor design can achieve an efficiency gain in terms of the AT criterion by a factor 6-7 compared to flexible architectures. According to this study, for a typical video codec it is needed 100mm²/GOPS for flexible architectures, and 15 mm²/GOPS for adapted programmable architectures.

3.3 New Architectural Trends

The latest dedicated processors use SIMD and VLIW architectural schemes and their variations to achieve very high parallelism. Figure 8 shows the architectural models applied in contemporary multimedia processors and several promising approaches.

Multimedia Processor	Clock [MHz]	GOPS	Key Characteristics
TI MVP (TMS320C80)	50	2	Flexible programmable MPEG-1 encoder/decoder MPEG-2 decoder H.261 codec
IIT VCP	80	2	Flexible programmable MPEG-1 encoder/decoder MPEG-2 decoder H.261 codec
NEC VSP3	300	1.5	Adapted programmable H.261 codec
C-Cube VideoRISC2	60	2.5	Adapted programmable MPEG-1 encoder/decoder
Matsushita VDSP2	100	2	Adapted programmable MPEG-2 encoder (requires external motion estimation)
Array Microsystems VideoFlow	50	1	Adapted programmable MPEG-1 encoder (requires External motion estimation and Huffman encoder) MPEG-2 decoder

Table 2. Programmable multimedia processors.

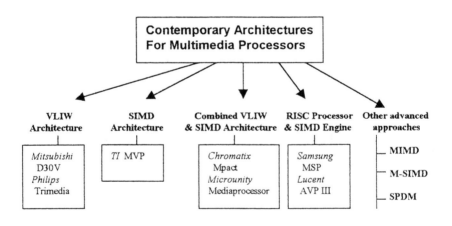

Figure 8. The architectural models applied in advanced multimedia processors.

The two commonly used parallel schemes, the SIMD and the VLIW, are described next.

The SIMD parallel computer organization, applied in multimedia processors, typically uses a single control unit (or master processor), a number of processing elements (PEs) and shared memory among the PEs, as shown in Figure 9 [11]. An interconnection network, such as crossbar switch, is used to interconnect the control processor, all PEs, and shared memory. The control processor evaluates every instruction. If it is a scalar or program control operation, the scalar processor will directly execute it. If the instruction is a vector operation, it will be broadcast to all the PEs for parallel execution. Partitioned data sets are distributed to the shared memory modules before starting the program execution. Then, the same instruction is executed by all the PEs in the same cycle, but on different data elements.

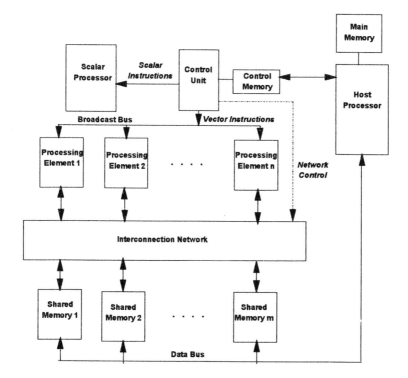

Figure 9. A general SIMD architectural model applied in multimedia processors.

The VLIW architectural model is used in the latest dedicated multimedia processors. A typical VLIW architecture uses long instruction words with more than hundreds of bits in length. The idea behind VLIW concept is to reduce the number of cycles per instruction required for execution of highly complex and parallel algorithms by the use of multiple independent functional units that are directly controlled by long instruction words. This concept is illustrated in Figure 10, where multiple functional units operate in parallel under control of a long instruction. All functional units share a common large register file [11]. Different fields of the long instruction word contain opcodes to activate different functional units. Programs written for conventional 32-bit instruction word computers must be compacted to fit the VLIW instructions. This code compaction is typically done by a special compiler, which can predict branch outcomes, called trace scheduling.

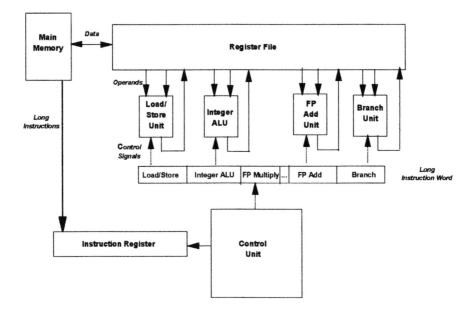

Figure 10. The very-long-instruction-word (VLIW) architectural model applied in dedicated multimedia processors.

Both approaches, SIMD and VLIW, require a giant routing network of buses and crossbar switches. VLIW machines fetch one large instruction per clock cycle and execute all operations on different ALUs. The advantage of this approach is that the ALUs can be specialized to fit the requirements of a given set of applications. However, these architectures use of silicon is inefficient, because of the area taken by the huge interconnection network and hundreds of pipeline data paths.

Another approach consists of combining a RISC processor with a SIMD machine that operates as a vector processor. A SIMD engine simply executes a conventional 32-bit instruction per clock cycle. This instruction processes a single vector of data points, which execute on a set of identical ALUs of a single pipeline. The data vector is treated as a single number for operand access and memory references. The advantage of this approach includes an efficient use of silicon, because only one pipeline has to be implemented, rather than hundreds.

The next generation of programmable multimedia processors incorporates increased parallelism by combining SIMD, VLIW, and some other hybrid architectural schemes. For example, the Mitsubishi D30V and Philips Semiconductor's Trimedia use the VLIW architecture to boost the performance of their video processors. The Chromatix Mpact multimedia processor combines both VLIW and SIMD concepts. The Lucent's AVP III chip uses a RISC processor and an SIMD engine for highly parallel operations, and has dedicated functional units for motion estimation and variable-length encoding and decoding.

Samsung's Multimedia Signal Processor (MSP) combines a traditional RISC controller with an SIMD vector processor (VP) and special-purpose hardware engines. The RISC processor runs the RTOS, performs overall system management and control, and some scalar media processing. The VP processor performs high-performance signal processing. Special-purpose hardware units handle some other functions that cannot be performed efficiently in the other two units.

Mediaprocessor from Microunity Systems Engineering (Sunnyvale, CA) combines a 128-bit load-and-store RISC engine (VLIW concept) with a SIMD-like variation, called single-instruction-group-data (SIGD) parallelism. The architecture also includes a large register file allowing tens of instructions to be executed in parallel. In addition, it also has an execution pipeline that can be either deep (superpipelined), wide (superscalar), or both [7].

Promising Approaches. For the performance and functionality that will be required in next five years, several new approaches are evolving (see Fig. 8).

Multiple-instruction, multiple-data (MIMD) architectures offer 10 to 100 times more throughput than existing VLIW and SIMD architectures. In the MIMD approach, multiple instructions are executed in parallel on multiple data, requiring a control unit for each data path. This requires a significant increase in silicon area to implement control unit for each data path. In addition, a major practical limitation of the MIMD approach is that its implicit asynchronous nature increases the complexity of software development.

Due to these limitations of the MIMD architectures, other hybrid solutions are currently studied. One approach is referred to as *multiple single-instruction, multiple-data (M-SIMD)* or SIMD clustering. In this approach, several SIMD clusters are used, each of which consists of a specific number of data paths and an associated control unit. The data paths within each cluster operate as a SIMD array, while the clusters operate in the MIMD mode.

Another promising approach, referred to as *single-program, multiple-data (SPDM)*, combines SIMD and MIMD architectural features. The SIMD nature of this architecture is in the fact that it executes a single program or a task at a time, while the MIMD feature is because the data paths operate asynchronously.

4.   General-Purpose Processors and Their Support for Multimedia

The real-time multimedia processing on PCs and workstations is still handled by dedicated multimedia processors. However, the advanced GP processors provide an efficient support for certain multimedia applications. These processors can provide software-only solutions for many multimedia functions, which may significantly reduce the cost of the system.

GP processors apply the SIMD approach, described in previous section, by sharing their existing integer or floating-point data paths with a SIMD coprocessor. All leading processor vendors have recently designed GP processors that support multimedia, as shown in Figure 1. The main differences among these processors are in the way that they reconfigure the internal register file structure to accommodate SIMD operations, and the multimedia instructions they choose to add.

4.1 Generic Operations in Multimedia Processing

The instruction mix of multimedia extensions of GP processors varies depending on their application focus. Table 3, adapted from [5], shows typical arithmetic operations required for the main functional blocks of the image and video compression standards, their complexity, inherent parallelism, and the speed-up achieved by current GP processors based on the SIMD approach.

Function	Operations	Complexity	Parallelism
Color transformation (RGB-YUV) Preprocessing and Postprocessing	$\Sigma C_i X_i$, *clip()* $(X_i+X_j)/2$ $(1/4)\Sigma X_i$	Constant for every pixel	Highly parallel
FDCT and IDCT	$ax+b$ $\Sigma C_i X_i$	Either constant or a function of the average number of non-zero DCT coefficients	Depends on the implementation of FDCT or IDCT
Quantization	X_i/C_i	Constant for every pixel	Highly parallel
Dequantization	$X_i C_i$	Function of the average number of non-zero DCT coefficients	Highly parallel
Motion estimation (Encoder)	$\Sigma\|X_i-Y_i\|$ or $\Sigma(X_i-Y_i)^2$ $\min(a,b)$	Depends on the selected motion estimation algorithm	Highly parallel both data-intensive and instruction-intensive processing
Motion compensation (Decoder)	X_i+cX_j Block copies Pixel interpolations	Block copies with pixel interpolations	Highly parallel
VLC (Huffman) Encoding/Decoding	Data shifts Comparisons	Function of the average number of symbols in the bitstream	Fully sequential

Table 3. Generic operations needed for multimedia compression.

The following conclusions can be made from Table 3, that can be used as the main guidelines when specifying multimedia extensions for GP processors [5]:

- Input data and coefficients are typically 8-bit and 16-bit data elements.
- There is no need for floating-point operations.
- The multiply-accumulate operation is very common, but most of multiplications are with constants.
- Saturation arithmetic, where the result is clipped to the maximum or minimum value of a predefined range, is common in many operations.

With the exception of the Huffman (variable length) encoder and decoder, all other operations can be parallelized. Therefore, contemporary GP processors take advantage of this fact by applying the SIMD approach t these operations. An SIMD coprocessor typically performs up to four identical arithmetic or logic operations on different integer-type data. This approach can significantly boost the performance of the GP processors in handling multimedia applications with inherent parallelism (video compression and decompression, image filtering, etc.).

In addition to the arithmetic operations, video processing requires efficient data addressing and I/O processing, which is implemented in some GP processors.

Several contemporary GP processors with multimedia extensions are described in the following sections.

4.2 Intel MMX Technology

Intel MMX technology for Intel Pentium processors is targeted to accelerate multimedia and communications applications, especially on the Internet. The fundamental architectural concept in the MMX system consists of the parallel, SIMD-like operation on small data elements (8 and 16 bits). The MMX system extends the basic integer instructions: *add, subtract, multiply, compare, and shift* into SIMD versions. These instructions perform parallel operations on multiple data elements packed into new 64-bit data types (8x8 bit, 4x16 bit, or 2x32 bit fixed-point elements). The MMX instructions also support saturation arithmetic, described in Section 4.1, which is important for multimedia applications.

The following example of *image composition* illustrates how the SIMD concept has been implemented in Intel MMX system [12]. In this example, fade-in-fade-out effect in video production is performed between two images A and B to produce the final image R as a weighted average of A and B:

$$R = A * fade + B * (1 - fade) = fade * (A - B) + B \qquad (3)$$

where *fade* is gradually changing from 1 to 0 across few video frames, and thus generating fade-in-fade-out effect. Let's assume that the frames are in RGB format, where R, G, and B components are not interleaved. In that case, the MMX processor can access four elements of both frames A and B in a single memory access, subtract them in parallel, and then multiple the result with the fade factor in parallel, as illustrated in Figure 11. The MMX code performing this operation is shown in Figure 12.

Performance results for the Pentium processor with MMX technology, reported in [12], show the improvement between 65% to 370% over the same Pentium processor without MMX technology. For example, MPEG-1 video decompression speed-up with MMX is about 80%, while some other applications, such as image filtering speedup 370%.

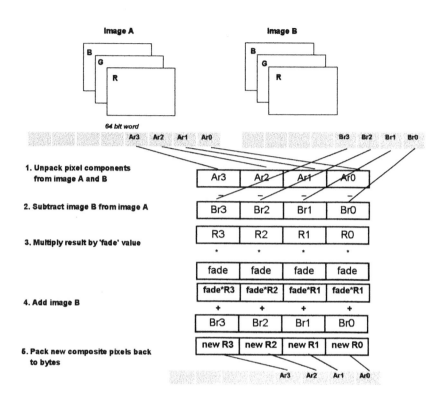

Figure 11. Image composition - fade-in-fade-out effect - performed by MMX system [12].

```
pxor        mm7,mm7         ; zero out mm7
movq        mm3,fade_val    ; load 4 times replicated fade value
movd        mm0,image A     ; load 4 red pixel components from image A
movd        mm1,image B     ; load 4 red pixel components from image B
punpcklbw   mm0,mm7         ; unpack 4 pixels to 16 bits
punpcklbw   mm1,mm7         ; unpack 4 pixels to 16 bits
psubw       mm0,mm1         ; subtract image B from A
pmulhw      mm0,mm3         ; multiply result by fade values
paddw       mm0,mm1         ; add result to image B
packuswb    mm0,mm7         ; pack 16-bit result back to bytes
```

Figure 12. MMX code performing fade-in-fade-out effect [12].

4.3 Sun's Visual Instruction Set

Sun has developed Visual Instruction Set (VIS) for its UltraSPARC processors, which provides graphics and image processing capabilities needed for multimedia applications [13],[14]. The VIS supports new data types used for video processing: pixels and fixed data. Pixels consist of four 8-bit unsigned integers contained in a 32-bit word, while fixed data consist of either four 16-bit fixed-point components, of two 32-bit fixed-point components both contained in a 64-bit word. The SIMD concept has also been applied for some arithmetic and logic instructions (multiplication, addition, subtraction, and logical evaluations), providing parallel operation on four pixels.

An innovative concept, applied in the UltraSPARC, is the *motion estimation instruction* (PDIST), implemented in hardware rather than software. The hardware-implemented instruction PDIST computes the sum of the absolute differences between two 8-pixel vectors, which would require about 48 operations on most processors. Accumulating the error for a 16x16 block requires only 32 PDIST instructions; this operation typically requires 1500 conventional instructions. The hardware implementation of the PDIST (pixel distance) instruction is shown in Figure 13. The circuitry consists of three 4:2 adders, two 11-bit adders, and a 53-bit incrementer. It operates on 8-bit pixels, stored in a pair of double-precision registers, and produces the result in a single-cycle operation.

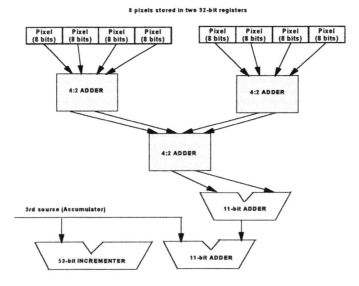

Figure 13. The implementation of the motion estimation instruction in UltraSPARC processor.

As reported in [2],[14], the VIS provides four times or higher speedup for most of the time-critical computations for video decompression, including IDCT, motion estimation, and color conversion. According to an analysis, reported in [2], a 200-MHz UltraSPARC processor is capable of decoding MPEG-2 video of 720x480 pixels resolution at 30 fps entirely in software.

4.4 Other General-Purpose Processors

The majority of contemporary general-purpose processors also support multimedia applications (Fig. 1). They all apply similar concepts, such as support for new data types needed for multimedia processing, and SIMD-like parallel execution of arithmetic and logic operations.

HP PA7100LC Processor

Hewlett-Packard has introduced the PA7100LC processor and its successor HP-PA RISC2 with support for multimedia [15]. The processor has two ALU units, which allows a parallelism of four 16-bit operations per cycle. Implementing the color conversation step together with the color recovery step has enhanced the graphics subsystem. Color conversation converts between YCbCr and the RGB color formats, while color recovery allows 24-bit RGB color that had been "color compressed" into 8 bits to be converted back to 24-bit color before being displayed (dithering operation). This enhancement reduces the display operation in MPEG decoding. The memory controller and the I/O controller have been integrated, which significantly reduces the overhead in the memory to frame buffer bandwidth.

DEC Alpha 21164 Processor and MVI Extensions

The Alpha architecture has been enhanced with Motion Video Instruction (MVI) extensions [16]. The MVI consists of three classes of instructions: pixel-error instruction (PERR), Max/Min, and Pack/Unpack instructions. The PERR motion estimation instruction computes the sum of absolute value of differences of eight pairs of bytes. It replaces nine traditional operations. The Max and Min instructions allow efficient clamping of pixel values to the maximum or minimum values, which is convenient for image and video processing applications. The Pack and Unpack instructions expand and contract the data width on bytes and words. Initial results indicate that MVI improves MPEG-2 compression performance for more than 400%, compared to the Alpha 21164 processor without MVI [16].

MIPS V Processor and SGI MDMX Extensions

MIPS V processor support multimedia applications through its instruction-set architecture (ISA) extensions and MIPS Digital Media Extensions (MDMX). Like on the other processors, ISA extensions use new data types (8 bits and 16 bits) and a

SIMD approach to perform some arithmetic and logical operations in parallel. MIPS ISA extensions, unlike on other processors, also provide support for single-precision floating-point operations, which are useful for front-end image and video synthesis. MDMX extensions, nicknamed Mad Max, use the innovation from the DSP world, by providing an accumulator with extra precision to support the width required by intermediate calculations. Unlike DSPs, MDMX implements a vector accumulator to take advantage of the SIMD aspect of the instruction set.

4.5 Performance Analysis

In summary, GP processors that support multimedia, apply new integer data types, well suited for multimedia, new multimedia instructions, and an SIMD architecture for parallel execution of identical instructions on different data.

An example, adapted from [2], shows how a GP processor with an SIMD coprocessor can speedup the MPEG-2 decoding. In the example in Section 2, we calculated the complexity of a typical MPEG-2 decoder, and the obtained results were in the range 609-740 MOPS. However, in most GP processors integer multiplication has a higher complexity than other instructions, and therefore we will assume that one multiplication is equivalent to 4 generic operations. In this case, the complexity of the MPEG-2 decoder becomes 735 to 876 MOPS for a bit rate of 4 Mbps.

As indicated earlier, the block 1 - bit stream parsing and Huffman decoder, cannot be paralellized, and its complexity remains the same – 12 MOPS. However, operations in all the other blocks can be parallelized by a factor 4, assuming an SIMD coprocessor that executes four identical parallel operations on different data. The complexity of the MPEG-2 decoder, implemented on such GP processor, becomes in the range 194 to 227 MOPS, as illustrated in Table 4.

MPEG-2 Functions	Complexity [MOPS]	Parallel Implementation on a GP Processor Using a SIMD coprocessor
Parser & VLC	12	12
Dequantization	14	4
IDCT	206	52
Motion Compensation	143-274	36-69
YUV to RGB Conversion	360	90
TOTAL COMPLEXITY	735-876	194-227

Table 4. The complexity of the MPEG-2 decoder and its implementation on a GP processor with an SIMD coprocessor.

Similarly, for an increased bit rate of 8 Mbps, the total MPEG-2 complexity on a GP processor with an SIMD coprocessor becomes 220-250 MOPS, and for 16 Mbps, is in the range 320-352 MOPS [2].

Contemporary GP processors use superscalar RISC architectures, in which the number of executed instructions is at least 2 x Clock Frequency. Therefore, a 200 MHz processor can execute about 400 MOPS, which suggests that a software-only MPEG-2 decoder can be easily implemented. However, according to Table 1, MPEG encoders require 3,000 to 22,000 MOPS, and even their parallel implementation using an SIMD approach, will require around 1,000 MOPS. This still cannot be achieved with GP processors, and dedicated multimedia processors must be used.

5. CONCLUSIONS

In summary, general-purpose designers have recently realized that they should begin investing some of the available chip real estate to support multimedia. As we hurtle further into the multimedia revolution, we should expect that new generation of GP processors will devote more and more transistors to multimedia. How far and how fast this process will go will be determined by the market demand. By the end of this decade we may see a complete MPEG decoder, large frame buffers, a variety of functional units for video, image, and audio processing, and much more, all packed within a single processor chip.

On the other hand, computationally intensive multimedia functions, such as MPEG encoding, HDTV codecs, 3D processing, and virtual reality, will still require dedicated processors for a long time to come. Therefore, we can expect that general-purpose processors that support multimedia and dedicated multimedia processors will coexist for some time.

References

1. P. Pirsch, N. Demassieux, and W. Gehrke, "VLSI Architectures for Video Compression – A Survey", Proceedings of the IEEE, Vol. 83, No. 2, February 1995, pp. 220-246.
2. C-G. Zhou, L. Kohn, D. Rice, I. Kabir, A. Jabbi, and X-P. Hu, "MPEG Video Decoding with the UltraSPARC Visual Instruction Set", Proceedings of the IEEE Compcon, San Francisco, CA, March 1995, pp. 470-475.

3. W.B. Pennenbaker and J.L. Mitchell, "JPEG Still Image Data Compression Standard", Van Nostrant Reinhold, New York, 1993.

4. H. Fujiwara, M.L. Liou, M-T. Sun, K-M. Yang, M. Maruyama, K. Shomura, and K. Ohyama, "An All-ASCI Implementation of a Low Bit-rate Video Codec", IEEE Trans. On Circuits and Systems for Video Technology, Vol. 2, No. 2, June 1992, pp. 123-134.

5. V. Bhaskaran and K. Konstantinides, "Image and Video Compression Standards – Algorithms and Architectures", Kluwer Academic Publishers, Boston, MA, 1995.

6. K. Guttag, R.J. Gove, and J.R. Van Aken, "A Single-Chip Multiprocessor For Multimedia: The MVP", IEEE Computer Graphics & Applications, November 1992, pp. 53-64.

7. B. Cole, "New Processors Up Multimedia's Punch", Electronic Engineering Times, February 3, 1997, pp. 71.

8. W. Lee, Y. Kim, R.J. Gove, and C.J. Reed, "MediaStation 5000: Integrating Video and Audio", IEEE MultiMedia, Vol. 1, No. 2, Summer 1994, pp. 50-61.

9. B. Ackland, "The Role of VLSI in Multimedia", IEEE J. Solid-State Circuits, Vol. 29, December 1992, pp. 1886-1893.

10. T. Akari et al., "Video DSP Architecture for MPEG2 Codec", Proceedings of ICASSP, Vol. 2, IEEE Press, 1994, pp. 417-420.

11. K. Hwang, "Advanced Computer Architecture with Parallel Programming", McGraw-Hill, 1993.

12. A. Peleg, S. Wilkie, and U. Weiser, "Intel MMX for Multimedia PCs", Communications of the ACM, Vol. 40, No. 1, January 1997, pp. 25-38.

13. M. Tremblay, J.M. O'Connor, V. Narayanan, and H. Liang, "VIS Speeds New Media Processing", IEEE Micro, Vol. 16, No. 4, August 1996, pp. 10-20.

14. L. Kohn, G. Maturana, M. Tremblay, A. Prabhu, and G. Zyner, "The Visual Instruction Set (VIS) in UltraSPARC", Proceedings of the IEEE Compcon, San Francisco, CA, March 1995, pp. 462-469.

15. R.B. Lee, "Realtime MPEG Video via Software Decompression on a PA-RISC Processor", Proceedings of the IEEE Compcon, San Francisco, CA, March 1995, pp. 186-192.

16. P. Bannon and A. Jain, "MVI Instructions Boost Alpha Processor", Electronic Engineering Times, February 3, 1997, pp. 74.

PART II

MULTIMEDIA SERVERS

2

Dvds: Much Needed "Shot in the Arm" for Video Servers

VIJNAN SHASTRI   vshastri@cedt.iisc.ernet.in
CEDT, Indian Institute of Science, Bangalore-560 012, India

P. VENKAT RANGAN   venkat@cs.ucsd.edu
Department of Computer Science and Engineering, University of California, San Diego, CA, 92093-0114, USA

SRIHARI SAMPATH-KUMAR   srihari@cs.wustl.edu
Department of Computer Science, Washington University, St. Louis, MO 63130, USA

Abstract.   The release of DVD-ROMs (Digital Versatile Disk—Read Only Memory), capable of storing an entire 133 minute MPEG-2 movie, coupled with the gradual deployment of high speed networks will give a much needed impetus to Video-on-Demand systems, especially movie-on-demand services. Various memory components such as DVD-ROMs, magnetic RAID towers, and RAM are available, each with different storage and bandwidth capabilities, and each with different costs. To design a video server, we need to optimize the cost factor, yet meet the massive storage, high bandwidth and continuity requirements of video stream delivery.

In the first part of this paper we compare DVD-ROM and RAID systems on the basis of two factors—a storage factor and a bandwidth factor. We work out relations to calculate capacity requirements and costs, of these systems given the demands of video delivery. We then propose an architecture for a video server where we deploy three layers of memory functioning as video pumps: DVD-ROM towers, RAID towers, and RAM. We then work out expressions to determine the migration strategy of a movie between these layers of storage so as to optimize on the cost of storage while satisfying the performance requirements. We then show the method by which the amount of storage required for each type of memory in the three layers can be fixed, knowing the usage pattern.

In the second part of the paper, we discuss the implementation of a video pump where there is a need to integrate scheduling, admission control, VBR stream management, and handling of VCR-like requests such as fast-forward, fast-reverse and pause. We first work out general relations for calculation of the service time of a request knowing the seek overheads and playback rates. We then show that, surprisingly, the C-SCAN algorithm, which incurs the least amount of seek overhead and therefore has a lesser cycle time, is twice as efficient as SCAN in terms of buffer space requirements. We then propose a 'full-load' admission control and scheduling algorithm that operates on a constant cycle time basis. We test the validity of this scheme though a the simulator which we have built based on our disk model and use it to extract parameters such as disk bandwidth utilization factor and buffer sizes needed for a VBR load scenario.

Keywords: digital versatile disk, video servers, admission control, scheduling

1.0.   Introduction

Digital video servers are rapidly emerging on the internet and various other networks. Current incarnations of video servers are however severely limited in the following manner.

- The videos are just small clips such as trailers and advertisements. Typical total sizes accommodated by video servers are a few tens of gigabytes that translates to a few tens of hours.

- The streaming of video either is not continuous or breaks down for even a small number of users. Typically, maximum of a few tens of users can be supported simultaneously by video servers.

In comparison, a full service video server has the following requirements:

- The total storage requirement of a full service video server runs to thousands of gigabytes (thousands of hour long movies).
- The storage servers should support thousands of viewers accessing and viewing movies in a personalized fashion without noticeable degradation in either the response time or the throughput to each viewer. The viewers would expect very low delays in the reaction of the video server to VCR-like commands. Hence, there is a need for storage devices that access data at very high speeds and serve data at very high rates to a large audience.

A range of storage devices that vary in storage capacity, access speed, data transfer rate, and cost are available to choose from. At one end we have a set of high capacity, but relatively low speed and low cost devices such as tape drives. At the other end, we have a set of high speed and high cost, but relatively low capacity devices such as RAM. Wholly using high performance, expensive RAM would mean an enormous investment cost and suboptimal usage of RAM resources. For example a 1000 Gbyte RAM storage server would cost $10 million which amortized over a thousand users would mean $10,000 per user. On the other hand, Deployment of only the low cost devices would mean low performance. To compensate for this low performance, the storage devices would have to be replicated to a large extent thereby losing the cost advantage.

How do we tackle this situation?

Usually not all videos have uniform access levels. Some are hot and some others are cold, relatively speaking. Storing the hot movies on the fast storage and the cold ones on cheap storage is efficient and economical. Thus, a range of storage devices need to be deployed. However the access levels for each movie may change over time. The configuration of these storage devices should allow the migration of movies from one set of devices to another adaptively, according to changes in the number of viewers accessing the movies. In other words, the movie is cached in a layer to meet the increased demand for it. Such migration strategies are needed in order to minimize the cost and maximize the performance. Numerous investigations in the past have revealed that a hierarchy of storage devices have to be deployed in order to meet the above demands. Determining the optimal configuration of the storage hierarchy is a complex task as it involves the optimization of multiple parameters such as cost, service rate, and storage capacity.

However, the emergence of DVDs (Digital Versatile Disks) has the potential to solve the most important of these problems. In this paper, we introduce DVDs and develop design methodologies for optimally configuring large scale video servers for applications such as movie-on-demand.

2.0. Related work

Various configurations have been proposed. The commonality is that there is a hierarchy of tape library, disk bank, and RAM.

- Doganata and Tantawi [6] have discussed cost issues in a video server by considering a hierarchy of tape drives, Disk drives and expanded storage (RAM).
- Chang and Zakhor [3] have discussed cost issues in VBR servers by considering CTL (constant time length), CDL (Constant Data Length) and a hybrid scheme.
- Yu et al. [25] have proposed GSS (Grouped Sweeping Scheduling) algorithm as the optimal way of servicing requests for multimedia streams using magnetic disks.
- Traditionally, the elements of the storage hierarchy have been tape drives, disks, and RAM. Tape drives perform poorly when it comes to minimizing access delays and maximizing data transfer rates. Also, loading tapes into their drives is cumbersome, and tape drives are not inexpensive: e.g., 18 GB Metrum RSP-2150 tape drive with 2 Mbps transfer rate can cost upto $32 K. Thus, the deployment of large scale storage servers has been plagued with such problems.

3.0. Our contributions

- We are proposing a new architecture in which a large bank of DVD-ROMs constitute the primary storage medium both in parallel with RAIDs and RAM. The DVD-ROMs serve to feed users either through RAIDs, or RAMs, or directly. Consequently the relationship between DVD-ROMs, RAID, and RAM is not strictly hierarchical (Section 4.0). In the next section, we outline a generic framework to determine the amount of storage that must be available at each layer in the hierarchy.
- We quantify the performance and cost of DVD-ROMs and compare them with that of RAID and RAM (Section 4.2).
- We present rules for migrating videos when their popularity levels and viewership levels change. We then determine the conditions to be satisfied for the migration of a given movie from one level of storage to another (Section 4.3).
- Given a viewership pattern (number of videos and their usage statistics), we develop a systematic design methodology for an optimal storage configuration (Section 5.0). Based on the results of the previous subsections, we then determine the storage requirements needed at each layer for setting up a video server with known viewership patterns.
- We then work out the expression for the service time of a request in a video pump (Section 7.0) and prove that, surprisingly, C-SCAN is twice as optimal as SCAN in terms of buffer size requirements (Section 7.2).
- Finally, we propose a 'full-load' admission control algorithm which uses the concept of dummy requests to keep the cycle time constant. We have developed a simulator which we use to extract parameters such as buffer sizes needed and the disk bandwidth utilization factor in order to handle VBR streams such as MPEG-2. The algorithm handles disk scheduling, admission control of VBR streams, and implementation of VCR-like requests from the user. We discuss the design and implementation in detail (Section 8.0).

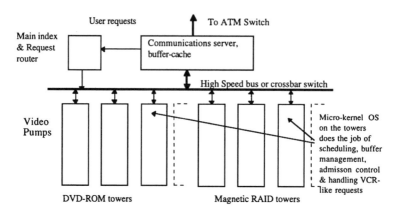

Figure 4.0.   Architecture of a video-on-demand (movie) server.

4.0.   The system architecture

DVD-ROMs (Digital Versatile Disks) are a result of an improvement in CD-ROM technology. The combination of improved optics, more efficient data coding, error correction and channel modulation allow single layer discs with a capacity of over 4.7 thousand million bytes (gigabytes). That is more than 7 times the capacity of a CD-ROM. Furthermore, DVD discs run at over 10 times the (fixed) CD rate. In digital video applications, the data read-out rate can be carried, to match the instantaneous data rate demanded by the particular application.

DVD-ROMs will soon hit the market with capacities of initially 4.7 GB and later in capacities of 8.5 GB, 10 GB and 17 GB. They are targeted for MPEG-2 (average bit rate: 5 Mbits/sec) based video storage with audio channels and will initially have transfer rates of 10 Mbits/sec. With each DVD-ROM capable of holding about 133 minutes of MPEG-2 Video, they will become the standard distribution medium for both MPEG-1 (data rates of 1.2 Mbits/sec) and MPEG-2 movies. In the deployment of Video-on-demand-systems, the cost of the Video server is a critical issue. The architecture of a video server is illustrated in figure 4.0. DVD-ROM drives will inevitably be part of the storage hierarchy in movie servers—consisting of DVD-ROM systems, magnetic RAID systems and RAM caches.

DVD-ROMs have transfer rates of 10 Mbits/s (1.25 Mbytes/sec). Thus, DVD-ROMs can easily handle up to 7 MPEG-1 streams and with the inevitable increase in transfer speeds they will be able to handle multiple MPEG-2 streams as well. MPEG-2 streams can have a variable bit rate of 4 Mbits/s–10 Mbits/s but have an average bit rate of 5–6 Mbits/s.

We assume a storage hierarchy of three storage components:

- **DVD-ROM drives:** DVD-ROMs function as the primary storage media. Each DVD-ROM has a minimum storage capacity of 4.7 Gbytes and has a transfer rate of 1.25 MB/s (10 Mbits/s). The cost (eventually) of each DVD-ROM drive is roughly \$250. Each DVD-ROM can hold 133 minutes of MPEG-2 data.

- **Magnetic RAID towers:** The RAID (Redundant Array of Inexpensive Disks) are composed of magnetic disks. The RAID functions as the primary cache storage. Each RAID drive typically holds a disk of 1 Gbyte storage capacity and has a data transfer rate of 5 MB/s (40 Mbits/s). The cost of each drive is approximately $250. Thus, RAID drives cost the same as DVD-ROM drives, have one-fourth the storage capacity and four-times the transfer rate of DVD-ROM drives.
- **RAM:** RAM serves as the secondary cache storage. The data transfer rate of RAM is 100 MB/s and the cost per megabyte is $10. Thus, RAM is forty times more expensive than RAID and is twenty times as fast.

The number of drives that we deploy (DVD-ROM cluster or magnetic RAID system) should satisfy two conditions:

a) **Storage requirements:** The total storage capacity of the drives should be at least the amount of storage needed for storing all the movies being accessed by the viewers.
b) **Bandwidth requirements:** The drives should be capable of servicing all the viewers in terms of the output data rate.

4.1. Terminology and preliminary definitions

The interesting parameters associated with a storage medium are cost per drive, drive transfer rate, storage capacity, and playback rate. These symbols and values of these parameters are summarized in Table 4.0 and we will refer them throughout the paper.

When analyzing cost factors, we refer to the cost per drive and do not look at it from the cost per byte point of view. This is because, in a magnetic drive, the medium is inseparable

Table 4.0. Parameters and their values used in this paper.

Parameter	Magnetic drive	DVD-ROM drive
Cost per drive	C_d^M, $250	C_m^{DVD}, $250
Capacity per drive (in MB)	S^M, 1 GB	S^{DVD}, 4.7 GB
Transfer rate of drive	R^M, 5 MB/s (40 Mbits/s)	R^{DVD} 0.625 MB/s (10 Mbits/s)
Total number of users (and hence number of streams)	N(Typical value 1000)	
Megabytes (MB) of storage per movie (133 minutes)	M, 4.7 GB—MPEG-2, 1.2 GB—MPEG-1	
Storage needed to service N users (as a fraction of $N * M$)	f	
Data transfer rate per user	R, 5 Mbits/s—MPEG-2, 1.2 Mbits/s MPEG-1	
Cost of RAM per MB	C^{RAM}, $10 per MB	
Number of drives needed	D	
Superscript to represent either DVD-ROM or magnetic drives	i	

from the drive, and hence it is certainly logical to refer to the cost per drive. The same is true of the DVD-ROM drive.

The parameter f is used as a measure to quantify the load from a bandwidth point-of-view. It is the ratio of the number of movies being accessed to the total number of users. In the worst case, when N users are accessing N **different** movies, f will be 1. If N users are accessing $\frac{N}{2}$ different movies, f will be 0.5.

Parameter 'D' is the number of drives (either magnetic or DVD-ROMs) needed to satisfy either storage or playback (bandwidth) requirements. The rest of the parameters are self-explanatory.

The bandwidth factor. The number of drives needed to satisfy the bandwidth requirement is the smallest integer not less than the ratio of the total required video data rate to the data rate of the drive. The total required data rate is $(N * R)$ where N is the number of viewers and R is the mean output data rate for a movie. If the data transfer rate of the drive is R^i where 'i' is the type of drive (magnetic or DVD-ROM), the number of drives, D must satisfy the following condition:

$$D \geq \left\lceil \frac{N * R}{R^i} \right\rceil$$

As the value of N is usually very large (in the order of thousands) $\lceil \frac{N*R}{R^i} \rceil \cong \frac{N*R}{R^i}$.

Therefore, the above relation simplifies to:

$$D \geq \frac{N * R}{R^i} \qquad (1)$$

In the rest of the paper we will refer to the above condition as the ***bandwidth factor***.

The storage factor. The number of drives needed to satisfy the storage requirement is the smallest integer not less than the ratio of: the *storage requirement* needed to store *all the movies* to the *storage capacity of the drive* in question. The total storage needed for all the movies is given by $(f * N * M)$ where f is the ratio of the number of distinct movies being watched to the total number of number of viewers. Let the storage capacity of the drive be S^i where i is the type of drive used.

Hence, the number of drives, D, must satisfy the following condition:

$$D \geq \left\lceil \frac{f * N * M}{S^i} \right\rceil$$

Similar to the assertion made previously, $D \geq \lceil \frac{f*N*M}{S^i} \rceil \cong \frac{f*N*M}{S^i}$ as N is very large.

Therefore the above relation reduces to

$$D \geq \frac{f * N * R}{S^i} \qquad (2)$$

In the rest of the paper, we will refer to the above condition as the ***storage factor***.

4.2. The cost of a set of drives

We have defined in the previous section two factors which affect the choice of number of drives.

- The number of different movies that are to be offered on the set of drives. This determines the storage factor.
- The number of users that are to be served from this set of drives. This determines the bandwidth factor.

When we assemble a set of drives, this set must meet both the storage factor requirement as well as the bandwidth factor requirements. Hence the number of drives we need to assemble is dictated by their maximum:

$$\textbf{max}(\textit{Number of drives needed to meet the storage factor,}$$
$$\textit{Number of drives installed due to bandwidth factor}) \tag{3}$$

Using (1) and (2) we have

$$D = \max\left(\frac{f * N * M}{S^i}, \frac{N * R}{R^i}\right) \tag{4}$$

Hence the cost of this set of drives is:

$$\max\left(\frac{f * N * M * C_d^i}{S^i}, \frac{N * R * C_d^i}{R^i}\right) \tag{5}$$

Note that in the above discussion *we are considering the overall storage **and** bandwidth requirements of a set of drives.*

When we talk about the status of a single movie within a particular layer (DVD-ROM/RAID), we note that:

- When we decide to store a single movie within a certain layer, we have to first satisfy at least the storage factor (by deploying a certain number of drive(s)).
- This one copy of the movie is able to satisfy a certain bandwidth factor.
- We then may need to replicate the movie in that layer when the bandwidth demand exceeds the bandwidth factor of that set of drives.

Thus within a set of drives, (magnetic or DVD-ROM), the cost of storage of a *single movie* due to the bandwidth factor dominates when (from (5))

$$\frac{n * R}{R^i} * C_d^i > \frac{M * C_d^i}{S^i}$$
$$\text{i.e., when } n > \frac{M * R^i}{R * S^i} \tag{6}$$

The value of n is 33 for magnetic disks and 2 for DVD-ROM drives using values in Table 4.0 (for MPEG-2 streams).

We have so far discussed about the issues concerning storage due storage and bandwidth factors *within* a set of drives (a memory layer). In the next section we discuss the conditions under which a movie must migrate from one layer to the other due to the bandwidth factor.

4.3. Conditions for migration of a movie from one layer of the hierarchy to the next

The layered view of different memory types is shown in figure 4.2. As we move up in the hierarchy, the storage costs increase but bandwidth costs decrease and as we move down the converse is true. In other words, it is more ***economical*** to service a movie from an upper layer relative to the current one when the number of users requesting that movie crosses a certain threshold.

In this section, we quantify under what load conditions a movie must migrate from the DVD-ROM cluster to the magnetic RAID cluster and from the magnetic RAID cluster to RAM.

We have seen in the previous section that the movie 'begins life' in a particular memory layer due to the storage factor but then may have to be replicated due to the bandwidth factor.

The condition for a movie to migrate from one layer to the next upper layer is the following:

When the cost of storage due to the bandwidth factor in the lower layer is more than the cost of storage due to the storage factor in the upper layer, the movie must migrate from the lower layer to the upper layer.

That is:

cost of storage due to bandwidth factor in lower layer > cost of storage due to storage factor in upper layer.

The condition for migration from DVD-ROM to RAID system can be stated as follows:

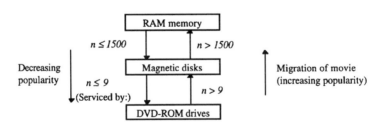

n is the number of users (requests) per movie

Figure 4.2.   Showing logical view of the memory hierarchy in a video pump.

cost of storage due to the bandwidth factor on DVD-ROM > Cost of Storage on RAID due to the storage factor

i.e., $\dfrac{n * R}{R^{\text{DVD}}} * C_d^{\text{DVD}} > \dfrac{M * C_d^M}{S^M}$

If we assume that $C_d^{\text{DVD}} = C_d^M$, then this simplifies to:

$$n > \frac{M * R^{\text{DVD}}}{R * S^M} \tag{7}$$

Taking values for parameters as before, we get: $n > 9$

Hence, a movie must migrate from the DVD-ROM cluster to the magnetic RAID cluster when the number of requests for a particular movie exceeds **nine**.

The condition for migration from RAID to RAM is:

cost of storage due to the bandwidth factor on RAID > Cost of Storage in RAM

$\dfrac{n * R}{R^M} * C_d^M > M * C^{\text{RAM}}$

A movie migrates from the RAID array to the RAM on the server when it becomes cheaper to store the movie in RAM than on the magnetic RAID array, i.e., when the following expression is true:

$$\text{i.e., } n > \frac{M * C^{\text{RAM}} * R^M}{R * C_d^M} \tag{8}$$

Substituting values from Table 4.0, we get: $n > 1500$

Thus, unless the demand for a movie is as much as 1500, *it is not cost effective to cache entire movies in RAM.*

The converse of (8) is also true, i.e., a movie that resides on the in RAM must be serviced by the RAID system if (8) is violated.

In working out relation (8), we have assumed that the movie is not striped if a RAID configuration of magnetic disk cluster is used. Striping enables better load balancing *within* the magnetic disk cluster. Thus slightly higher threshold values of *n* maybe obtained. In other words, migration of a particular movie may not be required if there is sufficient unused bandwidth (in the magnetic disk layer as a whole) *and* the movie has been suitably striped. However, Unlike traditional systems, striping of multimedia data poses to be especially difficult due to the continuity requirement *coupled* with the *dynamic variation in the load patterns*. A detailed discussion is beyond the scope of this paper but this is an active research subject and has been addressed in [15] and [24].

In the above relation we don't consider the cost of other components involved in deploying magnetic storage systems such as RAID and SCSI controllers, or the cost of memory controllers in installing RAM. The idea is to come up with estimates rather than exact figures. Note that the converse of relations (7) and (8) is also true, i.e., a movie residing in an upper layer moves *down* to the lower layer (i.e., get serviced by the lower layer) when (7) or (8) are violated.

Table 4.3. Sumarizes the results for migration of a movie from one layer to the next.

Migration of movie	Expression	Value of 'n' (# users per movie)
From DVD-ROM layer to RAID	$n > \frac{M * R^{DVD}}{R * S^M}$	9
From RAID to RAM	$n > \frac{M * C^{RAM} * R^M}{R * C_d^M}$	1500

Cost of buffers.   While calculating storage costs we have only considered the cost of the drives. We have not looked at the cost of buffers required in main memory to support the continuity requirement of playback streams. The size (and hence their cost) of these buffers are substantial in video servers. However their precise contribution to the cost depends on several factors: the disk characteristics such as seek time, the scheduling algorithm employed, the type of streams that are served (MPEG-1 or MPEG-2) and the load on the disk. We look at these issues in Section 7.0 onwards, where we focus on buffer design in addition to other, scheduler-design related issues.

In summary, we have derived relations for costs of storage (expressions (4) and (5)) on all levels and worked out expressions for the migration of a movie from one layer of the hierarchy to the next. The results are presented in Table 4.3. In the Section 5.0, we look at how much of each type of storage is required for at each level.

5.0.   Storage requirements of each layer of the memory hierarchy

In this section, we look at the amount of storage required for each of the layers (figure 4.2) such that the overall storage is optimized for cost. In order to carry this out, the usage pattern (i.e., how many users request for each of the movies stored on the server) must be known. A clear picture of such usage patterns will emerge only after such movie servers are installed. However we can make some reasonable assumptions of the usage patterns and come up with estimates for the sizes of the three layers of storage.

We will assume the that the usage pattern follows a general behavior as shown in figure 5.0. For our estimate of storage, we use the values shown in Table 5.0. Note that this is the usage pattern under full-load conditions.

Table 5.0 implies that 30% of the users are watching the three most popular movies, 20% are watching the next 20 most popular movies and so on. We assume that the percentage of users in each category are uniformly distributed among the movies in that category.

Table 5.0. Percentage of users and popularity of movies.

Category	% of users	Number of movies requested
1	30%	3
2	20%	10
3	15%	50
4	35%	Remaining movies

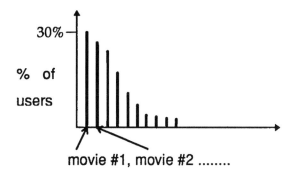

Figure 5.0.   Shows the probable usage pattern a movie-on-demand system.

Assuming movie server with a repository of 1000 movies, and all other parameters as in Table 4.0, we can get an estimate (using relations (7) and (8)) of storage requirements at each level for 3 communities (in terms of size) of users, 1000, 5000 and 10000. The results are tabulated in Table 5.1. for a MPEG-2 based server.
The steps used in the calculation are as follows:

- We first determine 'n', the number of users per movie for all the categories in Table 5.0.
- We then determine from (7) and (8) which of the layers services each category.
- From (5) we then determine the number of drives for each layer thus giving number of DVD-ROM drives, magnetic drives and RAM.

The calculation for the first row is detailed below:

Category (1) of Table 5.1.   30% $\Rightarrow$ 300 users for 3 movies, i.e., $n = 300/3 = 100$ users per movie. This category will therefore be serviced by the RAID storage (from (7) and (8)).
   3 movies $\Rightarrow 3*4.7 = 14.1$ GB of storage.
   The amount of storage needed is (from (4)) $= \max(14.1, \frac{300*0.625}{5}) = 38$ drives—magnetic.
Category (2).   20% $\Rightarrow$ 200 users for 10 movies, i.e., $n = 200/10 = 20$ users per movie—serviced by magnetic RAID storage.
   Storage needed is $\max(4.7*10, \frac{200*0.625}{1.25}) = 47$ drives magnetic.

Table 5.1.   Amount of storage required at each of the three levels of the hierarchy.

Total number of users	RAM	Magnetic storage	DVD-ROM storage
1000	—	85 GB (85 drives 1 GB each)	2350 GB (500 drives 4.7 GB each)
5000	—	548 GB (548 drives)	1776 GB (378 drives)
10000	15 GB	485 GB (485 drives)	2056 GB (438 drives)

Category (3).   15% $\Rightarrow$ 150 users for 50 movies, i.e., $n = 150/50 = 3$ users per movie—
serviced by DVD-ROM (from (7)).

Storage needed is max($\frac{150*4.7}{4.7}$, $\frac{150*0.625}{1.25}$) = 150 DVD-ROM *drives.*

Category (4).   35% $\Rightarrow$ 350 users for 950 movies, i.e., $n = 350/950 = 1$ user per movie—
serviced by DVD-ROM (from (7)).

Here we take the minimum requirement, i.e., 350 DVD-ROM drives (into which the a
subset of the 950 movies is loaded) $\Rightarrow$ 1645 GB *of storage.*

Similarly the amount of storage for the two other communities (5000 and 10000 users)
is also calculated. Note that the entry in the last column (for DVD-ROM drives) is the
minimum required as seen from a load (number of requests) point of view. We assume that
the movies are loaded in the lowest layer (DVD-ROM) either manually or automatically .
This means that at no time are all 1000 movies present in the memory system—this is also
not necessary.

6.0.   Summary of results in this section

We conclude the first part of the paper, having completed the investigations into the design of the memory hierarchy of a video server from the cost/performance point of view.
Summarizing the main contributions till now:

- We have defined two parameters: the storage factor and the bandwidth factor—using
  which we derive expressions for a cost of set of drives.
- We have then derived relations to determine the factors under which a movie should
  migrate from one layer to the next in the memory hierarchy. The memory hierarchy
  consists of DVD-ROMs, magnetic RAID systems and RAM.
- We have used these results to determine the amount of storage of each type, given a
  community of users and their usage pattern.

In the next section we discuss the scheduling, buffer size and admission control aspects
of a video server that is able to handle VCR-like requests from users.

7.0.   Scheduling and buffer optimization in video pumps

In our architecture of a VoD server, both the DVD-ROM towers and magnetic RAID towers
act as Video pumps (figure 4.0). These pumps handle pure video requests and do not handle
aperiodic non-video requests. The operating system, indexing, and other information about
the movie database (of each tower) resides on a separate disk on each of the towers. The
operating system (a micro-kernel OS) is responsible for disk scheduling, admission control,
buffer management and transport of the retrieved video data to the main controller, in
addition to handling VCR-like requests generated by users.

Thus in a DVD video pump, video stream retrieval is characterized by periodic requests
for data that sustain for long periods of time and its delivery demands that continuity
of the stream be maintained, and the process of servicing the requests $s_1, s_2, s_3, \ldots, s_n$

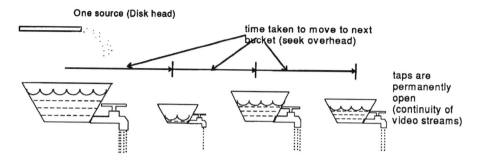

Figure 7.0. An analogy for multiple request streams.

proceeds typically in periodic rounds. In each round the disk-head seeks to the starting sector corresponding to a particular request, retrieves a certain number of sectors (proportional to the playback rate of that request) then seeks to the next request, retrieves the required number of sectors, and so on, until all requests have been serviced. It then begins a new round. We will refer to the time to service a round as the '*cycle time*'. There exists a buffer for each request whose size is *proportional* to the playback rate.

We draw the following analogy:

Suppose we have many buckets (see figure 7.0) of water (*buffers*) whose outlet taps are open *permanently* (*continuous playback*).The rate of outflow is different in the different buckets (*differing playback rates for multiple request streams*). The size of the bucket is proportional to the rate of outflow. Then the problem of scheduling is for one to run between the buckets (*head movement & seek overhead*) and keep filling them such that:

- They are never empty, even for a moment (*continuity of playback*).
- They never overflow (*buffer overflow*).
- One uses the <u>minimum</u> size of buckets, *yet maintaining* the continuity of outflows (*buffer size optimization and continuity requirement of multimedia streams*).
- The sum of the outflows from the taps does not exceed the inflow from the source (*overload*).
- If a new bucket is introduced, (provided the above condition is satisfied) this does not disrupt the outflow (*continuity*) from the other taps (*admission control*).
- When the outflow from the taps continuously varies then this corresponds to **VBR** (*Variable Bit Rate*) *stream playback*.
- In a VBR scenario, there will be (albeit temporarily) demands for outflow greater than the inflow. This temporary demand can be met if all the buckets have enough *extra* water to satisfy this demand. (*extra buffer size*).

Earlier work [9, 18, 19, 22, 25] has addressed the above questions in the context of magnetic disks and the scattered nature of placement of sectors. Several disk-scheduling algorithms for magnetic disks have been proposed for implementing multimedia storage: FCFS (First Come First Serve), SCAN, SCAN-EDF(SCAN with Earliest Deadline First),

GSS (Grouped Sweeping Scheduling) and C-SCAN (Circular-SCAN). The popular SCAN algorithm sorts the requests in increasing order of seek distances and services them: moving from inner to outer periphery and then from outer to inner periphery, servicing them in reverse order. The SCAN- EDF services the requests in the order of earliest deadline but employs SCAN to sort the requests which have the same deadline. GSS organizes the requests in groups and employs SCAN within the groups. The C-SCAN operates like SCAN in one sweep, from inner to outer for example, but does an idle seek from outer to inner to begin a new cycle.

For multimedia streams, it is the continuity requirement and optimization of buffer sizes which is of prime concern. For traditional streams it is the response time (latency) which is most important. Buffer optimization is achieved through shorter round times which are in turn achieved by seek optimization—but seek optimization leads to longer response times. Thus there is a tradeoff between these two conflicting requirements. All the above algorithms seek to find the best trade-off between the two. All these algorithms have considered a scenario where requests to the disk consist of both normal aperiodic requests as well as multimedia streams.

To handle VBR streams, a variety of schemes have been proposed [1, 3]. They are derived from the CTL (constant time length) or CDL (Constant Data Length) schemes.

In this section:

- We first work out a relation to calculate the service time for each request knowing the playback rate for each request a priori and the seek overheads (from the seek characteristic of the drive).
- We show that the total buffer size is proportional to the to seek overhead, we then compare scheduling algorithms and prove that, surprisingly, C-SCAN is optimal over SCAN.
- We then propose a 'full-load' admission control algorithm that admits new requests without disrupting the continuity of playback of other requests.
- We discuss the implementation of this algorithm and also show that this algorithm supports operations such as fast forward, reverse, etc.
- We discuss scheduling and related issues in a general way first and then discuss the difference between magnetic drives and DVD-ROM drives.

An example for three requests (with different playback rates) is shown in figure 7.1. During the service time, both retrieval and playback take place. The rest of the time only playback takes place and this repeats periodically. For this periodicity to occur, *time to playback the retrieved data (which is proportional to their respective playback rates) is the same for all the request streams*. In the figure, playback rate of s_1 > playback rate of s_2 > playback rate of s_3.

Our first objective is to provide a relation by which a server can *calculate the service time for each request, which will then enable us to calculate the buffer requirement for each request stream* given that:

- The seek overheads are known (this can be got from the sector-distance vs. seek-time characteristic).
- The playback rate r_i for each request stream s_i is known.

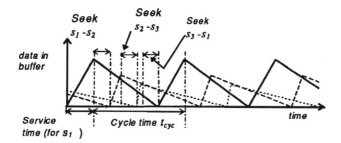

Figure 7.1. Servicing multiple requests—Buffer contents.

The symbols used in the equations that follow are summarized in Table 7.0.
In order to maintain continuity of playback we can write, for all request streams:

$$playback\ rate = \frac{data\ retrieved\ for\ that\ stream\ in\ a\ round}{cycle\ time} \tag{9}$$

The above equation assumes:

- that the playback requirements of each round are exactly met and hence progressive accumulation of data in the buffers with every successive round does not occur.
- that the sectors pertaining to a request stream are read in one go, in a round. This follows from the assumption that sectors belonging to a video stream are stored continuously.

We will refer to the time that the head spends reading the sectors belonging to a request (in a round) as the '*service time*'.

Table 7.0. Symbols used in this section.

Symbol	Parameter
s_i	The ith request stream
n	Number of request stream
r_i	Playback rate of ith request stream
R	Transfer rate of drive
t_{cyc}	Total time to service all requests in a round
t_i^r	Service time for the ith request (synonym: retrieval time)
t_i^s	Time to seek from the previous request stream to the ith request stream
u	Disk Bandwidth utilization factor = Sum of all the playback rates
T_{seek}	Total seek overhead $\sum^n t_i^s$

Now,

$$amount\ of\ data\ transferred = drivetransferrate * service\ time$$
$$= R * t_i^s \tag{10}$$

$$cycle\ time = sum\ of\ all\ seek\ overheads\ for\ all\ requests$$
$$+\ sum\ of\ service\ time\ of\ all\ requests$$

i.e., $\quad t_{\text{cyc}} = \sum^n t_i^s + \sum^n t_i^r \tag{11}$

(9) becomes $\quad \forall s_i, r_i = \dfrac{R * t_i^r}{\sum^n t_i^s + \sum^n t_i^r} \tag{12}$

It is also true that the service time of each request is proportional to its playback rate: i.e.,

$$t_i^r \propto r_i \tag{13}$$

(This can be shown from (12), if we take two values of i say, $r_1 = \frac{R*t_1^r}{t_{\text{cyc}}}$ and $r_2 = \frac{R*t_2^r}{t_{\text{cyc}}}$, dividing we get $\frac{t_1^r}{t_2^r} = \frac{r_1}{r_2}$).

Hence, if t_j^r is the service time for the request stream 'j', we can represent all other t_i^r as a multiple (or fraction) of t_j^r as follows:

$$t_i^r = \left(\frac{r_i}{r_j}\right) * t_j^r \tag{14}$$

Substituting in (12) we have,

$$r_j = \frac{R * t_j^r}{\sum^n t_j^s + \frac{t_j^r * \sum^n r_i}{r_j}} \tag{15}$$

simplifying, we get the required service time for request s_j

$$t_j^r = \frac{r_j * \sum^n t_i^s}{R - \sum^n r_i} \tag{16}$$

We will simplify the notation by using:

$$\sum^n t_i^s = T_{\text{seek}} \quad \text{(The total seek overhead)}$$

and expressing the sum of the playback rates $= \sum^n r_i$ in terms of the disk transfer rate R as $u * R$ where u is the disk bandwidth utilization factor.

So Eq. (16) becomes $t_j^r = \frac{r_j * T_{\text{seek}}}{R - u * R}$

The **total buffer space B** is $=$ Disk transfer rate $*$ sum of the service times of all requests $= R * \sum^n t_j^r$.

We finally have,

$$B = R * \sum_{}^{n} \frac{r_j * T_{seek}}{R - u * R} = \frac{u * R * T_{seek}}{1 - u} \tag{17}$$

In words,

$$Total\ buffer\ space = \frac{Sum\ of\ playback\ rates * Total\ seek\ overhead}{1 - \dfrac{Sum\ of\ playback\ rates}{Disk\ transfer\ rate}}$$

We will use (17) repeatedly in the following sections for analysis.

We observe from (17) that:

The total buffer size is proportional to the total seek overhead T_{seek} and inversely proportional to the bandwidth utilization factor u.

Thus *a scheduling algorithm that minimizes* $\sum^n t_i^d$ *will also minimize* t_i^r *and (therefore all* t_i^r). This further leads to the conclusion that *a scheduling algorithm that minimizes* $\sum^n t_i^d$ **also minimizes the buffer requirements for each of the requests (and hence for the entire system)**.

Equation (17), offers a computationally easy method for the server to determine the service time and buffer size requirement for each request in terms of known quantities.

In the following discussion we will use the above relations to implement the C-SCAN scheduling algorithm and also show that it is more efficient than SCAN.

7.1. The C-SCAN algorithm for DVD video pumps

The scan algorithm continuously sweeps the disk from left to right and right to left and 'picks up' the sectors corresponding to each of the request streams as it does the sweeps.

Our measurement of the seek time vs. seek distance curve for CD-ROM drives is shown in figure 7.2 and for magnetic disks in figure 7.3. DVD-ROM drives also will have similar

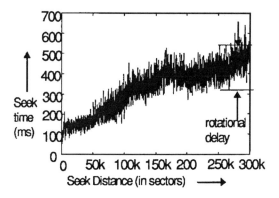

Figure 7.2.   Seek profile of a CDROM drive.

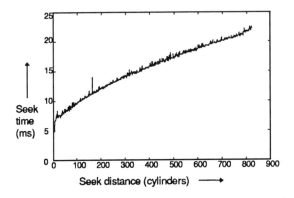

Figure 7.3. Seek profile for a magnetic disk.

curves as CD-ROM drives with the large order of seek times. The reason is the large moment of inertia of the Optical head (due to the complex lens-prism arrangement) and the very fine distances between tracks and the consequent difficulty in 'locking onto' the correct segment in the single-track spiral.

The saw-tooth variations are due to the rotational delay. Also, the saw-tooth band is narrow for smaller seek distances and broader for larger seek distances. This is due to the fact that the rotational speed is greater on the inner tracks than on the outer tracks (since it is a Constant Linear Velocity—CLV disk). For the purpose of discussion without losing generality, we can approximate this curve as a line as shown in figure 7.3.

Hence we write the approximation for the seek time as the equation for a line as (with slope $= \alpha$ and constant $= \beta$)

$$t_s = \alpha * d_s + \beta \tag{18}$$

For CD-ROM drives, the values of α *and* β *are* **0.0012 ms/sector and 100 ms** *respectively.* *DVD-ROM drives will have approximately similar values.* For magnetic drives, the α value is **0.02 ms/cylinder and** $\beta \cong$ **8 ms**.

Now, Consider an example of four requests s_1, s_2, s_3 and s_4 which arrive in that order. But if we sort the requests according their relative positions from the center of the disk, the order is s_1, s_3, s_2, s_4 with s_1 closest to the center of the disk (say leftmost) and s_4 being the farthest from the center (rightmost). This is illustrated in figure 7.4.

In a round robin algorithm, the sequence of servicing in a round will be $s_1, s_2, s_3, s_4, s_1, \ldots$ and the total seek overhead (per round) is $8\alpha * d_m + 4\beta$. (See figure 7.5).

In a SCAN, the service order will be $s_1, s_3, s_2, s_4, s_2, s_3, s_1, s_3 \ldots$ and the seek overhead will be $6\alpha * d_m + 6\beta$. However, the intermediate request streams are serviced twice. Once in the left-to-right sweep of the head and then on the right-to-left sweep. (See figure 7.5).

If the seek time vs. seek distance curve had started from the origin then the SCAN algorithm would have been optimal (in terms of buffer space requirements). This not being the case, leads us to prove (in the following section) that C-SCAN, where the head scans from left to right and services all the requests then sweeps back from right to left (idle seek)

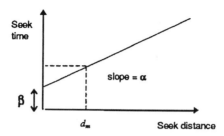

Figure 7.4. Approximation of the curve shown in figures 7.2 and 7.3.

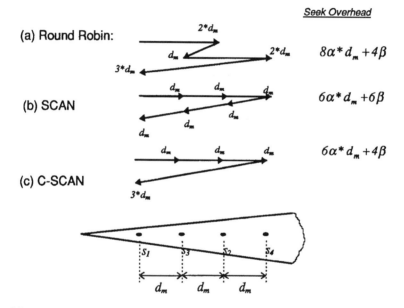

Figure 7.5. Movement of the head (and the seek overhead) for different algorithms.

without reading and starts another round. Hence the service order for the above example will be $s_1, s_2, s_3, s_4, s_1, \ldots$ and so on and the total seek overhead is $6\alpha * d_m + 4\beta$.

Since the cycle time in C-SCAN is less than in SCAN this offers the advantage that *startup-delay (when a new user is admitted) and servicing VCR-like requests from the user is faster than in SCAN.* We will look at this point later in Section 8.0.

7.2.   *Proof of optimality in terms of buffer usage of C-SCAN over SCAN*

Here we prove that C-SCAN is optimal as compared to SCAN in terms of buffer size needed.

Let the number of requests be 'n', their playback rates be 'r' (all equal) and the seek distance between the requests be 'd_m'.

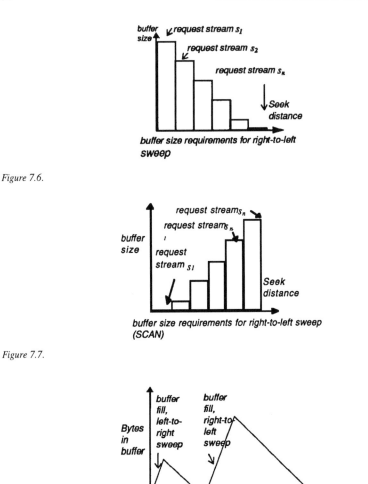

Figure 7.6.

Figure 7.7.

Figure 7.8.

In the SCAN algorithm, the buffer sizes that must be reserved for each of the request streams varies in the left-to-right and right-to-left sweep and is depicted in figures 7.5 and 7.6 respectively. The request streams which are located near the center of the extremes need equal sized-buffers allotted for the two sweeps whereas the request streams located near the end of the sweep require unequal sized buffers for the two sweeps. The process of buffer fills and buffer consumption for a channel which is nearer the right extreme is shown in figure 7.7.

In the C-SCAN algorithm since the all request streams have the same cycle time ('symmetrical'), the buffer sizes are all equal.

We have to prove that the total size of buffers in SCAN is more than the total size of the buffers in the C-SCAN algorithm.

For the following analysis we assume that the request streams are equally spaced from each other at a seek distance of d_m, the playback rate for all the streams is r_m, and the service time of request stream s_k is t_k.

The SCAN algorithm. There are $(n - 1)$ gaps between the 'n' requests and hence,

$$\textit{The total seek overhead} = \textit{seek overhead for the left-to-right sweep}$$
$$+ \textit{seek overhead for the right-to-left sweep}$$
$$= (2(n - 1) * (\alpha * d_m + \beta))$$

The service time for request 'k', for **both** sweeps is (from (16))

$$t_k = \frac{r_m * (2(n - 1) * (\alpha * d_m + \beta))}{R - n * r_m} \tag{19}$$

We also note that the total service times for all requests is the same and is t_k.

$$\textit{The total buffer space is therefore} = \textit{number of requests} * \textit{transfer rate} * \textit{service time}$$
$$= \frac{n * R * r_m * (2(n - 1) * (\alpha * d_m + \beta))}{R - n * r_m}$$

The C-SCAN algorithm. In the C-SCAN algorithm with the same request stream scenario,

$$\textit{The total seek overhead is} = 2(n - 1) * \alpha * d_m + n * \beta$$

The total buffer space requirement is

$$= \frac{n * R * r_m [2 * (n - 1) * \alpha * d_m + n * \beta]}{R - r_m * n} \tag{20}$$

If C-SCAN is optimal as compared to SCAN, then (19) > (20) must be true, i.e., after simplifying we get

$$2 * (n - 1) * \beta > n * \beta$$

which gives:

$$n > 2$$

Which implies that *when the number request streams is greater than two*, **C-SCAN uses lesser total buffer space than the buffer space used in SCAN.**

If we compare the ratio of the total buffer usage in SCAN to that in C-SCAN we have (from (19) and (20))

$$\frac{Total\ Buffer\ size\ in\ SCAN}{Total\ Buffer\ size\ in\ C\text{-}SCAN} = \frac{\dfrac{n * R * r_m * (2(n-1) * (\alpha * d_m + \beta))}{R - n * r_m}}{\dfrac{n * R * r_m[2 * (n-1) * \alpha * d_m + n * \beta)]}{R - n * r_m}}$$

$$= \frac{2(n-1) * (\alpha * d_m + \beta)}{2 * (n-1) * (\alpha * d_m + n * \beta)}$$

For **large** values of **n**,

- $n - 1 \cong n$.
- Large n implies that the *distance between requests reduces* and the contribution of α can be neglected as compared to the contribution by the β term. (Use of actual values shows that this is indeed true.)

Thus the above ratio simplifies to:

$$\frac{Total\ Buffer\ size\ in\ SCAN}{Total\ Buffer\ size\ in\ C\text{-}SCAN} = \frac{2n * (\alpha * d_m + \beta)}{2n * \alpha * d_m + n * \beta)} = 2$$

Thus for large values of 'n' the buffer size required for C-SCAN is twice as much as C-SCAN.

This is illustrated in the following section where we use numerical values to compare SCAN and C-SCAN to see actual values of buffer sizes.

In the above, for simplicity we have assumed that the requests are equally spaced. However, the values are the same even if the requests are unequally spaced provided the end points of the sweep are the same and the number of requests are the same. We have also verified this experimentally. This is because:

- The total contribution (to the seek overhead) of the α term during a round depends only on the *end-to-end distance traveled by the disk head* and not on the number of requests in between or the spacing between them.
- The total contribution due to the β terms depends only the *number of requests* and not on the spacing between them.

7.3. *Estimating the size of buffers in main memory*

We use the results of the previous section and known values to work out values buffer sizes for both C-SCAN and SCAN.

The point to note is: In a video pump, the environment is specific—a video pump is *not* a general-purpose computing system. Hence, optimizing RAM buffer size (in main memory) at run-time to benefit other processes on the system (as is the case in a general computing system) *is not important*. What *is important* is to answer the question: *How much of RAM needs to be installed specifically to buffer video data?*

This question is answered by assuming worst-case design conditions (i.e., maximum load) and using the relations developed above.

For DVD-ROM drives. For CD-ROM drives we have seen that typical values for α and β (from Section 7.1) are **0.0012 ms/*sector*** and **100 ms**. These values will be the same for DVD-ROM drives too.

We choose a DVD-ROM of transfer rate—10 Mbits/s (1.25 Mbytes/s). Hence this drive can support 8 MPEG-1 streams (each of 1.2 Mbits/s). We assume that all the eight requests are spaced uniformly over the disk (from each other) implying that the distance (in terms of sectors between them is $\frac{300000}{8}$ = 37500 sectors. This is because there are approximately 300000 sectors on the disk. The playback rate of MPEG-1 is 1.2 Mbits/s or 0.15 MB/s.

for **SCAN** using (21) the total buffer size is

$$= \frac{8 * 0.15 * 1.25 * (2 * (8 - 1) * (0.0012 * 37.5 + 0.1))}{1.25 - 8 * 0.15} \text{ Mbytes}$$

$$= \textbf{61 Mbytes}$$

for **C-SCAN** using (22) the total buffer size is

$$= \frac{8 * 0.15 * 1.25 * (2 * (8 - 1) * (0.0012 * 37.5 + 8 * 0.1))}{1.25 - 8 * 0.15} \text{ Mbytes}$$

$$= \textbf{36 MBytes}$$

For magnetic disks. We assume that maximum transfer rate of a magnetic drive is 5 MB/s. Hence a maximum of 32 streams off MPEG-1 can be supported.

We use the following values $\alpha = 0.02$ ms/*cylinder*, $\beta = 8$ ms.

for **SCAN** using (21) the total buffer size is

$$= \frac{32 * 5 * 0.15 * (2 * (32 - 1) * (0.02 * 0.026 + 0.008))}{5 - 32 * 0.15} \text{ Mbytes}$$

$$= \textbf{62 MBytes}$$

for **C-SCAN** using (22) the total buffer size is

$$= \frac{32 * 5 * 0.15 * (2 * (32 - 1) * (0.02 * 0.026 + 32 * 0.008))}{5 - 32 * 0.15} \text{ Mbytes}$$

$$= \textbf{35 MBytes}$$

It can be seen from the above that clearly C-SCAN is better than SCAN for video pumps. The shorter round time (cycle time) of C-SCAN also means that VCR-like requests from the user will suffer lesser latency. We will deal with this in more detail in a subsequent section.

Note. In our analysis we have considered the buffers to be circular. The size of buffers in both the algorithms doubles if circular buffers are not assumed. We also do not look at re-use of buffer space segments where data has already been consumed-in which case further savings on buffer sizes can be achieved.

8.0.   Admission control, handling VCR-like requests and VBR stream management

In this section we propose an algorithm for disk head scheduling and admission control that guarantees continuity requirements, is able manage VBR (Variable Bit Rate) streams such as MPEG-2 and is able to handle VCR-like requests such as fast-forward, fast-reverse and pause. We have developed a simulator which can be used to extract various parameters such as extra buffer sizes needed to handle VBR streams and the disk bandwidth utilization factor u needed for given load conditions. We discuss the design and implementation details of this algorithm.

As we have pointed out in Section 7.3, buffers in memory on the Video pump have to be designed considering the worst case load. This is the basis for our admission control algorithm.

We propose that:

- If we do not allow for buffer overruns or underflows, then we must provide for empty slots (**dummy requests**) to allow for the unused bandwidth of the server and any new request must be 'allotted' *from* this pool and any request leaving the server will be allotted *to* this pool.
- We will call this as the 'dummy request pool' which will always make **the *server operate under full-load conditions***. By full-load we mean the disk head will constantly seek from left to right and right to left (idle sweep) and the sum of the data rates of all requests (dummy and actual) will be nearly equal to the disk transfer rate and the number of dummy requests is the maximum possible number of requests to the server.
- What will be dynamic is *the proportion of dummy requests to the proportion of actual requests*. In other words, all the calculations will be under full load conditions.
- Hence in this scheme, the *key issue is*: *once we decide the cycle time (see figure **7**.1), it remains constant regardless of the number of __actual__ requests. We emphasize that the concept of the dummy request pool is notional and we use it simply to calculate the cycle time.*

We implement this in the following way:

- In order to calculate the total cycle time we need to estimate the seek time component and the service time component.
- The seek time component is decided based on the number of requests that we wish to service. We estimate n the number of requests as follows: If $r_{average}$ is the average playback rate of any request stream then $n = \lfloor \frac{R}{r_{average}} \rfloor$ (the maximum number of request streams that can be supported).
- The service time component of the cycle time is calculated by fixing the *Disk Utilization factor*. A higher utilization factor enables the server to meet temporary demands in bandwidth that exceed the disk bandwidth (which occurs in a VBR scenario). However

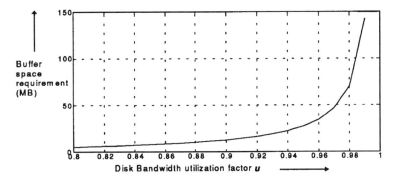

Figure 8.0. Buffer function for DVD-ROM as a function of *u* (8 request streams).

too large a value for the utilization factor also lengthens the cycle time which means that buffer sizes increase exponentially and requests such as fast-forward and fast-reverse suffer a larger latency. Here lies the trade-off.

- In each round, unused cycle time (for dummy requests) is used to fill the buffers. The 'extra' amount of service time is divided proportional to emptiness of the buffers of the requests.

Before discussing further details, we examine the effect of the Disk Utilization factor *u* on the buffer size. We use Eq. (17) to plot *u* vs. buffer size needed for a DVD-ROM drive with same characteristics as earlier. The plot is shown in figure 8.0.

In a VBR scenario, the load on the disk fluctuates and in some rounds, the total bandwidth requirement can exceed that of the disk. This situation can be handled if there are adequate number of extra bytes in the buffers of each stream. Recall our bucket analogy. The question arises as to how much should this extra size of buffers be? As already mentioned above, in our algorithm, we are maintaining the cycle time constant. In some of the cycles we use the unused disk bandwidth (of dummy requests) to fill (by equal amounts) the buffers corresponding each of the requests to take care of sudden demands in bandwidth.

To estimate the correct the value of *u*, we have simulated a scheduler that operates according to the steps outlined above and uses the approximation of the disk model of figure 7.4. We also use this to track buffer sizes and work out other parameters such as the maximum extra buffer size needed to sustain sporadic demands for bandwidth. The playback demands on the simulator are streams with a VBR characteristic. The playback rate for each request stream in every round is generated randomly. We ensure that the lower bound on this bitrate is r_{low} and the upper bound is $2 * r_{low}$. With an average bit rate of $r_{average}$.

We choose a magnetic disk and look at MPEG-2 VBR streams for the analysis. The following are the parameters:

Disk bandwidth: 6 MB/s (48 Mbits/s). Total contribution of the α terms is 0.017 s . $\beta =$ 0.015 s.

Playback streams: MPEG-2 with bit rate varying from 4 Mbits/s to 8 Mbits/s with an average of 6 Mbits/s.

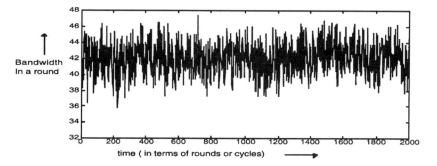

Figure 8.1.   Variation of total bandwidth of 7 VBR streams in a round.

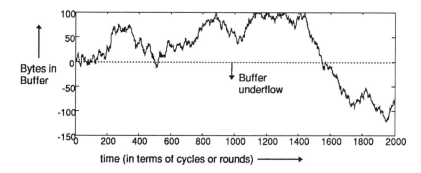

Figure 8.2.   Illustrates buffer (size unlimited) underflow for 87.5% utilization factor.

Thus we can serve $\frac{48}{6} - 1 = 7$ streams. This requires a bandwidth utilization of $\frac{7*6*100}{48}$ $= 87.5\%$.

The cycle time is: **1.096 s.**

The buffer size required (using C-SCAN) is **5.1 MB.**

We run the simulator for 2000 rounds which is equivalent to about 1 hour of MPEG-2 playback.

The variation of the total playback bit rate per cycle (which is generated randomly in our simulator) is illustrated in figure 8.1. The buffer function is shown in figure 8.2. We observe that the buffers suffer from heavy underflow. We purposely fix a high upper bound (100 MB) on the *extra* buffer size to observe this. This points to the fact that the disk bandwidth utilization factor u that we have chosen is inadequate.

We find through the simulator that if we choose a 90% utilization factor (resulting in a buffer space of 6.6 MB) and provide for an *additional* buffer space of 3 MB, buffer underflows are completely avoided. The buffer function for these conditions is illustrated in figure 8.3. This increase in u also results in an increase in the cycle time to **1.37 s.** This is the worst-case delay that the user will suffer in response to a VCR-like request.

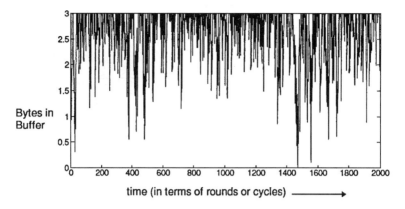

Figure 8.3. Buffer (Limited size) function with 90% disk utilization.

The simulator can be used to calculate the required utilization factor **u** and buffer sizes needed for any given load conditions and disk characteristics which can obtained through a seek time measurement.

Buffer costs. Our simulator can be used to quickly extract buffer size requirements. These values together with the results in sections 1 to 6 will enable the calculation of the overall cost and design parameters, migration criteria for a particular configuration and load scenarios. Tables 8.0 and 8.1 give an idea of these sizes for typical load conditions for DVD-ROM and magnetic disk systems. *The high costs of buffers relative to drive costs suggest strongly that buffer re-use algorithms can play a crucila role and could lower costs substantially in video servers.*

Table 8.0. Overview of buffer costs for typical MPEG-1 loads.

	Values for MPEG-1 streams at 1.2 Mbit/s		
Disk type	Disk parameters	Number of streams	Buffer size/cost
DVD-ROM	1.8 MB/s (12X speed)	10 ($u = 84\%$)	15 MB ($150)
Magnetic disk	6 MB/s	36 ($u = 90\%$)	22 MB ($220)

Table 8.1. Overview of buffer costs for typical MPEG-2 VBR loads.

	Values for MPEG-2 VBR streams at an average of 6 MB/s		
Disk type	Disk parameters	Number of streams	Buffer size/cost
DVD-ROM	1.8 MB/s (12X speed)	2($u = 87\%$)	15 MB ($150)
Magnetic disk	6 MB/s	7($u = 90\%$)	8 MB ($80)

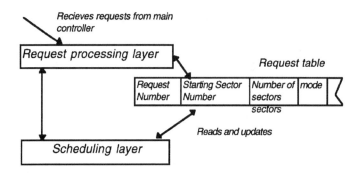

Figure 8.4. Implementation of admission control.

Further implementation details are as follows.

- The scheduler software running on the server is divided into two layers: the request processing layer and the layer responsible for data retrieval. See figure 8.4.
- They share a common data structure known as the request table, each entry of which contains the request number, starting sector for that request, number of sectors to be retrieved for that request (calculated from the service time) and other fields such as the mode (normal, fast-forward, fast-reverse or pause).
- The entries in the table are inserted and deleted in C-SCAN order.
- An index for the movie on the disk is maintained as shown in figure 8.0. It is used by the scheduling layer to calculate the service time for each request before each round.
- The request processing layer receives requests from the request router, and using the index information, makes or deletes appropriate entries in the request table.
- The new requests are admitted only at the beginning of a cycle (round) depending on whether bandwidth is available or not.
- When there is a request for fast-forward, for instance, the request processing layer changes the mode flag for that request. The scheduler then calculates the starting sector for that request, for a new round by skipping a certain number of sectors (which it determines from the steam index of figure 8.0).
- The general flow of the scheduler is shown in figure 8.3.

The stream index. The index of the stored movie is vital for the implementation of the above algorithm. In MPEG streams the GOP (Group of Pictures) is the unit of random access. Hence all VCR-like requests such as fast forward, and fast-reverse need to do these operations at GOP boundaries. This is true even if the stream is a system stream, i.e., if it is embedded in the pack-packet architecture of MPEG. Each movie (stream) must have a table with the entries as shown in figure 8.5, indexed by the GOP number.

Size of the index. Usually in MPEG, the number of frames per GOP is about 15. This implies that on the average 2 GOP/s are retrieved to maintain the 30 frames/s rate of full screen—full motion video. Hence for a 2 hour movie we will have $2 * 60 ** 60 * 2 = 14400$ GOPs. Assuming that there are 32 bytes per entry in the table, the table size will be 460,800 bytes—a negligible overhead.

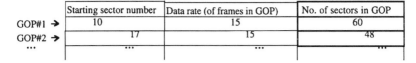

	Starting sector number	Data rate (of frames in GOP)	No. of sectors in GOP
GOP#1 →	10	15	60
GOP#2 →	17	15	48
...	...	...	...

Figure 8.5.   Table showing structure of the stream index.

Processing of VCR-like requests by the scheduling layer.   As mentioned earlier, the request layer uses the mode flag in the request table to inform the scheduling layer that the user has asked for a fast-forward, fast-reverse or pause. Let us look at fast-forward first. In normal mode, the scheduling layer retrieves successive GOPs belonging to the stream. When the scheduling layer sees that the mode flag has changed to *fast-forward*, instead of entering the sector number corresponding to the successive GOP to be retrieved, it skips a pre-determined number of GOPs and enters (in the request table), the corresponding sector number, obtained from the index. This is made more clear in figure 8.2 where we assume for simplicity that a constant number of GOPs are retrieved in each round for the stream (i.e., it is a Constant Bit rate stream). In figure 8.2, three GOPs are skipped for both the fast-forward and fast-reverse operations. We also note that for fast-reverse, although in successive rounds the GOPs retrieved are previous ones, in a round they are successive GOPs. An important point to keep in mind is that the VCR-like operations do not change the bandwidth requirements from the disc—they only change the retrieval sequence for the stream and hence will incur more seek overhead (since non-consecutive GOPs are retrieved).

Startup-delay and latency to VCR-like requests.   While admitting new requests or while handling VCR-like requests the user will experience a delay before the request is serviced. The worst-case latency is one cycle time and the average is half this value. Hence the C-SCAN algorithm is advantageous from this point of view as well since it incurs the least cycle time.

Summary of results and conclusions of Sections 7.0 and 8.0

- We have worked out a simple relation to calculate the service time for a request in a multiple request scenario in a video pump. The number of request streams that can be serviced depends only on the playback rates of these streams and the disk transfer rate, and is independent of the scheduling algorithm.
- Seek optimization serves to reduce buffer sizes for the request streams and we prove that the algorithm that does this best is the C-SCAN algorithm. C-SCAN also yields shorter cycle times which will reduce the latency to VCR-like requests from the user. We estimate buffer sizes using the relations.
- We propose a 'full-load' admission control algorithm that uses the concept dummy requests resulting in a constant round time.
- We provide for extra buffers to meet sporadic bandwidth demands that are more than the disk bandwidth. We use a simulator from which for a given load scenario, we extract the disk bandwidth utilization factor and the sizes of these additional buffers.

- The scheduling algorithm relies on a stream index to implement operations such as fast forward and fast-reverse. The stream index reflects the structure of the movie (stored in MPEG format) on the disk.

Conclusion

In this paper we have looked at a comprehensive set of issues in the implementation of a video server: We first looked at cost of implementation of a video server using a memory hierarchy of DVD-ROM drives, magnetic RAID arrays and RAM memory. We have given relations by which we work out conditions by which a video migrates from one-layer to the next. We then given relations and methods by which the amount of storage at each layer can be calculated to optimize cost/performance.

In the next section, we have addressed the issues of buffer management, scheduling and admission control and their implementation in Video pumps. We first derive relations by which the service times for each request can be calculated. We then prove that C-SCAN is the best algorithm in a Video-pump. We then discuss the implementation of a constant round time scheduling algorithm in a Video pump where we use a simulator to extract various parameters such as buffer sizes and the disk utilization factor for given load conditions. We finally discuss implementation of VCR-like requests from the user using a stream index.

References

1. E. Biersack et al., "Constant data length retrieval for video servers with variable bit rate streams," IEEE Multimedia (ICMCS'96) Hiroshima, pp. 151–155, 1996.
2. BYTE magazine, June '95, Jan. '95, Feb. '95, Aug. '96.
3. E. Chang and A. Zakhor, "Cost analysis for VBR video servers," SPIE/IS&T Multimedia Computing and Networking, pp. 381–398, 1996.
4. P. Pin-Shan Chen, "The compact disk ROM: How it works," IEEE Spectrum, pp. 44–54, April 1988.
5. A. Dan and D. Sitaram, "Generalized interval caching policy for mixed interactive and long video workloads," SPIE/IS&T Multimedia Computing and Networking, pp. 344–351, 1996.
6. Y.N. Doganata and A.N. Tantawi, "Making a cost-effective video server," IEEE Multimedia, pp. 22–30, Winter 1994.
7. Electronic Design, Sept. '94, June '94.
8. D.J. Gemmel, J. Han, R.J. Beaton, and S. Christodulakis, "Delay sensitive multimedia on disks," IEEE Multimedia, pp. 56–66, Fall 1994.
9. D.J. Gemmel, V.M. Harrick, D.D. Kandlur, P.V. Rangan, and L. Rowe, "Multimedia storage servers—A tutorial," IEEE Computer, Vol. 28, No. 25, May 1995.
10. http://www.visblelight.com/mpeg/resource/faq/496dvd.txt, Chad Fogg's Unofficial DVD Technical Specification.
11. http://www.disktrend.com, Market reports of magnetic and optical drives.
12. http://www.philips.com/pbm/laseroptics/dvd.htm
13. http://www.toshiba.com/tacp/SD
14. B. Ozden et al., "A low-cost storage server for movie on demand databases," Proceedings of the Twentieth International Conference on Very Large Databases, Santiago, Sept. 1994.
15. B. Ozden et al., "Disk striping in video server environments," IEEE Multimedia (ICMCS '96), pp. 580–589, 1996.
16. David A. Patterson and John L. Hennessey, Computer Architecture a Quantitative Approach, Morgan Kaufmann Publishing, CA.
17. PC Magazine, March '95, July '96.
18. P.V. Rangan and Harrick Vin, "Designing file systems for digital audio and video," Proceedings of the 13th ACM symposium on Operating Systems Principles (SOSP'91) Operating Systems Review, pp. 69–79.

19. P.V. Rangan et al., "Designing an on-demand multimedia service," IEEE Communications Magazine, pp. 56–64, July 1992.
20. P.V. Rangan and V.M. Harrick, "Efficient storage techniques for digital continuous media," IEEE Transactions on Knowledge and Data Engineering, Vol. 5, No. 4, Aug. 1993.
21. C. Ruemmler and J. Wilkes, "An introduction to disk drive modeling," IEEE Computer, Vol. 27, No. 3, pp. 69–74, March 1994.
22. R. Steinmetz, "Multimedia file systems survey: Approaches for continuous media disk scheduling," Computer Communications, pp. 133–144, March 1995.
23. H.M. Vin, A. Goyal, and P. Goyal, "Algorithms for designing multimedia servers," Computer Communications, pp. 192–203, March 1995.
24. H.M. Vin, Sriram S. Rao, and P. Goyal, "Optimizing the placement of multimedia objects on disk arrays," IEEE Multimedia (ICMCS '95), Washington, pp. 158–165.
25. Philip Yu, M. Chen, and D. Kandlur, "Grouped sweeping scheduling for DASD-based multimedia storage management," Multimedia Systems Journal, pp. 99–109, 1993.

3

Mitra: A Scalable Continuous Media Server*

SHAHRAM GHANDEHARIZADEH   shahram@research.panasonic.com
ROGER ZIMMERMANN, WEIFENG SHI AND REZA REJAIE
DOUG IERARDI   ierardi@cs.usc.edu
TA-WEI LI
Computer Science Department, University of Southern California, Los Angeles, California 90089

Abstract. Mitra is a scalable storage manager that supports the display of continuous media data types, e.g., audio and video clips. It is a software based system that employs off-the-shelf hardware components. Its present hardware platform is a cluster of multi-disk workstations, connected using an ATM switch. Mitra supports the display of a mix of media types. To reduce the cost of storage, it supports a hierarchical organization of storage devices and stages the frequently accessed objects on the magnetic disks. For the number of displays to scale as a function of additional disks, Mitra employs staggered striping. It implements three strategies to maximize the number of simultaneous displays supported by each disk. First, the EVEREST file system allows different files (corresponding to objects of different media types) to be retrieved at different block size granularities. Second, the FIXB algorithm recognizes the different zones of a disk and guarantees a continuous display while harnessing the average disk transfer rate. Third, Mitra implements the Grouped Sweeping Scheme (GSS) to minimize the impact of disk seeks on the available disk bandwidth.

In addition to reporting on implementation details of Mitra, we present performance results that demonstrate the scalability characteristics of the system. We compare the obtained results with theoretical expectations based on the bandwidth of participating disks. Mitra attains between 65% to 100% of the theoretical expectations.

Keywords: video, zoned disks, scalable servers, multi-disk hardware platforms, striping, file system management

1.   Introduction

The past few years have witnessed many design studies describing different components of a server that supports continuous media data types, such as audio and video. The novelty of these studies is attributed to two requirements of continuous media that are different from traditional textual and record-based data. First, the retrieval and display of continuous media are subject to real-time constraints that impact both (a) the storage, scheduling and delivery of data, and (b) the manner in which multiple users may share resources. If the resources are not shared and scheduled properly then a display might starve for data, resulting in disruptions and delays that translate into jitter with video and random noises with audio. These disruptions and delays are termed *hiccups*. Second, objects of this media type are typically large in size. For example, a two hour MPEG-2 encoded video requiring 4 Megabits per second (Mbps) for its display is 3.6 Gigabyte in size. Three minutes of uncompressed CD quality audio with a 1.4 Mbps bandwidth requirement is 31.5 Megabyte

*This research was supported in part by a Hewlett-Packard unrestricted cash/equipment gift, and the National Science Foundation under grants IRI-9203389 and IRI-9258362 (NYI award).

(MByte) in size. The same audio clip in MPEG-encoded format might require 0.38 Mbps for its display and is 8.44 Mbyte.

Mitra is a realization of several promising design concepts described in the literature. Its primary contributions are two-fold: (1) to demonstrate the feasibility of these designs, and (2) to achieve the non-trivial task of gluing these together into a system that is both high performance and scalable. Mitra is a software based system that can be ported to alternative hardware platforms. It **guarantees** simultaneous display of a collection of different media types as long as the bandwidth required by the display of each media type is constant (isochronous). For example, Mitra can display both CD-quality audio clips with a 1.34 Mbps bandwidth requirement and MPEG-2 encoded streams with 4 Mbps bandwidth requirement (two different media types) at the same time as long as the bandwidth required by each display is constant. Moreover, Mitra can display those media types whose bandwidth requirements might exceed that of a single disk drive (e.g., uncompressed NTSC CCIR 601 video clips requiring 270 Mbps for their display) in support of high-end applications that cannot tolerate the use of compression techniques.

Due to their large size, continuous media objects are almost always disk resident. Hence, the limiting resource in Mitra is the available disk bandwidth, i.e., traditional I/O bottleneck phenomena. Mitra is scalable because it can service a higher number of simultaneous displays as a function of additional disk bandwidth. The key technical idea that supports this functionality is to distribute the workload imposed by each display evenly across the available disks using staggered striping [3] to avoid the formation of hot spots and bottleneck disks.

Mitra is high performance because it implements techniques that maximize the number of displays supported by each disk. This is accomplished in two ways. First, Mitra minimizes both the number of seeks incurred when reading a block (using EVEREST [18]) and the amount of time attributed to each seek (using GSS [33]). Second, it maximizes the transfer rate of multi-zone disks by utilizing the bandwidth of different zones in an intelligent manner (FIXB [19]). Mitra's file system is EVEREST. As compared with other file systems, EVEREST provides two functionalities. First, it enables Mitra to retrieve different files at different block size granularities. This minimizes the percentage of disk bandwidth that is wasted when Mitra displays objects that have different bandwidth requirements. Second, it avoids the fragmentation of disk space when supporting a hierarchy of storage devices [4] where different objects are swapped in and out of the available disk space over time. GSS minimizes the amount of time attributed to each seek by optimizing the disk scheduling algorithm. Finally, FIXB in combination with EVEREST enables Mitra to guarantee a continuous display while harnessing the average transfer rate of multi-zone disks [31, 16]. FIXB enables Mitra to strike a compromise between the percentage of wasted disk space and how much of its transfer rate is harnessed. With each of these techniques, there are tradeoffs associated with the choices of values for system parameters. Although these tradeoffs have been investigated using analytical and simulation studies, Mitra's key contribution is to demonstrate that these analyses hold true in practice. It shows that one does not have to rewrite software to support diverse applications with different performance objectives (startup latency versus throughput versus wasted disk space). Instead, there is a single system, where different choices of parameters support different application requirements.

Table 1. Parameters and their definition.

Parameter	Definition
η	Number of media types
$\mathcal{R}_C(M_i)$	Bandwidth required to display objects of media type i
$\mathcal{R}_D$	Bandwidth of a disk
$\mathcal{B}(M_i)$	Block size for media type i
D	Total number of disks
d	Number of disks that constitute a cluster
$\mathcal{C}$	Number of clusters recognized by the system
g	Number of groups with GSS
k	Stride with staggered striping
$\mathcal{N}$	Number of simultaneous displays supported by the system
S	Maximum height of sections with EVEREST
ω	Number of contiguous buddies of section height i that form a section of height $i+1$

Several related studies have described the implementation of continuous media servers[1]. These can be categorized into single-disk and multi-disk systems. The single-disk systems include [1, 8, 26, 30]. These pioneering studies were instrumental in identifying the requirements of continuous media. They developed scheduling policies for retrieving blocks from disk into memory to support a continuous display. (Mitra employs these policies as detailed in Section 3.) Compared with Mitra, most of them strive to be general purpose and support traditional file system accesses in addition to a best-effort delivery of continuous media. Thus, none strive to maximize the number of displays supported by a disk using alternative disk scheduling policies, techniques that harness the average transfer rate of disk zones, or strategies that constrained the physical file layout. The multi-disk systems include: Streaming RAID [32], Fellini [28], and Minnesota's VOD server [23]. None claims to support either the display of a mix of media types or a hierarchical storage structure, nor do they describe the implementation of a file system that ensures contiguous layout of a block on the disk storage medium. (The authors of Fellini identify the design of a file system such as the one developed for Mitra as an important research direction in [29].) Moreover, all three systems employ disk arrays where the number of disks that are treated as a single logical disk is pre-determined by the hardware. Mitra differs in that the number of disks that are treated as one logical disk is NOT hardware dependent. Instead, it is determined by the bandwidth requirement of a media type. Indeed, if one analyzes two different displays with each accessing a different media type, one display might treat two disks as one logical disk while the other might treat five disks as one logical disk. This has a significant impact on the number of simultaneous displays supported by the system as detailed in Section 4.

Streaming RAID implements GSS to maximize the bandwidth of a disk array and employs memory-sharing to minimize the amount of memory required at the server. It develops analytical models similar to [12, 14] to estimate the performance of the system with alternative configuration parameters. Fellini analyzes constraint placement of data to enhance

Table 2. Defining terms.

Mbps	Megabits per second
Block	Amount of data retrieved per time period on behalf of a PM displaying an object of media type i. Its size varies depending on the media type and is denoted as $\mathcal{B}(M_i)$
Fragment	Fraction of a block assigned to one disk of a cluster that contains the block. All fragments of a block are equi-sized
Time period	The amount of time required to display a block at a station. This time is fixed for all media types, independent of their bandwidth requirement
Page	Basic unit of allocation with EVEREST, also termed sections of height 0
Startup latency	Amount of time elapsed from when a PM issues a request for an object to the onset of the display

the performance of the system with multi-zone disks. The design appears to be similar to FIXB. Fellini describes several designs to support VCR features such as Fast Forward and Rewind. (We hint at Mitra's designs to support this functionality in Section 5 and do not detail them due to lack of space.) Neither Fellini nor Streaming RAID present performance numbers from their system. Minnesota's VOD server differs from both Mitra and the other two multi-disk systems in that it does not have a centralized scheduler. Hence, it cannot guarantee a continuous display. However, [23] presents performance numbers to demonstrate that a mass storage system can display continuous media.

The rest of this paper is organized as follows. In Section 2, we provide an overview of the software components of Mitra and its current hardware platform. Section 3 describes the alternative components of the system (EVEREST, GSS, FIXB, and staggered striping) and how they interact with each other to guarantee a continuous display. Section 4 presents experimental performance results from Mitra. As a yard stick, we compare these numbers with theoretical expectations based on the available disk bandwidth [14, 15]. The obtained results: (1) demonstrate the scalability of the system, (2) show that Mitra attains between 65% to 100% of the theoretical expectations. Our future research directions are presented in Section 5.

2. An overview of Mitra

Mitra employs a hierarchical organization of storage devices to minimize the cost of providing on-line access to a large volume of data. It is currently operational on a cluster of HP 9000/735 workstations. It employs a HP Magneto Optical Juke-box as its tertiary storage device. Each workstation consists of a 125 MHz PA-RISC CPU, 80 MByte of memory, and four Seagate ST31200W magnetic disks. Mitra employs the HP-UX operating system (version 9.07) and is portable to other hardware platforms. While 15 disks can be attached to the fast and wide SCSI-2 bus of each workstation, we attached four disks to this chain because additional disks would exhaust the bandwidth of this bus. It is undesirable to exhaust the bandwidth of the SCSI-2 bus for several reasons. First, it would cause the underlying hardware platform to not scale as a function of additional disks. Mitra is a software system and if its underlying hardware platform does not scale then the entire system would not scale. Second, it renders the service time of each disk unpredictable, resulting in hiccups.

Mitra consists of three software components:

1. Scheduler: This component schedules the retrieval of the blocks of a referenced object in support of a hiccup-free display at a PM. In addition, it manages the disk bandwidth and performs admission control. Currently, Scheduler includes an implementation of EVEREST, staggered striping, and techniques to manage the tertiary storage device. It also has a simple relational storage manager to insert, and retrieve information from a *catalog*. For each media type, the catalog contains the bandwidth requirement of that media type and its block size. For each presentation, the catalog contains its name, whether it is disk resident (if so, the name of EVEREST files that represent this clip), the cluster and zone that contains its first block, and its media type.
2. Mass storage Device Manager (DM): Performs either disk or tertiary read/write operations.
3. Presentation Manager (PM): Displays either a video or an audio clip. It might interface with hardware components to minimize the CPU requirement of a display. For example, to display an MPEG-2 clip, the PM might employ either a program or a hardware-card to decode and display the clip. The PM implements the PM-driven scheduling policy of Section 3.1.3 to control the flow of data from the Scheduler.

Mitra uses UDP for communication between the process instantiation of these components. UDP is an unreliable transmission protocol. Mitra implements a light-weight kernel, named HP-NOSE. HP-NOSE supports a window-based protocol to facilitate reliable transmission of messages among processes. In addition, it implements the threads with shared memory, ports that multiplex messages using a single HP-UX socket, and semaphores for synchronizing multiple threads that share memory. An instantiation of this kernel is active per Mitra process.

For a given configuration, the following processes are active: one Scheduler process, a DM process per mass storage read/write device, and one PM process per active client. For example, in our twelve disk configuration with a magneto optical juke box, there are sixteen active processes: fifteen DM processes, and one Scheduler process (see figure 1). There are two active DM processes for the magneto juke-box because it consists of two read/write devices (and 32 optical platters that might be swapped in and out of these two devices).

The combination of the Scheduler with DM processes implements asynchronous read/write operations on a mass storage device (which is otherwise unavailable with HP-UX 9.07). This is achieved as follows. When the Scheduler intends to read a block from a device (say a disk), it sends a message to the DM that manages this disk to read the block. Moreover, it requests the DM to transmit its block to a destination port address (e.g., the destination might correspond to the PM process that displays this block) and issue a done message to the Scheduler. There are several reasons for not routing data blocks to active PMs using the Scheduler. First, it would waste the network bandwidth with multiple transmissions of a block. Second, it would limit the scalability of the system because the processing capability of the workstation that supports the Scheduler process would determine the overall throughput of the system. CPU processing is required because a transmitted data block

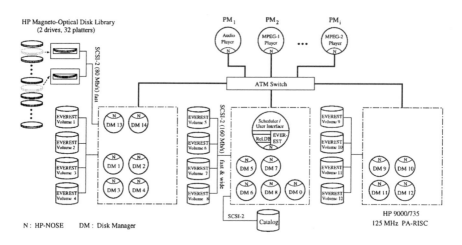

Figure 1. Hardware and software organization of Mitra. Note: While 15 disks can be attached to the fast and wide SCSI-2 bus of each workstation, we attached four disks because additional disks would exhaust the bandwidth of this bus.

is copied many times by different layers of software that implement the Scheduler process: HP-UX, HP-NOSE, and the Scheduler.

While the interaction between the different processes and threads is interesting, we do not report on them due to lack of space.

3. Continuous display with Mitra

We start by describing the implementation techniques of Mitra for a configuration that treats the d available disks as a single disk drive. This discussion introduces EVEREST [18], Mitra's file system, and motivates a PM-driven scheduling paradigm that provides feedback from a PM to the Scheduler to control the rate of data production. Subsequently, we discuss an implementation of the staggered striping [3] technique.

3.1. One disk configuration

To simplify the discussion and without loss of generality, conceptualize the d disks as a single disk with the aggregate transfer rate of d disks. When we state that a block is assigned to the disk, we imply that the block is declustered [3, 10] across the d disks. Each piece of this block is termed a *fragment*. Moreover, when we state a DM reads a block from the disk, we imply that d DM processes are activated simultaneously to produce the fragments that constitute the block.

To display an object X of media type M_i (say CD-quality audio) with bandwidth requirement $\mathcal{R}_C(M_i)$ (1.34 Mbps), Mitra conceptualizes X as consisting of r blocks: $X_0, X_1, \ldots, X_{r-1}$. Assuming a block size of $\mathcal{B}(M_i)$, the display time of a block, termed a *time period* [15], equals $\frac{B(M_i)}{\mathcal{R}_C(M_i)}$. Assuming that the system is idle, when a PM references object X, the Scheduler performs two tasks. First, it issues a read request for X_0 to the DM. It also provides the network address of the PM, requesting the DM to forward X_0 directly to the PM. Second, after a pre-specified delay, it sends a control message to the PM to initiate the display of X_0. This delay is due to the implementation of both GSS [33] (detailed below) and FIXB [19] (described in Section 3.1.2). Once the PM receives a block, it waits for a control message from the Scheduler before initiating the display. The Scheduler requests the DM to transmit the next block of X (i.e., X_1) in the next time period to the PM. This enables the PM to provide for a smooth transition between the two blocks to provide for a hiccup-free display. With the current design, a PM requires enough memory to cache at least two blocks of data.

Given a database that consists of η different media types (say $\eta = 2$, MPEG-2 and CD-quality audio), the block size of each media type is determined such that the display time of a block (i.e., the duration of a time period at the Scheduler) is fixed for all media types. This is done as follows. First, one media type M_i (say CD-quality audio) with bandwidth requirement $\mathcal{R}_C(M_i)$ (1.34 Mbps) defines the base block size $B(M_i)$ (say 512 KByte). The block size of other media types is a function of their bandwidth, $\mathcal{R}_C(M_i)$, and $B(M_i)$. For each media type M_j, its block size is:

$$B(M_j) = \frac{\mathcal{R}_C(M_j)}{\mathcal{R}_C(M_i)} \times B(M_i)$$

In our example, the block size for MPEG-2 (4 Mbps) objects would be 1521.74 KByte.

In an implementation of a file system, the physical characteristics of a magnetic disk determines the granularity for the size of a block. With almost all disk manufacturers, the granularity is limited to $\frac{1}{2}$ KByte[2]. Mitra rounds up the block size of each object of a media type to the nearest $\frac{1}{2}$ KByte. Thus, in our example, the block size for MPEG-2 object would be 1522 KByte. However, Mitra does not adjust the duration of a time period to reflect this rounding up. Thus, for each time period, the system produces more data on behalf of a display as compared to the amount that the display consumes. The amount of accumulated data is dependent on both the number of blocks that constitute a clip and what fraction of each block is not displayed per time period. For example, with a two hour MPEG-2 video object, a display would have accumulated 622.7 KByte of data at the end of the display. Section 3.1.3 describes a scheduling paradigm that prevents the Scheduler from producing data should the amount of cached data become significant.

Mitra supports the display of $\mathcal{N}$ objects by multiplexing the disk bandwidth among $\mathcal{N}$ block retrievals. Its admission control policy ensures that the service time of these $\mathcal{N}$ block retrievals does not exceed the duration of a time period. The service time of the disk to retrieve a block of media type i is a function of $B(M_i)$, the disk transfer rate, rotational latency, and seek time. Mitra opens each disk in RAW mode [22]. We used the SCSI commands to interrogate the physical characteristics of each disk to determine its track sizes, seek characteristics, number of zones, and transfer rate of each zone. (To gather this information, one requires neither specialized hardware nor the use of the assembly programming language, see [16] for a detailed description of these techniques.) The Scheduler reads this information from a configuration file during its startup.

The Scheduler maintains the duration of a time period using a global variable and supports a linked list of requests that are currently active. In addition to other information, an element of this list records the service time of the disk to retrieve a block of the file referenced by this display. Mitra minimizes the impact of seeks incurred when retrieving blocks of different objects by implementing the GSS algorithm. With GSS, a time period might be partitioned into g groups. In its simplest form, GSS is configured with one group ($g = 1$). With $g = 1$, a PM begins to consume the block that was retrieved on its behalf during time period ℓ at the beginning of time period $\ell + 1$. This enables the disk scheduling algorithm to minimize the impact of seeks by retrieving the blocks referenced during a time period using a scan policy. Mitra implements this by synchronizing the display of the first block of an object (X_0) at the PM with the end of the time period that retrieved X_0. Once the display of X_0 is synchronized, the display of the other blocks are automatically synchronized due to a fixed duration for each time period. The synchronization of X_0 is achieved as follows. A PM does not initiate the display of X_0 until it receives a control message from the Scheduler. The Scheduler generates this message at the beginning of the time period that retrieved X_1.

With $g > 1$, Mitra partitions a time period into g equi-sized intervals. The Scheduler assigns a display to a single group and the display remains with this group until its display is complete. The retrieval of blocks assigned to a single group employs the elevator scheduling algorithm. This is implemented as follows. Assuming that group G_i retrieves a block of X per time period, the display of X_0 is started when the disk subsystem begins to service group G_{i+1}.

3.1.1. File system design.
The current implementation of Mitra assumes that a PM does not perform complex operations such as Fast-Forward, Fast-Rewind or Pause operations. Upon the arrival of a request for object X belonging to media type M_X, the admission control policy of the Scheduler is as follows. First, the Scheduler checks to see if another scheduled display is beginning the display of X, i.e., references X_0. If so, these two new requests are combined with each other into one. This enables Mitra to multiplex a single stream among multiple PMs. If no other stream is referencing X_0, starting with the current active group, the Scheduler locates the group with sufficient idle time to accommodate the retrieval of a block of size $\mathcal{B}(M_i)$. The implementation details of this policy are contained in Appendix A. If no group can accommodate the retrieval of this request, the Scheduler queues this request and examines the possibility of admitting it during the next time period.

With η media types, Mitra's file system might be forced to manage η different block sizes. Moreover, the blocks of different objects might be staged from the tertiary storage device onto magnetic disk storage on demand. A block should be stored contiguously on disk. Otherwise, the disk would incur seeks when reading a block, reducing disk bandwidth. Moreover, it might result in hiccups because the retrieval time of a block might become unpredictable. To ensure a contiguous layout of a block, we considered four alternative approaches: disk partitioning, extent-based [2, 5, 21], multiple block sizes, and an approximate contiguous layout of a file. We chose the final approach, resulting in the design and implementation of the EVEREST file system. Below, we describe each of the other three approaches and our reasons for abandoning them.

With disk partitioning, assuming η media types with η different block sizes, the available disk space is partitioned into η regions, one region per media type. A region i corresponds to media type i. The space of this region is partitioned into fix sized blocks, corresponding to $\mathcal{B}(M_i)$. The objects of media type i compete for the available blocks of this region. The amount of space allocated to a region i might be estimated as a function of both the size and frequency of access of objects of media type i [13]. However, partitioning of disk space is inappropriate for a dynamic environment where the frequency of access to the different media types might change as a function of time. This is because when a region becomes cold, its space should be made available to a region that has become hot. Otherwise, the hot region might start to exhibit a thrashing [6] behavior that would increase the number of retrievals from the tertiary storage device. This motivates a re-organization process to re-arrange disk space. This process would be time consuming due to the overhead associated with performing I/O operations.

With an extent-based design, a fixed contiguous chunk of disk space, termed an extent, is partitioned into fix-sized blocks. Two or more extents might have different page sizes. Both the size of an extent and the number of extents with a pre-specified block size (i.e., for a media type) is fixed at system configuration time. A single file may span one or more extents. However, an extent may contain no more than a single file. With this design, an object of a media type i is assigned one or more extents with block size $\mathcal{B}(M_i)$. In addition to suffering from the limitations associated with disk partitioning, this approach suffers from internal fragmentation with the last extent of an object being only partially occupied. This would waste disk space, increasing the number of references to the tertiary storage device.

With the Multiple Bock Size approach (MBS), the system is configured based on the media type with the lowest bandwidth requirement, say M_1. MBS requires the block size of each of media type j to be a multiple of $\mathcal{B}(M_1)$, i.e., $\mathcal{B}(M_j) = \lceil \frac{\mathcal{B}(M_j)}{\mathcal{B}(M_1)} \rceil \mathcal{B}(M_1)$. This might simplify the management of disk space to: 1) avoid its fragmentation, and 2) ensure the contiguous layout of each block of an object. However, MBS might waste disk bandwidth by forcing the disk to: (1) retrieve more data on behalf of a PM per time period due to rounding up of block size, and (2) remain idle during other time periods to avoid an overflow of memory at the PM. These are best illustrated using an example. Assume two media types MPEG-1 and MPEG-2 objects with bandwidth requirements of 1.5 Mbps and 4 Mbps, respectively. With this approach, the block size of the system is chosen based on MPEG-1 objects. Assume, it is chosen to be 512 KByte, $\mathcal{B}(\text{MPEG-1}) = 512$ KByte. This implies that $\mathcal{B}(\text{MPEG-2}) = 1365.33$ KByte. MBS would increase $\mathcal{B}(\text{MPEG-2})$ to equal 1536 KByte. To avoid excessive amount of accumulated data at a PM displaying an MPEG-2 clip, the Scheduler might skip the retrieval of data one time period every nine time periods using the PM-driven scheduling paradigm of Section 3.1.3. The Scheduler may not employ this idle slot to service another request because it is required during the next time period to retrieve the next block of current MPEG-2 display. If all active requests are MPEG-2 video clips and a time period supports nine displays with $\mathcal{B}(\text{MPEG-2}) = 1536$ KByte then, with $\mathcal{B}(\text{MPEG-2}) = 1365.33$ KByte, the system would support ten simultaneous displays (10% improvement in performance). In summary, the block size for a media type should approximate its theoretical value in order to maximize the number of simultaneous displays.

The final approach, and the one used by Mitra, employs the buddy algorithm to approximate a contiguous layout of a file on the disk without wasting disk space. The number of contiguous chunks that constitute a file is a fixed function of the file size and the configuration of the buddy algorithm. Based on this information, Mitra can either (1) prevent a block from overlapping two non-contiguous chunks or (2) allow a block to overlap two chunks and require the PM to cache enough data to hide the seeks associated with the retrieval of these blocks. Currently, Mitra implements the first approach. To illustrate the second approach, if a file consists of five contiguous chunks then at most four blocks of this file might span two different chunks. This implies that the retrieval of four blocks will incur seeks with at most one seek per block retrieval. To avoid hiccups, the Scheduler should delay the display of the data at the PM until it has cached enough data to hide the latency associated with four seeks. The amount of cached data is not significant. For example, assuming a maximum seek time of 20 milliseconds, with MPEG-2 objects (4 Mbps), the PM should cache 10 KByte to hide each seek. However, this approach complicates the admission control policy because the retrieval of a block might incur either one or zero seeks.

EVEREST. With EVEREST, the basic unit of allocation is a page,[3] also termed *sections* of height 0. EVEREST organizes these sections as a tree to form larger, contiguous sections. As illustrated in figure 2, only sections of size(page) $\times \omega^i$ (for $i \geq 0$) are valid, where the base ω is a system configuration parameter. If a section consists of ω^i pages then i is said to be the height of the section. The system can combine ω height i sections that are buddies (physically adjacent) to construct a section of height $i + 1$.

To illustrate, the disk in figure 2 consists of 16 pages. The system is configured with $\omega = 2$. Thus, the size of a section may vary from 1, 2, 4, 8, up to 16 pages. In essence, a binary tree is imposed upon the sequence of pages. The maximum height, computed by[4] $S = \lceil \log_\omega (\lfloor \frac{Capacity}{size(page)} \rfloor) \rceil$, is 4. With this organization imposed upon the device, sections of height $i \geq 0$ cannot start at just any page number, but only at offsets that are multiples of ω^i. This restriction ensures that any section, with the exception of the one at height S, has a total of $\omega - 1$ adjacent *buddy* sections of the same size at all times. With the base 2 organization of figure 2, each section has one buddy.

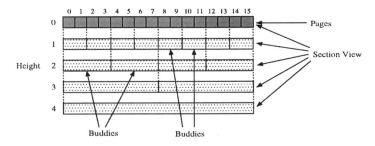

Figure 2. Physical division of disk space into pages and the corresponding logical view of the sections with an example base of $\omega = 2$.

With EVEREST, a portion of the available disk space is allocated to objects. The remainder, should any exist, is free. The sections that constitute the available space are handled by a *free list*. This free list is actually maintained as a sequence of lists, one for each section height. The information about an unused section of height i is enqueued in the list that handles sections of that height. In order to simplify object allocation, the following *bounded list length property* is always maintained: For each height $i = 0, \ldots, S$, at most $\omega - 1$ free sections of i are allowed. Informally, this property implies that whenever there exists sufficient free space at the free list of height i, EVEREST *must* compact these free sections into sections of a larger height[5].

The process of staging an object from tertiary onto available disk space is as follows. The first step is to check, whether the total number of pages in all the sections on the free list is either greater than or equal to the number of pages (denoted no-of-pages(X)) that the new object X requires. If this is not the case then one or more victim objects are elected and deleted. (The procedure for selecting a victim is based on heat [17]. The deletion of a victim object is described further below.) Assuming enough free space is available at this point, X is divided into its corresponding sections as follows. First, the number $m = $ no-of-pages(X) is converted to base ω. For example, if $\omega = 2$, and no-of-pages(X) = 13_{10} then its binary representation is 1101_2. The full representation of such a converted number is $m = d_{j-1} \times \omega^{j-1} + \cdots + d_2 \times \omega^2 + d_1 \times \omega^1 + d_0 \times \omega^0$. In our example, the number 1101_2 can be written as $1 \times 2^3 + 1 \times 2^2 + 0 \times 2^1 + 1 \times 2^0$. In general, for every digit d_i that is non-zero, d_i sections are allocated from height i of the free list on behalf of X. In our example, X requires 1 section from height 0, no sections from height 1, 1 section from height 2, and 1 section from height 3.

For each object, the number v of contiguous pieces is equal to the number of one's in the binary representation of m, or with a general base ω, $v = \sum_{i=0}^{j} d_i$ (where j is the total number of digits). Note that v is always bounded by $\omega \lceil \log_\omega m \rceil$. For any object, v defines the maximum number of sections occupied by the object. (The minimum is 1 if all v sections are physically adjacent.) A complication arises when no section at the right height exists. For example, suppose that a section of size ω^i is required, but the smallest section larger than ω^i on the free list is of size ω^j ($j > i$). In this case, the section of size ω^j can be split into ω sections of size ω^{j-1}. If $j - 1 = i$, then $\omega - 1$ of these are enqueued on the list of height i and the remainder is allocated. However, if $j - 1 > i$ then $\omega - 1$ of these sections are again enqueued at level $j - 1$, and the splitting procedure is repeated on the remaining section. It is easy to see that, whenever the total amount of free space on these lists is sufficient to accommodate the object, then for each section that the object occupies, there is always a section of the appropriate size, or larger, on the list. This splitting procedure will guarantee that the appropriate number of sections, each of the right size, will be allocated, and that the bounded list length property is never violated.

When there is insufficient free disk space to materialize an object, then one or more victim objects (with copies on tertiary) are removed from the disk. Reclaiming the space of a victim requires two steps for each of its sections. First, the section must be appended to the free list at the appropriate height. The second step ensures that the bounded list length property is not violated. Therefore, whenever a section is enqueued in the free list at height i and the number of sections at that height is equal to or greater than ω, then ω sections must be combined into one section at height $i + 1$. If the list at $i + 1$ now violates bounded list length property, then once again space must be compacted and moved to section $i + 2$. This procedure might be repeated several times. It terminates when the length of the list for a higher height is less than ω.

Compaction of ω free sections into a larger section is simple when they are buddies; in this case, the combined space is already contiguous. Otherwise, the system might be forced to exchange one occupied section of an object with one on the free list in order to ensure contiguity of an appropriate sequence of ω sections at the same height. The following algorithm achieves space-contiguity among ω free sections at height i.

1. Check if there are at least ω sections for height i on the free list. If not, stop.
2. Select the first section (denoted s_j) and record its page-number (i.e., the offset on the disk drive). The goal is to free $\omega - 1$ sections that are buddies of s_j.
3. Calculate the page-numbers of s_j's buddies. EVEREST's division of disk space guarantees the existence of $\omega - 1$ buddy sections physically adjacent to s_j.
4. For every buddy $s_k, k \leq 0 \leq \omega - 1, k \neq j$, if it exists on the free list then mark it.
5. Any of the s_k unmarked buddies currently store parts of other object(s). The space must be re-arranged by swapping these s_k sections with those on the free list. Note that for every buddy section that should be freed there exists a section on the free list. After swapping space between every unmarked buddy section and a free list section, enough contiguous space has been acquired to create a section at height $i + 1$ of the free list.
6. Go back to Step 1.

To illustrate, consider the organization of space in figure 3(a). The initial set of disk resident objects is $\{X, Y, Z\}$ and the system is configured with $\omega = 2$. In figure 3(a), two sections are on the free list at height 0 and 1 (addresses 7 and 14 respectively), and Z is

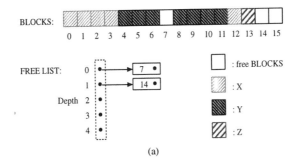

(a)

Figure 3. Deallocation of an object. The example sequence shows the removal of object Z from the initial disk resident object set $\{X, Y, Z\}$. Base two, $\omega = 2$. (a) Two sections are on the free list already (7 and 14) and object Z is deallocated. (b) Sections 7 and 13 should be combined, however they are not contiguous. (c) The buddy of section 7 is 6. Data must move from 6 to 13. (d) Sections 6 and 7 are contiguous and can be combined. (e) The buddy of section 6 is 4. Data must move from (4, 5) to (14, 15). (f) Sections 4 and 6 are now adjacent and can be combined. (g) The final view of the disk and the free list after removal of Z.

(Continued on next page.)

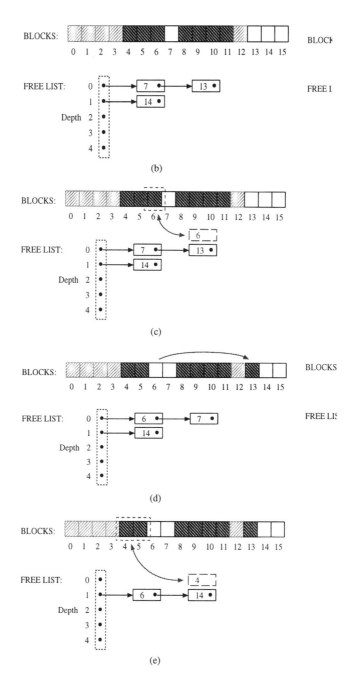

Figure 3. (Continues.)

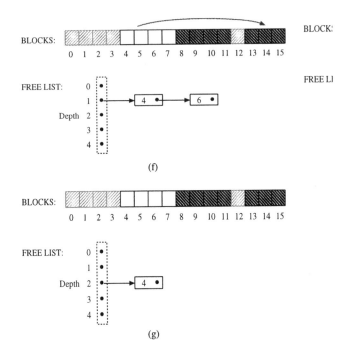

Figure 3. (*Continued.*)

the victim object that is deleted. Once page 13 is placed on the free list in figure 3(b), the number of sections at height 0 is increased to ω and it must be compacted according to Step 1. As sections 7 and 13 are not contiguous, section 13 is elected to be swapped with section 7's buddy, i.e., section 6 (figure 3(c)). In figure 3(d), the data of section 6 is moved to section 13 and section 6 is now on the free list. The compaction of sections 6 and 7 results in a new section with address 6 at height 1 of the free list. Once again, a list of length two at height 1 violates the bounded list length property and pages (4, 5) are identified as the buddy of section 6 in figure 3(e). After moving the data in figure 3(f) from pages (4, 5) to (14, 15), another compaction is performed with the final state of the disk space emerging as in figure 3(g).

Once all sections of a deallocated object are on the free list, the iterative algorithm above is run on each list, from the lowest to the highest height. The previous algorithm is somewhat simplified because it does not support the following scenario: a section at height i is not on the free list, however, it has been broken down to a lower height (say $i - 1$) and not all subsections have been used. One of them is still on the free list at height $i - 1$. In these cases, the free list for height $i - 1$ should be updated with care because those free sections have moved to new locations. In addition, note that the algorithm described above actually performs more work than is strictly necessary. A single section of a small height, for example, may end up being read and written several times as its section is combined into larger and larger sections. This is eliminated in the following manner. The algorithm is first performed "virtually"—that is, in main memory, as a compaction algorithm on the free lists. Once completed, the entire sequence of operations that have been performed determines the ultimate destination of each of the modified sections. The Scheduler constructs a list of these sections. This list is inserted into a queue of house keeping I/Os. Associated with each element of the queue is an estimated amount of time required to perform the task. Whenever the Scheduler locates one or more idle slots in the time period, it analyzes the queue of work for the element that can be processed using the available time. (Idle slots might be available with a workload that has completely utilized the number of idle slots due to the PM-driven scheduling paradigm of Section 3.1.3.)

The value of ω impacts the frequency of preventive operations. If ω is set to its minimum value (i.e., $\omega = 2$), then preventive operations would be invoked frequently because every time a new section is enqueued there is a 50% chance for a height of the free list to consist of two sections (violates the bounded list length property). Increasing the value of ω will therefore "relax" the system because it reduces the probability that an insertion to the free list would violate the bounded list length property. However, this would increase the expected number of bytes migrated per preventive operation. For example, at the extreme value of $\omega = n$ (where n is the total number of pages), the organization of blocks will consist of two levels, and for all practical purpose, EVEREST reduces to a standard file system that manages fix-sized pages.

The design of EVEREST suffers from the following limitation: the overhead of its preventive operations may become significant if many objects are swapped in and out of the disk drive. This occurs when the working set of an application cannot become resident on the disk drive.

In our implementation of EVEREST, it was not possible to fix the number of disk pages as an exact power of ω. The most important implication of an arbitrary number of pages is that some sections may not have the correct number of buddies ($\omega - 1$ of them). However, we can always move those sections to one end of the disk—for example, to the side with the highest page-offsets. Then instead of choosing the first section in Step 2 in the object deallocation algorithm, Mitra chooses the one with the lowest page-number. This ensures that the sections towards the critical end of the disk—that might not have the correct number of buddies—are never used in both Steps 4 and 5 of the algorithm.

Our implementation enables a process to retrieve a file using block sizes that are at the granularity of $\frac{1}{2}$ KByte. For example, EVEREST might be configured with a 64 KByte page size. One process might read a file at the granularity of 1365.50 KByte blocks, while another might read a second file at the granularity of 512 KByte.

The design of EVEREST is related to the buddy system proposed in [24, 25] for an efficient main memory storage allocator (DRAM). The difference is that EVEREST satisfies a request for b pages by allocating a number of sections such that their total number of pages equals b. The storage allocator algorithm, on the other hand, will allocate *one* section that is rounded up to $2^{\lceil lg\,b \rceil}$ pages, resulting in fragmentation and motivating the need for either a re-organization process or a garbage collector [21]. The primary advantage of the elaborate object deallocation technique of EVEREST is that it avoids both internal and external fragmentation of space as described for traditional buddy systems (see [21]).

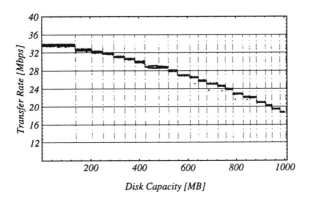

Figure 4.   Zone characteristics of the seagate ST31200W magnetic disk.

3.1.2. Multi-zone disks.   A trend in the area of magnetic disk technology is the concept of *zoning*. It increases the storage capacity of each disk. However, it results in a disk with variable transfer rates with different regions of the disk providing different transfer rates. Figure 4 shows the transfer rate of the 23 different zones that constitute each of the Seagate disks. (Techniques employed to gather these numbers are reported in [16].)

A file system that does not recognize the different zones might be forced to assume the bandwidth of the slowest zone as the overall transfer rate of the disk in order to guarantee a continuous display. In [19], we described two alternative techniques to support continuous display of audio and video objects using multi-zone disks, namely, FIXed Block size (FIXB) and VARiable Block size (VARB). These two techniques harness the average transfer rate of zones. Mitra currently implements FIXB[6]. It organizes an EVEREST file system on each region of the disk drive. Next, it assigns the blocks of each object to the zones in a round-robin manner. The blocks of each object that are assigned to a zone are stored as a single EVEREST file. In the catalog, Mitra maintains the identity of each EVER-EST file that constitute a clip, its block size, and the zone that contains the first block of this clip.

The Scheduler scans the disk in one direction, say starting with the outermost zone moving inward. It recognizes m different zones, however, only one zone is active per time period. A global variable Z_{Active} denotes the identity of the active zone. The bandwidth of each zone is multiplexed among all active displays. Once the disk reads data from the innermost zone, it is repositioned to the outermost zone to start another sweep. The time to perform on weep is denoted as T_{scan}. The block size is chosen such that the amount of data produced by Mitra for a PM during one T_{scan} equals the amount of data consumed at the PM. This requires the faster zones to compensate for the slower zones. As demonstrated in figure 5, data accumulates at the PM when outermost zones are active at the Scheduler and decreases when reading blocks from the innermost zones. In this figure, $T_{\text{Mux}}(Z_i)$ denotes the duration of a time that a zone is active. It is longer for the innermost zone due to their low transfer rate. In essence, FIXB employs memory to compensate for the slow zones using the transfer rate of the fastest zones, harnessing the average disk transfer rate.

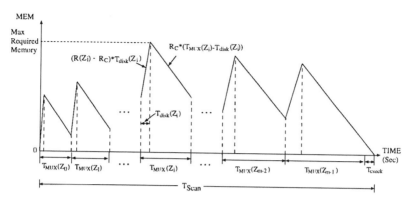

Figure 5. Memory requirement with FIXB.

If X_0 is assigned to a zone other than the outermost one (say Z_{X_0}) then its display may not start at the end of the time period that the system retrieves X_0 (i.e., $T_{MUX}(Z_{X_0})$). This is because both the retrieval and display of data on behalf of a PM is synchronized relative to the transfer rate of the outermost zone to ensure that the amount of data produced during one sweep is equivalent to that consumed. If the display is not delayed, then the PM might run out of data and incur hiccups. By delaying the display at a PM, the system can avoid hiccups. In [19], we detail analytical models to compute the duration of a delay based on the identity of Z_{X_0}.

A drawback of recognizing a large number of zones is a higher startup latency. Mitra can reduce the number of zones by logically treating one or more adjacent zones as a single logical zone. This is achieved by overlaying a single EVEREST file system on these zones. Mitra assumes the transfer rate of the slowest participating zone as the transfer rate of the logical zone to guarantee hiccup-free displays.

3.1.3. PM-driven scheduling.
The duration of a time period might exceed the disk service time to retrieve $\mathcal{N}$ blocks on behalf of $\mathcal{N}$ active displays. This is because: 1) Mitra assumes the transfer rate of a logical zone to equal the transfer rate of the slowest participating physical zone, and 2) the $\mathcal{N}$ retrieved blocks might physically reside in the fastest participating zone (by luck). When this happens, the Scheduler may either (1) busy-wait until the end of the time period, (2) employ the idle slot for house keeping activities, i.e., migrate sections in support of the bounded list length property, or 3) proceed with the retrieval of blocks that should be retrieved during the next time period. The third approach minimizes the average startup latency of the system (as demonstrated in Section 4). However, it causes the Scheduler to produce data at a faster rate on behalf of an active PM. This motivates an implementation of a PM-driven scheduling paradigm where the Scheduler accepts skip messages from a PM when the PM starts to run out of memory.

With this paradigm, a PM maintains a data buffer with a low and a high water mark. These two water marks are a percentage of the total memory available to the PM. Once the high water mark is reached, the PM generates a skip message to inform the Scheduler that it should not produce data on behalf of this PM for a fixed number of time periods (say Y time periods). Y must be a multiple of the number of logical zones recognized on a disk (otherwise, Y is rounded to $\lfloor \frac{Y}{m} \rfloor$). This is due to the round-robin assignment of blocks of each object to the zones where a display cannot simply skip one zone when $m > 1$. The number of time periods is dependent on the amount of data that falls between the low and high water marks, i.e., the number of blocks cached. It must correspond to at least one sweep of the zones (T_{scan}) to enable the PM to issue a skip message. During the next Y time periods, the Scheduler produces no data on behalf of the PM while the display consumes data from buffers local to the PM. After Y time periods, the Scheduler starts to produce data for this PM.

The choice of a value for the low and high water marks at the PM are important. The difference between the total available memory and the high water mark should be at least one block due to possible race conditions attributed to networking delays between the PM and the Scheduler. For example, the Scheduler might produce a block for the PM at the same time that the PM is generating the skip message. Similarly, the low water mark should not be zero (its minimum value must be one block). This would eliminate the possibility of the PM running out of data (resulting in hiccups) due to networking delays.

3.2. Staggered striping

Staggered striping was originally presented in [3, 14]. This section describes its implementation in Mitra. With staggered striping, Mitra does not treat all the available disks (say D disks) as a single logical disk. Instead, it constructs *clusters* of disks, with each treated as a single logical disk. Assuming that the database consists of η media types, Mitra registers for each media type M_i: (1) the number of disks that constitute a cluster for this media type, termed $d(M_i)$, and (2) the block size for M_i, i.e., $B(M_i)$. (The tradeoff associated with alternative values for $d(M_i)$ and $B(M_i)$ is reported in Section 4.) Mitra constructs logical clusters (instead of physical ones) using a fixed stride value (k). This is achieved as follows. When loading an object (say X) of media type M_X, the first block of X (X_0) recognizes a cluster as consisting of $d(M_X)$ adjacent disks starting with an arbitrary disk (say disk_a). Mitra declusters X_0 into $d(M_X)$ fragments and assigns each fragments to a disk starting with disk_a: disk_a, $\mathrm{disk}_{(a+1) \bmod D}$, $\ldots$, $\mathrm{disk}_{(a+d(M_X)) \bmod D}$. For example, in figure 6, X_0 is declustered into three fragments $d(M_X) = 3$ and assigned to a logical cluster starting with disk 4. It places the remaining blocks of X such that the first disk that contains the first fragment of block X_j is shifted k disks to the right relative to that of block X_{j-1}. Thus, in our example, the placement of X_1 would start with disk_b where $b = (a + k) \bmod D$. The placement of X_2 starts with $\mathrm{disk}_{(b+k) \bmod D}$. In figure 6, $k = 1$. Thus, X_1 is declustered across disks 5, 6, and 7 while X_2 is declustered across disks 6, 7, and 8. With m zones per disk, the assignment of blocks to the zones of clusters continues to follow a round-robin assignment. For example, if X_0 is assigned to zone Z_i of disks a to $(a + d(M_X)) \bmod D$, X_1 is assigned to zone $Z_{(i+1) \bmod m}$ of disks b to $(b + k) \bmod D$. This process repeats until all blocks of X are assigned to disks and zones. One EVEREST file contains all fragments of X assigned to zone i of disk j. Thus,

Time Interval	\- Disks - 0	1	2	3	4	5	6	7	8	9	10	11
0	Y0.0	Y0.1	Y0.2	Y0.3	X0.0	X0.1	X0.2					
1		Y1.0	Y1.1	Y1.2	Y1.3	X1.0	X1.1	X1.2				
2			Y2.0	Y2.1	Y2.2	Y2.3	X2.0	X2.1	X2.2			
3				Y3.0	Y3.1	Y3.2	Y3.3	X3.0	X3.1	X3.2		
4					Y4.0	Y4.1	Y4.2	Y4.3	X4.0	X4.1	X4.2	
5						Y5.0	Y5.1	Y5.2	Y5.3	X5.0	X5.1	X5.2
6	X6.2						Y6.0	Y6.1	Y6.2	Y6.3	X6.0	X6.1
7	X7.1	X0.2						Y7.0	Y7.1	Y7.2	Y7.3	X7.0
8	X8.0	X8.1	X8.2						Y8.0	Y8.1	Y8.2	Y8.3
9	Y9.3	X9.0	X9.1	X9.2						Y9.0	Y9.1	Y9.2
10	Y10.2	Y10.3	X10.0	X10.1	X10.2						Y10.0	Y10.1
11	Y11.1	Y11.2	Y11.3	X11.0	X11.1	X11.2						Y11.0
12	Y12.0	Y12.1	Y2.2	Y12.3	X12.0	X12.1	X12.2					
13		Y13.0	Y13.1	Y13.2	Y13.3	X13.0	X13.1	X13.2				
14			Y14.0	Y14.1	Y4.2	Y14.3	X14.0	X14.1	X14.2			

Figure 6. Staggered striping for two media types.

a total of $D \times m$ files might represent object X. Once object X is loaded, Mitra registers with the catalog the following information: (1) the disk and zone that the assignment of X_0 started with, (2) X's media type, and (3) the identity of each file that contains different fragments of X.

While the value of $d(M_i)$ might differ for the alternative media types, k is a constant for all media types. For example, in figure 6, the media type of object X requires the bandwidth of three disks while that of Y requires four disks. However, the value of $k = 1$ for both objects.

To display an object X, the Scheduler uses the catalog to determine: (1) X's media type, i.e., the value of $d(M_X)$ for this object, (2) the disk that contains the first fragment of X_0 (say disk$_a$), and (3) the zone that contains X_0 (say Z_{X_0}). Once the active zone equals Z_{X_0} and $d(M_X)$ disks starting with disk$_a$ (i.e., disk$_a$, disk$_{(a+1) \bmod D}$, ..., disk$_{(a+d(M_X)) \bmod D}$) have sufficient bandwidth to retrieve the fragments of X_0, the Scheduler initiates the retrieval of X_0. During the next time period, this display shifts k disks to the right and the next active zone to retrieve X_1. This process repeats until all blocks of X have been retrieved and transmitted to the PM.

4. Performance evaluation

This section presents performance numbers that demonstrate the scalability characteristics of Mitra. We start with an overview of the experimental design employed for this evaluation. Next, we focus on a single disk configuration of Mitra to demonstrate the tradeoff associated with its alternative optimization techniques. Finally, we present the performance of Mitra as a function of the number of disks in the system and their logical organization as clusters. In all experiments, the entire system was dedicated to Mitra with no other users accessing the workstations.

4.1. Experimental design

A problem when designing this evaluation study was the number of variables that could be manipulated: block size, number of groups with GSS, mix of media types, mix of requests, the number of participating disks, the number of disks that constitute a cluster per media type, the bandwidth of each disk as a function of the number of participating disks, closed versus open evaluation, the role of the tertiary storage device, the size of database, frequency of access to objects that constitute the database, etc. We spent weeks analyzing alternative ways of conducting this study. It was obvious that we had to reduce the number of manipulated parameters to obtain meaningful results. As a starting point, we decided to: (1) ignore the role of tertiary storage device and focus on the performance of Mitra during a steady state where all referenced objects are disk resident, and (2) focus on a single media type. Moreover, we partitioned this study into two parts. While the first focused on the performance of a single disk and the implementation techniques that enhance its performance, the second focuses on the scalability characteristics of Mitra as a function of additional disks.

The target database and its workload were based on a WWW page that ranks the top fifty songs every week[7]. We chose the top 22 songs of January 1995 to construct both the benchmark database and its workload. (We could not use all fifty because the total size of the top 22 audio clips exhausted the storage capacity of one disk Mitra configuration.) Figure 7(a) and (b) shows the frequency of access to the clips and the size of each clip in seconds, respectively. The size of the database was fixed for all experiments.

We employed a closed evaluation model with a zero think time. With this model, a workload generator process is aware of the number of simultaneous displays supported by a configuration of Mitra (say $\mathcal{N}$). It dispatches $\mathcal{N}$ requests for object displays to Mitra. (Two or more requests may reference the same object, see below.) As soon as Mitra is done with the display of a request, the workload generator issues another request to the Scheduler (zero think time). The distribution of request references to clips is based on figure 7(a). This is as follows. We normalized the number of votes to the 22 clips as a function of the total number of vote for these objects. The workload generator employs this distribution to construct a queue of requests that reference the 22 clips. This queue of requests is randomized to result in a non-deterministic reference pattern. However, it might be the case that two or more

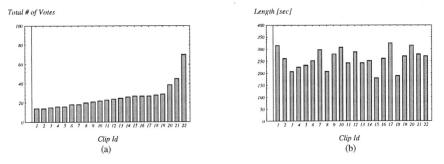

Figure 7. Characteristics of the CD audio clips. (a) Number of votes for each clips. (b) Length [in seconds] of each clip.

Table 3. Fixed parameters.

Seagate ST31200W	
Capacity	1.0 gigabyte
Revolutions per minute	5400
Maximum seek time	21.2 millisecond
Maximum rotational latency	11.1 millisecond
Number of zones	23 (see figure 5)
Database Characteristics *CD Quality Audio*	
Sampling rate	44,100 per second
Resolution	16 bits
Channels	2 (stereo)
Bandwidth requirement	1.3458 Mbps

requests reference the same clip (e.g., the popular clip) at the same time. In all experiments Mitra was configured NOT to multiplex a single stream to service these requests.

This experimental design consists of three states: warmup, steady state, and shutdown. During the system warmup (shutdown), Mitra starts to become fully utilized (idle). In our experiments, we focused on the performance of Mitra during a steady state by collecting no statistics during both system warmup and shutdown.

4.2. One disk configuration

We analyzed the performance of Mitra with a single disk to observe the impact of: 1) alternative mode of operation with the PM-driven scheduling paradigm, 2) block size, 3) different number of groups with GSS, and 4) multiple zones. In the first experiment, we configured the system with 384 KByte block size, $g = 1$, a single zone, with the low and high water marks set to 1 and 2 respectively. In theory, the number of guaranteed simultaneous displays supported by our target disk is 12. This is computed based on the transfer rate of the slowest zone, i.e., 18 Mbps, to capture the worst case scenario where all blocks retrieved during a time period reside in this zone. Mitra realized these theoretical expectations successfully. However, during a time period, the referenced blocks might be scattered across the disk surface, causing the system to observe the average disk transfer rate (26 Mbps). This results in a number of idle slots per time period. The PM-driven scheduling approach to proceed with the retrieval of blocks for the next time period (see Section 3.1.3) reduces the average latency when compared with busy waiting (0.3 seconds compared with 2.4 seconds). This paradigm enhances the probability of a new request locating an idle slot during the current time period.

In the second experiment, we changed the block size from 32 KByte to 64, 128, and 256 KByte. (The remaining parameters are unchanged as compared with the first experiment.) As the block size increases, Mitra supports a higher number of simultaneous displays (6, 8, 10, and 12 displays, respectively). The maximum number of simultaneous displays supported by the available disk bandwidth is 13 and can be realized with a block size of 625 KByte[8]. The explanation for this is as follows. With magnetic disks, the block size impacts the percentage of wasted disk bandwidth attributed to seek and rotational delays. As the block size increases, the impact of these delays becomes less significant, allowing the disk to support a higher number of simultaneous displays [9].

The number of groups (g) with GSS impacts the seek times incurred by the disk when retrieving blocks during a time period. In general, small values of g minimize the seek time. The number of groups (g) has an impact with small block sizes where the seek time is significant. This impact becomes negligible with large block sizes. For example, with a 64 KByte block size, Mitra supports 6 displays with six groups, 7 displays with three groups, and 8 displays with one group. However, with a 384 KByte block, Mitra supports 11 displays with eleven groups, and 12 displays with one group. This block size is large enough to render the seek time insignificant when compared with the transfer time of a block.

In a final experiment, EVEREST was configured to recognize all the 23 zones of the disk. The block size was 539 KByte to guarantee a continuous display with FIXB. In this case, Mitra can store only twelve clips (instead of 22) on the disk because once the storage capacity of the smallest zone is exhausted, no additional clips can be stored (due to a round-robin assignment of blocks to zones). With this configuration, Mitra supports 17 displays with an average startup latency of 35.9 seconds. The higher number of simultaneous displays (as compared to 12 in the previous experiments) is due to the design of FIXB that enables Mitra to harness the average disk transfer rate. The higher startup latency is because a display must wait until the zone containing its first block is activated. The number of logical zones recognized by Mitra is a tradeoff between the number of displays supported by the system, the average startup latency and the percentage of wasted disk space. We now report on several experiments that demonstrate this tradeoff. In the first experiment, we configured EVEREST to recognize two logical zones. The first logical zone consists of zones Z_0 to Z_{11} while the second consists of the remaining physical zones. In this case, Mitra can store 15 clips on the disk. With this configuration, while the number of simultaneous displays is reduced to 14, the average startup latency is reduced to 0.22 seconds. In a second experiment, we configured EVEREST to recognize one logical zones consisting of only the nine outermost zones. With this configuration, Mitra can store twelve clips on the disk because EVEREST has eliminated the storage capacity of the 14 innermost zones. This increases the transfer rate, allowing Mitra to support 19 displays with an average startup latency of 2 seconds. The higher startup latency is due to a longer duration of a time period. In [19], we detail a planner that determines system parameters to satisfy the performance objectives of an application (it desired throughput and maximum startup latency tolerated by its clients).

4.3. Multi-disk configuration

In these experiments, the following system parameters are fixed: block size is 384 KByte, GSS is configured with a single group ($g = 1$), and a single logical zone spans all 23 physical zones of each disk. We analyzed the performance of Mitra as a function of additional disks by varying D from 1 to 2, 4, 8, and 12. For each configuration, we analyzed the

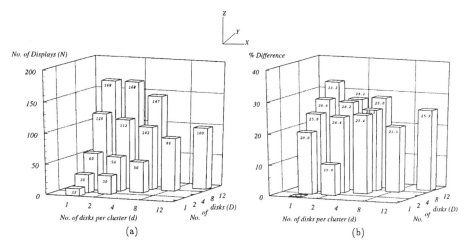

Figure 8.   Performance of Mitra as a function of D and d ($k = d$). (a) Number of simultaneous displays. (b) Percentage difference between theoretical expectations and obtained results from Mitra.

performance of Mitra as a function of the number of disks that constitute a cluster (i.e., d). In all experiments, the stride (k) equals to d. For example, with a 12 disk configuration ($D = 12$), a cluster may consist of two disks ($d = 2$). With this configuration, stride would also equal to two ($k = 2$). Obviously, the choice of d and k has a significant impact on the obtained results. We analyze the performance of Mitra for those values of d and k that are reasonable[9]. For example, with $D = 12$, it would be unreasonable to configure Mitra with $d = k = 8$ because it would force the bandwidth of four disks to sit idle because the database consists of a single media type. With $d = k = 8$, the performance of Mitra with $D = 12$ would be reduced to that with $D = 8$. Figure 8(a) presents the number of simultaneous displays supported by Mitra as a function of D and d. In this figure, the number of disks available to Mitra is varied on the y-axis, the number of disks that constitute a cluster is varied on the x-axis, and the throughput of the system is reported on the z-axis.

As the number of disks in the system (D) increases from 1 to 12 with $d = k = 1$, the throughput of the system increases super linearly (the throughput of Mitra with $D = 12$ is fourteen times higher than that with $D = 1$). This is because the average transfer rate of each disk increases as a function of D. The explanation for this is as follows. In this experiment, the size of the database is fixed and the EVEREST file system organizes files on a disk starting with the outermost zone, i.e., fastest zone. The amount of data assigned to each disk shrinks as D increases. With $D = 1$, the innermost zone of the disk contains data, while with $D = 12$, only the three outermost zones contain data. The average transfer rate of the three outermost zones is higher than the average transfer rate of all 23 zones of a disk (see figure 5).

In figure 8(b), for a given hardware platform (fixed D), the throughput of Mitra drops as d increases. For example with $D = 12$, Mitra's throughput drops from 168 streams to 100 as d increases from 1 to 12. This is because the percentage of wasted disk bandwidth increases as d increases in value [14]. To observe this, note that both the maximum seek time and rotational latency are fixed. Moreover, they waste disk bandwidth. The percentage of wasted disk bandwidth is a function of these two values along with the amount of data read from each disk drive per time period. As d increases in value, the amount of data retrieved from each disk decreases because a block is declustered across a larger number of disks. This wastes a higher percentage of disk bandwidth, resulting in a lower throughput.

For each choice of D, we located the slowest participating zone of the disks that contains data. This zone is the same for all disks due to the round-robin assignment of blocks of each object to disks. We computed expected performance of Mitra as a function of this zone's transfer rate for each configuration (using the analytical models of [14, 15]). Next, we examined how closely Mitra approximates these theoretical expectations. Figure 8(b) presents the percentage difference between the measured results and theoretical expecta-tions. Each value of this figure is computed based on: $1 - \frac{Measured}{Theory}$. With $D = 1$, the system approximates the theoretical expectation with 100% accuracy. With $D > 1$, Mitra's performance is anywhere from 10% to 35% lower than its theoretical expectations. Part of this is due to loss of network packets using UDP and their retransmission with HP-NOSE. However, there are other factors (e.g., SCSI-2 bus, software overhead, system bus arbitration, HP-UX scheduling of processes, etc.,) that might contribute to this difference. These delays are expected with a software based system (based on previous experience with Gamma [7] and Omega [11]) because the system does not have complete control on the underlying hardware.

A limitation associated with values of d smaller than D is that the placement of data is constrained with staggered striping. This results in a higher average startup latency (see figure 9(a)). In addition, it increases the amount of memory required at each PM even with the PM-driven scheduling paradigm (see figure 9(b)). Consider each observation in turn. The average startup latency is higher because a display must wait until the cluster containing its first subobject has sufficient bandwidth to retrieve its referenced block. Similarly, each PM requires a larger amount of memory because the Scheduler cannot simply skip one time

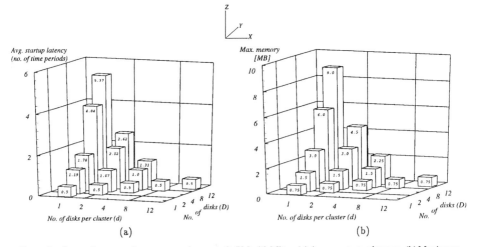

Figure 9. Startup latency and memory requirement of a PM with Mitra. (a) Average startup latency. (b) Maximum amount of memory required at a PM.

period on its behalf. Its next block resides on the cluster adjacent to the currently active cluster. Assuming the system consists of C clusters, a PM must cache enough data so that the Scheduler skips multiples of C time periods on behalf of this PM.

5. Conclusion and future research directions

Mitra is a scalable storage manager that support the display a mix of continuous media data types. Its primary contribution is a demonstration of several design concepts and how they are glued together to attain high performance. Its performance demonstrates that an implementation can approximate its theoretical expectations.

As part of our future research direction, we are extending Mitra in several novel directions. First, we have introduced techniques to support on-line re-organization of data when new disks are added to a system that has been in operation for a while [20]. These technique modify the placement of data to incorporate new disks (both their storage and bandwidth) without interrupting service. Second, we are investigating several designs based on request-migration and object replication to minimize the startup latency of the system [14]. Third, we are evaluating techniques that speedup the rate of display to support VCR functionalities such as fast-forward and fast-rewind. These techniques are tightly tied to those of the second objective that minimize the startup latency of a display. Finally, we are investigating distributed buffer pool management technique to facilitate sharing of a single stream among multiple PMs that are displaying the same presentation. The buffer pool is distributed across the available DMs. However, its content is controlled by the Scheduler.

Appendix A: Admission control with GSS

This appendix details the implementation of the Scheduler's admission policy with GSS. A building component is a function, termed seek(# cyl), that estimates the disk seek time. Its input is the number of cylinders traversed by the seek operation. Its output is an estimate of the time required to perform the seek operation using the models of [16]. Assuming CYL cylinders for the disk and n displays assigned to a group G_i, we assume that the n blocks are $\frac{CYL}{n}$ cylinders apart.

The Scheduler maintains the amount of idle time left for each group G_i. With a new request for object X, the scheduler retrieves from the catalog the record corresponding to X to determine its media type, M_X. Next, it retrieves from the catalog the record corresponding to media type M_X to determine $\mathcal{B}(M_X)$. Starting with the current group G_i, the Scheduler compares the idle time of G_i with the disk service time to retrieve a block of size $\mathcal{B}(M_X)$. The disk service time with G_i is:

$$S_{\text{disk}}(G_i) = \frac{\mathcal{B}(M_X)}{\mathcal{R}_D} + \text{max rotational latency} + \text{seek(CYL)}$$

It assumes the maximum seek time (i.e., seek(CYL)) because the blocks to be retrieved during G_i have already been scheduled and the new request cannot benefit from the scan policy. Assuming that G_i is servicing $n - 1$ requests and its idle time can accommodate

$S_{\text{disk}}(G_i)$, its idle time is reduced by $S_{\text{disk}}(G_i)$. Prior to initiating the retrieval of blocks that belong to group G_{i+1}, the scheduler adjusts the idle time of group G_i to reflect that the active requests can benefit from the scan policy. Thus, the idle time of G_i is adjusted as follows:

$$\text{idle}(G_i) = \text{idle}(G_i) - \left[\text{seek(CYL)} + (n-1) \times \text{seek}\left(\frac{\text{CYL}}{n-1}\right) \right]$$
$$+ \left[n \times \text{seek}\left(\frac{\text{CYL}}{n}\right) \right]$$

The subtracted portion reflects the maximum seek time of the request that was just scheduled and the seek time of $n-1$ other active requests. The added portion reflects the n seeks incurred during the next time period by this group with each $\frac{\text{CYL}}{n}$ cylinders apart.

If current group G_i has insufficient idle time, the Scheduler proceeds to check the idle time of other groups G_j where $j = (i+1) \bmod g$, $0 < j < g$ and $j \neq i$. Assuming that G_j is servicing $n-1$ active requests, the disk service time with G_j is:

$$S_{\text{disk}}(G_j) = \frac{\mathcal{B}(M_X)}{\mathcal{R}_D} + \text{max rotational latency}$$
$$+ \left[n \times \text{seek}\left(\frac{\text{CYL}}{n}\right) \right] - \left[(n-1) \times \text{seek}\left(\frac{\text{CYL}}{n-1}\right) \right]$$

If the idle time of G_j is greater than $S_{\text{disk}}(G_j)$, then the new request is assigned to G_j and its idle time is subtracted by $S_{\text{disk}}(G_j)$.

Notes

1. We do not report on commercial systems due to lack of their implementation detail, see [27] for an overview of these systems.
2. With the buffered interface of the HP-UX file system, one might read and write a single byte. This functionality is supported by a buffer pool manager that translates this byte read/write to a $\frac{1}{2}$ KByte read/write against the physical device.
3. The size of a page has no impact on the granularity at which a process might read a section. This is detailed below.
4. To simplify the discussion, assume that the total number of pages is a power of ω. The general case can be handled similarly and is described below.
5. A lazy variant of this scheme would allow these lists to grow longer and do compaction upon demand, i.e., when large contiguous pages are required. This would be complicated as a variety of choices might exist when merging pages. This would require the system to employ heuristic techniques to guide the search space of this merging process. However, to simplify the description we focus on an implementation that observes the invariant described above.
6. We intend to implement VARB in the near future.
7. This web site is maintained by Daniel Tobias (http://www.softdisk.com/comp/hits/). The ranking of the clips is determined through voting by the Internet community, via E-mail.
8. Thirteen is computed based on the bandwidth of the innermost zone, consumption rate of CD-quality audio, and maximum seek and rotational latency times.
9. However, the results are presented such that one can estimate the performance of the system with unreasonable choice of d and k values.

References

1. D.P. Anderson, Y. Osawa, and R. Govindan, "Real-time disk storage and retrieval of digital audio/video data," IEEE Transactions on Computer Systems, 1992.
2. M.M. Astrahan, M.W. Blasgen, D.D. Chamberlin, and et al, "System R: Relational approach to database management," ACM Transactions on Database Systems, Vol. 1, No. 2, pp. 97–137, June 1976.
3. S. Berson, S. Ghandeharizadeh, R. Muntz, and X. Ju, "Staggered striping in multimedia information systems," in Proceedings of the ACM SIGMOD International Conference on Management of Data, 1994.
4. M. Carey, L. Haas, and M. Livny, "Tapes hold data, too: Challenges of tuples on tertiary storage," in Proceedings of the ACM SIGMOD International Conference on Management of Data, pp. 413–417, 1993.
5. H.T. Chou, D.J. DeWitt, R. Katz, and T. Klug, "Design and implementation of the Wisconsin storage system," Software Practices and Experience, Vol. 15, No. 10, 1985.
6. P.J. Denning, "Working sets past and present," IEEE Transactions on Software Engineering, Vol. SE-6, No. 6, pp. 64–84, Jan. 1980.
7. D. DeWitt, S. Ghandeharizadeh, D. Schneider, A. Bricker, H. Hsiao, and R. Rasmussen, "The gamma database machine project," IEEE Transactions on Knowledge and Data Engineering, Vol. 1, No. 2, March 1990.
8. J. Gemmell, H. Beaton, and S. Christodoulakis, "Delay sensitive multimedia on disks," IEEE Multimedia, 1994.
9. D.J. Gemmell, H. Vin, D.D. Kandlur, P. Rangan, and L. Rowe, "Multimedia storage servers: A tutorial," IEEE Computer, Vol. 28, No. 5, pp. 40–51, May 1995.
10. S. Ghandeharizadeh, L. Ramos, Z. Asad, and W. Qureshi, "Object placement in parallel hypermedia systems," in Proceedings of the International Conference on Very Large Databases, 1991.
11. S. Ghandeharizadeh, V. Choi, C. Ker, and K. Lin, "Omega: A parallel object-based system," in Proceedings of the International Conference on Parallel and Distributed Information Systems, Dec. 1992.
12. S. Ghandeharizadeh and L. Ramos, "Continuous retrieval of multimedia data using parallelism," IEEE Transactions on Knowledge and Data Engineering, Vol. 5, No. 4, Aug. 1993.
13. S. Ghandeharizadeh and D. Ierardi, "Management of disk space with REBATE," Proceedings of the Third International Conference on Information and Knowledge Management (CIKM), Nov. 1994.
14. S. Ghandeharizadeh and S.H. Kim, "Striping in multi-disk video servers," in SPIE International Symposium on Photonics Technologies and Systems for Voice, Video, and Data Communications, Philadelphia, Pennsylvania, Oct. 1995.
15. S. Ghandeharizadeh, S.H. Kim, and C. Shahabi, "On configuring a single disk continuous media server," in Proceedings of the ACM SIGMETRICS, 1995.
16. S. Ghandeharizadh, J. Stone, and R. Zimmermann, "Techniques to quantify SCSI-2 disk subsystem specifications for multimedia," Technical Report USC-CS-TR95-610, USC, 1995.
17. S. Ghandeharizadeh, D. Ierardi, D.H. Kim, and R. Zimmermann, "Placement of data in multi-zone disk drives," in Second International Baltic Workshop on Databases and Information Systems, June 1996.
18. S. Ghandeharizadeh, D. Ierardi, and R. Zimmermann, "An on-line algorithm to optimize file layout in a dynamic environment," Information Processing Letters, No. 57, pp. 75–81, 1996.
19. S. Ghandeharizadeh, S.H. Kim, C. Shahabi, and R. Zimmermann, "Placement of Continuous Media in Multi-Zone Disks," Multimedia Information Storage and Management, S. Chung (Ed.), Kluwer, 1996.
20. S. Ghandeharizadeh and D. Kim, "On-line re-organization of data in continuous media servers," Multimedia Tools and Applications, Jan. 1997.
21. J. Gray and A. Reuter, Transaction Processing: Concepts and Techniques, Morgan Kaufmann, pp. 682–684, 1993.
22. Hewlett-Packard Co. How HP-UX Works: Concepts for the System Administrator, 1991.
23. J. Hsieh, M. Lin, J. Liu, D. Du, and T. Ruwart, "Performance of a mass storage system for video-on-demand," Journal of Parallel and Distributed Computing, Vol. 30, pp. 147–167, 1995.
24. K.C. Knowlton, "A fast storage allocator," Communications of the ACM, Vol. 8, No. 10, pp. 623–625, Oct. 1965.
25. H.R. Lewis and L. Denenberg, Data Structures & Their Algorithms, Harper Collins, Chapter 10, pp. 367–372, 1991.

26. P. Lougher and D. Shepherd, "The design and implementation of a continuous media storage server, network and operating system support for digital audio and video," in Proceedings of the 3rd International Workshop, La Jolla CA, Springer Verlag, pp. 69–80, 1992.

27. K. Natarajan, "Video servers take root," in IEEE Spectrum, pp. 66–69, April 1995.

28. B. Özden, R. Rastogi, and A. Silberschatz, "Fellini-a file system for continuous media," Technical Report 113880–941028–30, AT&T Bell Laboratories, Murray Hill, 1994.

29. B. Özden, R. Rastogi, and A. Silberschatz, "The storage and retrieval of continuous media data," Multimedia Database Systems, V.S. Subrahmanian and S. Jojodia (Eds.), Springer, 1996.

30. R. Rooholamini and V. Cherassky, "ATM based multimedia servers," IEEE Multimedia, Vol. 2, No. 1, pp. 39–53, 1995.

31. C. Ruemmler and J. Wilkes, "An introduction to disk drive modeling," IEEE Computer, March 1994.

32. F.A. Tobagi, J. Pang, R. Baird, and M. Gang, "Streaming RAID-A disk array management system for video files," in First ACM Conference on Multimedia, Aug. 1993.

33. P.S. Yu, M.-S. Chen, and D.D. Kandlur, "Grouped sweeping scheduling for DASD-based multimedia storage management," Multimedia Systems, Vol. 1, No. 1, pp. 99–109, Jan. 1993.

4

Multimedia Caching Strategies for Heterogeneous Application and Server Environments

ASIT DAN   asit@watson.ibm.com
DINKAR SITARAM   sitaram@watson.ibm.com
IBM Research Division, T.J. Watson Research Center, Hawthorne, NY 10532

Abstract.   In a multimedia system, *storage* and *bandwidth* are critical resources since any presentation requires a large volume of data to be delivered in real-time. Caching of multimedia documents in local storage can alleviate large retrieval bandwidth requirements. An important requirement for a multimedia caching policy is to guarantee continuous delivery even when a stream is served from cache. It should also cope with dynamic changes in workload and heterogeneity arising from large and small multimedia files. The proposed *Generalized Interval Caching* (GIC) policy, that caches intervals between successive streams of a large file as well as entire small files, satisfies all the above criteria. A caching policy needs to cope with additional challenges in a large scale distributed multimedia environment consisting of many heterogeneous servers. The issues include a) routing of requests to ensure good cache hits in each server, and b) balancing of loads across servers. For routing of requests, we introduce the notion of an *asset group* and propose an affinity routing policy based on this concept. Finally, we adapt the GIC policy for load balancing across servers.

Keywords: multimedia caching, interval caching, affinity routing, asset group

1.   Introduction

The rapid development and deployment of large scale multimedia applications have been hindered by the lack of available server and network delivery bandwidth (BW). The multimedia files are large in comparison with the requirements of most traditional applications, and hence, require a large space for storage and a large BW for transport [2, 5, 8, 19]. While new networking infrastructures are being deployed at a slow pace to tackle this problem, the delivery BW and storage space will continue to remain critical resources for such applications. The presentation of multimedia objects require a guarantee on the available BW [1, 7, 10, 33]. This makes proper usage of such critical resources even more challenging. Caching of multimedia documents in a local storage can reduce the requirement of retrieval BW. For example, storage of frequently used documents in the client nodes can reduce the requirement of expensive network BW for retrieval from remote servers. Similarly, storage of documents shared by many users in the server memory can reduce disk retrieval BW.

Traditional caching policies employed for non-multimedia applications are not appropriate for multimedia applications. Block-level caching policies (e.g., LRU) that cache unrelated sets of blocks instead of complete multimedia objects can not guarantee continuous delivery of streams. Hence, in a multimedia environment, large multimedia objects (e.g., movie) need to be cached in their entirety. Also, the traditional policies such as LRU and CLOCK [15] are based on the concept of a *hot set* of data which is much smaller in size than the total set of data. This is also true for the database buffer management policies that exploit the semantics of queries in identifying a hot-set [3, 9, 35]. Generalizing the concept of a hot set in a multimedia environment (i.e., storing the most frequently accessed videos in the cache) may not be very useful since multimedia objects are large. Additionally, detecting changes in the frequency of access to various multimedia objects is difficult; bringing newly hot objects into the cache may require a large amount of time [4].

A number of caching policies have been proposed specifically for multimedia environments [4, 8, 17, 21, 30, 34]. These policies exploit the unique access characteristics to multimedia documents: multiple clients access the same (popular) documents sequentially separated by small time intervals. Hence, the blocks retrieved by one client can be reused by other closely following clients[1]. The proposed policy in [4, 11], referred to as the *Generalized Interval Caching* (GIC) policy, additionally analyzes the stream dependencies explicitly. By associating placement and replacement of data blocks with retrieval streams, the GIC policy ensures continuous delivery of data. It opportunistically caches the shortest intervals between successive streams to maximize the number of streams served from the cache. The GIC policy outperforms the policy of caching the hottest videos in terms of cache hit ratio. More importantly, it adapts to the dynamic changes in workload.

Multimedia applications can be quite diverse in terms of the sizes of the accessed documents. In a movie-on-demand application a single long video may be watched for a long duration (say two hours). In contrast, in a multimedia database system, say for previewing movie trailers, many small video clips may be retrieved in response to client commands. In a general environment, the mix of applications accessing various types of document may vary greatly with time. Additionally for all applications, access patterns may change rapidly with time (e.g., with the time of the day, or in response to the availability of new videos in the above mentioned applications). The caching policies need to handle the very different characteristics of different applications. Hence, it is necessary for multimedia caching policies to perform well under all workloads containing both large as well as small video objects. The proposed GIC policy in [11] caches effectively both the small intervals of large files as well as entire small files and performs well under all workloads.

Another important requirement of multimedia environment is support of VCR control operations (e.g., PAUSE, RESUME) by clients. VCR control interrupts the sequential reading of multimedia files, and hence, optimizations exploited in caching policies. Note that the problem of dealing with VCR control arises as well in other aspects of multimedia operations (e.g., batching, load balancing). Hence, a general policy is required in a multimedia environment for dealing with VCR control operations and the resulting unpredictable BW requirement. In [7, 10, 12], a general policy of setting aside a portion of the server capacity for dealing with VCR operations is proposed. This can be integrated with the GIC policy as shown later. The access patterns generated by VCR control operations (e.g., skip) can also be exploited by the caching policy [29].

A related aspect of caching is prefetching of blocks to be accessed by a single stream, rather than sharing of retrieved blocks across streams. Prefetching of blocks (also referred to as *buffering* in [8]) can mask the variance in response time (e.g., disk response time) and hence, can avoid jitter in presentation. Prefetching is also used to smooth the burstiness introduced by data compression in a single long data stream [18, 36] or composite multimedia documents [25, 40]. The policies in [18, 36] address optimal delivery schedules consisting of piecewise constant rate such that neither the prefetching of data overflows the client buffer, nor does the chosen delivery rate cause buffer underflow. Prefetching for smoothing burstiness in the end-to-end delivery path for retrieving composite documents is addressed in [25, 40]. Finally, prefetching can be employed to avoid jitter in retrieving composite documents stored across multiple devices [38, 40].

The remainder of the paper is organized as follows. In Section 2, we describe in detail the GIC policy and demonstrate its effectiveness under various multimedia workloads. The additional challenges of caching in a distributed server environment are addressed in the subsequent sections. Section 3 introduces the concept of an asset group which is used in conjuction with the affinity routing of requests for improving cache hit ratio in distributed server nodes. If the cache can be shared by multiple storage devices or servers, the appropriate caching of contents can reduce the load imbalance across devices or servers. In Section 4, we propose extensions to the basic GIC policy for load balancing across storage devices. Section 5 contains a summary of results and conclusions.

2.   Generalized interval caching policy

The Generalized Interval Caching policy integrates the concept of stream aware cache management for caching intervals in large video objects as well as temporal locality in retaining short video objects. The main idea behind the GIC policy is illustrated in figure 1 [11]. The small arrow marked S_{ij} shows the playback positions of stream j on video object i. The example shows various streams reading large movies 1 and 2, and video clips 3 and 4. In the interval caching policy [4], the data blocks between a pair of consecutive streams S_{ij} and $S_{i(j+1)}$ accessing the same video object is referred to as an *interval*. The two streams associated with an interval are referred to as the *preceding* and the *following* streams. By caching a running interval, the following stream can be served from the cache using the blocks brought in by the preceding stream. The size of an interval is estimated as the time difference between the two streams in reading the same block. The number of blocks needed to store a running interval (i.e., interval size time the playback rate) is defined to be the cache requirement of an interval. To maximize the number of streams served from cache, the interval caching policy orders the intervals in terms of interval size and caches the shortest intervals.

For small video objects that are not being accessed concurrently, the definition of an interval is extended as follows. In figure 1 arrow S_{32} represents a stream presently reading small video object 3 and arrow S_{31} represents the position that would have been reached by the previous stream accessing object 3 if the object had been larger. (S_{31}, S_{32}) is defined to form an interval for objects 3 even though stream S_{31} has already terminated. The interval size in this case is defined to be the time-interval between two successive accesses on the same object. However, the cache requirement is equal to the size of the object and is smaller than the interval size times the data rate. Therefore, if the interval is selected for caching, the entire video object will be cached. The anticipated interval size for an object can be estimated from the sizes of the previous intervals. In the GIC policy, the size of the last interval is assumed to be the anticipated interval size. The GIC policy thus caches intervals

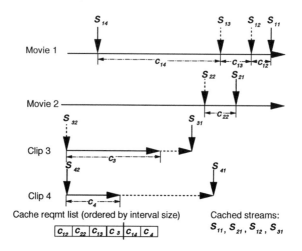

Figure 1. Illustration of GIC policy.

which may be either video segments or entire video objects. The policy maximizes the number of streams served from the cache by ordering all intervals (current or anticipated) in terms of increasing interval size (see, figure 1) and allocating cache to as many of the intervals as possible. The ability to choose a small set of intervals from a large set of samples allows the policy to exploit the variations in interval size due to the statistical variations in inter-arrival times. The GIC policy also incurs low implementation overhead since changes in the interval list may occur only due to the arrival of a new stream or termination of a current stream. Therefore, algorithms for reordering the interval list and allocation and deallocation of cache to intervals are executed only at the times of arrival and ending of a playback stream.

In the remainder of the section, we discuss further details of implementation of the GIC policy. We next describe a general workload that captures the earlier described complexities (e.g., interactive sessions, movie-on-demand, dynamic load changes) which need to be addressed by a multimedia caching policy. Subsequently, we demonstrate the superior performance of the GIC policy under various workload scenarios.

2.1. Implementation details of the GIC policy

Recall that under the GIC policy, intervals are created and destroyed only during OPEN and CLOSE operations on files. When an OPEN request is received, it is necessary to decide whether or not to cache the newly formed interval. Upon a CLOSE request, an interval will be destroyed, possibly allowing caching of another interval. The interval may also be destroyed or recreated upon pause and resume (i.e., VCR control operations). The OPEN, CLOSE and VCR control operations are detailed in the following subsections.

2.1.1. Starting of a new client request. Figure 2 details the procedure to decide whether or not a new interval (formed by an OPEN request) is to be cached.

OPEN:
```
Form new interval with previous stream;
Compute interval size
    and cache requirement;
Reorder interval list;
If not already cached
    If space available,
        Cache this new interval;
    else if this interval is smaller
        than existing cached intervals
      and sufficient cache space
            can be released
        Release cache space from
            larger intervals;
        Cache this new interval;
```

Figure 2.   Details of OPEN request in generalized interval caching policy.

As shown in figure 2, the GIC policy first computes the interval size of the new interval and its cache requirement. If the request is for a frequently requested small object, all the blocks of the object may already be in the cache, allowing the request to be served from the cache. If the interval is not already cached, it is necessary to determine if it is desirable to cache the interval. The GIC policy attempts to retain the blocks with the lowest interval size, since these are the most frequently referenced object segments. Hence, the policy computes the total cache space available in (less desirable) intervals with a larger interval size and the free pool. If the cache requirement of the new interval is smaller than this space, it can be cached by allocating blocks from the free pool and by deleting the less desirable larger intervals (if needed). Note that deleting an existing cached interval requires switching the stream reading this cached interval to disk.

Caching a real interval implies that the blocks brought in by the current stream will be retained only until they are read and discarded by the concurrent following stream. In contrast, allocating cache to a predicted interval causes the corresponding multimedia object to be retained in the cache for reuse by an anticipated following stream. A flag is associated with an interval to determine whether or not it is a predicted interval.

2.1.2. Ending of a client request.

When a CLOSE request is received, indicating that the client is no longer viewing the current stream, the interval formed by the current stream and its preceding stream no longer exists. Figure 3 describes the subsequent steps executed by the GIC policy. First, the policy deletes the interval in which the client was the following stream and the GIC policy releases the space allocated to the interval. The newly released space may make it possible to cache another interval. Hence, the GIC policy considers the smallest uncached interval to determine if it should be allocated cache. The algorithm used is the same as that during the arrival of a new stream.

CLOSE:

```
If following stream of a real interval
    Delete the interval;
    Free allocated cache;
    If next largest interval can
                be cached
        Cache next largest interval;
```

Figure 3.   Details of CLOSE request in generalized interval caching policy.

2.1.3. Switching of streams between disk and cache.   In the previous steps, a stream may need to be switched from disk to cache or vice versa. Switching streams is not a high-overhead operation and can be accomplished using two state flags associated with each stream. The `source` state flag can take on two values—DISK or CACHE—that indicates whether the stream is being served from disk or from cache, respectively. During block retrieval, the `source` flag is consulted to see whether the next block for the stream should be retrieved from the disk or from the cache. The `block_disposal` state flag can take on two values—DELETE or RETAIN. Initially, the `block_disposal` flag is set to DELETE. This indicates that blocks retrieved for the stream should be deleted after transmission to the client. If it is determined that an interval should be cached, the `block_disposal` flag of the preceding stream of the interval is set to RETAIN. This causes the blocks retrieved for the preceeding stream to be retained so that they can be used by the following stream. Switching streams between disks and cache can be accomplished by appropriately setting the values of the flags.

2.1.4. VCR control.   Video-on-demand systems may allow clients to pause and restart viewing at arbitrary times. This results in change in stream dependencies, which affect the caching decisions taken by the GIC policy. The challenges posed by the VCR control operations and the resulting unpredictable BW requirements are general problems in any multimedia environment, even in the absence of caching. If resources are released during a pause, they may not be available in general at the time of a resume request. On the other hand, not releasing resources leads to inefficient usage of resources. In [10] it is proposed that pause and resume requests be handled by setting aside a small pool of channels (i.e., resources needed for delivering a stream) called *contingency channels*. Under the contingency channel method, upon a pause, resources are released immediately either to the contingency pool or to an waiting request. The resume requests are served using resources from this contingency channel pool. The method provides a *statistical guarantee* that with high probability (e.g., 99%) a resume request can be serviced within a small pre-specified delay. It is shown in [7] that this method is more efficient than reserving resources for all paused streams.

The contingency channel method can easily be integrated with the GIC policy. The pausing of a sole following stream reading from the cache poses no problem other than deleting the cached interval. However, pausing of a preceding stream results in further actions. Its following stream may need to be switched to disk. If both a paused stream and its following stream have been reading from the cache the two intervals can be merged into a single interval, i.e., the blocks previously read by the paused stream continue to be cached. If the GIC policy favors another interval over this merged interval the total cache allocated to the merged interval will be freed and its following stream will be moved to disk. The caching algorithm then reallocates this cache to other interval(s) to be cached. Upon resume, a new stream is needed to serve this request. Sometimes, the resumed stream may lie in the middle of a cached interval, and it will immediately be served from the cache. Otherwise the contingency capacity is used to serve it from disk and the GIC policy is re-run as before to determine if the newly created interval should be cached.

2.2. Workload

We now describe the workload used to study the effectiveness of the GIC policy [11]. In a general multimedia environment, two types of applications may be present. In *interactive* applications, short video objects may be displayed in response to frequent client queries. Example of such applications are news-on-demand applications where users may view short video news clips, and shopping applications where users browse short product advertisements before making a purchase. On the other hand, in a *non-interactive* application such as movie-on-demand, client interactions are infrequent and the length of the displayed video objects are typically very long. A general multimedia workload is generated by combining an interactive workload (representing interactive applications) and a non-interactive workload. The arrival process of new client requests is modeled as a Poisson process with a mean inter-arrival time of T seconds. Upon arrival, client sessions are randomly classified as interactive or non-interactive in accordance with an *interactive probability*.

2.2.1. Interactive workload. A general multimedia environment may contain various different interactive applications (e.g., catalog shopping, news-on-demand, educational training). For an interactive application, clients establish a session during which it selects various short clips interactively. It is assumed that the video objects are selected according to an access distribution. The interactive workload is thus defined by the following parameters:

Video object access skew: Access to small video objects is assumed to be skewed so that 80% of the accesses are to 20% of the video objects.
Video object length distribution: It is assumed that the length of the short video objects is distributed uniformly between L_{min} and L_{max}.
Viewing time per individual clip: In many interactive applications *video banners* consisting of a short clip are repeatedly displayed (e.g., a logo that is shown until the client makes a selection). This kind of behavior is modeled by assuming that each clip is viewed for a random viewing time T_v. Viewing time is assumed to be independent of the length of a clip, and can be smaller than the playback duration of an entire clip, with a minimum of 5 seconds.
Client session duration: Client sessions are assumed to be of length T_s, with clients repeatedly selecting clips until the length of the session exceeds T_s.

2.2.2. Long video workload. Clients executing a movie-on-demand application are assumed to select long video objects according to a Zipf distribution with parameter 0.271

that fits empirical data on video rental frequencies well [42]. It is assumed that the server contains N_l long video objects of length L_l.

2.3.   Evaluation of the GIC policy

The analysis of the interval caching policy can be related to the general problem of obtaining order statistics, and obtaining explicit expressions may be quite a difficult task [4]. Hence, simulation is used to study the effectiveness of the GIC policy. The server considered is a single server with a single set of striped disks with a pre-specified bandwidth. The change in disk load due to arrival and ending of client requests, or switching between cache and disk are modeled explicitly. However, it is not necessary to model individual block I/Os. Any request for a video that would cause the disk bandwidth to exceed the disk capacity is rejected. The cache is modeled as a collection of 1MB blocks. Hence the cache space required for cachable segments is always rounded up to the nearest megabyte. The required length of the simulation is estimated through trial runs, made using the method of batch means.   It is found that with a simulation duration of 8 hours, and after ignoring the initial transient (1.5 hours), 99% confidence intervals of less than 10% can be obtained for important quantities such as the average number of streams reading from the cache. Thus the simulations are run, in general, for 8 hours.

2.3.1. Workload parameters.   Figure 4 shows the default workload parameters chosen for evaluation of the GIC policy. The request interarrival time, T, is chosen so as to correspond to a server simultaneously serving on an average 400 streams. This value is typical of the range of active clients expected for future video-on-demand servers [16]. Various mixtures of interactive and long video workloads are modeled by varying the *interactive probability*. From the duration of interactive sessions and the length of videos, it can be seen that with the default value, 50% of all I/O requests are made by the interactive sessions. All videos are assumed to be MPEG-1 with a delivery rate of 192 KB/s. Hence, the total amount of

Parameter	Default value
Number of clips	500
Length of clips	1 to 30 sec.
Average viewing time	30 sec.
Interactive sess. length	30 min.
Number of long videos	92
Length of long videos	90 min.
Request inter-arrival time	6.25 sec.
Interactive prob.	0.8

Figure 4.   Default workload parameters for analysis of GIC policy.

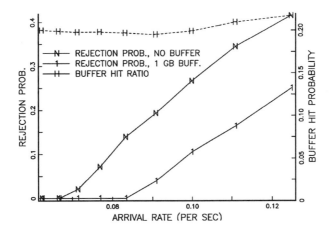

Figure 5.   Rejection probability; 400 stream disk capacity.

storage required per movie is one GB. For interactive applications, the total size of (all video clips in) the video catalog is 125 minutes. The number of video clips was varied in the simulation to study its impact on the server capacity. Experiments varying other parameters are reported in [11].

2.3.2. Admission control.   Caching increases the number of streams that can be served by a video server. The server capacity can be defined as the request rate that can be supported with no or a small rejection probability. Figure 5 shows the rejection probability as a function of the arrival rate for a system with a disk capacity of 400 streams. The curve plotted with 'N' is for a system without any cache while the curve plotted with '1' is for a system with 1 GB cache. In both cases, the rejection probability is 0 in the region where the system capacity is not exceeded. After this point the rejection rate rises approximately linearly. It can be seen that the 1GB cache has increased the system capacity by 25%, considering the arrival rates where the rejection probabilities become non-zero. (0.067/sec and 0.085/sec). The curve plotted with 'H' shows the corresponding overall cache hit ratios. The cache hit ratio is defined as the number of reads served from the cache as a fraction of the total number of reads. It can be seen from the graph that the hit ratio (which is approximately constant) is 0.22. Estimation of server capacity as a function of hit ratio translates to a 25% increase, which matches with the earlier estimate considering the non-zero rejection probability points. Hence, only the cache hit ratio is studied in the subsequent experiments.

2.3.3. Cache hit ratios.   The GIC policy performs well under a wide range of workload parameters. We first consider the base mixed workload in figures 6(a) and (b). Figure 6(a) shows the variation in the overall cache hit ratio as a function of the cache size. The two curves are for interactive library sizes of 500 clips and 1250 clips. For a given cache size, as expected, the overall hit ratio with 500 clips is higher than that with 1250 clips since with a smaller number of clips, a larger fraction of the accesses falls on the clips

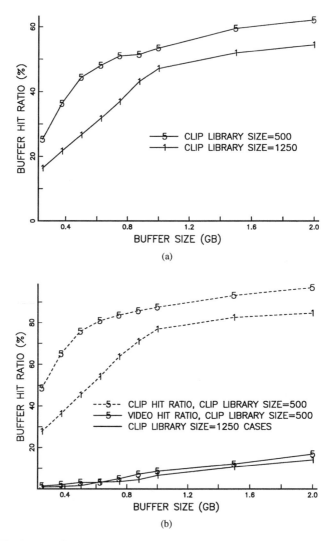

Figure 6. GIC policy under base mixed workload. (a) Overall cache hit ratio. (b) Interactive and movic cache hit ratios.

retained in the cache. The hit ratios of the individual components of the workload are shown in figure 6(b). The clip hit ratio shown in the figure is defined as the fraction of clip reads satisfied from the cache. Similarly, the movie hit ratio is the fraction of movie reads serviced from the cache. The clip hit ratio is higher, since access to the short videos are more likely to be found in the cache, and only the shortest intervals of long videos are satisfied from the cache. However, both clip and movie hit ratios are smaller for the workload with 1250 clips.

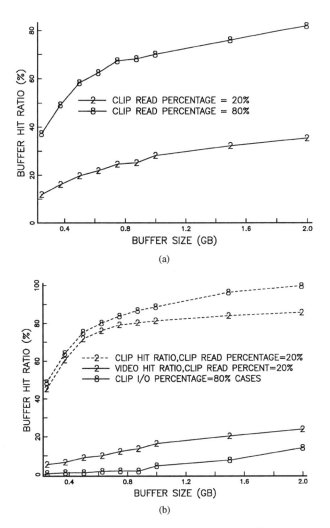

Figure 7. Effect of varying interactive fraction. (a) Overall cache hit ratio. (b) Interactive and movie cache hit ratios.

We next consider the impact of varying the workload mix on the GIC policy. Figure 7(a) shows the variation of the overall cache hit ratio with the cache size for different fractions of short video clips. The interactive library size contains 500 clips as in the base workload. However, the workloads differ in the fraction of accesses to the short clips, 20% and 80%, respectively. The workload with a higher fraction of accesses (80%) to interactive clips has a much larger cache hit ratio, since by caching the hot clips in a small amount of cache, a larger fraction of the accesses can be served from the cache. Figure 7(b) shows the interactive clips hit ratios and the movie hit ratio separately for the above values of access

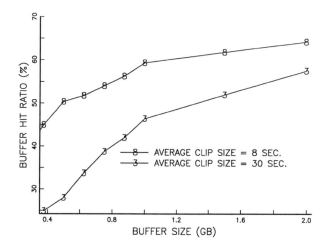

Figure 8.   Effect of varying average clip size on overall cache hit ratio.

to interactive clips. The dotted lines are for the interactive clips while the solid lines are
for the movies. As before, in both cases the clip hit ratio is higher than the movie hit ratio.
However, the clip hit ratio for the 80% read case is higher than that for the 20% read case
while the relationship is reversed for the movie hit ratios. This is because with a lower clip
access frequency a smaller number of hot clips are retained in the cache. This results in a
lower clip cache hit ratio and a higher movie cache hit ratio.

Figure 8 plots the cache hit ratio against the cache size for two different values of average
clip size (8 seconds and 30 seconds). The cache hit ratio with an average clip size of
8 seconds is higher than that for an average clip size of 30 seconds, since less cache is
required for smaller clip size. The difference in cache hit ratios is most marked at smaller
cache sizes. For larger cache sizes, hot clips can be retained in both cases.

3.   Affinity routing for multimedia applications

In the earlier section, we demonstrated that the GIC policy is effective in coping with
heterogeneous workloads, however, in a single server environment. In a distributed server
environment, a caching policy may need to address additional concerns, such as, routing of
requests and load balancing across server nodes for efficient system operation.

In a large scale single server system, caching policy exploits economies of scale [22],
since cache reuse is more likely with a larger number of concurrent requests. However,
such large scale systems may be built with a large number of nodes. A typical distributed
server (see figure 9) consists of a set of front-end nodes that retrieve video data from shared
disks or storage servers [28, 30, 41]. The cache is partitioned across the server nodes,
e.g., front-end nodes and possibly storage server nodes. If different requests are served by
different nodes without any coordination with the caching policy, the cache hit ratio will be
quite low. The principle of caching is reuse, and therefore, if related requests are not served

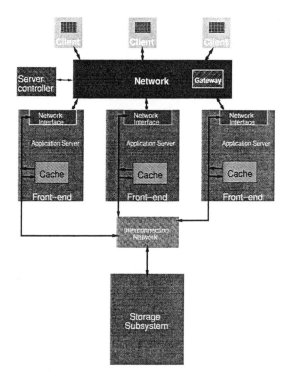

Figure 9. Distributed server environment.

by the same nodes, reuse will be low. This coordination in serving of related requests is referred to as *affinity routing*.

In this section, we will describe in detail the operations of a distributed multimedia server, and subsequently, how the GIC policy can be adapted to such an environment. The extension embraces two new concepts: i) *path based* routing, i.e., routing based on the availability of a complete path up to the front-end nodes which may include cache, and ii) *asset group*, i.e., logical grouping of small related files that may be accessed from the same client session. We subsequently demonstrate the effectiveness of this policy via simulations.

3.1. Issues in affinity routing

The *server controller* in figure 9 receives client requests for setting up of an application session and selects the server to which the request is to be routed [13, 22, 28, 30]. To guarantee continuous delivery, the server controller reserves bandwidth on all the components needed to deliver a video (referred to as a *logical channel* or *path*). Hence, the server controller is also responsible for admission control. It keeps track of available resources (e.g., disk bandwidth, CPU) on each server. Application specific client requests and additional processing (e.g., catalog search) are handled by the application server [14]. After establishment of an application session, all subsequent client requests are routed directly to the selected application server. For an interactive application, it may be necessary to switch the session to another node with available bandwidth if it is not possible to serve a future requests in the current node. For example, resource requirements may change as future video clips may not be present in the cache, and no additional resources may be available in that node. Also, during a long running session, the capacity of a node may change due to failure of one or more components. The switching is done in coordination with the server controller.

Path based routing. The bottleneck in such distributed systems may be in the storage subsystem, the interconnection network or the front-end nodes. Front-end node caching can improve the performance of the system by reducing the needed retrieval bandwidth from the storage subsystem. However, if the server controller routes requests at random to front-ends, front-end caching will not be effective since the resulting cache hit ratio will be very low.

Hence, it is necessary for the server controller to route application requests taking into account the access affinity of front-end nodes. Affinity routing has been proposed in various environments (e.g., file system [39], database [43]) for improving the cache hit ratio at the front-end nodes of a distributed server. As mentioned earlier, in a multimedia environment, setting up a logical channel requires reserving bandwidth on the entire path to the client (e.g., front-end, network interface). Therefore, unlike traditional applications it is not enough to consider only the access affinity for improving cache hit or balancing of front-end node utilization across nodes. The server controller additionally has to take into account the availability of all resources needed to form a logical channel. In this paper, we propose a *path based affinity* routing policy that takes into account the bottleneck resources when routing requests.

Asset group. For access to long videos (e.g., movies) affinity can be based on the identity of videos. However, affinity routing based on the identity of the clip during interactive sessions will lead to frequent switching of front-end nodes. This is undesirable since setting up a logical channel across network and server nodes may introduce a large latency, and incurs processing overheads. Also, as in transaction processing, the application server builds up state of the client (i.e., items purchased so far in browsing through a shopping mall), and switching front-end nodes would require distributed application processing. In many applications, only a subset of the video clips on the server are accessed during a session (e.g., shopping clips of a particular store). Related short clips which are most likely to be accessed together during a single session can be logically grouped into an *asset group*. Routing of application sessions based on the affinity to an asset group will avoid undesirable switching. The incoming application specifies the likely asset group(s) it would access.

The incoming application will be routed to a node as follows:

1. First consider only the nodes that have one or more applications accessing the same asset group(s). Order the nodes in terms of affinity, i.e., the number of application sessions

accessing the same asset group(s). Select a node in order that has enough available resources to set up a logical channel, where the source could be the disks or the cache.[2]

2. Otherwise, consider only those nodes that retain in their cache some of the clips of the asset groups(s) associated with the current application. Note that no active application sessions accessing the requested asset group(s) are being served by these nodes. Select any node with sufficient resources for setting up a logical channel.

3. Otherwise use any node for setting up a new channel that will reduce imbalance in available capacity.

4. If no bandwidth is available in any of the node reject this request.

For an interactive application, if a future request can not be satisfied by the current node, the above algorithm is reexecuted to select a new node for the application. An interactive application may have to wait if no bandwidth is currently available in any of the nodes. Alternatively, contingency capacity (as described in the earlier section for coping with VCR control operations) may be used. In our simulations, we will count only the sessions that are served without any such delay to estimate the effective server capacity.

3.2. Simulation parameters

We next study via simulation the effectiveness of the proposed affinity routing policy. Figure 10(a) shows the default values of the workload parameters as described in Section 2. The clips are assumed to be distributed evenly over the asset groups, i.e., each asset group contains both hot and cold clips. The effective server capacity and the cache hit ratio are used to measure system performance. These estimates are derived from sample statistics gathered every 5 minutes of the number of active streams, the number of streams being served from the cache, and the number of sessions completed successfully. The cache hit ratio is measured as the ratio of the number of I/Os being served from the cache to the total number of I/Os. Before gathering performance estimates, the experiment is run for 40 minutes to allow the simulated system to stabilize. Subsequently, the statistics are collected for 30 minutes.

Parameter	Default value
Number of clips	560
Length of clips	1 to 60 sec.
Interactive sess. length	30 min.
Number of asset groups	8
Number of long videos	100
Length of long videos	30 min.
Request inter-arrival time	1.4 sec.

(a)

Resource	Total capacity
Disk B/W	1024 streams
Cache Size	288 MB
Network capacity	1280 streams

(b)

Figure 10.   Default values. (a) Simulation parameters. (b) Server capacities.

3.3. System configurations

The performance of the affinity routing policy is studied by comparing the cache hit ratio and throughput of a distributed server using the policy against that of an idealized large server. It is assumed that in the idealized server the resources needed to set up a logical channel: network interface, front-end node, cache, disk B/W are well matched. The capacities of the idealized server are shown in figure 10(b). The cache size of 288 MB is sufficient to store a 30 minute 1.2 Mb/s video. The network capacity of 1280 streams can match a cache hit ratio of at least 20%.

Two different types of distributed server configurations are studied to demonstrate the robustness of the policy. Under a *symmetric configuration*, the total system capacity is divided amongst the nodes equally. Note however, that due to the unpredictable cache hit ratio, the required front-end node capacity and network interface capacity cannot be predicted in advance. Hence it is impossible to design a distributed server configuration where all the resource capacities are matched, even if all the resources are divided equally. The experimental results assume that only the network capacity is equally divided amongst all the nodes, with other parameters being varied in order to study their impact.

The distributed server may also be built using many heterogeneous nodes. In our experiments, by dividing the resources unequally amongst the nodes, a large number of *asymmetric configurations* can be generated. In the following, to limit the scope of the experiments, only a specific type of asymmetric configuration is considered. It is assumed that the system consists of two types of nodes, and the capacity of the larger nodes are three times those of the smaller nodes. The results can easily be generalized for other configurations.

3.4. Affinity routing without constraint on front-end node capacity

We first assume that the capacity (e.g., CPU) of the front-end node is not a bottleneck resource. However, disk BW and the network interface (i.e., adapter) BW could be the bottleneck resources. Hence, the routing is based on the available network interface capacity, whether or not the stream can be served from the cache of its associated affinity nodes and the total available disk BW in the system. Figure 11(a) shows the performance of the affinity routing policy as the number of nodes in the server is varied. Three different workloads with different mix of interactive and long video applications are studied. The server capacity is measured as the number of applications sessions served without any delay. As can be seen from the graphs, under all three workloads affinity routing is quite effective for a small number of nodes, and even for a large number of nodes, (i.e., 32) a reasonable cache hit is obtained (see, figure 11(b)). Affinity routing tries to avoid replication of cache entries (particularly of short clips) [39, 43]. Affinity routing also helps to create small intervals in long videos, and hence, improves the cache hit probabilities for long videos. If the workload is dominated by access to long videos (20% clip access case), the fragmentation of B/W implies that hottest long videos are served by multiple nodes, and hence, cache hit probability degrades. However, since the network interface BW is the bottleneck resource, the change in cache hit has negligible effect on the effective server capacity (see, figure 11(a)).

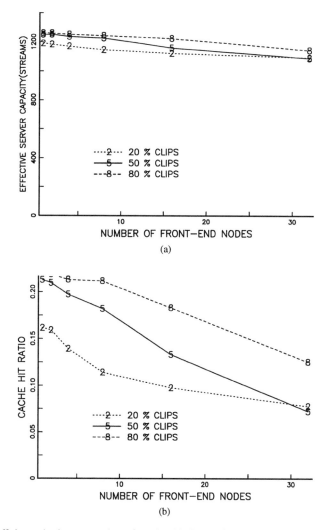

Figure 11. Affinity routing in a symmetric configuration; No front-end node bottleneck. (a) Server capacity. (b) Cache hit ratio.

Figure 12(a) compares the server capacity under affinity and random routing of sessions[3] for an workload consisting of 50% clip access. For interactive workload, to avoid switching overhead, once the initial session is established, all subsequent clips are accessed through the same front-end node. Switching occurs only when the stream in a session was served from the cache, subsequent access to a clip can not be served from the same cache and no capacity is available in the current node. Note that a truly random routing (i.e., without any such concept of an asset group) will cause the cache hit to degrade

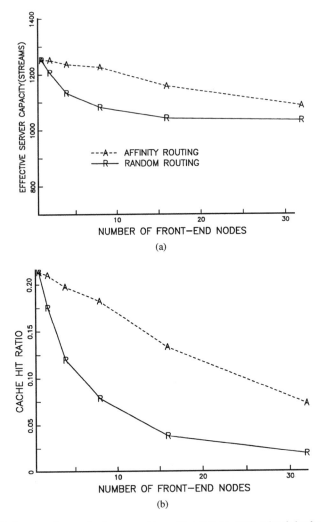

Figure 12. Affinity vs. random routing in a symmetric configuration; No front-end node bottleneck. (a) System capacity. (b) Cache hit ratio.

further. In any case, the cache hit is significantly lower under a random routing policy (see figure 12(b)). For a small number of nodes the affinity routing performs significantly better than the random routing policy. The performance improvement of an affinity routing policy over the random routing policy is shown in figure 13. The improvement in server capacity is as high as 14% in this example. For a large number of nodes it is difficult to concentrate the accesses to the same videos in the same nodes. As noted earlier, only after a substantial degradation in cache hit the disk BW becomes a bottleneck resource.

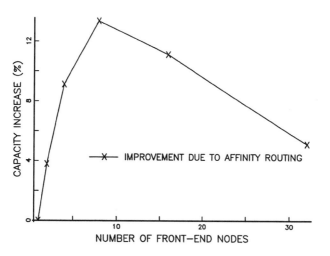

Figure 13.   Improvement in system capacity: Affinity vs. random routing

3.5.   Mismatch in front-end node capacity

Matching front-end node capacity to other resources is a difficult task in any configuration. First, cache hit is truly unpredictable. The demand on front-end node capacity comes from various sources. The application server has its own front-end node requirement (separate from the task of delivery of data). Serving a stream from disks requires front-end node MIPS for both I/O operations and delivery of data over the network. In contrast, serving of data from cache requires front-end node MIPS only for delivery of data over the network. We will assume that the front-end node MIPS requirement for serving a stream from cache is half of that of serving it from a disk. In a video database environment, the admission control policy makes sure that all the resources are available before a session is accepted [1, 7, 10, 33]. The front-end node scheduling policy schedules front-end node among various tasks (e.g., stream data delivery, application) so as provide smooth delivery of data to the clients [32].

Depending on the cost of various system resources, front-end node can be over or under configured. In figure 14(a) the front-end node capacity per front-end node is being varied. As can be seen, the overall server capacity improves with the increase in server capacity. Increasing capacity per node (of all resources) allows more similar applications to be routed to the same nodes resulting in higher cache hit probability (see figure 14(b)). However, beyond a certain point front-end node is over configured and other resources (network interface capacity) becomes a bottleneck. This clearly demonstrates the challenge in matching various system resources. A routing policy has to be aware of this mismatch in resources.

3.6.   Asymmetric configurations

Asymmetric configuration implies cache also needs to be divided across nodes in asymmetric manner. However, the cache hit is rarely proportional to the size of the cache. This

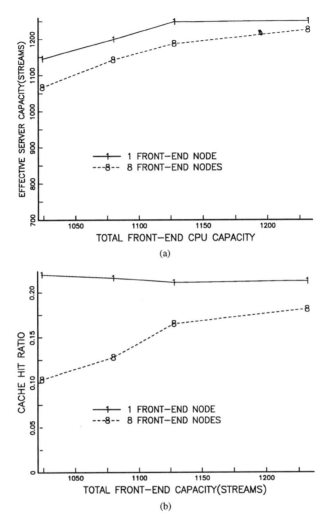

Figure 14.   Mismatch in network interface and front-end node capacity; Symmetric configuration. (a) System capacity. (b) Cache hit ratio.

creates further challenges in matching various resources. On the other hand, asymmetric configurations provide an opportunity for concentrating a larger number of requests to its ·larger nodes resulting in higher overall cache hit probability.

   As in the earlier case, we will first explore system configurations where the front-end node is not a bottleneck resource. The network interface capacity is divided unequally, i.e., the capacity of a larger node is three times that of a smaller node. Figures 15(a) and 15(b) show the capacity and cache hit for such a configuration. As mentioned earlier, the larger node size provides a greater opportunity for assigning the hot videos to a smaller set of nodes, and

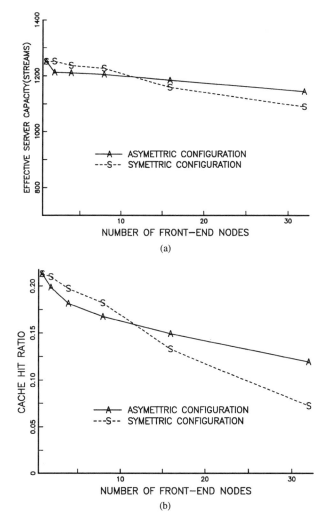

Figure 15. Affinity routing in an asymmetric configuration; No front-end node bottleneck. (a) System capacity. (b) Cache hit ratio.

hence, a greater cache hit and server capacity (see 32 node case). However, for a smaller number of nodes, this makes little difference in the over all cache hit ratio or server capacity.

We next consider a case where front-end nodes can be bottleneck resources. Figure 16(a) compares the overall server capacity as the front-end node capacity is increased in both larger and smaller nodes. Since the network interface capacity and the cache hits are different in different nodes the increase in front-end node capacity by the same percentage in all nodes may not be the best configuration. Therefore, we show two other cases marked by 'L' and 'S', where only the front-end node capacity of the larger and smaller nodes are varied,

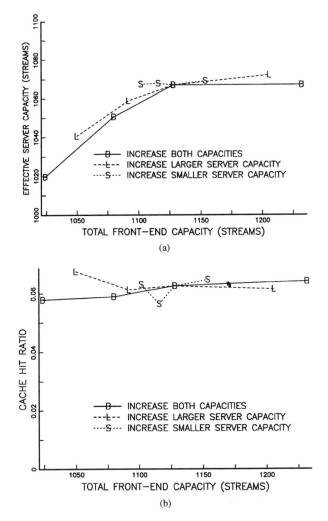

Figure 16. Mismatch in network interface and front-end node capacity; Asymmetric configuration. (a) System capacity. (b) Cache hit ratio.

respectively. The front-end node capacity of the other type of nodes (smaller and larger, respectively) are kept constant to a value that approximately matches the cache hit ratio. Figure 16(b) shows the corresponding cache hit ratios.

3.7. *Variation in workload*

Cache hit depends very much on workload partitionability as well as the mix of applications. To show the robustness of the proposed affinity routing policy, we compare the server

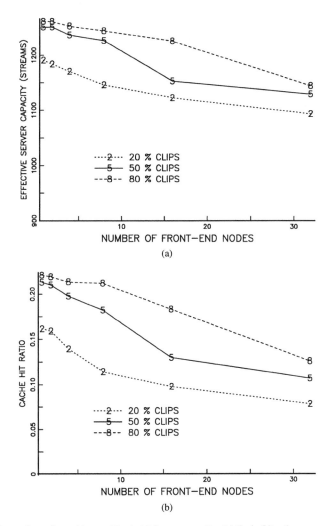

Figure 17.   Interactive vs long video workload. (a) System capacity. (b) Cache hit ratio.

performance (effective capacity and cache hit, respectively) for three different workloads in figures 17(a) and (b). The degradation is small with the increase in the number of nodes in all three cases.

Figures 18(a) and (b) show the effective server capacity and cache hit as the clips are divided across varied number of asset groups. Increasing the number of asset groups, allows the applications to be routed evenly (or to better match the capacity of nodes in an asymmetric configuration) across all nodes, particularly for a large number of nodes. For a smaller number of asset groups, an asset group is cached in multiple nodes resulting in replication of cached clips and hence, lower cache hit probability.

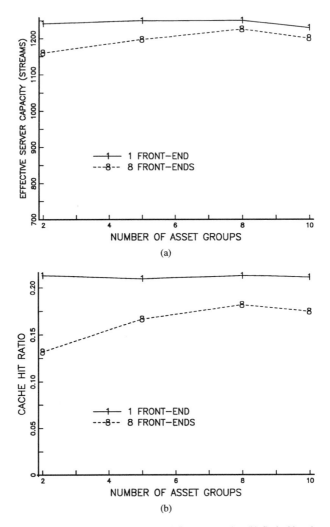

Figure 18.   Workload partionability into asset groups. (a) System capacity. (b) Cache hit ratio.

4.   Caching for load balancing across servers

In the previous section, we proposed extensions to the GIC policy for dealing with routing of related requests to various front-end nodes. Another important issue a caching policy needs to address in a distributed environment is the fragmentation of BW of storage devices. Load imbalance across storage devices may occur depending upon the file placement and current popularity of various files. If multiple storage devices share a common cache, the load imbalance can be reduced by properly managing the content of the cache. In this section, we describe how the GIC policy can be adapted for this purpose.

4.1. Issues in large scale storage server

A distributed multimedia server is likely to contain multiple storage groups or subsystems [6]. Aggregating multiple physical devices into a single logical device, and striping multimedia files over the logical device, is a widely used technique for balancing the load over the individual physical devices [27]. However, in practical environments, it may not be possible to combine all the physical devices in the system into a single storage group [6]. Real systems are likely to contain heterogeneous devices (e.g., disks of different types) and it is difficult to stripe over devices of different types due to mismatch in capacities (storage and BW). Hence, it is natural to have multiple striping groups, each containing devices of a single type. Some multimedia objects may be small, and thus it may be difficult to stripe over a very large number of devices. It has also been shown that in a system with multiple striping groups, high availability can be achieved by replicating a small number of popular videos [6].

The access rates to the videos stored in different striping groups may not be uniform. This will result in load imbalance across different storage devices and hence, in inefficient usage. Requests for videos on storage devices that are loaded to their capacity will be rejected even though sufficient bandwidth may be available on other storage devices. Caching can be used to balance the load on the storage devices, thereby increasing the effective throughput of the system. Load balancing for improving server throughput and response time has been studied in various environments. In the file server context, static replication has been proposed as a way to achieve both high availability and load balancing [24, 39]. In multimedia systems, such policies will incur a higher storage overhead since multimedia files are relatively large. However, replicating only frequently used files [37, 39] can reduce this storage overhead where advance knowledge of access patterns of the applications is available [5, 26]. For efficient usage of device capacities, the static placement of files should take into consideration both the BW and storage space utilizations [5]. Static placement alone cannot cope with sudden load surges, and a dynamic policy for dealing with sudden fluctuations in load is still needed. Placement and dynamic load balancing are complementary approaches since good initial placement makes the job of load balancing easier.

Load balancing by caching (i.e., dynamically replicating) of video segments in disk has been proposed in [6]. In this paper, we consider a complementary policy of caching in memory. First, we propose a modification to the GIC policy that balances the load among multiple storage devices. This is referred to as the *Caching for Load Balancing* (CLB) policy. Subsequently, the CLB policy is shown to be effective in reducing load imbalance across servers, and hence, to increase the effective throughput of the overall system.

4.2. Overview fo the CLB policy

As described earlier, the GIC policy attempts to maximize the number of streams served from the cache by retaining the smallest intervals. In a single storage server environment, the total system capacity expressed in the number of streams is increased by serving additional streams from the cache. In a distributed system with multiple storage devices simply maximizing the number of streams served from the cache is not adequate. Caching streams from the lightly loaded devices takes away valuable cache space that could be used for further reduction of load on the bottleneck devices. Therefore, the GIC policy needs to take into account the load on the different storage devices and should cache only the streams from highly loaded devices. In the paper, we consider a disk to be heavily loaded if its load is greater than the average load over all the disks.

Under an overload condition where rejection of requests is unavoidable, the objective of the caching policy needs to be changed. It may be preferable to minimize the rejection instead of balancing the load (and hence, balancing the rejection) across storage devices. Rejection is minimized by caching only the streams from overloaded storage devices using the basic GIC policy. Since the basic GIC policy maximizes the number of streams served from cache of the overloaded devices, the number of rejected requests is also minimized. The overall algorithm is bimodal. In the normal state, it balances the load, and under overload, it minimizes rejection. The overload condition is detected whenever a request is to be rejected. Alternatively, in the absence of any rejection, the algorithm switches to the normal state.

4.3.   Simulation parameters

The performance of the proposed CLB policy is studied via simulation. Default parameters for the workload are shown in figures 19(a) and (b). Each logical disk is assumed to contain one asset group with short clips. The access rates to the asset groups is non-uniform and is given by a Zipf distribution with the parameter 0.271. The access frequency to clips within each asset group is skewed (80-20). The request inter-arrival time is set to 3.6 seconds representing a server with approximately 500 users. The other default values are the same as those used in Section 3. The effective server capacity, average disk load, the number of cached streams of each disk and load imbalance between the disks are measured. The load imbalance between the disks is defined as follows. Let d_M be the average load of the most highly loaded disk, and d_m be the average load of the least highly loaded disk. The load imbalance (expressed as a percentage) is then defined as $100(d_M - d_m)/d_m$. These measures are derived from 5-minute sample statistics as in the earlier sections.

Parameter	Default value
Number of clips	560
Length of clips	1 to 60 sec.
Interactive sess. length	30 min.
Number of asset groups	Number of disks
Number of long videos	100
Length of long videos	30 min.
Request inter-arrival time	3.6 sec.

(a)

Resource	Total capacity
Disk B/W	512 streams
Cache Size	288 MB

(b)

Figure 19.   Default parameters. (a) Simulation parameters. (b) Server capacities.

4.4. System configurations

A distributed system with multiple storage devices with a single shared cache is assumed for studying the effectiveness of the CLB policy. The total bandwidth of 512 streams is divided equally amongst the storage devices. The number of storage devices (logical striping group) is varied from 2 to 6 in various experiments. Initial placement of files attempts to balance the expected load by allocating the long videos (that are ordered by their frequencies) in a round-robin among the storage devices. The asset groups are allocated in a similar round-robin manner. However, to create a controlled load imbalance the most highly accessed asset groups and the most highly accessed long videos are placed on the same storage device. The results can be generalized to other placements.

In the following sections, we first study the impact of the CLB policy in terms of its ability to balance the load among the storage devices in the system. Subsequently, we consider the improvement in effective throughput under this policy.

4.5. Impact of CLB—base workload

We first consider the impact of cache based load-balancing in a system with two storage devices. Figure 20(a) shows the storage device load in terms of the average number of streams reading from storage devices as a function of time. The dashed lines represent the storage device load without caching; the solid lines show the storage device load when caching is used to balance the load. Examination of the dashed lines shows that without caching, there is a load imbalance among the storage devices with storage device 1 being more heavily loaded than storage device 2. Under the CLB policy, it can be seen that the load imbalance is much less, i.e., the solid lines are much closer together. The CLB policy caches a relatively larger number of streams from storage device 1 than from storage device 2. Figure 20(b) shows the average number of cached streams per storage device.

4.6. Performance of the CLB policy under varying workload

We now show that the proposed CLB policy is robust with respect to variation in workload parameters. Figure 21(a) shows that the CLB policy works well under a wide range of arrival rates. The x-axis represents the arrival rate while the y-axis represents the average load on each storage device. The arrival rate is varied from a value of low load to a value where rejections just begins to occur. As in the earlier case, the dotted and solid lines represent the average load on the storage devices expressed in streams with and without caching, respectively. The solid lines are closer to each other demonstrating good load balancing under the CLB policy.

Figure 21(b) shows how the CLB policy copes with varying amounts of load imbalance between the storage devices. The load imbalance is varied by changing the parameter of the Zipf distribution used for generating the access frequencies. Here, the x-axis represents the load imbalance between the storage devices while the y-axis represents the average load per storage device. The CLB policy reduces substantially the load imbalance between the storage devices for a wide range of workload imbalances; with the imbalance being eliminated completely at lower values.

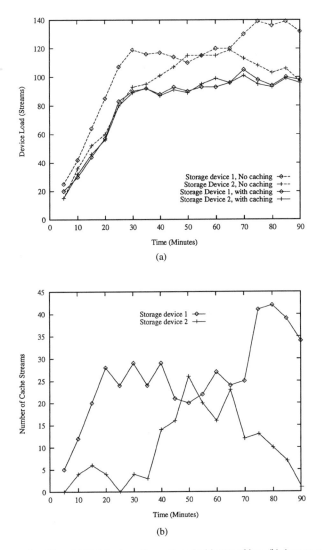

Figure 20. Impact of caching. (a) Disk load vs. time with and without caching. (b) Average number of cache streams vs time.

The higher imbalance in load can be reduced significantly only with a larger amount of cache. Figure 22(a) shows the load imbalance as a function of cache size for a workload with 40% initial imbalance (the same as the extreme point in figure 21(b)). As before, the closer solid lines imply less imbalance. The load imbalance tends to increase with a higher number of storage devices, as the bandwidth gets severely fragmented. Figure 22(b)

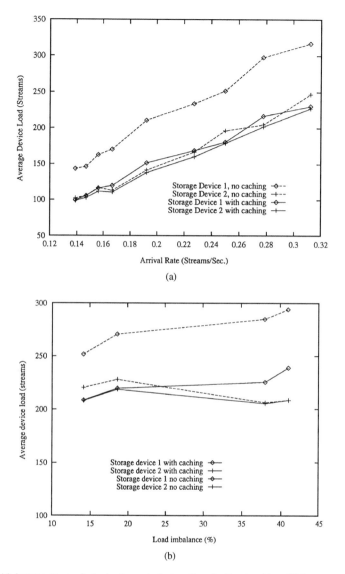

Figure 21. (a) Average storage device load vs arrival rate with and without caching. (b) Average storage device load with varying load imbalance under caching.

plots the load imbalance against the number of storage devices in the system. For each configuration of the storage device, the Zipf parameters is chosen such that the initial load imbalance between the heavily and lightly loaded devices is 18% (see earlier definition of load imbalance). It can be seen that in all cases, the load imbalance under the CLB policy is quite low ($< 6\%$).

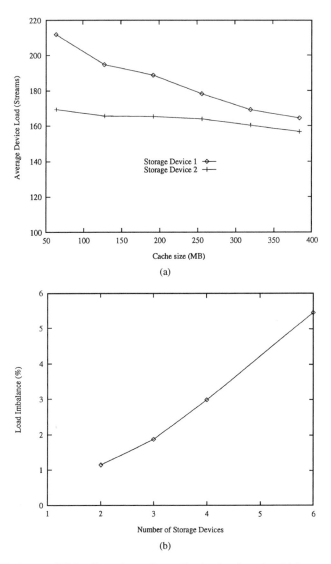

Figure 22. Effectiveness of CLB policy under varying workload and configuration. (a) Average storage device load vs cache size. (b) Load imbalance vs number of storage devices; 18% imbalance in workload.

4.7. Increase in effective throughput

The load balancing results in an increase in effective throughput. Figure 23 compares the rejection ratios for systems with and without any cache. The rejection ratio is expressed as a percentage and plotted against the arrival rate. It can be seen that both with and without

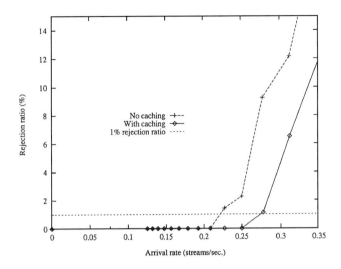

Figure 23.   Rejection ratio vs arrival rate with and without caching.

caching, the rejection rate is initially zero and beyond a certain point (referred to as the break-point) begins to rise, indicating overload on the bottleneck device. The rejection ratio is lower with caching than without caching. The break-point occurs for a lower arrival rate without caching. The system capacity is typically defined as the arrival rate that can be supported with a pre-specified (say 1%) rejection ratio. It can be seen that caching has increased the capacity of the system by approximately 20% for zero rejection tolerance.

5. Conclusions

Storage and retrieval of large multimedia documents demand large storage space as well as large bandwidth for real-time delivery. As a result, storage and bandwidth are critical resources in a large scale multimedia system. The requirement in retrieval bandwidth can be reduced by caching multimedia documents in local storage (memory). Multimedia applications can also be quite diverse; examples include movie-on-demand applications where long videos are played back with little user interactions, as well as multimedia database applications where relatively short clips are displayed in response to frequent user requests. Hence, the workloads differ greatly in terms of the requirement in file sizes, number of videos and other parameters. Additionally, application requirements may vary greatly with time. VCR control operations (e.g., PAUSE and RESUME) that change the sequential access to the files poses further challenges to a caching policy.

In this paper, we propose the *Generalized Interval Caching* (GIC) policy for handling diverse workloads. The GIC policy caches small intervals in large videos as well as entire small objects so as to maximize the cache hit ratio. It automatically adapts to changes in workload. Additionally, the GIC policy can be integrated with the policy of setting aside contingency capacity for supporting VCR control operations. To study the effectiveness of the GIC policy, we proposed a multimedia workload that captures the requirements of diverse applications. The GIC policy is shown to be effective in such an environment using simulations.

In a distributed server environment containing many front-end nodes and storage devices, the cache is partitioned across nodes. The GIC policy can be used to manage the cache within each node. However, affinity routing of related requests to the same server nodes is needed to achieve a good cache hit ratio. We propose an affinity routing policy based on two new concepts i) *path based routing* which takes into account the availability of bandwidth on each server component needed to deliver a video, and ii) grouping of related small files (e.g., clips needed by an application) into *asset groups*. The effectiveness of the proposed affinity routing policy is next demonstrated using simulation.

A distributed server may also contain multiple storage devices or servers. Depending on the placement of multimedia files across the storage devices and non-uniform access to them, load imbalance may develop among the storage devices. In such environments, caching can reduce load imbalance, thus increasing the effective capacity of the system. We further propose an extension of the GIC policy, called the *Caching for Load Balancing* policy, that preferentially caches the videos on the heavily loaded disks to balance the load. The CLB policy is also shown to be effective over a wide range of workloads using simulation.

Notes

1. An alternative ways to exploit closely following streams in a long video is to group or batch related requests and serve using a single stream [7, 10, 20, 21]. Batching is integrated with the caching policy in [21].
2. It is assumed in our experiments that the identity of the video to be accessed is known only for long videos. The identity of the clips to be accessed are not known in advance for an interactive session.
3. Random routing is used only for initial session establishment. Subsequent requests within the same session still go to the same node, i.e., is based on asset group.

References

1. D.P. Anderson, "Metascheduling for continuous media," ACM Transactions on Computer Systems, Vol. 11, No. 3, pp. 226–252, Aug. 1993.
2. S. Chaudhuri, S. Ghandeharizadeh, and C. Shahabi, "Avoiding Retrieval Contention for Composite Multimedia Objects," Research Report 95-618, University of Southern California, 1995.
3. H.T. Chou and D.J. Dewitt, "An evaluation of buffer management strategies for relation database systems," Proc. 11th VLDB Conf., Stockholm, Sweden, 1985.
4. A. Dan and D. Sitaram, "Buffer Management Policy for an On-Demand Video Server," IBM Research Report, RC 19347, Yorktown Heights, NY, 1994.
5. A. Dan and D. Sitaram, "An online video placement policy based on bandwidth to space ratio (BSR)," Proc. ACM SIGMOD, San Jose, CA, May 1995, pp. 376–385.
6. A. Dan, M. Kienzle, and D. Sitaram, "Dynamic policy of segment replication for load-balancing in video-on-demand servers," ACM Multimedia Systems, Vol. 3, No. 3, pp. 93–103, July 1995.
7. A. Dan, P. Shahabuddin, D. Sitaram, and D. Towsley, "Channel allocation under batching and VCR control in video-on-demand servers," Journal of Parallel and Distributed Computing, Vol. 30, No. 2, pp. 168–179, Nov. 1995.
8. A. Dan, D. Dias, R. Mukherjee, D. Sitaram, and R. Tewari, "Buffering and caching in large scale video servers," in Proceedings of IEEE CompCon, pp. 217–224, 1995.

9. A. Dan, P.S. Yu, and J.Y. Chung, "Characterization of database access pattern for analytic prediction of buffer hit probability," The VLDB Journal, Vol. 4, No. 1, pp. 127–154, Jan. 1995.

10. A. Dan and D. Sitaram, and P. Shahabuddin, "Dynamic batching policies for an on-demand video server," ACM Multimedia Systems, Vol. 4, No. 3, pp. 112–121, June 1996.

11. A. Dan and D. Sitaram, "A generalized interval caching policy for mixed interactive and long video environments," Multimedia Computing and Networking, San Joes, Jan. 1996.

12. J. Dey, J. Salehi, J. Kurose, and D. Towsley, "Providing VCR capabilities in large-scale video servers," Proceedings of ACM Multimedia Conference, pp. 25–32, 1994.

13. "Digital equipment corporation enters video-on-demand market," Digital Video Server News, Oct. 19, 1993.

14. K. DuLac, "Video pump interface recommendation to DAVIC," DAVIC/CFP/004, Dec. 1994.

15. W. Effelsberg and T. Haerder, "Principles of database buffer management," ACM Trans. Database Systems, Vol. 9, No. 4, pp. 560–595, Dec. 1984.

16. Electronic Engineering Times, p. 72, March 15, 1993.

17. M.L. Escobar-Molano, S. Ghandeharizadeh, and D. Ierardi, "An Optimal Memory Management Algorithm for Continuous Display of Structured Video Objects," Research Report 95-602, University of Southern California, 1995.

18. W. Feng, F. Jahanian, and S, Sechrest. "An optimal bandwidth allocation for the delivery of compressed prerecorded video," Technical Report CSE-TR-260-95, University of Michigan, Aug. 1995.

19. E.A. Fox, "The coming revolution in interactive digital video," Communication of the ACM, Vol. 7, pp. 794–801, July 1989.

20. L. Golubchik, J.C.-S. Lui, and R.R. Muntz "Reducing I/O demand in video-on-demand storage servers," Proceedings of ACM SIGMETRICS/Performance'95, Ottawa, Canada, May 1995.

21. M. Kamath, K. Ramamritham, and D. Towsley, "Continuous media sharing in multimedia database systems," Proc. Fourth Intl. Conf. on Database Systems for Advanced Applications, Singapore, April 10–13, 1995.

22. M. Kienzle, A. Dan, D. Sitaram, and W. Tetzlaff, "The effect of video server topology on contingency capacity requirements" Multimedia Computing and Networking, San Jose, Jan. 1996.

23. A. Laursen, J. Olkin, and M. Porter, "Oracle media server. Providing consumer based interactive access to multimedia data," in Proceedings of ACM SIGMOD, pp. 470–477, 1994.

24. B. Liskov et al., "Replication in the harp file system," ACM Symp. on Operating Systems Principles, pp. 226–238, 1991.

25. T.D.C. Little and A. Ghafoor, "Multimedia synchronization protocols for broadband integrated services," IEEE JSAC, Vol. 9, No. 9, pp. 1368–1382, Dec. 1991.

26. T.D.C. Little and D. Venkatesh, "Popularity-based assignment of movies to storage devices in a video-on-demand system," Multimedia Systems, Vol. 2, pp. 280–287, 1995.

27. M. Livny, S. Khoshafian, and H. Boral, "Multi-disk management algorithms," Performance Evaluation Review, Vol. 15, pp. 69–77, May 1987.

28. "Microsoft's interactive television strategy," Microsoft Directions, July 1994.

29. F. Moser, A. Krais, and W. Klas, "L/MRP, A buffer management strategy for interactive continuous data flows in a multimedia DBMS," Proc. 21st VLDB Conference, Zurich, Switzerland, 1995.

30. "nCube breaks new ground with oracle media server," Gartner Group Research Notes, Dec. 27, 1993.

31. R. Ng and J. Yong, "Maximizing buffer and disk utilizations for news-on-demand," Proc. VLDB, pp. 451–462, 1994.

32. K.K. Ramakrishnan, L. Vaitzblit, C. Gray, U. Vahalia, D. Ting, P. Tzelnic, S. Glaser, and W. Duso, "Operating system support for a video-on-demand file service." Multimedia Systems, Vol. 3, No. 2, pp. 53–65, May 1995.

33. P.V. Rangan, H.M. Vin, and S. Ramanathan, "Designing an on-demand multimedia service," IEEE Communication Magazine, Vol. 30, pp. 56–65, July 1992.

34. D. Rotem and J.L. Zhao, "Buffer management for video database systems," Proc. ICDE, pp. 439–448, 1995.

35. G.M. Sacco and M. Schkolnick, "Buffer management in relational database systems," ACM Trans. Database Systems, Vol. 11, No. 4, pp. 473–498, Dec. 1986.

36. J. Salehi, J.F. Kurose, Z.L. Zhang, and D. Towsley. "Supporting stored video: Reducing rate variability and end-to end resource reservation through optimal smoothing," Technical Report Umass-TR-95-98, University of Massachusetts, Amherst, Nov. 1995.

37. M. Satyanarayanan et al., "Coda: A highly available file system for a distributed workstation environment," IEEE Trans. on Computers, Special Issue on Fault-Tolerant Computing, April 1990.

38. C. Shahabi and S. Ghandeharizadeh, "Continuous display of presentations sharing clips," ACM Multimedia Systems, pp. 76–90, 1995.

39. D. Sitaram, A. Dan, and P.S. Yu, "Issues in the design of multi server file systems to cope with load skew," IEEE PDIS Conference, Jan. 1993.

40. J. Song, A. Dan, and D. Sitaram, "JINSIL: A system for presentation of composite multimedia objects in a distributed environment," IBM Research Report, RC 20476.

41. W. Tetzlaff and R. Flynn, "Elements of scalable video servers," Proc. CompCon95, pp. 239–248, 1995.

42. Video Store Magazine, Dec. 13, 1992.

43. P. Yu and A. Dan, "Performance analysis of affinity clustering on transaction processing coupling architecture," IEEE Transactions on Knowledge and Data Engineering, Vol. 6, No. 5, pp. 764–785, Oct. 1994.

PART III

MULTIMEDIA DATABASES

5

Benchmarking Multimedia Databases

A. DESAI NARASIMHALU   desai@iss.nus.sg
MOHAN S. KANKANHALLI   mohan@iss.nus.sg
JIANKANG WU   jiankang@iss.nus.sg
Institute of Systems Science, National University of Singapore, Singapore 119597

Abstract. Multimedia technologies are being adopted both in the professional and commercial world with great enthusiasm. This has led to a significant interest in the research and development of multimedia databases. However, none of these efforts have really addressed the issues related to the benchmarking of multimedia databases. We analyze the problem of benchmarking multimedia databases in this paper and suggest a methodology.

Keywords: benchmarking, multimedia database, information retrieval, hypermedia, context-based retrieval

1. Introduction

With the exponential growth of multimedia data comes the challenge of managing this information in a controlled, organized and efficient manner. The database researchers have set their sights on addressing the fresh challenges offered by the management of multimedia data [14]. While there are well known metrics for benchmarking traditional databases either in terms of performance of access methods & query optimization [2] or in terms of transaction throughput power [1], there has been no similar attempt for multimedia databases.

We define the problem in Section 2. Section 3 presents the benchmarking measures for the different retrieval techniques used by a multimedia database system. Section 4 provides a methodology for the overall benchmarking of a multimedia database system. Section 5 provides a brief summary and the future work. Some examples used in developing this methodology are presented in the appendix.

2. Definition of the problem

Multimedia database engines can be complex systems. In this section we will first define the types of retrieval mechanisms available to us and then go on to formulate the definition of the problem of benchmarking multimedia database systems.

2.1. Retrieval as a function of data and query

Multimedia databases can contain attribute data, content data and structure data. Let us discuss this using a multimedia document on *people of different nations*, as an example. The name of a country, its population, area and GNP are examples of attribute data. The

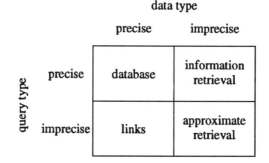

Figure 1.   Relationship among data, query and types of retrieval.

types of terrain, the face images of peoples living in that country, the flag of the country and the trademarks of companies in that country are examples of content data.

Content data are normally expressed in terms of features such as shape, color and texture. Certain types of content data such as a video shot of the terrain may be represented using spatio-temporal features. Structures are used to represent the relationship such as those among the country, its states, their counties, their towns and villages. Structures are also used to define navigation among objects or an object and the information about it.

Queries can be classified as well-formulated or *precise queries* and ill-formulated or *imprecise queries*. Queries expressed in SQL and similar tools are examples of well formulated queries. Queries that fall under this category are normally those addressing the attribute data or those using the attribute data to get the content or structure data if such associations exist.

Imprecise queries consist of two types. The first type of imprecise queries arise mostly because of a user's lack of focus and is prevalent in browsing applications using multimedia data. The second type of imprecise queries arise due to either the user's inability to express the content data accurately or user's preference to refer to content data using everyday language. Subjective descriptors such as 'beautiful' and 'thin', which are both abstract and relative abound in everyday language.

We suggest that the retrieval techniques practiced today can be related to the nature of query and data. We present this in figure 1.

All the traditional retrieval techniques used for *on-line transaction processing* (OLTP) applications based on their attribute data have collectively been called *database retrieval technology*. This technology handles precise queries on precise data sets. Thus, in answer to a query on the names of employees earning 10,500 dollars per month would be null (or a zero set) if no such employee exists. The retrieval techniques used for handling structure data of the first type, i.e., representing relationships such as *part-of* and *is-a*, fall under this category. *Information Retrieval* (IR) techniques, on the other hand, have been addressing collections of text document databases [8]. In such databases, the queries are very precise, they are made up of words and the semantics of the words in a query is very clear. Documents are also made of definitive words. However, the different roles played by the same word in different documents makes the collection of data in the document space less precise. Link based retrieval techniques such as *hypertext* and *hypermedia* [11] have been used to handle the imprecise queries of the first type defined above, to look for precise data. There is as yet no "label" attached to the retrieval techniques that handle imprecise query of the second kind on a collection of data that in itself is imprecise. The popular term in usage is *content-based retrieval*.

However, content based retrieval will also include information retrieval. Content based retrieval covers the right half of the table or the second column in total and not the bottom right quadrant. We like to suggest the phrase *approximate retrieval* (AR), to refer to those retrieval techniques that belong to the bottom right quadrant. We will use the above taxonomy in the following discussions on benchmarking multimedia databases.

2.2. *Definition of benchmarking of multimedia databases*

A multimedia database application could use any permutation and combination of the above four classes of retrieval techniques and hence our statement at the beginning of Section 2 that multimedia database engines can be complex systems. Clearly, speed of response is an important aspect of benchmarking any database system. This should be assiduously pursued and studied with respect to different levels of scaling up of data collections.

A second component that has been often used as a measure is the expressive power of a query language. Expressive power, in effect, determines the range of queries that an application can use. This is primarily a metric for the query language and not for a retrieval engine. Thus, even when retrieval engines are capable of handling any type of query, a query language may inhibit certain types of queries due to limitations in either the underlying model (such as relational algebra or calculus), or the syntax and semantics of the query language. Hence, we will not consider the range of queries as a measure given that there is now a trend towards using customized 'application programming interfaces' (API) for queries as compared to using structured or other query languages. This assumption can only affect the range of ad hoc queries and not API driven queries.

Multimedia database systems introduce a new concept called the *quality of result* to a query. This is due to the necessity of approximate retrieval for multimedia data. This is especially important in the context of the queries on imprecise data collections and assumes an even more important role when the queries are also imprecise. Quality was never an issue in database engines developed for OLTP applications. They simply returned an answer that satisfied the conditionals in the query or returned a null. Hence, the quality dimension was completely ignored. Given the prevalence of imprecise nature of both data and queries in multimedia databases, quality takes on a greater role than speed given that incorrect response however fast it is, will be of little value.

Hence, the benchmark of a multimedia retrieval engine can be thought of as a quality of service metric:

$$QOS = f(\text{Speed, Quality of answer}). \tag{1}$$

In the rest of the paper, we will formulate a measure for QOS and suggest a methodology to evaluate this metric.

3. Benchmarkings for different retrieval methods

There are standard metrics for conventional retrieval methods. We will mention them here. But we will certainly devote more discussion on metrics for links and approximate retrieval.

3.1. Benchmarking for database retrieval methods

There are examples of *DebitCredit* [1] and other test standards. These emerged primarily as measures of speed of response for scaled up collections and were typically measured in terms of number of transactions per unit time. The results here will depend on optimization of resources and tools such as buffer management and evaluation of join. The metric for OLTP type of applications T_{DB} is *Transaction per Second*, where transactions are generally speaking, queries. In *DebitCredit*, it is quantified by measuring the elapsed time for two standard batch transactions and throughput for an interactive transaction. A plot of T_{DB} vs. database size will provide the performance of the database engine with respect to database size. Although the database community has considered the *utilization* issue which counts the overhead for generating a useful query result, there has been no benchmark for the quality of retrieval.

3.2. Benchmarking of information retrieval methods

An *Information Retrieval* (IR) system returns a set of relevant objects (usually text documents) for any query. The objects not returned are considered irrelevant. Hence an IR system can also be called as a *Boolean* system since any object can either be relevant or not relevant for a particular query. Assume that we have a database D having n objects (documents):

$$D = \{o_i \mid i = 1, 2, \ldots, n\}$$

where o_i is a database object or a document. For a given query q we have the following:

1. *Ideal system response*: This assumes that an ideal IR system I exists. The response of this ideal IR system is the *ideal* or the desired response. The ideal response can be considered to be two sets which can be considered as a partition on the database D induced by query q:

$$R_q^I = \{o_j \mid (o_j \in D) \wedge (o_j \text{ is relevant})\}$$
$$N_q^I = \{o_k \mid (o_k \in D) \wedge (o_k \text{ is not relevant})\}$$

such that

$$R_q^I \cap N_q^I = \phi$$
$$R_q^I \cup N_q^I = D$$

Note that the ideal response can be considered as the *ground truth*. This can be a corpus which is a collection of known objects with known ideal responses to some known queries.

2. *Test system response*: This is the response actually provided by an IR system E being benchmarked. This system also partitions D for the same query q:

$$R_q^E = \{o_u \,|(o_u \in D) \wedge (o_u \text{ is relevant according to } E)\}$$
$$N_q^E = \{o_v \,|(o_v \in D) \wedge (o_v \text{ is not relevant according to } E)\}$$

such that

$$R_q^E \cap N_q^E = \phi$$
$$R_q^E \cup N_q^E = D$$

Given R_q^I, N_q^I, R_q^E and N_q^E, the IR community has the following two well known measures for benchmarking:

- **Recall:** The *recall* for query q is defined as:

$$\frac{\|R_q^E \cap R_q^I\|}{\|R_q^I\|}$$

  where $\| \cdot \|$ indicates the cardinality of the set.
- **Precision:** The *precision* for query q is defined as:

$$\frac{\|R_q^E \cap R_q^I\|}{\|R_q^E\|}$$

Relevance of retrieved documents with respect to a query measured in terms of precision and recall have continued to be the commonly accepted metrics. There is, however, a growing disillusionment among the IR community that these two measure somehow do not tell the whole story but there is yet to emerge alternatives to these two measures. Speed of retrieval T_{IR} for IR has to be measured differently from that for database technology. This is primarily because the application environment does not have the same volume of transactions and the retrieval process is more interactive due to the imprecise nature of the data collection.

$$T_{IR} = \frac{\text{No. of query terms}}{\text{Response time}} \tag{2}$$

Quality of output from IR systems can be measured as follows.

$$Q_{IR} = W_{PR} * \text{precision} + W_{RE} * \text{recall} \tag{3}$$

where, W_{PR} is the weightage for precision and W_{RE} is the weightage for recall. Then, the overall quality of service can be defined as:

$$QOS_{IR} = T_{IR} * Q_{IR} \qquad (4)$$

TREC, the annual *Text Retrieval Conference* organized by the *National Institute of Standards and Technology* (NIST) in the United States continues to be the key forum for benchmarking both commercial and academic IR systems [3]. This conference aims to bring IR groups together to discuss their work on a new large test collection. The participants of TREC employ a variety of retrieval techniques, including methods using automatic thesaurii, sophisticated term weighting, natural language techniques, relevance feedback, and advanced pattern matching. These methods are run through a common evaluation package in order for the groups to compare the effectiveness of different techniques and to discuss how differences between the systems affected performance.

Thus, the emphasis of this exercise is to benchmark the different IR methods on increasingly large and common collections. It is important to note that these two metrics relate to the quality of the answer to a query. Although TREC participants may record the time taken to get a result, quality measures have assumed a more important role in this benchmarking exercise.

TREC is now considering corpuses in languages other than English. A complementary forum called the *Message Understanding Conference* (MUC) is likely to produce results that may impact information retrieval methods.

3.3. Benchmarking links

We have not come across any attempts to benchmark significant sized collections of hyperlinks. We list below the measures that could be used for retrieval methods for links.

3.3.1. Speed as a measure.   The time, T_{LI}, to fetch immediate (or next level) information associated with a link is definitely an immediate measure to consider. This measure will be affected by the quality of schemes such as buffer management and cluster management on the disk.

In addition, the time taken to reach distant information, T_{LD}, can also be a measure. This measure will be affected by the design of the information structures. If there are too many levels of nesting before reaching a desired information, then this measure will suffer. It will also be poor when retrieval on structures is not complemented by other retrieval methods. The speed of response, T_L, is defined as:

$$T_L = \frac{W_{LI} * N_{LI} * T_{LI} + W_{LD} * N_{LD} * T_{LD}}{W_{LI} * N_{LI} + W_{LD} * N_{LD}} \qquad (5)$$

where W_{LD} is the relative importance of distant transactions, N_{LD} is the number of distant transactions, W_{LI} is the relative importance of immediate transactions and N_{LI} is the number of immediate transactions.

3.3.2. Quality as a measure.   The ability to find a piece of information is one measure of quality. This can be represented by the ratio Q_L, between the number of successful retrievals of information to the total number of queries.

$$Q_L = \frac{\text{No. of successful retrievals}}{\text{Total No. of queries}} \qquad (6)$$

No retrieval method employing links can afford to keep all possible links all the time. Hence, it is desirable to generate links when they are not predefined. This is a difficult task and is dependent on the extent of supporting information available to a link retrieval method.

3.3.3. A wholistic measure for link based system.   A total quality measure for link based system can be defined to be,

$$QOS_L = T_L * Q_L \qquad (7)$$

3.4.   Benchmarks for approximate retrieval methods

Benchmarks for the approximate retrieval methods are the least understood or established. Hence we will devote more discussion to this topic. The imprecise representation of data will have to be converted into some objective measures represented in terms of numbers or alphanumeric characters. This transformation may employ concepts such as fuzzy mapping, fuzzy set theory, classification using traditional clustering techniques and more recent methods using neural nets, and classification trees.

3.4.1. Speed as a measure.   AR methods will in general use data from more than one dimension for retrieval. The features that identify a country from its flag may use color and the spatial location of the different colors as the two features or dimensions for retrieval. The difference between AR and other retrieval methods, more often, lies in the fact that most features take on continuous values. For example, while there are only a finite number of words in a corpus of text, the number of face images in a face database can be very large and the shape feature like "moment invariants" (say for the nose, eyes, mouth and chin) can assume continuous values. Speed of response will continue to be an important measure. However, AR methods may need to be evaluated with greater emphasis on the quality of the response rather than the speed. The speed, T_{AR}, can be measured by:

$$T_{AR} = \frac{\text{No. of features in query}}{\text{Response time}} \qquad (8)$$

3.4.2. Quality as a measure.   Quality of response has been a subject of discussion even as early as 1968 [5]. The measures presented here will apply to the qualitative aspects of an AR system. The ranked list of objects in response to a query (based on some features) is referred to as the *response set*. The objects that are useful and relevant to the query are called *relevant objects*.

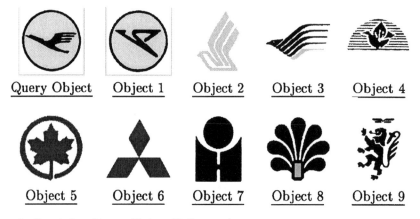

Figure 2.   Some trademark image objects used in the example.

To illustrate the importance of quality of result for AR techniques, we will present an example now. This example will also serve as a vehicle to present certain important aspects of the quality of a retrieval result. Assume that we have a database of different trademark shape images. A typical query to this system would be to obtain all images in the database which are *similar in shape* to a query trademark shape image. So it uses an AR technique which utilizes shape similarity computation between two images. It answers any shape-similarity query by computing the similarity between the query trademark shape image and all the trademark shape images in the database and presents them in a ranked list in the decreasing order of similarity to the query image. We also refer to an image (i.e., a trademark shape) as an object. Object i is represented as o_i in the following discussion and in general, it refers to a multimedia object. Assume that the query object o_q is a bird. Let the four objects o_1, o_2, o_3 and o_4 (all of them are stylized versions of birds) be the relevant objects in the database for the query object o_q. Let us also assume that for the four relevant objects, the ith object is expected to appear in ith rank in a response set. So the o_1 is the most similar object to the query bird image, the o_2 is the next-most similar object followed by o_3 and finally o_4 is the least similar relevant object. This also implies that all other objects in the response sets constitute noise and are irrelevant. Figure 2 shows the query object o_q, all the relevant objects (o_1 through o_4) and some of the irrelevant objects (o_5 through o_9) in the database. We will use two response sets for our discussions below. The use of two response sets will help illustrate the concepts discussed better than the use of a single response set.

The following observations on relevant objects in ranked response sets obtained for the same query from two different retrieval engines will be used to discuss the new performance metrics (or measures).

- **Observation 1:** The same set of objects may appear in different orders in the two response sets (Order).

Example 1.

Response set 1: $o_1, o_2, o_3, o_4, \ldots$
Response set 2: $o_2, o_4, o_3, o_1, \ldots$

In this example, the first system correctly retrieves the four relevant objects in descending order of similarity. The second system has retrieved the four relevant objects at the top of the list but they have not been retrieved in a descending order of similarity. Hence the quality of the second system is not good as that of the first system.

- **Observation 2:** The same set of objects while appearing in the same order may have different ranks in the two response sets (Rank).

Example 2.

Response set 1: $o_1, o_2, o_3, o_4, \ldots$
Response set 2: $o_7, o_1, o_2, o_3, o_4, \ldots$

In this example, the first system has performed ideal retrieval. The second system has retrieved an irrelevant shape as the most similar shape and the next four objects are the same as in the ideal response. Hence, even though the second system obtains the correct order, the ranks of the individual objects are not correct. Hence the second system response is of an inferior quality.

- **Observation 3:** The same set of objects while appearing in the same order may have different spreads (Spread).

Example 3.

Response set 1: $o_1, o_7, o_2, o_3, o_4, \ldots$
Response set 2: $o_1, o_2, o_8, o_9, o_5, o_3, o_4, \ldots$

This example shows while the order can be preserved, the number of objects to be considered can vary for all relevant abjects to appear in the response. In this case, both systems have retrieved the relevant objects in a correct order, but the second system response has more irrelevant objects. Hence the spread of the ranked list which encompasses the relevant objects is larger for the second system which is less desirable.

- **Observation 4:** The same set of objects while having the same Spread may have different displacements of individual objects in the two response sets (Displace).

Example 4.

Response set 1: $o_1, o_7, o_2, o_6, o_3, o_4, \ldots$
Response set 2: $o_1, o_7, o_6, o_2, o_3, o_4, \ldots$

Here, the number of objects appearing between the first relevant object and the last relevant object on the ranked list is the same. However, the displacement (from the ideal position) of the individual relevant objects are different. For the first system o_2 is displaced by one position while o_3 and o_4 are displaced by two positions. For the second case o_2, o_3 and o_4 are displaced by two positions each. Hence the response of the second system is of a lesser quality than that of the first system.

Taking these observations in account, we will now classify all types of AR systems into two categories. We will define the measures for a response set and then define the measures for calibrating an AR system. The preliminary version of these ideas were first presented in [7].

3.4.3. Types of AR systems.   Depending on the type of the response set produced, we can classify AR systems into two categories:

1. **Continuous:** A continuous AR system returns a ranked list of object as the response to any query. Essentially, for any query q, it computes a relevance measure (often a *similarity measure* based on content of multimedia objects) for all the objects in the database and returns the set of objects in a ranked manner where the rank indicates the relative relevance to the query. The first object in the ranked list is the most relevant object for the query (most *similar* object for similarity retrieval) and the last object in the list is the least relevant object. More formally, assume that we have a database D having n objects:

$$D = \{o_i \mid i = 1, 2, \ldots, n\}$$

where o_i is a multimedia object such as text, image, audio or video. For the continuous AR system, we also have a *Relevance Function S*, which for a given query q assigns a relevance measure s_i^q to every every object o_i in the database i.e., it is a function $S : D \times Q \rightarrow [0, 1]$ such that $S(o_i, q)$ is the relevance measure of object o_i for query q. Q is the set of all queries. Note that $[0, 1]$ is a closed subset of $\Re$, the set of real numbers. Also note that:

$$S(o_i, q) = 0.0 \Rightarrow o_i \text{ is totally irrelevant for query } q$$
$$S(o_i, q) = 1.0 \Rightarrow o_i \text{ is totally relevant for query } q$$

For a given query q we have the following:

(a) *Ideal system response*: This assumes that an ideal continuous AR system I which has the associated relevance function S^I exists. The ideal response to a query q can be considered to be a *ranked* list:

$$L_q^I = \left(o_1^I, o_2^I, o_3^I, \ldots, o_n^I\right)$$

where L_q^I is a ranked list such that:

$$S^I\left(o_1^I, q\right) \geq S^I\left(o_2^I, q\right) \geq S^I\left(o_3^I, q\right) \cdots \geq S^I\left(o_n^I, q\right)$$

Therefore the first ranked element o_1^I is the most relevant object in the database for query q and the last element o_n^I is the least relevant. The ranking is done using the relevance function S^I. Note that S^I induces a partial order on the objects of D. Most often, this relevance function is a similarity measure based upon some feature of the objects. It is clear that this is the "ideal" or the desired ranking of the objects in the database.

(b) *Test system response:* This is the response actually provided by an AR system E, with the associated relevance function $\mathcal{S}^E$, being benchmarked. What this system returns is also a ranked list:

$$L_q^E = \left(o_1^E, o_2^E, o_3^E, \ldots, o_n^E \right)$$

which is ranked in the descending order of relevance by the relevance function $\mathcal{S}^E$. Therefore, $\mathcal{S}^E(o_1^E, q) \geq \mathcal{S}^E(o_2^E, q) \geq \mathcal{S}^E(o_3^E, q) \cdots \geq \mathcal{S}^E(o_n^E, q)$.

Precision and recall are not adequate to capture the performance of an AR system since they cannot account for the *order, rank, spread* and the *displacement* aspects of response sets. We therefore need new measures for benchmarking AR systems performance. In order to come up with new measures, we adopt the following two principles:

(a) *Principle 1*: If an object is displaced from its "ideal rank" for an AR system, then the penalty is symmetric with respect to moving up or down the list. That is to say that the penalty for displacement around the ideal position is the same whether the displacement increases or decreases the rank.
(b) *Principle 2*: The penalty of an object displaced from its "ideal rank" is directly proportional to its relevancy measure. This is intuitive because given equal displacements, the displacement of an object with a higher relevancy measure is less desirable than for an object with a lower relevancy measure. Also, this is reasonable since the relevancy measure is the *basis* for the ranking.

Based on these two principles and the four observations noted in Section 3.4.2, we propose the following two measures:

- **Order:** The *order* of a response set is defined as the size of the longest consecutive subsequence of objects appearing in their ideal order (not the ideal rank). This basically measures one aspect of the quality of the relevance function of the AR system being benchmarked. For a database of size n, the ideal order is n. This measure captures the Order aspect of response sets described in Section 3.4.2.
- **Weighted displacement:** For an object o_i^E, the displacement $d_q(o_i^E)$ for a query q is defined as:

$$d_q\left(o_i^E\right) = \left| \left(\text{Rank}\left(o_i^E\right) \text{ in } L_q^I\right) - \left(\text{Rank}\left(o_i^E\right) \text{ in } L_q^E\right) \right|$$

The displacement indicates the amount an object has moved from its ideal rank. We define the performance measure *weighted displacement*, ω_q^E, for a query q by weighting the displacement with the ideal relevance measure:

$$\omega_q^E = \sum_{i=1}^{n} \mathcal{S}^I\left(o_i^E, q\right) d_q\left(o_i^E\right)$$

Note that ω_q^E is 0 if the ideal response is returned by AR system E. Also, this measure incorporates the two principles described above. Moreover, it captures the Rank (through $\mathcal{S}^I$) and Displace (through $d_q(o_i^E)$) of Section 3.4.2. Note that Spread is not relevant in case of an continuous AR system since the spread will be n for all responses.

2. **Mixed:** A mixed AR system has characteristics of both Boolean IR systems and continuous AR engines. The mixed AR system returns a response set consisting of two subsets—a set of relevant objects and a set of irrelevant objects for any query. Moreover, for the set of relevant objects, it also returns a ranked list of objects based on the relevance function for that query. Again, assume that we have a database D having n multimedia objects:

$$D = \{o_i \mid i = 1, 2, \ldots, n\}.$$

Like in the case of the continuous AR system, we also have a *Relevance Function S*, which for a given query q assigns a relevance measure s_i^q to every every object o_i in the database. It is a function $S : D \times Q \rightarrow [0, 1]$ such that $S(o_i, q)$ is the relevance measure of object o_i for query q. Again, Q is the set of all queries. For a given query q we have the following:

(a) *Ideal system response*: This assumes that an ideal AR system I exists. The ideal response can be considered to consist of two sets which is as a partition on the database induced by query q:

$$R_q^I = \{o_j \mid (o_j \in D) \wedge (o_j \text{ is relevant})\}$$
$$N_q^I = \{o_k \mid (o_k \in D) \wedge (o_k \text{ is not relevant})\}$$

such that

$$R_q^I \cap N_q^I = \phi$$
$$R_q^I \cup N_q^I = D$$

In addition, the set of relevant objects, R_q^I, has an associated ranked list L_q^I:

$$L_q^I = \left(o_1^I, o_2^I, o_3^I, \ldots, o_x^I\right) \quad \text{for some } x \leq n,$$

such that:

$$S^I\left(o_1^I, q\right) \geq S^I\left(o_2^I, q\right) \geq S^I\left(o_3^I, q\right) \cdots \geq S^I\left(o_x^I, q\right)$$

This means that there are x relevant objects for the query q ranked in a descending order of relevance.

(b) *Test system response*: This is the response actually provided by a mixed AR system E being benchmarked. What this system returns is a ranked list:

$$L_q^E = \left(o_1^E, o_2^E, o_3^E, \ldots, o_n^E\right)$$

which is ranked in the descending order of relevance by the relevance function S^E. Therefore, $S^E(o_1^E, q) \geq S^E(o_2^E, q) \geq S^E(o_3^E, q) \cdots \geq S^E(o_n^E, q)$. Now, as far as the relevant and non-relevant sets go, there are two scenarios for the mixed AR system response:

i. **Size thresholding:** In this case, the relevant number of objects for query q from the response set L_q^E is considered to be ℓ. This means that the top ℓ objects of the ranked list L_q^E are relevant for the query. Formally, the relevant set of objects R_q^E is:

$$R_q^E = \left\{ o_j^E \mid \left(o_j^E \in L_q^E \right) \wedge \left(j \leq \ell \right) \right\} \quad \text{where } \ell \leq n$$

Note that it is reasonable to have $\ell \leq x$ because the ideal system I returns x relevant objects, but this may not always be the case. The set of irrelevant objects N_q^E is defined as:

$$N_q^E = \left\{ o_k^E \mid \left(o_k^E \in L_q^E \right) \wedge \left(o_k^E \notin R_q^E \right) \right\}$$

For the case of size thresholding, we propose three performance measures which can be used:

- **Order:** The *order* of a response set is defined as the size of the longest consecutive subsequence of *relevant objects* (according to I) appearing in their ideal order (but not necessarily possessing the ideal rank). This basically measures one aspect of the quality of the relevance function of the AR system being benchmarked. The ideal order is ℓ if $\ell < x$ and is x if $\ell \geq x$. This measure captures the Order aspect of response sets described in Section 3.4.2.

- **Rank:** The *rank* of a response set is defined as the sum of the ranks (positions) of the relevant objects appearing in the system response relevant set. If an object appears in the ideal response set R_q^I but does not appear in the system relevant set R_q^E, it is assumed to have a rank of $\ell + 1$. The ideal rank will be $\frac{\ell(\ell+1)}{2}$ if $\ell < x$. If $\ell \geq x$, then the ideal rank is $\frac{x(x+1)}{2}$.

- **Fill ratio:** The *fill ratio* is defined to be the ratio of the number of actually relevant objects appearing in R_q^E to the number of objects in R_q^E which is ℓ. Therefore,

$$\text{Fill ratio} = \begin{cases} \frac{\|\chi\|}{\ell} & \text{if } \ell < x \\ \frac{\|\chi\|}{x} & \text{if } \ell \geq x \end{cases}$$

where

$$\chi = \left\{ o_j \mid o_j \in \left(R_q^I \cap R_q^E \right) \right\}$$

ii. **Object thresholding:** If the last relevant object o_x^I of L_q^I appears at the $\hbar$th position of L_q^E, then we threshold L_q^E by $\hbar$. So the response set is thresholded such that the last (ideally) relevant object appears in the set. In other words, the relevant number of objects is $\hbar$ such that the *last* object o_x^I of the ideal response ranked list L_q^I appears in the $\hbar$th position of system E's response. So, formally the relevant set of objects R_q^E is:

$$R_q^E = \left\{ o_j^E \mid \left(o_j^E \in L_q^E \right) \wedge \left(j \leq \hbar \right) \right\}$$

where

$$\hbar = \text{Rank of } \left(o_x^I \in L_q^I \right) \text{ in } L_q^E$$

The set of irrelevant objects N_q^E is defined as:

$$N_q^E = \left\{ o_k^E \mid \left(o_k^E \in L_q^E \right) \wedge \left(o_k^E \notin R_q^E \right) \right\}$$

For the case of object thresholding, we propose three performance measures which can be used:

- **Order:** The *order* of a response set is defined as the size of the longest consecutive subsequence of relevant objects appearing in their ideal order. This again measures one aspect of the quality of the relevance function of the AR system being benchmarked. The ideal order is x. This measure captures the Order aspect of response sets described in Section 3.4.2.

- **Spread:** The *spread* of a response set is the threshold at which all the objects in R_q^I appear in R_q^E. In other words, the spread is exactly equal to $\hbar$. This measure captures the Spread aspect described in Section 3.4.2.

- **Weighted displacement:** For an object o_i^E, the displacement $d_q(o_i^E)$ for a query q is defined as:

$$d_q\left(o_i^E\right) = \left|\left(\text{Rank}\left(o_i^E\right) \text{ in } L_q^I\right) - \left(\text{Rank}\left(o_i^E\right) \text{ in } L_q^E\right)\right|$$

The displacement indicates the amount an object has moved from its ideal rank. We define the performance measure *weighted displacement*, ω_q^E, by weighting the displacement with the ideal relevance measure:

$$\omega_q^E = \sum_{i=1}^{n} \mathcal{S}^I\left(o_i^E, q\right) d_q\left(o_i^E\right)$$

Note that ω_q^E is 0 if the ideal response is returned by RLIR engine E. This measure incorporates the two principles described earlier. It also captures the Rank and Displace of Section 3.4.2.

3.4.4. Quality measures for calibrating an AR system. Measures for calibrating an AR system will assume the existence of an ideal AR system that produces the Expected Response Set (ERS). ERS is the ideal answer to a query. Hence ERS will become the reference result against which results from all other AR systems will be evaluated. Such evaluations can then be used to calibrate the AR system under test. We can define relative measures which show how well a system E performs with respect to a particular measure against the ideal system I. We define the relative measures in the range [0, 1]. A relative measure closer to unity indicates a better (more "ideal") response and hence is of better quality. We have defined the new measures in the last section. We will now show how to compute the relative measure for each of the type of AR system:

1. **Continuous AR system:**

   - **Order:** Since the ideal order for a database of size n is equal to n (the largest possible), the relative order for a query q can be defined as:

     $$\text{Relative order}_q = \frac{\text{Order of engine } E \text{ for query } q}{n}$$

- **Weighted displacement:** Since the ideal weighted displacement is 0, the relative weighted displacement for a query q can be defined as:

$$\text{Relative weighted displacement}_q = \frac{\omega_q^E}{\Omega}$$

where

$$\Omega = \begin{cases} \frac{n^2}{2} & \text{if } n \text{ is even} \\ \frac{n^2-1}{2} & \text{if } n \text{ is odd} \end{cases}$$

for a database of size n. Note that it can be proved that Ω is the largest weighted displacement possible assuming all objects have the highest weight of unity [10].

2. **Size thresholded mixed AR system:**

- **Order:** Since the ideal order for a database of size n is equal to ℓ, the relative order for a query q can be defined as:

$$\text{Relative order}_q = \begin{cases} \frac{\text{order of } E \text{ for query } q}{\ell} & \text{if } \ell < x \\ \frac{\text{order of } E \text{ for query } q}{x} & \text{if } \ell \geq x \end{cases}$$

- **Rank:** This can be computed as the ratio of the ideal rank to the engine rank:

$$\text{Relative rank} = \frac{\text{Rank}(R_q^I)}{\text{Rank}(R_q^E)}$$

- **Fill ratio:** Since the fill ratio of the ideal system is 1 and that of the system response is less than or equal to 1, the relative fill ratio is equal to the fill ratio.

3. **Object thresholded mixed AR system:**

- **Order:** Since the ideal order for a database of size n is equal to x, the relative order can be defined as:

$$\text{Relative order}_q = \frac{\text{Order of } E \text{ for query } q}{x}$$

- **Spread:** The relative spread is the ratio of the spread of the ideal response to that of the system response:

$$\text{Relative spread}_q = \frac{\|L_q^I\|}{\hbar}$$

- **weighted displacement:** Since the ideal weighted displacement is 0, the relative weighted displacement can be defined as:

$$\text{Relative weighted displacement}_q = \frac{\omega_q^E}{\Omega}$$

where

$$\Omega = \begin{cases} \frac{n^2}{2} & \text{if } n \text{ is even} \\ \frac{n^2-1}{2} & \text{if } n \text{ is odd} \end{cases}$$

for a database of size n.

3.4.5. Overall measure for AR method. The measures defined earlier can be combined to derive an overall figure of merit by using a weighted combination of the individual measures. The quality AR of an AR system can be computed as:

$$Q_{AR} = \frac{\sum(W_i * M_i)}{\sum W_i} \quad \text{for } i = 1 \ldots N \tag{9}$$

where M_i is the appropriate relative measure i (e.g., for an object-thresholded mixed AR system, it will be relative order, relative spread and relative weighted displacement), W_i is the relative importance of the measure i and N is the total number of measures appropriate for that AR system. Then the overall quality of service can be defined as:

$$QOS_{AR} = T_{AR} * Q_{AR} \tag{10}$$

3.5. Complete benchmark for multimedia databases

We have described the benchmarks for each of the different retrieval methods in Sections 3.1. to 3.4. Different multimedia database applications may use one or more of the retrieval methods in some permutation. The combination of retrieval methods may be used either independently or in some interdependent manner. The independent combination will use the different retrieval method to get the answers to different parts of a complex query. The results are usually collated into different parts of the response to a query. The overall benchmark for such an application will be,

$$QOS_{MMDB} = \frac{W_Q * \prod(Q_i)}{W_T * \max(T_i)} \tag{11}$$

where W_T is the importance of time of response, W_Q is the importance of quality, Q_i is the quality measure of the ith retrieval technique, T_i is the speed measure of the ith retrieval technique. The simplest form of interdependent usage may be to use the results from one retrieval method as the input to another retrieval method. In such a case, the overall benchmark may be represented as follows.

$$QOS_{MMDB} = \frac{W_Q * \prod(Q_i)}{W_T * \sum(T_i)} \tag{12}$$

The graph in figure 3 shows the desired region into which we would like to see the systems fall.

4.   A methodology for benchmarking of multimedia databases

The benchmarking of multimedia databases use the time and quality measures that were discussed in Section 3 on what we call a multimedia database engine. Such an engine may be just one of the four types of retrieval methods or some permutation and combination of the four types.

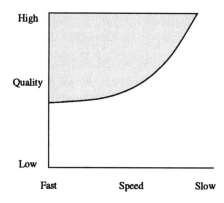

Figure 3. Desired region in quality-speed plane.

4.1. Scalability with respect to time

This is a fairly straightforward method. One can start with certain number of records in the database and then scale up using multiples of same quantity. Then a plot of time (or speed) of response versus the database size for the same query will give us a good idea of scalability of the engine with respect to time.

4.2. Scalability with respect to quality

The measures for quality for each of the retrieval methods has been presented in Section 3. We will discuss how these can be used for the different types of retrieval methods.

4.2.1. Database technology.   Since quality has not been a factor for consideration in database technologies used in OLTP applications, we do not suggest any methodology.

4.2.2. Information retrieval.   TREC has been attempting to set up testing standards and hence we will keep our discussion on this topic to a minimum. The following quality related tests may be desirable in addition to what TREC has been carrying out. It would be desirable to construct corpuses containing different roles of words capable of playing multiple roles, and to set up the queries corresponding to each of these roles. The different parts of speech will be the set of roles that words can assume.

The corpuses, roles and queries will be determined by the type of applications. For example, applications using corpuses containing name databases would be interested only in those words that play the role of noun phrase. Applications using corpuses containing sports information would be interested in noun phrases and verbs.

The method for such testing can be designed using an iterative two step process. We will first define the two step process.

The first step will be to choose a word that plays the most types of roles and to generate documents and queries corresponding to each of these roles. This will give the different IR algorithms and methodologies an opportunity to refine themselves against this test data.

The second step would be to choose additional words that play the same set of roles and corresponding documents and queries to test the IR methods against this "scaled up corpus."

Later iterations of this two step process should increasingly bring in other words, documents and queries that correspond to other types of roles as dictated by the type of application. The testing can be said to be completed when sufficient corpus and queries have been generated and tested corresponding to all the common (and necessary) roles.

4.2.3. Links. Benchmarking the links for quality can be set up as a test set of information to be retrieved against queries on links and then computing the quality measure mentioned in Section 3.3.

4.2.4. Approximate retrieval methods. The benchmarking of quality of retrieval from AR methods can be set up in two steps: evaluation of individual features, and overall testing. Evaluation of approximate retrieval is application-type dependent. It must be done against a given set of objects—the *test data set*. The sample data set specifies a sequence of objects which should be retrieved for every given sample. To define a test data set for approximate retrieval, let us define the ideal retrieval. It must be clearly understood that for any AR query, there is a "context" associated with it. This context can vary from person to person and perhaps it can vary with time for the same person. The response to a query can then vary depending on the context. So for AR, the 'right answer' to a query can vary depending on the context. This makes the task of evaluating an AR system very difficult. Therefore, in order to benchmark various AR systems, one needs to fix a context for every query and then obtain a corresponding *ideal retrieval result.* For any given sample, the ideal retrieval result should exactly follow designer's expectation of similarity—all similar data items must be retrieved and be ordered from the most similar to the least similar. In order to perform a fair evaluation, it is necessary to have a large set of queries, contexts and the associated ideal retrieval results. These are in turn driven by the specific application area which the AR system purports to address. Moreover, for ideal approximate retrieval, the test data set should consist test data (and associated queries) for both individual features and the overall retrieval. The system should be tuned using individual features and then tested for overall retrieval. The test data should be used to evaluate the measures presented in Section 3.5. We give a brief description of the use of this methodology for real applications in the appendix.

4.2.5. Combined retrieval techniques. The individual retrieval techniques should be first tested to obtain their individual performance measures. The results can be used to tune the different retrieval techniques. Once the individual retrieval techniques are tested, then they will remain unaltered unless the range of values of the individual features change. The next step is to change the weights for combining the results obtained from each of the component retrieval techniques. The combined result is the overall benchmark and can be used to modify the weights until the desired performance levels are obtained.

5.   Future work

We have provided a taxonomy of retrieval methods in this paper and defined the measures for benchmarking each of the methods and combinations of these methods. We have also outlined a methodology for benchmarking multimedia database applications.

Our further research is on refining the quantitative measures and defining the test environments for benchmarks. We would like to propose that some international body work towards MREC (Multimedia Retrieval and Evaluation Conference) along the lines of TREC, which would essentially try to establish benchmarking data and standards for multimedia databases. A good starting point may be the MIRA effort being undertaken in the EC which works on evaluation frameworks for interactive multimedia information retrieval applications [4]. We strongly feel that the multimedia database community should have standard test data sets, standard queries and the *ideal* retrieval output for each of these queries. Perhaps one database will not be enough, several would be needed for the different types/features of multimedia data and also for overall combined retrieval in various applications. In the long run, standard data sets, queries and known ground truth will be the only way to judge the accuracy and utility of different retrieval engines. Moreover, common collections for each type of multimedia data type should be built up. Reporting research results based on massive data sets should also be made mandatory. Fortunately this is already happening in certain niche areas like the NIST standard databases for human face images and handwriting images.

Acknowledgments

We thank our colleagues at ISS for critiquing the ideas presented. In particular, we thank Ang Yew Hock, Lam Chian Prong, Ngair Teow Hin and Limsoon Wong for their help. Mohan S. Kankanhalli and Jiankang Wu's work has been supported by the *Real World Computing Partnership* of Japan.

Appendix: Applications

The benchmarking procedure defined in Section 4 using the measures defined in Section 3 are being employed for testing applications built around multimedia database engines developed at the Institute of Systems Science.

FACE application

The FACE application was reported in [12]. It used image features and text descriptions as the two dimensions. The image features were defined both as crisp sets and fuzzy sets on six facial features: chin, eyes, eyebrow, nose, mouth, and hair. A set of artificially composed facial images are created to form a test data set. In the test data set, there are faces with one, two, or more different facial features. The test is conducted in two steps: Firstly, quality of retrieval is tested against individual facial features. For example, to test retrieval on eyes, a subset of test image data set with different eyes are used. Samples for the test is arbitrarily chosen from the set. Retrieval results are evaluated subjectively by several (10 in our test) people.

The second step is the overall test. It is conducted against all facial features. Figure 4 gives an example of a set of faces with change in one or more features. On the bottom-right side, there is a "similarity retrieval" panel to control the weightage among facial features.

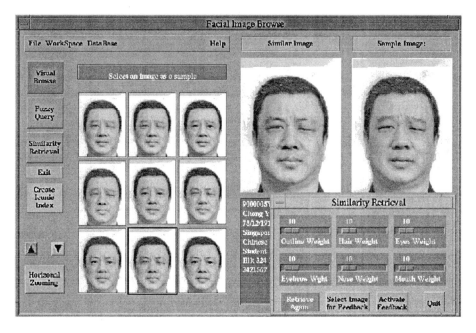

Figure 4.

Here, all weightage are equally set to 10. The nine images on the left are retrieval result
with the first being the sample. Comparing with the sample, the differences of other eight
images are listed in the table, where "small" "medium" stand for "small difference" and
"medium difference":

	Eyes	Eyebrow	Nose	Mouth	Chin	Hair
1	Same	Same	Same	Small	Same	Same
2	Medium	Same	Same	Small	Same	Same
3	Same	Same	Small	Small	Same	Same
4	Medium	Same	Small	Same	Same	Same
5	Same	Medium	Same	Small	Same	Same
6	Same	Medium	Small	Small	Same	Same
7	Medium	Medium	Same	Same	Same	Same
8	Medium	Medium	Small	Same	Same	Same

Such test sets were used for refining the image database engine used in the system. The
fuzzy retrieval engine also used similar tests except that the membership of a feature was
not limited to one set only. These engines are of the *AR type*. The text retrieval engine
used in the system was tested along the quality measures reported in Section 3.2. The text
retrieval engine uses the *IR method*. The iconic browsing uses the *link method*.

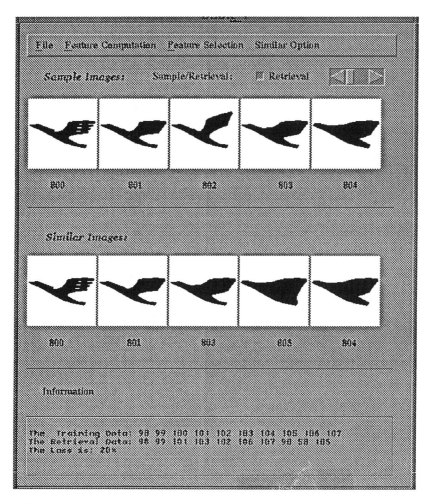

Figure 5.

Trademark application

The trademark application consisted of device mark (local and global shape measures) retrieval, phonetic retrieval, word-in mark retrieval and retrieval by meaning. The retrieval engines used in this application are reported in [13, 14]. While we have different engines for using color as a feature [6], we have not yet integrated this into the present trademark application. The device mark uses the *AR method*. The phonetics retrieval, word-in mark retrieval and the retrieval by meaning are all based on the *IR method*.

To test the quality of retrieval for device mark shape, three levels of test data sets have been created: mathematically created geometric patterns, actual device marks and their variations, complicated device marks. In the first class of test patterns, the variations can be exactly controlled by the program used to create these patterns. For example, one series of geometric patterns consists of a circle, an octagon, a hexagon, a pentagon, a square, and a triangle. Figure 5 shows the test results using the second class of test patterns. The images shown in the first row belong to one test series with the first as the sample for retrieval. Neighboring images are more similar than distant ones. The second row shows retrieval result. By comparing these two rows, different quality measures are computed.

We can see, from figure 5, that in the test data set displayed in the first row, the bird in the third image is indeed more similar to the bird in the sample image (the first one) than that in the fourth and fifth. This test data set is selected from the view point of perception and by consideration of user requirements. The system uses shape similarity for retrieval. The bird in the third test image has its wings open wider, so its shape is surely different from the sample. The quantitative measures of *order* and *weighted displacement* provide a tool for the fine tuning of the system. The third class of test data sets consists of actual trademarks selected by trademark officers. This test data set is for the final test stage to see if the system can bring out potentially conflicting trademarks from the databases with respect to all possible aspects.

References

1. Anon et. al., "A measure of transaction processing power," Readings in Database Systems, M. Stonebraker (Ed.), Morgan Kaufmann Publishers, Inc.: San Mateo, CA, pp. 300–312, 1988.
2. D. Bitton and C. Turbyfill, "A Retrospective on the wisconsin benchmark," Readings in Database Systems, M. Stonebraker (Ed.), Morgan Kaufmann Publishers, Inc.: San Mateo, CA, pp. 280–299, 1988.
3. http://potomac.ncsl.nist.gov:80/TREC/
4. http://www.dcs.gla.ac.uk/mira/
5. F.W. Lancaster, Information Retrieval Systems, John Wiley, 1968.
6. B.M. Mehtre, M.S. Kankanhalli, A.D. Narasimhalu, and C.M. Guo, "Color matching for image retrieval," Pattern Recognition Letters, Vol. 16, pp. 325–331, 1995.
7. A.D. Narasimhalu, "Beyond recall and precision: Additional measures for multimedia applications and services," MIRO Workshop, Glasgow, Sept. 1995.
8. G. Salton and M.J. McGill, Introduction to Modern Information Retrieval, McGraw-Hill Advanced Computer Science Series, Auckland, 1983.
9. G. Salton, The State of Retrieval System Evaluation, Information Processing and Management, Vol. 28, No. 4, pp. 441–449, 1992.
10. L. Wong, Personal Communication, 1995.
11. P. Wright, "Cognitive overheads and prostheses: Some issues in evaluating hypertexts," Proceedings of Third ACM Conference on Hypertext, San Antonio, Texas, Dec. 1991, pp. 1–12.
12. J.K. Wu, Y.H. Ang, C.P. Lam, H.H. Loh, and A.D. Narasimhalu, "Inference and retrieval of facial images," ACM Multimedia Journal, Vol. 2, No. 1, pp. 1–14, 1994.
13. J.K. Wu, B.M. Mehtre, Y.J. Gao, P.C. Lam, and A.D. Narasimhalu, "STAR—A multimedia database system for trademark registration," Applications of Databases, Lecture Notes in Computer Science, Vol. 819, pp. 109–122, W. Litwin and T. Risch (Eds.), Proc. First International Conference on Applications of Databases—ADB 94', Springer-Verlag, 1994.
14. J.K. Wu, A.D. Narasimhalu, B.M. Mehtre, C.P. Lam, and Y.J. Gao, "CORE: A content-based retrieval engine for multimedia databases," ACM Multimedia Systems, Vol. 3, pp. 3–25, 1995.

6

Four Promising Multimedia Databases and Their Embodiments

Y. YAGINUMA, T. YATABE, T. SATOU, J. TATEMURA AND M. SAKAUCHI
Institute of Industrial Science, University of Tokyo, Roppongi 7-22-1, Minato-ku, Tokyo 106, Japan

Abstract. Multimedia database systems have become more and more important as the tool to extract and generate additional values from multimedia 'Contents'. In this paper, four multimedia database systems are proposed from the view point of promising contents sources; the Network multimedia databases, the Stream MM database systems, the Library MM database systems, and the Real world MM database systems. Important problems to be solved, i.e., 'what to do', are also discussed for each databases. Three concrete multimedia systems by authors' research group, are then introduced and discussed as the embodiments of these multimedia systems; (1) the open Global Image Retrieval and Linking System, GIRLS, for mediation WWW data pace as the network MM database systems, (2) the flexible multimedia database platform GOLS, and (3) the higher level authoring system for the Stream MM environments.

Keywords: muiltimedia database, image retrieval, multimedia platform, authoring

1. Introduction

Multimedia systems are expected as promising carrying vehicles for creating new services and businesses in the coming twenty-one century. Generally, they are consisted of three major components; "Contents" in the form of video, voice and images, "Distribution" for communication tools and "Platform" for various types of utilization. Especially, "Contents" which include multimedia soft, video soft, etc., are important to generate additional values directly for the users. On the other hand, 'Multimedia Database Systems' have been defined in the narrow sense as tools for querying efficiently multimedia data. However, the concept and role of 'Multimedia database systems' should be extended here in order to be responsible for 'contents' to generate new services.

In this paper, we consider Multimedia Database Systems as the tools to extract and generate additional values from multimedia 'Contents' with putting emphasis on the mediator functions between users and contents.

Firstly, promising multimedia data contents sources of 'On the network', 'In the digital broadcasting stream', 'In the library', and 'In the Real World' will be discussed. Four types of multimedia database systems are then proposed corresponding each contents source environments; the Network multimedia databases, the Stream MM database systems, the Library MM database systems, and the Real world MM database systems. Important problems to be solved, i.e., 'what to do', are also discussed for each databases. Three concrete multimedia systems by authors' research group, are then introduced and discussed as the embodiments of these multimedia systems; (1) the open Global Image Retrieval and Linking System, GIRLS, for mediation WWW data pace as the network MM database

systems, (2) the flexible multimedia database platform GOLS, and (3) the higher level
authoring system for the Stream MM environments.

2. Four promising multimedia database systems

What are the basic functions (what to do) of the multimedia database systems to provide
users with additional values from 'contents?' Before discussing this, we need to imagine
where promising multimedia contents in the coming multimedia society are generated and
accumulated. Though it's difficult to predict these Where's precisely, we propose here the
four Where's (fields) considering the various related situations; namely, 'On the network',
'In the digital broadcasting', 'In the library' and 'In the real world', and define four types
of multimedia database systems corresponding to them.

(1) *On the network*: The 'internet' data services including the WWW are now becoming
    more and more popular. Tremendous amount of severs provide multimedia information
    even in the form of video and images. This means that most databases hereafter will be
    scattered where contents are generated and such situations will grow uncontrollably.
    Such dispersed databases should be called here the 'Network Multimedia DB' as one
    of our most promising targets as shown in figure 1.
    There are many 'what to do' for this network multimedia DB. We believe, however,
    mediator functions, which inform users what kind of data are in the network, or where

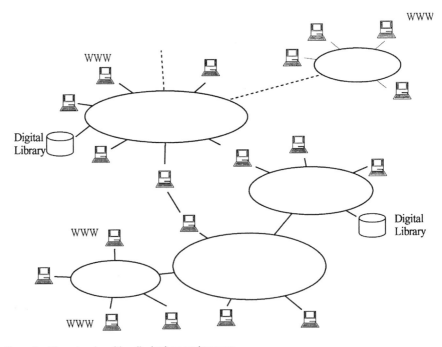

Figure 1. The network multimedia database environment.

is their useful or desired information, and help to collect and relate them to the user's applications, are the most important. Such 'contexing' of the network multimedia data should be the main function in the database. Their typical and first step trials examples are the 'Yahoo' directory service or another search engines for text data. Various trials and functions, however, will be required for more general multimedia data in the network.

As the embodiment of this network multimedia database system GIRLS(Global Image Retrieval and Linking Systems) for images on the WWW by authors' group is introduced in **3**.

(2) *In the digital broadcasting*: Needless to say, one of the typical leaders of multimedia contents providers is broadcasting. Commercial-based satellite digital broadcasting with over 100 channels have already started or will soon start in USA, Japan, Europe and Asia. Another digital broadcasting in the form of CATV, ordinary TV, or Fibernet Communication also have already been or will be planed within less than ten years. In such situations, where we'll be able to enjoy hundreds or thousands of broadcasting channels, much more user-oriented and intelligent access to the tremendous amount of 'contents stream' will be required as shown in figure 2. Let's call this situation as 'Stream-type Multimedia DB'.

In this stream-type Multimedia DB, the mediator functions would be also most important for users, which help them to pick up useful and required data from the stream and to make their own customized contents for new service and business.

Satellite, CATV, Ordinary Broadcasting · ·

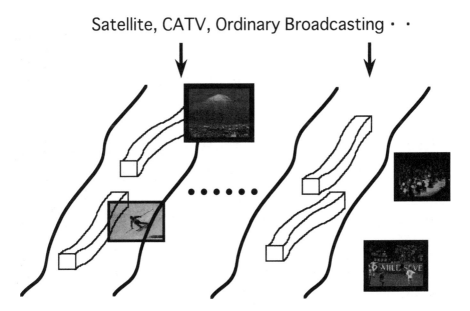

Digital Broadcasting:->Multimedia stream

Figure 2.   The stream multimedia database environment.

As the embodiments of these stream multimedia database systems, two concrete systems by authors' research group will be introduced in **4** and **5**.

(3) *In the Library*: Such library-type databases as digital libraries, electronic catalogs et al., are of course important targets of the Multimedia DB in the narrow and ordinary sense. We call this type as 'Library Multimedia DB'.

This type of systems has been main targets for Multimedia DB. Many researches including flexible and powerful 'retrieval' functions etc., have been done during two decades [1, 17].

(4) *In the Real World*: We Japanese, suffered sever earthquake damage at Kobe in January, 1995. This tragedy taught us importance of realtime acquisition of our city information for disaster mitigation. Multimedia communication technology enables us to establish a new type of databases which collect and analyze realtime situations (video information) to tell us 'What's going on in the city'. Let's call this type as 'Real World Multimedia DB', as shown in figure 3.

Though this type of systems have not been considered as multimedia databases, they have promising possibility to realize new services and businesses with real time integration of real world situations and existing another databases. Expecting fields in this category include disaster mitigation, intelligent transport systems (ITS), advanced environment management, advanced utilization of high resolution satellite

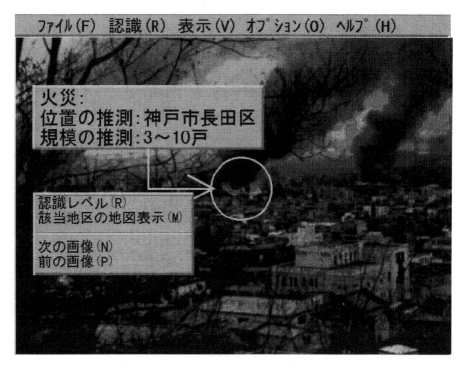

Figure 3.   The real world multimedia database environment.

images etc. Author's group started, in 1994, the research project to realize so called 'Multimedia Geographical Information System' by integrating ordinary map data and realtime city video data from robot cameras. Some details are reported in Ref. [7].

3.   Global image retrieval and linking system in the network MM environments

In the network multimedia database systems shown in figure 1, 'contexing' of the data space is the most important function as described in **2**. GIRLS (the Global Image Retrieval and Linking System) for the image data in the WWW [13] has been developed as the embodiment of such database systems.

In GIRLS, a search robot named BOYS automatically gathers typical images and layout information and URL from the WWW to construct the database for retrieval and linking based on the image contents as shown in figure 4.

Though over 100 search robots are working for text data, a very few robots including BOYS are for images and video. The system provides users with open functions including retrieval of images or Logo's in the WWW data space, linkage to the original home pages with images imagined by users, feedback to the retrieval performance, or participating in the retrieval command creation etc. In the example of the GIRLS operation in figure 5, similarity retrieval results to the given layout home page are shown. GIRLS are now growing towards more friendly mediator functions in the network multimedia database environments.

4.   Flexible multimedia platform GOLS for stream-type multimedia data environments

The second concrete example is a flexible Multimedia Platform GOLS supporting various functions for the 'stream-type' multimedia databases. GOLS [9, 10] provides many functions including database acquisition from images and videos, object-oriented database

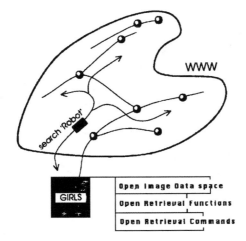

Figure 4.   Open image retrieval system GIRLS.

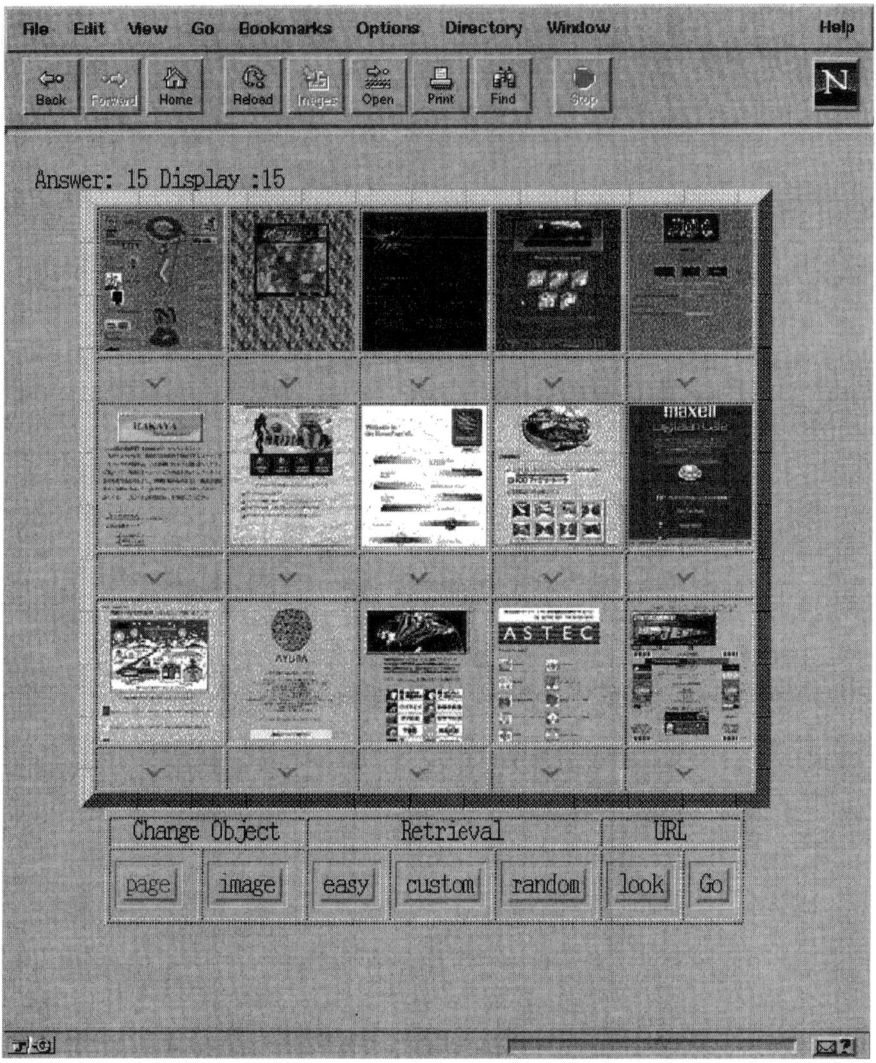

Figure 5. The similarity retrieval results to the given layout home page.

managements, and powerful database presentations with unique GUI. Acquisition of a desired set of video scene from live TV broadcasting programs (Live Hypermedia) is one typical example of GOLS functions.

Figure 6 gives the concept of the live hypermedia in GOLS. The model in GOLS for recognition accepts a set of segments in a shot, detects the scene categories, and extracts objects in the shot of video. In the live hypermedia, information nodes and links between them are dynamically determined corresponding to the structure of the recognition models.

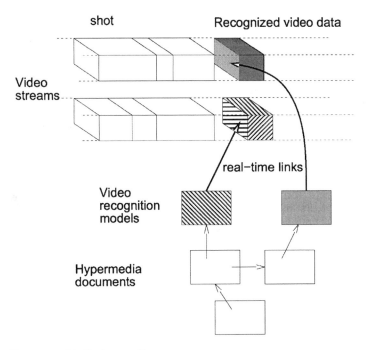

Figure 6.   The concept of the live hypermedia.

A state-transition type expression [11] is proposed to describe flexible and compound models for recognition on live hypermedia. The system can detect not only TV program categories but also their contents.

The model for recognition is implemented by Video Scene Description Language (VSDL) and the state-transition model. The VSDL realizes primitive description of shots. The state-transition model infers contents of shots using the primitive description. Object-oriented approach is adopted in the model construction process, in order to improve the modularity and reusability of the models.

VSDL [1] was developed for automatic detection of TV shots. Users can describe TV scenes or objects they want to pick up or select by the language VSDL. VSDL predicates include description of video scene by features of color segments (color, area, position, etc.), relations to another segment, motion vector, and camera effects.

A user describes what to pick up with VSDL. In real time, the GOLS checks for matches between this description and the given live TV images. When it found a match, it picks the corresponding video scenes up into the system.

The state-transition model was originally proposed by our research group in order to realize flexible and reusable models for recognition of drawings [11]. In GOLS, this model has been improved and extended to adopt video data recognition. A primitive data (e.g., a segment for video scene generated by color image processing) is called as a *token*. Each token is given a *state*. The state is changed from one to another according to arrows between the states.

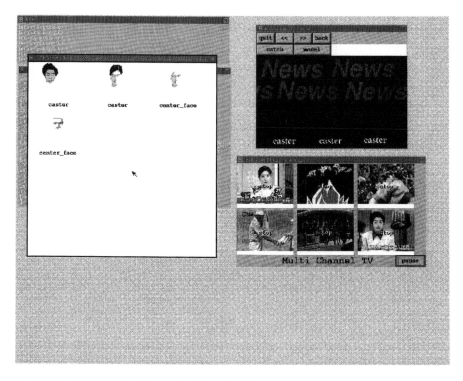

Figure 7.   Example of database object manipulation using GOLS.

Let's consider the human TV caster recognition in the shot for example. The state can be changed to 'seg_skin', 'seg_face', ..., 'caster', etc., in accordance with bottom-up and/or top-down recognition rules given for each state-transition link. In this manner, the structure of segments can be recognized by this type of models. The model consists of a set of the transition rules. Each rule describes a condition to change from one state to another. The condition consists of the VSDL predicates and Prolog predicates.

The inference engine interprets the rules and updates the state of each token. Interpretation strategy is a combination of bottom-up and top-down analysis. At first, bottom-up rules are

Table 1.   The retrieval accuracy.

Model	Strict		Coarse	
	Recall	Precision	Recall	Precision
News	0.57	1.00	0.99	0.55
Sumo	0.67	0.95	0.84	0.47
Golf	0.63	0.71	0.87	0.45

Figure 8. Results of the content-based retrieval.

invoked and token states are updated until no more state can be changed. Then top-down rules are invoked to further more updating.

Merit of this model expression lies in its modularity: rule sets can be easily replaced according to a recognition target. In fact, over 80% of the experimental models for commercial TV broadcastings are found reasonable.

Figure 7 presents an example GOLS operation. GOLS picks up the desired newscaster video scene from the live TV broadcast programs shown in the lower right window. Then it recognizes the contents of the scene and generated "video parts," which are shown in the upper left window. A GOLS user can utilize this video parts to design the new card type hyper-media shown in the upper right window.

To demonstrate the effectiveness of the GOLS or Live Hypermedia, experimental evaluation of the Recall rate and the Precision rate (video scene pick-up performance) for commercial TV broadcasting programs using the GOLS models has been done successfully, whose results are shown in Table 1.

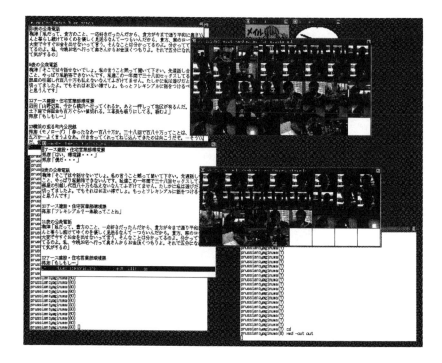

Figure 9.   Example of content-based editing.

5.   A higher-level authoring system for stream-type MM environments

The third example is also related to the stream-type MM database.

In order to realize more flexible and user-oriented access and utilization of stream-type multimedia DB's, advanced methods of making higher data models for video data in the DB are required. Many trials using image or video recognition techniques have been done for this targets. They have not necessarily, however, been successful because of difficulty of image understanding. A new approach to overcome this problem using multiple media synchronization proposed by author's research group, is introduced here.

Many video data have corresponding video, sounds and relevant documents. TV drama programs, for example, have related video sounds and scenario documents. Our idea is to realize logical synchronization between these related multiple media using DP matching techniques. Several numbers of related patterns are first extracted from each medium, and then optimal matching for these patterns is carried out using modified DP matching technique [14, 15]. The scene change pattern in the video, voice or female voice patterns and word arrangement pattern in the scenario document are selected for this related 'patterns'.

Once, these logical synchronization has been carried out, document data, which have much higher symbolic and abstracted representation than video data, can be used as a kind of structure or content navigator for video. For example, intelligent access to video scenes including the specified person (character) can be successfully realized with the Recall rate of about 90–97% for typical TV dramas.

Figure 8 shows the retrieval results of a specified person who is laughing. The user interface of the system is written using HTML. In this version, the retrieval is realized not only by the name of the person but also by the action of the person.

Figure 9 shows another example of user-oriented content-based editing for TV drama video. A user can easily realize his/her own video authoring just using much easier word-processor editing functions, because sentences in the scenario documents have now tight timing synchronization with video stream. This user-oriented access and authoring system for video is now growing toward more flexible and effective video database mediator.

6. Conclusions

Four types of promising multimedia databases are introduced and importance of the mediator functions in these databases have been identified as important research directions. Three concrete multimedia database systems with unique mediator functions, the image data mediator GIRLS on the WWW, the stream-type multimedia database platform GOLS and the intelligent access and authoring system using multiple media synchronization have been introduced with experimental evaluation results and concrete multimedia database applications.

We expect various trials will be done toward this multimedia DB mediators.

References

1. Yiong Gong and Masao Sakauchi, "A method for color image classification using the color and motion features of moving images," Proceedings of Second International Conference on Automation Robotics and Computer Vision (ICARV) '92, 1992.
2. N. Nakamura, S. Abe, Y. Ohsawa, and M. Sakauchi, "The MD-tree: An efficient data management structure for spatial objects," IEEE Trans. on Knowledge and Data Engineering, Vol. 5, No. 4, pp. 682–694, 1993.
3. M. Sakauchi, "Image retrieval techniques," The Journals of the IEICE, Vol. 71, No. 9, 1988.
4. M. Sakauchi, "Image and multimedia data-base," The Journal of the Institute of Television Engineers of Japan, Vol. 46, No. 11, pp. 1474–1479, 1992.
5. M. Sakauchi, "Image retrieval and image understanding," IEEE Multi-media Computing Magazine, Vol. 1, No. 1, pp. 79–81, 1994.
6. M. Sakauchi and S. Satoh, "Data model generation in image database system," Transaction of IEICE of Japan, Vol. J74-D-I, No. 8, pp. 545–554, 1991.
7. M. Sakauchi, Y. Ohsawa, and T. Sagara, "Construction and application of multimedia geographical database," Journal of Institute of Geographical Information Systems of Japan, Vol. 3, No. 2, pp. 53–58, 1995.
8. M. Sakauchi, T. Satou, and Y. Yaginuma, "Multimedia database systems for the contents mediator," Transaction of IEICE, Vol. E79-D, No. 6, pp. 641–646, 1996.
9. T. Satou and M. Sakauchi, "Data acquisition in live hyper media," Proc. of IEEE International Conference on Multimedia Computing and Systems, pp. 175–181, 1995.
10. T. Satou and M. Sakauchi, "Video information acquisition on live hypermedia," Transaction of IEICE, Vol. J79-D-II, No. 4, pp. 559–567, 1996.

11. S. Satoh, Y. Ohsawa, and M. Sakauchi, "A proposal of drawing image understanding system applicable to various target drawings," Transactions of Information Processing Society of Japan, Vol. 33, No. 9, pp. 1092–1102, 1992.

12. S. Satoh, H. Moh, and M. Sakauchi, "A drawing image understanding system cooperating with rule generation supporting using man-machine interaction," IEICE Transaction on Information and Systems, Vol. E77-D, No. 7, 1994.

13. H. Takaha, T. Yatabe, T. Satou, and M. Sakauchi, "Open image retrieval system GIRLS on WWW," Technical Report of IEICE, Vol. IE95-11, pp. 1–8, 1995.

14. Y. Yaginuma and M. Sakauchi, "A proposal of a video editing method using synchronized scenario document," Transaction of IEICE, Vol. J79-D-II, No. 4, pp. 547–558, 1996.

15. Y. Yaginuma and M. Sakauchi, "A proposal of the synchronization method between drama image," Sound and Scenario Document Using DP Matching, Transaction of IEICE, Vol. J79-D-II, No. 5, pp. 747–755, 1996.

16. Y. Yaginuma, M. Kageyama, and M. Sakauchi, "Synchronization between image, sound and scenario document using DP matching," Proc. of 1994 IAPA Workshop on Machine Vision Applications, pp. 115–118, 1994.

17. J. Yamane and M. Sakauchi, "A construction of a new image database system which realizes fully automated image keyword extraction," IEICE Transactions on Information and Systems, Vol. E76-D, No. 10, pp. 1216–1233, 1993.

7

An Annotation Engine for Supporting Video Database Population

MARCO CARRER
LEONARDO LIGRESTI
GULRUKH AHANGER
THOMAS D.C. LITTLE   tdcl@bu.edu
Multimedia Communications Laboratory, Department of Electrical and Computer Engineering, Boston University,
Boston, Massachusetts 02215, USA

Abstract.   Segmentation, video data modeling, and annotation are indispensable operations necessary for creating and populating a video database. To support such video databases, annotation data can be collected as metadata for the database and subsequently used for indexing and query evaluation. In this paper we describe the design and development of a video annotation engine, called **Vane**, intended to solve this problem as a domain-independent video annotation application.

Using the Vane tool, the annotation of raw video data is achieved through metadata collection. This process, which is performed semi-automatically, produces tailored SGML documents whose purpose is to describe information about the video content. These documents constitute the metadatabase component of the video database. The video data model which has been developed for the metadata, is as open as possible for multiple domain-specific applications. The tool is currently in use to annotate a video archive comprised of educational and news video content.

Keywords: video annotation, video segmentation, video databases, metadata, SGML

1.   Introduction

In recent years interest in digital communications has substantially increased due to advances in end-user applications and the publicity of the Internet. The use of digital video is not far behind, although the infrastructure, particularly bandwidth, is not yet sufficient to compete with existing television technology. The availability of video as an accessible media leads to a new set of applications including video conferencing, video-telephony, movies-on-demand, and distance learning.

Most of these applications, however, assume the viability of constructing substantial databases of video content. A *video database system*, as defined here, is an entity which provides fast and efficient storage and retrieval of digital video across multiple application domains. For example, the common functional requirements for digital news video or movie storage and delivery are provided by such a system. In this context we expect specific domain information models to be associated with each application; however, significant common functionality will exist and be supported by a video database system.

The primary distinction of a video database by our definition is the ability to rapidly locate and retrieve video content. In contrast, an archive of video tapes is fraught with latencies that render most applications not viable. This "fast access" enables new applications of video information such as personalized news-on-demand and educational reuse of classroom instruction that would otherwise be content or feature-deficient. (For example, our experience found many students asking for a synopsis of a lecture rather than to review a two-hour video tape.) The goal of a video database application is to provide this fast access to the *information* in the video data. To accomplish this objective; however, an approach to characterizing this information must be developed. The video content (i.e., the information embedded in the video data) must be extracted from video data, stored, and managed. Techniques for this process can be static or dynamic, and manual or automated. Due to our desire to construct working systems, we focus on pragmatic alternatives. This steers us towards semi-automated techniques that apply shot boundary detection coupled with human annotation. Moreover, our motivation has been to create a tool for collecting a reusable universe of annotated, interconnected multimedia documents that can subsequently be translated, indexed, and stored in any database in any format. That is, we sought to "front-load" a multimedia database rich in video content.

There are existing solutions for providing video data collection and annotation (e.g., Refs. [7, 13]). However, because of the complexity of the problem, most of the proposed solutions are domain-specific, being optimized to work only on specific video content such as news, instruction, or specific categories of movies. To incorporate cross-domain annotation functionality in our annotation tool, we make use of SGML (Standard Generalized Markup Language). One important property of SGML for use in representing video data is its ability to define nested structures as required for hierarchical models of video data. Moreover, SGML context rules, even if very strict, are highly customizable through definitions in the DTD (document type definition) for video. Therefore, we establish a common nested structure across domains and simultaneously consider the properties of different domains. This is achieved by associating a DTD with each domain. All of the DTDs have common elements or objects, but the attributes associated with these elements differ with each domain. The metadata, therefore exist in an SGML-compliant format, making it easy to make post-annotation changes or enhancements to the annotated data without requiring a redefinition of the end-application data model. The collected data can also be readily translated to alternative representations (e.g., relational, object-oriented, or deductive data models), thus making it straightforward to populate a video database.

With this context, and the desire to construct a usable system, we set out to develop the Vane annotation tool. An additional requirement was to render an annotation solution that would not be bound to a particular application domain, yet could deal with, or could be tailored to, the nuances of each. The result is a system built on these concepts that can be used/tailored for any annotation and subsequent data model. The novelty in the work is the generic, flexible model and representation for capturing video content in a reusable way, and the subsequent implementation.

The remainder of the paper describes our technical solution to this problem. In Section 2 we introduce basic technologies required as a foundation for the annotation solution. In Section 3 technologies related to our work are discussed. In Section 4 we discuss the annotation tool. Section 5 describes the translation of collected annotations to a relational database format. Section 6 concludes the paper.

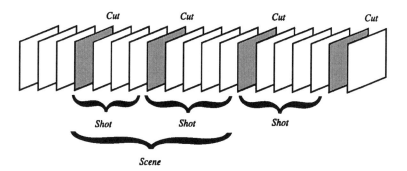

Figure 1. Segmentation of a video stream.

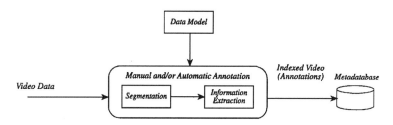

Figure 2. Data flow in the video annotation process.

2. The fundamentals of video annotation

When video and audio signals are brought into a digital system, they yield a format that is very different from alphanumeric data. Textual information supports concepts of alphabetical ordering, indexing, and searching on words or phrases. In contrast, video and audio data yield a format that does not provide straightforward access to its content. Ordering of the basic units for audio and video (sample and frame, respectively) is temporal. The analogous indexing or searching based on pattern matching is a much more difficult task, one that has yet to prove as complete and successful as vector-space text indexing.

Because of the lack of satisfactory techniques for extracting information from raw video or audio content, we seek alternative schemes for achieving the same goal of supporting indexing and query of content. Figure 2 illustrates the overall process of video annotation that we describe here [3].

For simplicity, we define the following terminology used throughout the paper. Raw digital video and audio data are aggregated and called *video data*. The content of the video and audio are referred to as *video information*, but are captured as *metadata*. Thus, video information describes the content of video data stored in the video database.

Video data, at a finest grain, are represented as individual frames (a finer decomposition is not significant in the context of video content as a whole). As such, any segmentation and feature extraction applicable to still images is relevant identification of the information contained in each still. We therefore, focus our attention on the information that is obtained by the juxtaposition of stills (i.e., shots), and the associated sound track, in a video composition.

The process of isolating small units of the video (segments) is also called segmentation. This process achieves a partition of the entire video stream into collections of frames whose characteristics are common. The criterion for automated segmentation is usually consistency in compressed-domain data size. Unfortunately, this does not guarantee a perfect mapping of frame collections to video information, nor does it guarantee the finest grain of decomposition, nor overlapping sets as is associated with stratification [2].

The next step in the process of video database construction is identification of the contents of the video or *information extraction* from the raw video data. Even if the logical partition of a video stream can help in dealing with raw video data, it is still very difficult to extract information from the raw data on-the-fly. All approaches reviewed from recent literature support the idea that in order to achieve fast data retrieval through queries, video information must be extracted from the raw video data and then stored in a different, more readily usable format which constitutes the input for the query engines. Information can be extracted automatically or manually. The new format must contain references to points in the physical video data so that a particular video segment (e.g., a news item, a movie), or a part of it, can be easily retrieved from the video database.

Of course, a suitable model must exist to bin the extracted information or to otherwise represent it in a manner that will lead to fast and efficient retrieval. Subsequently, the video information can be stored in this representation in the act of video database population.

2.1. Video segmentation

Before starting the annotation process, raw data are partitioned into elemental units called *shots*. These shots are essentially sequences of contiguous frames formed by a continuous recording process. However, because this definition yields some difficulties for edited material (shot boundaries are vague) and surveillance footage (shots correspond to interesting events), it can be modified to describe a contiguous sequence of frames whose content is common. Starting from this segmentation, shots can be used to build up a logical units called *scenes*, which are collections of contiguous shots (figure 1), and *sequences*, which are groups of scenes.

Shot detection within the raw data can be performed automatically using video segmentation techniques (e.g., [4, 12, 16–18, 24]). As a shot consists of one or more frames recorded contiguously and representing a continuous action in time and space [9], it can be completely defined by the timing of its beginning and ending points. This reduces the partitioning task to detecting shot boundaries (cuts) and identifying them by start and stop frame numbers. A variety of segmentation techniques can achieve this goal.

2.2. Information extraction

The operation of a video database implies the management of a large quantity of raw video data. The presence of this raw data does not significantly assist in indexing and search. In contrast, video *information* assists this process. Data that characterize the information contained in video data can be called *metadata* [6, 8, 11, 14]. Although any suitable representation can be used to represent metadata, text is commonly used. In the Vane implementation we make use of SGML markup to represent video metadata.

The problem becomes one of identifying information contained in the video data and associating them with tokens (metadata). Not surprisingly, humans are quite good at extracting information from video data, whereas it is difficult to get the same performance from an automaton. In the annotation process, a viewer takes notes, albeit biased, of the content of the video stream. During this process, the annotator can be assisted by a computer to provide a more regular representation to capture domain-specific information. For example, a football announcer might use a football-specific metadata schema to capture information about goals scored. In this role, the computer, and the annotation process, provides a consistent and repeatable process for collecting metadata for the application domain.

As metadata are also intended to be applied to query formulation as well as to information capture, they should facilitate indexing and searching techniques on the video content. That is, the metadata component of the video database system can be treated as a conventional text (token)-based database system. This in turn will provide random and direct access to the raw video content. Thus it is possible to search the annotation/metadata as well as locate specific video data elements.

Three types of indexing identified by Rowe [21] are bibliographic, structural, and content-based. The first one, which reflects the conventional method to catalog movies and papers, covers the annotation of objective fields such as title, keywords, and author. Structural indexing, in contrast, is based on a logical segmentation of the video data. For each of these three elements, a data model identifies a unique set of attributes whose values must be annotated according to the elemental video content. Thanks to a hierarchical organization, structural indexing is useful for the visualization of essential information and for fast searches. Content-based indexing is used when the annotation must be focused on objects that appear in the video, irregardless if they are people or things. Supporting one or more of these indexing schemes means building different structures for metadata, and leads to a different implementation of the annotation process.

At the end of the annotation process, raw video data should be indexed to support retrieval by the multimedia system/application for which they are intended. Requested information can be identified within the metadata which will also provide references and links to the archive where the video data are stored.

2.3. Related work

We believe that with current technologies video information must be converted to metadata to support effective database queries. Different approaches can be found in the literature for this process. The following is a summary of are related techniques.

Tonomura et al. [22] propose *Structured* video computing. Here the video stream is first analyzed and then automatically decomposed into shots. Each shot is indexed using features called *video indices* which are extracted from the video data. These indices include attributes such as camera information and representative colors. Subsequently, two different structures are built: a link structure that maintains relations between the shots and a content structure consisting of the textual descriptions related to the corresponding components of the video data.

Smith and Davenport [1, 9] propose partitioning video information into overlapping segments rather than disjoint shots. This technique facilitates multiple interpretation of segment content due to the overlap. The segments are called *strata*. With this scheme the concept of an object become more significant, as the objects, represented as strata, are independent of a strict hierarchical organization offered by a simple shot decomposition.

Tools have also been developed that consider image texture in the annotation and feature extraction process. Most rely on image processing and pattern recognition techniques. One example is *vision texture* [20] which extends the text-based concepts of sorting and similarity of alphanumeric data to the domain of images, video, and audio. With this scheme a user labels a part of an image, or of a video, and a texture model is used to propagate the label to other "visually similar" regions.

Metadata are commonly expressed using text-based tokens because of their ease of manipulation. An unusual approach is proposed by Davis [10] using icons. This approach, called *media streams* uses system-provided animated icons to describe elemental actions. Here the annotation step is performed by matching shot contents with one of the icons. Composition of icons can also achieve complex representations of shots.

Carreira et al. [7] developed a system to organize video for stored video delivery applications. The system, called the Video Broadcast Authoring Tool (VBAT) uses a simple hierarchical organization and graphic user interface that facilitates the collection of metadata. A post-processing step allows the VBAT to generate a video "table of contents" in HTML for subsequent viewing and video launch from a Web browser. The VBAT does not make use of content-based indexing techniques.

3. Related technologies

A number of related technologies are used in the construction of our annotation engine. In this section we introduce these technologies as essential for understanding how the Vane tool is constructed. These related technologies are the SGML standard used in metadata collection, Tcl/Tk used in interface design, and the MPEG video compression standard.

3.1. SGML

In the early 1980s, the International Standards Organization (ISO) proposed the Standard Generalized Markup Language, (SGML–ISO 8879), as a means for managing and organizing information. It was designed to increase the portability documents among computers and text-processing systems.

One of the tenets of SGML is the separation of document content from its rendering. This division is achieved with text *markup*: a series of instructions, mixed and embedded in the text of the document to provide the system with necessary processing rules for interpretation during presentation. *Procedural* markup is used in most electronic publishing systems, giving a typesetter the necessary directions to fit document text on the rendered page. SGML makes use of *generic* markup, also known as *descriptive* markup, rather than focusing on how the text should appear on the page. Generic markup defines the purpose of the text in a document. Data are broken into *elements*, that represent object semantics within the overall system. Elements are organized in a strict logical structure defining a hierarchical model for the document. To understand how SGML works, the relationship between the content and the structure of a document is viewed as two layers:

- **Structure:** The DTD, or Document Type Definition, establishes a document structure. It provides a framework for the types of elements that constitute a document. It also defines the hierarchy or relationships within the elements and sets the context rules that must be followed to ensure a consistent and logical structure in the documents.
- **Content:** Tagging is used to isolate the content within the document: by using *start* and *end* tags, logical elements can be delineated. With SGML, it is possible to associate attributes of arbitrary types to any element: user-defined or enumeration, numbers and strings. Elements can also be nested within other elements to define the organization of the document. As tags should strictly respect the set of context rules defined in the DTD, SGML parsers are required to ensure consistency and correctness of a document with respect to its DTD.

In summary, SGML enables the efficient storage and reuse of information, information sharing amongst users and applications, and information maintenance in storage. We apply SGML as a format to capture and characterize video information as metadata in the Vane tool.

3.2. Tcl/Tk

Tcl/Tk is a language developed by Ousterhout [19, 23] for rapid construction of user interfaces. It is comprised of the *Tcl* (Tool Command Language), a string-based command language and interpreter for the language, and the *Tk* (Tool Kit) which associates the *X* windows toolkit to Tcl. The latter defines Tcl commands that support the creation and manipulation of user interface widgets, extending the core of Tcl itself.

Tcl and Tk together also provide all functionalities of shell programs plus the ability to create graphical user interfaces (GUIs). They provide a high-level interface to a GUI toolkit, giving the possibility of implementing new interface design in a short time and hiding all the details faced by languages as C. As it is an interpreted language it does not need compilation, allowing programs to be tested and debugged quickly. For performance enhancement, libraries supporting new functions can be developed in C and pre-compiled for use with the developed application. In addition, there now exist Tcl/Tk interpreters that function within the context of Web browser software, making it possible to execute Tcl/Tk scripts in a platform-independent manner.

3.3. MPEG

A set of compression techniques developed by the Moving Pictures Experts Group (MPEG) have become a standard for the delivery of digital video for applications such as Video-on-Demand. At the moment they encompass: MPEG-1 (ISO/IEC 11172: Coding of moving pictures and associated audio—for digital storage media at up to about 1.5 Mb/s), MPEG-2 (ISO/IEC 13818) and MPEG-4 (an evolving standard). Their video and audio specifications give the semantics and syntax of encoded video and audio streams. The system specifications address the combination of audio and video into a single stream and their synchronization.

The video coding algorithms used are lossy compression schemes. The basic MPEG encoding scheme uses the prediction of motion from picture to picture, the use of Discrete Cosine Transforms, quantization, and Huffman coding to organize the redundancy in spatial directions. Pictures are encoded to yield three different frame types: I-frames which are encoded independently from other pictures, thus offering moderate compression but providing random access points into the compressed video data; P-frames whose encoding is based on the motion-compensated prediction from a past I or P-frame; and B-frames which are encoded by using of both past and future picture compensation [5, 15].

Each of these technologies is applied in the Vane tool, which we describe next.

4. The video annotation engine (Vane)

In Section 2 we described the fundamental role of annotation in the process of organizing and building a video databases. We also highlighted the difficulties that can be encountered due to encompassing multiple application or video content domains. One of the key objectives for the Vane tool is to accommodate different application domains from a common basis, i.e., via extensibility and customization rather than by a comprehensive but inflexible solution.

To this end, we have designed the Vane tool to be a domain-independent application with the ability to support different domain-specific data models without rewriting the tool itself. This has been accomplished through the use of SGML and an exploitation of its unique characteristic of separating the context rules from the information content. This will be illustrated in Section 4.1.

In the design of Vane we incorporated a high-level semi-automatic annotation process which is intended to extract the content and semantic value of a raw video stream. Fully-automatic techniques, which are still in their early stage of experimentation and which are implemented with image pattern/image recognition algorithms were not considered reliable enough to be used in a practical manner for large video data sets (e.g., hundreds of hours/gigabytes of video data). Current technology in this domain facilitates the retrieval of pictures from image archives using color and texture analysis. Efforts also seek to identify objects and track their movements within a video stream. However, these are not appropriate for our objectives. None are able to make the computer sensitive to the semantic value of a video. More sophisticated techniques are required to recognize the information expressed within raw video data. As illustrated in figure 3, we integrated a segmentation tool into Vane so that shot detection is automatically performed when the annotation of new video data is initiated.

In our implementation, the lack of knowledge by the system is compensated by the presence of a human (the *annotator*), whose role is fundamental in the collection of video information. The Vane tool, however, has been developed to support and assist the annotator as much as possible so that annotation is expedited and leads to canonical representation

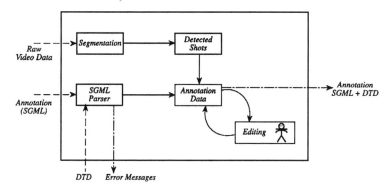

Figure 3. Data flow in the Vane tool.

of information as metadata within the application domain. It is therefore semi-automated. Finally, the Vane tool supports the playback of digital video in MPEG format with the conventional video shuttling functions.

The design of the Vane tool is decomposed into two parts dealing with metadata issues and user interface issues. The metadata issues include the definition of the format used for metadata, the specifications for its syntax and the tools necessary to deal with them. The user interface issues focus on assisting the annotator in the collection of video information as metadata. We describe these next.

4.1. Video data modeling

Before constructing the annotation tool, a suitable video data model was required. Our objective was to provide a flexible metadatabase able to be accessed by search engine and able to retrieve all interesting information sought (e.g., to support operations like information personalization). During the annotation process relevant content of the video must be extracted and annotated without loss of information. The optimization of the search engine to browse the whole metadatabase, or only a subset of it, leads to a system which can perform with different granularities and be able to satisfy different application needs. We model video information such that we can maintain both structural and content information. Such an approach must comprehend all types of indexes outlined by Rowe [21] (i.e., bibliographical, structural and content based) and indexes must be strictly associated to the objects they are expected to describe. Therefore, we define the metadata as *structural metadata* and *content metadata* as explained below:

Structural metadata. Video structure includes media-specific attributes such as recording rate, compression format, and resolution; and cinematographic structure such as frames, shots, sequences, and the spatio-temporal characterization of represented objects. These are further decomposed as:

- **Media-specific metadata:** Describing implementation-specific information (e.g., video compression format, playout rate, resolution).

- **Cinematographic structure metadata:** Describing creation-specific information (e.g., title, date recorded, video format, camera motion, lighting conditions, weather; shots, scenes, sequences; object spatio-temporal information).

Structural annotations organize linear video sequences as a hierarchy of frames, shots, and scenes [9]. This decomposition constitutes the simplest video structural model.

Content metadata. Video content metadata are concerned with objects and meaning in the video stream that appear within or across structural elements. Content metadata are further decomposed as:

- **Tangible objects:** Describing objects that appear as physical entities in the media stream (e.g., a dog, a disc).
- **Conceptual entities:** Describing events, actions, abstract objects, context, and concepts appearing in or resulting from the media stream (e.g., running, catching, tired, master).

Therefore, our annotation tool supports two types of objects: *structural objects* and *content objects*. The structural objects represent shots, scenes, sequences, format, etc., and the content objects represent the unstructured information. However, the content objects can be restricted by the structural boundaries. We include the concept of timeline so that content objects can represent strata as defined earlier [2] (figure 6).

In the requirements for the video data model we include object-oriented support, portability, embedded support for links and cross-references, and support for database query.

Given these requirements, the choice of SGML as the means to express and maintain metadata is natural. It is a text-based representation that is both lightweight and robust. Dealing with text is more straightforward and computationally less expensive than working directly with the time-dependent video or audio data, and intuitive concepts such as "equal to" and "similar to" are easily implementable. Moreover, SGML context rules, even if very strict, are highly customizable through the settings within a DTD. Furthermore, through its ELEMENT structure, object-oriented representation of concepts can be pursued. The advantage or operating with objects is that the metadata text file annotating the movie content will be easier to access and browse during database searches and data export. The support for links and cross-references is embedded in the SGML syntax, thanks to the ID attribute and the reference element REF, that can be associated with any element. All references are resolved during the post-processing achieved during data export when populating a database tailored to the application domain. The hypermedia link mechanism is useful to provide the user with other material related to the content of the video stream.

In SGML, the content of a document is separated from its structural definition. For this reason it is also possible to build a system that facilitates a dynamic document definition according to the annotator's needs and to the domain of the content to be annotated (we consider video content, which is unusual for SGML). Thus, it is possible, and we have achieved, a dynamic GUI based on a dynamic DTD. Each DTD for an application domain will have a common basis. Subsequently, tailored DTDs have augmentations reflecting the domain dependencies. In this manner we reduce the dependency of the system on the application domain allowing modifications to have little or no impact on the data model, database, or annotation engine.

The ability of SGML to nest several elements inside one another allows us to easily define a structured view of the video content. For example, a shot description can be nested inside a scene description.

It is clear that in this scenario where several types of video can be annotated the Vane tool will have to deal with different documents constituting the annotations. Each will refer to its own DTD. To ensure the consistency of SGML documents with the context rules specified by their own DTDs, we applied an SGML parser in the input stage of the tool. Among its functions is the notification of mismatches between the opened annotations and the corresponding DTD.

4.1.1. Model design. Given SGML as the language to represent video content, the video content model itself must be designed following the specifications given above. The analysis of the video content follows a structural decomposition. The object representing the whole video stream can be considered the largest container in which all objects are encompassed. Its subsequent logical decomposition is performed using the basic structural decomposition as sequences, scenes, and shots. The choice of three levels of video content results in the most straightforward generic decomposition. Additional levels, in our experience, yield excessive fragmentation and do not provide significant additional information. Subsequent query operations on a finer-grain decomposition would operate at a level which is not obviously useful. Moreover, at a finer grain, there can be an excessive burden on the metadata management system with the number of components represented. All three structural layers need not be annotated. For example, it is reasonable to only annotate shots and scenes.

The step following the identification of the three levels of the video information model is the organization of identified objects. Our approach proposes a hierarchical structure in which the shots, commonly representing the smallest unit of information comprise the leaves while scenes and sequences form intermediate nodes of the hierarchy. Therefore, the decomposition of the content of the video reflects the logical organization of the objects. Scenes are groups of shots whose content is considered common and, consequently, sequences are collection of scenes (figure 1).

The data model also includes support objects that encompass unstructured content data. This is achieved by annotating start and stop frames in which an object appears. A content object can belong to audio, video, graphics types or any composition thereof. For example, in the newscast domain an anchor person might reference a celebrity without showing the individual. We can annotate the individual associated with the audio medium. If desired all the annotations belonging to a particular object can be grouped together to form a stratum. Each object can be conceptually associated with any shot, scene, or segment by analyzing the time-line boundaries.

Consider the domain of educational video for this scheme. As instructional video typically follow an hierarchical organization (e.g., a lesson plan), they are organized in a hierarchical structure of topics and sub-topics and map well to the proposed model. A possible logical decomposition of educational video content can follow the following scheme: sequences represent daily class recordings, scenes represent topics within a class or lecture, and shots represent individual topics of a lesson. This logical decomposition simplifies the work of the annotation in its regular structure and facilitates the task of creating the query engine supporting the end retrieval application.

The basic purpose of Vane in this context is to provide infrastructure for collecting, annotating, and identifying structure and content in video data that will facilitate authoring and indexing at a later stage.

4.1.2. DTD design and syntax.   We applied these aforementioned concepts in the creation of a baseline DTD with the following syntax:

```
<!ELEMENT FULLDOC    - -   (ABSTRACT?, CATEGORY?, REF*, SEQUENCE*,
                            OBJECT*)>
<!ELEMENT SEQUENCE   - -   (ABSTRACT?, REF*, SCENE*)>
<!ELEMENT SCENE      - -   (ABSTRACT?, REF*, SHOT*)>
<!ELEMENT SHOT       - -   (ABSTRACT?, REF*, TRANSCR?)>
<!ELEMENT OBJECT     - -   (REF*, OBJECT*)>
<!ELEMENT ABSTRACT   - -   (#PCDATA & REF*)*>
<!ELEMENT TRANSCR    - -   (#PCDATA)>
<!ELEMENT REF        - 0   EMPTY>
<!ELEMENT CATEGORY   - -   (EDU | NEWS | MOVIE | DOC | SPORT)>
```

The previous lines constitute the basis of the definition of an SGML document. Each object and its role is defined as follows. An object is identified by and ELEMENT definition which is delimited by angle brackets. The element FULLDOC, which represents the whole video data stream, is defined in the first line. SEQUENCE, SCENE and SHOT assume the obvious interpretation. All elements except REF have both start and stop tags. REF, instead, has only the start tag. The content model for the element is enclosed in parentheses. For each of the possible contained elements, an occurrence indicator is also expressed. FULLDOC can have at most one of possibly no ABSTRACT - ? occurrence indicator. As expected, a FULLDOC can also have one or more SEQUENCEs as represented by "*". To support stratification, content OBJECTSs are considered part of FULLDOCs and each OBJECT can be composed of sub-objects. In the same manner, we specify that a SCENE can have one or more nested SHOT elements.

With this set of rules expressed above, we ensure that if, by error, a shot contains a scene then an error message results when the SGML document is checked by the SGML parser. Other definitions of the content model include the reserved word #PCDATA, which means that the element being defined may contain any valid character data. We choose this option for the elements ABSTRACT and TRANSCR which are to be expressed by plain text. The CATEGORY element, in contrast, can assume only one of the values expressed in the defined list. The same syntax is used to define the possible sub-categories.

Once the object definition, or element in the SGML terminology, is completed a set of attributes linked to each of these objects must be defined. The objects ABSTRACT, CATEGORY, REF, TRANSCR, even if defined as SGML elements, are meant to be attributes of the elements which contain them. They are not meant to be instantiated as stand-alone elements but are to be linked to any of the three elements that comprise the hierarchical structure. For the four main structural elements, FULLDOC, SEQUENCE, SCENE, and SHOT, we define a list of pre-defined attributes following the classification scheme of Section 4.1. For example, startf and stopf are attributes of the cinematographic structure indicating starting and ending frame numbers for a particular sequence. Combined with the frame rate attribute (frate) of the FULLDOC, they are used to recover the time reference from the raw video data file. The file attribute keeps the information describing where the raw video data are stored. The current implementation assumes that the file is stored locally but can be extended to support network scenarios. Finally, in the SHOT element, we introduce the transcr attribute to report the dialogue (e.g., closed captioning) present in the corresponding raw video data.

Another important attribute common to each element is the ID. This attribute constitutes the element identification and provides a mechanism for expressing cross-references. Its value is computed with a specific automatic coding. For example, the ID of the fourth shot of the second scene belonging to the first sequence will be: DOC1.SEQ1.SEC2.SHT4. Therefore, the shot position inside the hierarchy is comprehensible from the ID itself. If, instead, a reference to that shot is required, we use the REF element.

An example of a DTD used for news video annotation is shown in Appendix A. News consists of sub-categories (e.g., politics, sport, foreign, local) that are further subdivided. Upon loading a new video data file to be annotated, shots and shot breaks are located automatically by a cut detection algorithm. Because news delivery follows a single timeline, all shots belonging to a news item are contiguous. Therefore, we can associate a news item with the "scene" component. References to similar news items in other documents are stored as REFs. Additional content information about the news video is annotated as OBJECTs, whose attributes include name, type, metatype, time and date of creation, source from where obtained, and the popularity of a particular object (popularity is associated with news items for use in personalization).

4.1.3. Dynamic interface and metadata definition. In the previous section we presented the baseline DTD used by Vane. This DTD is extended for different application domains. As long as the syntax is correct, Vane is designed to adapt to different DTDs without reconstruction or recompilation. The following are a few examples of modifications to the DTD that the Vane tool will recognize:

- **Category definition:** As the CATEGORY attribute can assume only one value among a discrete set of possibilities (an enumeration), it was designed to keep the list of possibilities open to further additions. The same operation can be performed on each sub-category expansion (pull-down). CATEGORY, SUBCATEGORY and any other elements for which a set of possible values has been predefined, are shown by the interface as pop-up menus.
- **Attribute order:** The order of the attributes expressed in the attribute list of each element reflects the order of the entries presented by the interface. For a better customization of the annotation tool, the order can be changed and replaced with the one that best suits the annotator's needs.
- **Attribute definition:** Any other attribute considered relevant for the description of the video content in the domain under consideration, can be added to the main four elements: FULLDOC, SEQUENCE, SCENE, and SHOT. The interface of the tool will adapt itself accordingly to what is specified in the resultant DTD.

4.1.4. The role of the annotator.   The delineation of shots within an entire video data stream (e.g., a movie) is performed automatically by the segmentation algorithm provided with the tool. Here we assume that each camera break corresponds to change in the content of the video. (If not, the annotator can make corrections.) At this point the human annotator is required in the process and the delineated shots can be grouped on a logical basis. For example, in the educational domain the shots related to a lesson topic can be aggregated into the same "scene." Similarly we group related scenes into sequences. This activity is performed by the human expert with steering by the Vane tool. Forming such aggregates is possible when the related data are present as a contiguous set of frames. Subsequent reorganization (repurposing) of shots and scenes from the complete of pre-annotated content can be achieved at a later authoring stage. In this educational domain, shots that have the same title (e.g., in a lesson) can be automatically grouped together into a scene. The annotator also has opportunity to use the OBJECT representation of the content to encompass unstructured annotation data beyond enumerated fields.

The human annotator is clearly important in our annotation system. This leads to an apparent drawback of the subjective nature of human observation. To relieve the system from the dependence on this subjective factor, multiple annotations of the same video data can be obtained by different annotators. Afterwards, they can either be combined into a single annotated document or stored in the metadatabase and processed during the database search, merging the results obtained. Therefore, multiple interpretation can lead to additional detail available to support information retrieval.

Note however, if the validity of the information collected by the annotator is in question, it only bears on the retrieval process. That is, it in no way jeopardizes the validity of the raw video data. Once accessed, the raw data can be interpreted by the user.

4.2.   The Vane interface

The Vane user interface is the key component which links the video archive and the meta-database with the human annotator. It must provide meaningful and complete dialog boxes to the annotator to allow the insertion of relevant information. Moreover, it must be consistent with the metadata format and the document definition specified for the current annotation. The same is true for any query or browsing interface provided to the end-user, but with perhaps a more limited video of the database contents. Among the specifications of the video data model, we require the capability of dynamic definition and extension of the document. If new indices and new fields are entered in the document definition, the interface must be able to "build itself" accordingly, so that the annotator is steered to input information considered important to the application domain (figure 4). However, the interface presented is also consistent across domains. This characteristic increases the usability of the tool as a front-end to a multimedia database system and potentially decreases the learning time for an annotator.

The interface handles both raw video to be annotated and SGML documents already stored in the metadatabase. Outputs, on the other hand, are SGML documents, as the tool leaves the video archive untouched and does not perform any physical segmentation on the raw video data (video files are maintained as single entities). In the current implementation

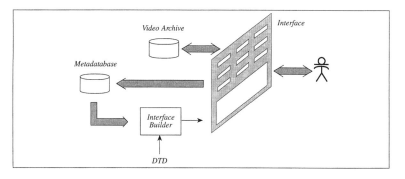

Figure 4. Role of the interface of the Vane tool.

of Vane the video formats accepted as input to the tool are MPEG-1 video and MPEG-1 system streams. However, there are no specific dependencies on the MPEG-1 format. To be able to access video data at random points, we maintain offsets to groups of pictures (GOPs) in an associated file. Whenever an annotator wants to play a video segment, the start and end frames and the GOP size of the segment are passed to the video delivery engine to initiate playout.

We designed the graphical user interface taking in consideration all the aspects investigated in the previous section. We decided to depict the aforementioned hierarchical structure by three colored horizontal bars in which each represents a level in the hierarchy (figure 5). For complete correspondence between the levels and for "at a glance" visualization of relations between the levels, each is represented with the same time scale. The longer the duration of a video, the longer the bars will be. This provides the ability to expand and shrink the time scale to fit the entire time-line onto the working area. The units on the time axes can either be number of frames, or time in hours, minutes, and seconds. A fourth bar has also been designed to represent the entire video stream is associated with the "full document". Its purpose is to summarize the main metadata for the current stream annotation and to provide an overview of the current tags.

A bottom-up approach is typically applied when a video stream is annotated from scratch. The annotation begins following automatic segmentation. As annotation proceeds, shots are

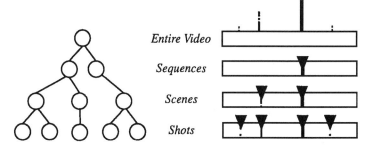

Figure 5. Design of the interface.

aggregated to scenes and ultimately sequences. Object annotation is graphically represented by additional bars in the sequence, scene, and shot hierarchy.

The shot boundary segmentation algorithm we developed for Vane is based on the analysis of the sizes of the frames. As I, B and P-frames use different compression schemes, they cannot be compared. Therefore, only I-frames are compared by the algorithm. The consequence is an error as large as one half of a GOP size which is tolerable for most information retrieval applications.

Graphically, segmentation results in a division of the shot bar. This concept is applied to the other bars as well, and the set of frames between two contiguous breaks is called a segment. An intuitive method for visualizing these segments was designed so that the start and stop points (frames) can be seen very easily. On each bar, we implemented colored arrows to identify breaks. On the shot bar arrows show the starting and ending frame of each shot; on the scene bar arrows indicate where shots are grouped together into scenes; on the sequence bar arrows show the aggregation of scenes. The top bar acts as a time ruler where references for each cuts are reported to have a complete view over the current logical decomposition (figure 5). We also found it useful to offer the ability to visualize any element attribute on the bars based on user preference. For example the "category" of the video can be seen on the top bar, the name of the sequences on the second, the ID on the third and the keywords on the fourth.

Separate dialog boxes, dynamically built using the scheme illustrated in figure 4, have been designed to let the annotator fill in all the fields defined in the current DTD. According to the domain, the different DTD will indicate a different interface for the collection of metadata. In addition, the top level, representing the video itself, can be annotated. The type of information that can be associated with it are bibliographical indices. All media-specific data on the video such as title and video category, or technical information as compression format or frame rate are required at this level.

The interface facilitates splitting shots to create multiple shots from an existing one. This action, which is often used during annotation, is called *break segment*. The inverse operation, joining two contiguous elements ("*join segments*") is also supported. Arrows, which represent breaks, are draggable in different position along the bars providing an simple method to change the start and stop frame of the elements (e.g., to tweak automatic segmentation results).

During the annotation, a simple means to create hypermedia links between different elements is provided. Link references can be placed inside transcripts and abstracts using SGML. These are facilitated by interface tools that do not require the annotator to memorize SGML commands and syntax. A similar reference scheme is used for objects.

4.3. Vane implementation

The Vane code is written using the Tcl/Tk scripting language described earlier. This choice was due to the large number of platforms which support this development environment. We used an SGI Indy running IRIX 5.3 for development and video playback. This platform allowed us to capture video in other formats as well, via built-in video capture hardware.

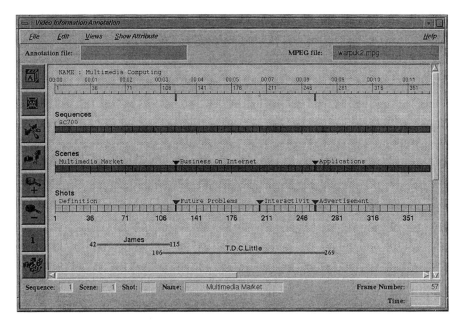

Figure 6.   Screen-shot of the Vane tool.

Figure 6 shows a screen shot of the interface in the main window after an annotation file, previously constructed, has been opened. In this particular case, the associated DTD applies to the educational domain.

Color coding is used again to help the user in identification of the relationships among the elements. Thus, the color of a bar is the same used for the arrow in the lower level and for the vertical mark on the first bar, the one related to the entire video. In this way, yellow vertical marks on the first bar indicate the presence of a shot (yellow bar) in that position; red marks indicate scenes while blue stands for sequences. An overview of the entire annotation can be obtained by the analysis of the first bar. A time ruler is drawn here with two different scales (frames per second and hours, minutes and seconds). Note that the object view is separate from the hierarchy. The content objects are represented along the timeline in the color green.

To change the structure of the tree representing the annotation, new arrows, corresponding to breaks, can be inserted and existing arrows can be moved or deleted. These actions can be performed using the toolbar on the left and acting subsequently on the bars. For example, after the "joining operator" has been picked up, the cursor changes and the user has only to click on the arrow that must be erased. The annotation data present on the left segment will then be merged with the one belonging to the next element. The result constitutes the data of the joined segment.

Zoom-in and zoom-out options allow different depth of magnification for the views. When the zoom does not allow a global view, the working area can be shifted via a horizontal

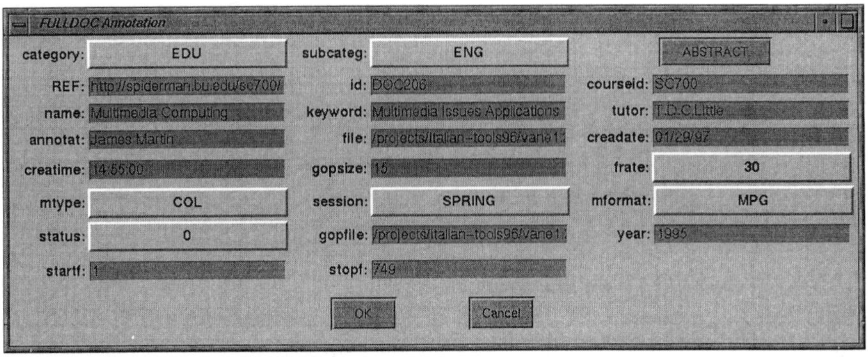

Figure 7. The annotation window.

scroll bar. To change the start or the stop frame of an element (sequence, scene or shot), the corresponding arrow can be moved simply selecting and dragging it along the bar. When this action is performed, a vertical line appears and follows the movements of the arrow so that the precise position of the cursor can be read on the ruler. At the bottom of the window, we also added a status bar which keeps track of the mouse position. This bar provides information such as the frame number, the field name and the identification number of the currently pointed element.

Each segment identified in the annotation can be selected by a mouse click. Subsequently it appears as a dedicated dialog box. Figure 7 shows the dialog box for the annotation of the whole video. In this example the fields that can be edited are related to the aforementioned educational DTD. A different DTD would result in a different automatic construction of the windows. The "Abstract" button will pop-up an additional window where the abstract of the segment can be entered. For the shot element we have also included a transcript window.

Objects belonging to unstructured data or defined as content objects are annotated by identifying the segments to which they belong. Each object in the interface is represented by a line and by clicking on a line a dedicated dialog box appears in which any data (description, type, origin, medium) concerning an object can be annotated.

5. Mapping of SGML content to a database schema

After video data have been collected and annotated, the resultant annotations are stored as metadata using SGML. This is a convenient format for encapsulating collected metadata and supporting reuse. However, it is a bulky format that is not tailored to application needs. For example, one might seek to create search indices on the objects represented in a video database as well as keywords found in the audio transcripts. Such a scenario is appropriate for accessing on-line news video. In this case, an appropriate database schema can be defined that is far more efficient in space and access time than the raw SGML format. An additional feature of this approach is the ability to support changes in the end-application requirements. For example, because the raw content and format is comprehensive, it can be translated to different output formats such as HTML 2 or HTML 3 by changes in the translator, not the content.

Based on an end-application requirement, the translation process can be defined. This will include mapping of tags to fields in a database schema, populating the data fields, and resolving hypertext references. In the following we describe one translation process that has been constructed to support SQL queries. The translator is called sgml2sql.

Sgml2sql is a conversion tool written to parse the SGML output of the Vane tool and to populate an SQL database. The sgml2sql implementation is modular in nature, built with the premise of supporting enhancements at the production side of the conversion. For example, a change of the database manager affects only the module which interfaces with the database.

Sgml2sql is written in Perl 5 and uses the DBD/DBI (database interface) to communicate with the database. Currently we are using the mSQL-DBD package and the mini SQL database. However, the choice of DBMS is not significant for our functionality. Sgml2sql first runs an SGML parser on the SGML file under conversion. The parser checks the SGML file and its associated DTD file for any inconsistencies. If no errors are found at this stage then the tool reads the DTD-to-database-map file, consisting of a mapping between various table attributes to the fields in the database. An example of the mapping between an DTD and database schema in figure 9 for an instructional database application is shown in the Table 1.

As seen in the table, metadata about the "fulldoc" (complete video document) is mapped to "course," scenes are mapped to "topics," and objects are mapped to "object" in the database schema. Some of the attributes of the video document such as format, medium, frame rate, video file name, GOP metadata file name are mapped to the physical layer schema (figure 10) for providing information to the video playout engine on how the data should be handled. We populate the "course-topic" field by assuming that all the topics in the video document belong to same course. This assumption is based on the fact that all video data which we are annotating are already authored, but if a topic from any other course is to be added or existing topic is to be deleted then this can be achieved in a separate authoring process. The "scene" start and stop frames are utilized to populate the "topic-object" table in the database. By comparing the start and stop frame boundaries of an object and the topics we can find which

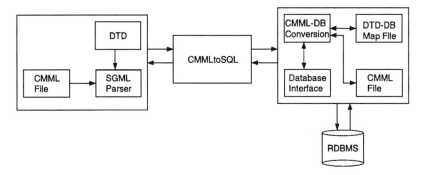

Figure 8.   Sgml2sql conversion tool architecture.

Table 1. Map between SGML and DB.

SGML attribute	DB field
fulldoc.id	course.course_id
fulldoc.courseid	course.title_id
fulldoc.name	course.title
fulldoc.tutor	course.instructor
fulldoc.gopsize	save for physical_map.gop_size
fulldoc.frate	save for physical_map.frame_rate
fulldoc.mtype	save for physical_map.mtype
fulldoc.session	course.session
fulldoc.mformat	save for physical_map.mformat
fulldoc.gopfile	save for physical_map.mfilename
fulldoc.year	course.year
(fulldoc).category	course.subcategory
(fulldoc).sequence	IGNORE
(fulldoc).object	new object table entry
sequence.(except SCENE)	IGNORE
scene	new topic entry, new course_topic entry
scene.id	topic.topic.id
scene.name	topic.title
scene.keyword	topic.keywords
scene.imgfile	topic.image_file
scene.frame	topic.frame_num
scene.time	topic.time
scene.date	topic.date
scene.populaty	topic.popularity
scene.startf	SAVE FOR POST PROCESS
scene.stopf	SAVE FOR POST PROCESS
(scene).ref	new object and topic_object entry
(scene).abstract	topic.abstract
(scene).transcr	uniquely-named file
(scene).shot	IGNORE
shot.*	IGNORE
object	new object
object.id	object.object_id
object.name	object.name
object.type	object.type
object.metatype	object.meta_type
object.time	object.time
object.date	object.date
object.medium	object.medium
object.origin	object.origin
object.populaty	object.popularity
object.file	new physical_map
object.startf	physical_map.start_frm
object.stopf	physical_map.stop_frm

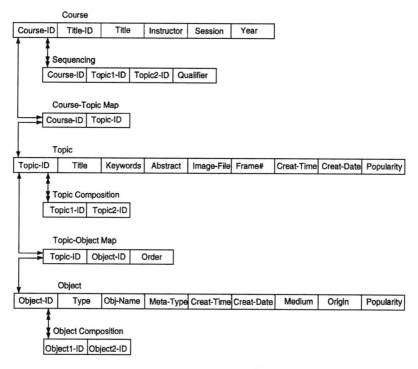

Figure 9. Instructional domain application-specific schema.

Physical Map

Object-ID	File-Name	Start-Frm	Stop-Frm	Frame-rate	GOP-File

Figure 10. Physical layer schema.

object belongs to what topic. In the future, if any changes to the database schema are made, only the map file needs to be changed. After loading in the relevant contents from the SGML annotation file, the database interface module writes the appropriate fields to the database.

6. Summary

The goal of this work is to facilitate the construction of large and useful video databases supporting fast access to raw video content. To this end, the Vane annotation tool was designed and constructed to provide a domain independent solution to metadata collection using SGML as a basis for the metadata model. In operation the tool interprets input DTDs to generate a view on a content model for a video domain and presents an interface tailored to that domain. In this manner, a single instance of the tool is appropriate for databases of news, educational materials, entertainment, or other video.

Vane is currently in use in the capture and annotation of a data set of over 500 hours of instructional video existing on VHS tapes at Boston University.

Appendix: A news video DTD

```
<!--Document Type Definition for Generalized WYSIWYG
 Example (FULLDOC)-->

<!ELEMENT FULLDOC   -- (ABSTRACT?,CATEGORY?,REF*,SEQUENCE*,OBJECT*)>
<!ELEMENT SEQUENCE  -- (ABSTRACT?,REF*,SCENE*)>
<!ELEMENT SCENE     -- (ABSTRACT?,REF*,SHOT*,TRANSCR?)>
<!ELEMENT SHOT      -- (ABSTRACT?,REF*,TRANSCR?)>
<!ELEMENT OBJECT    -- (REF*,OBJECT*)>
<!ELEMENT ABSTRACT  -- (#PCDATA & REF*)*>
<!ELEMENT TRANSCR   -- (#PCDATA)>
<!ELEMENT REF       -O EMPTY>
<!ELEMENT CATEGORY  -- (NEWS)>
<!ELEMENT SCCATOGR  -- (POLITICS | SPORT | FOREIGN | LOCAL)>
<!ELEMENT NEWS      -O EMPTY>
<!ELEMENT SPORT     -O EMPTY>
<!ELEMENT POLITICS  -O EMPTY>
<!ELEMENT FOREIGN   -O EMPTY>
<!ELEMENT LOCAL     -O EMPTY>


<!ATTLIST NEWS subcat (morning | mid-day | evening) morning>
<!ATTLIST SPORT subcat (basket | soccer | football | ski | baseball)
 basket>

<!ATTLIST FULLDOC
 id         CDATA                              #IMPLIED
 keyword    CDATA                              #IMPLIED
 anchor     CDATA                              #CURRENT
 producer   CDATA                              #IMPLIED
 location   CDATA                              #IMPLIED
 language   CDATA                              #IMPLIED
 annotat    CDATA                              #CURRENT
 country    CDATA                              #IMPLIED
 videofile  CDATA                              #REQUIRED
 creadate   CDATA                              #IMPLIED
 creatime   CDATA                              #IMPLIED
 frate      (30 | 24 | 15)                     30
 mtype      (col |BW)                          col
 mformat    (mpg | cosmo | qt | par | avi)     mpg
 startf     NUMBER                             1
 stopf      NUMBER                             #REQUIRED>
```

```
<!ATTLIST SEQUENCE
  id        CDATA    #IMPLIED
  name      CDATA    #REQUIRED
  keyword   CDATA    #CURRENT
  file      CDATA    #CURRENT
  startf    NUMBER   #REQUIRED
  stopf     NUMBER   #REQUIRED>

<!ATTLIST SCENE
  id        CDATA    #IMPLIED
  name      CDATA    #REQUIRED
  keyword   CDATA    #CURRENT
  populaty  CDATA    #IMPLIED
  startf    NUMBER   #REQUIRED
  stopf     NUMBER   #REQUIRED>

<!ATTLIST SHOT
  id        CDATA    #IMPLIED
  name      CDATA    #REQUIRED
  keyword   CDATA    #CURRENT
  startf    NUMBER   #REQUIRED
  stopf     NUMBER   #REQUIRED>

<!ATTLIST REF
  target    CDATA    #IMPLIED>

<!ATTLIST OBJECT
  id        CDATA    #REQUIRED
  name      CDATA    #REQUIRED
  type      CDATA    #IMPLIED
  metatype  CDATA    #IMPLIED
  time      CDATA    #IMPLIED
  date      CDATA    #IMPLIED
  medium    CDATA    #IMPLIED
  origin    CDATA    #IMPLIED
  populaty  CDATA    #IMPLIED
  startf    NUMBER   #REQUIRED
  stopf     NUMBER   #REQUIRED>
```

Acknowledgments

This work is supported in part by the National Science Foundation under Grant No. IRI-9502702. We extend our thanks to John Casebolt for implementing the SGML to SQL conversion utility and to William Klippgen for his support in the text-indexing area.

References

1. T.G. Aguierre Smith and N.C. Pincever, "Parsing movies in context," Proc. USENIX, pp. 157–168, Summer 1991.
2. T.G. Aguierre Smith and G. Davenport, "The stratification system: A design environment for random access video," in 3rd Intl. Workshop on Network and Operating System Support for Digital Audio and Video, Nov. 1992.
3. G. Ahanger and T.D.C. Little, "A survey of technologies for parsing and indexing digital video," Journal of Visual Communication and Image Representation, Vol. 7, No. 1, pp. 28–43, March 1996.
4. F. Arman, A. Hsu, and M-.Y. Chiu, "Image processing on compressed data for large video databases," in 1st ACM Intl. Conf. on Multimedia, pp. 267–272, Aug. 1993.
5. V. Bhaskaran and K. Konstantinides, Image and Video Compression Standards: Algorithms and Architectures, Kluwer Academic Publishers, 1995.
6. K. Böhm and T.C. Rakow, "Metadata for multimedia documents," SIGMOD Record, Vol. 23, No. 4, pp. 21–26, Dec. 1994.
7. M. Carreira, J. Casebolt, G. Desrosiers, and T.D.C. Little, "Capture-time indexing paradigm, authoring, tool, and browsing environment for digital broadcast video," Vol. SPIE 2417, pp. 380–388, May 1995.
8. F. Chen, M. Hearst, J. Kupiec, J. Pedersen, and L. Wilcox, "Metadata for mixed-media access," SIGMOD Record, Vol. 23, No. 4, pp. 64–71, Dec. 1994.
9. G. Davenport, T.A. Smith, and N. Pincever, "Cinematic primitives for multimedia," IEEE Computer Graphics and Applications, pp. 67–74, July 1991.
10. M. Davis, "Media streams: An iconic visual language for video annotation," Proc. IEEE Symposium on Visual Languages, pp. 196–202, 1993.
11. W.I. Grosky, F. Fotouhi, and I.K. Sethi, "Using metadata for the intelligent browsing of structured media objects," SIGMOD Record, Vol. 23, No. 4, pp. 49–56, Dec. 1994.
12. A. Hampapur, R. Jain, and T. Weymouth, "Digital video segmentation," in 2nd ACM Intl. Conf. on Multimedia, pp. 357–364, 1994.
13. R. Hjelsvold, S. Langorgen, R. Midtstraum, and O. Sandsta, "Integrated video archive tools," in 3rd ACM Intl. Multimedia Conf., pp. 5–9, Nov. 1995.
14. W. Klas and A. Sheth, "Metadata for digital media: Introduction to the special issue," SIGMOD Record, Vol. 23, No. 4, pp. 19–20, Dec. 1994.
15. W. Kou, Digital Image Compression: Algorithms and Standards, Kluwer Academic Publishers, 1995.
16. J. Lee and B.W. Dickinson, "Multiresolution video indexing for subband coded video databases," in IS&T/SPIE, Conference on Storage and Retrieval for Image and Video Databases, Feb. 1994.
17. A. Nagasaka and Y. Tanaka, "Automatic video indexing and full-video search for object appearances," in Visual Database Systems, II, E. Knuth and L.M. Wegner (Eds.), IFIP, Elsevier Science Publishers B.V., 1992, pp. 113–127.
18. K. Otsuji and Y. Tonomura, "Projection detecting filter for video cut detection," in 1st ACM Intl. Conf. on Multimedia, pp. 251–257, Aug. 1993.
19. J.K. Ousterhout, Tcl and the Tk Toolkit, Addison-Wesley Publishing Company, 1994.
20. R.W. Picard and T.P. Minka, "Vision texture for annotation," M.I.T. Media Laboratory Perceptual Computing Section Technical Report, Vol. 1, No. 302, pp. 3–14, 1995.
21. L.A. Rowe, J.S. Boreczky, and C.A. Eads, "Indexes for user access to large video databases," Vol. SPIE 2185, pp. 150–161, Feb. 1994.
22. Y. Tonomura, A. Akutsu, Y. Taniguchi, and G. Suzuki, "Structured video computing," IEEE Multimedia, pp. 34–43, Fall 1994.
23. B.B. Welch, Practical Programming in Tcl and Tk, Addison-Wesley Publishing Company: Upper Saddle River, New Jersey, 1995.
24. H.J. Zhang, A. Kankanhalli, and S.W. Smoliar, "Automatic partitioning of full-motion video," ACM/Springer Multimedia Systems, Vol. 1, No. 1, pp. 10–28, 1993.

8

Similarity is a Geometer

SIMONE SANTINI   ssantini@cs.ucsd.edu
*Department of Computer Science and Engineering, University of California, San Diego, 9500 Gilman Drive,
La Jolla, CA 92093-0114*

RAMESH JAIN   jain@ece.ucsd.edu
*Department of Electrical and Computer Engineering, University of California, San Diego, 9500 Gilman Drive,
La Jolla, CA 92093-0407*

Abstract.   Multimedia databases (in particular image databases) are different from traditional system since they cannot ignore the perceptual substratum on which the data come. There are several consequences of this fact. The most relevant for our purposes is that it is no longer possible to identify a well defined *meaning* of an image and, therefore, matching based on meaning is impossible. Matching should be replaced by similarity assessment and, in particular, by something close to human *preattentive* similarity.

   In this paper we propose a geometric model of similarity measurement that subsumes most of the models proposed for psychological similarity.

Keywords: image databases, similarity measures, Riemann geometry, search by content, query by visual example

1.   Introduction

Searching through the raw material of perception is something our systems are not very good at, yet. Before current systems can do anything useful, information must be abstracted from the perceptual substratum on which we receive it, and encoded in some convenient form. In a database—which is the system we are interested in—some particular piece of information is extracted from the sensorial data, and encoded in a form that makes retrieval efficient.

   A common example is a database with data about the employees of a company. The sensorial data in this case could be a form on which an employee wrote some information about herself. This form contains a lot of information: the color of the ink, the handwriting of the person, the fact that a poor fly was smashed on the top left corner of the page. A graphologist could also infer the sex of the applicant and (usually with negligible precision) something about his character. In addition, of course, there will be the information that the form required. When the data are entered into the database, all this information is filtered out by the operator, and the "relevant" information is encoded into a form which is completely abstracted from the sensorial support on which it originally rested. Note that there are two distinct but equally important aspects of this operation: on one hand information is filtered out and on the other hand information is encoded in a way that makes retrieval easy. The second aspect is connected to the first: keeping only selected information is essential for efficient encoding.

We are interested in building image databases. From this perspective, we should ask ourselves whether this type of encoding is feasible. We believe that, at least for a large class of databases, the answer is no. A simple example should convince the reader of this. In this moment, we are sitting at a table, writing the first draft of this paper, and, looking out of a window, we can see a tree. We could take a picture of what we are seeing, and enter it in an image database. At that time, the information contained in the picture could be encoded. We could, e.g., attach a label to the image that reads "a tree behind a window." But in the image that we have in front now there is a lot more than this. There is the shape of the tree, the color of its leaves, the size of the window (which, in this particular case, happens to be a French door), the fact that the tree is planted in the middle of a lawn, the fact that it is a warm and sunny day (although it is late October), and much more. If we just used the label "a tree outside a window" we would lose all the *perceptual* information: the information that makes the image we are seeing now different from all other images of trees behind other windows.

We are trying to build image databases in which it is possible to search images through their perceptual characteristics. These databases should operate directly on the image data, and require no encoding or labeling by an operator. Databases based on this idea, or on similar ideas, which we call *perceptual databases*, have received a lot of attention lately [9, 10, 12, 20, 21, 23, 32, 35, 41, 45]. This is, of course, a somewhat ideal situation, and in some practical applications we can expect that some information encoding will still be necessary. This is particularly true when images have a *cultural*, rather than perceptual, content. For instance, one of the figures in this paper contains the face of the President of the United States, Bill Clinton. The fact that he is the President of the United States, or even the fact that there is an entity called "United States" which has a president, are obviously cultural facts and, at the present time, there seems to be no feasible way to associate them to the images in a database. For this kind of information, labeling is necessary. In this paper, however, we will not consider this kind of similarity. We are interested in the information that we can extract from the images only, with that minimum of information about the state of the world that we can imagine an animal has. On a lighter note, we can state the same idea as the *cat principle*: you should not ask a perceptual database to recognize something that your cat can't.

One important consequence of our approach is the following: we believe that the fundamental operation in databases, *matching* an item against a query, has no meaning at the perceptual level, and therefore image databases should not use it [39, 40].

The reason why we believe this has to do with the isomorphism between a datum and its meaning, and with the representation of information. Before we talk about our approach, we will spend a few words on this problem.

A record in a traditional database is a sequence of symbols which encode the information in the record and which, syntactically, is generated following the rules of some grammar. The information, or meaning, of the record is a function of this representation which induces an isomorphism between representations and meanings. There can be many such functions and many different isomorphisms but, in databases, one of them is selected a priori and used as the "real" meaning of the record.

The information in a traditional database is obtained through the mechanical manipulation of symbols which have a combinatorial syntax and semantics, and for which the semantics respects the compositionality principle [26]. Let the meaning be a function $M : D \rightarrow T$, where D is the set of syntactically well-formed records and T is a meaning space that, for the purpose of our discussion, can be identified with the set of mappings from queries to {match, no-match}.

The compositionality property dictates that if a syntactically well-defined fragment of a record expands as

$$P \Rightarrow \alpha_1 P_1 \alpha_2 P_2 \cdots \alpha_n P_n \alpha_{n+1} \qquad (1)$$

where P and the P_is are nonterminal symbols of the grammar defining the records syntax, and the α_is are strings of terminal symbols, then the meaning of P is given by:

$$M[P] = f(M[P_1], \ldots, M[P_n]). \qquad (2)$$

The function f depends on the particular expansion rule that is being used, but not on the syntax of $P_1, \ldots, P_n$.

This type of encoding, and this relation between syntactic structure and meaning are not valid for perceptual-like data. Although in many important aspects the images in a database are different from what we see in the world[1], in one essential aspect the data we present to a multimedia database are the same as the sensorial impressions we receive from the world: the same data can be interpreted in many different ways, many isomorphisms are possible with many different meanings, and none (or very few) of these isomorphisms respect the compositionality principle.

The debate over whether symbols and syntactic manipulation are an appropriate model for reasoning and concept formation is still very active but, whatever its conclusion, it seems unlikely that anything resembling symbols come to us directly from perception. The reasons for this are many: images are continuous and, for natural stimuli, so are their meanings, the meaning of an image is an holistic property, and cannot be syntactically decomposed in the meaning of its parts, and so on.

Having postulates that image databases must deal with the sensorial aspects of the images, in all their richness and complexity, we have given up many of the common ways of representing meaning and information. Since we cannot assume that we can single out some particular aspects of the information contained in the image and represent those aspects alone, we cannot encode images in a syntactic and compositional form and this, in turn, makes matching an hopeless endeavor.

Not all practical image databases are equal with respect to this problem. For the purpose of this paper, it will be helpful to divide the databases in two classes, that we will call *restricted* and *unrestricted* databases. Restricted databases contain images from a well-defined domain or, in any case, images for which one particular meaning outweighs all the others. A database with only high-contrast frontal views of mechanical tools is an example of a restricted database, and so is a database of general images if we are only interested, say, in the color of the sky. In the latter case the images themselves are not restricted, but the isomorphism between images and meanings is. An unrestricted database, of course, is composed of images that are not restricted neither in content nor in interpretation. For instance, [38], [37], [29], and [2] can be considered *restricted* in our sense, while [23], [12], and [15] are *unrestricted*.

There is no place in the image to which we could ascribe the meaning or parts of it (from which particular part of a tree does its shape come from?). In an image of the sea at twilight, there is no pixel value that, alone, can tell us anything about the meaning of the image. Pixels of the same color as the deep blue sea could represent the asphalt in an urban scene on a bright day. Pixels with the same color of the sky in the top portion of the image could be a reflex in a foundry in the light of melting steel. The meaning "sky" comes from the structure of the whole image.

In these conditions, matching is very difficult, if not impossible. Matching is the operation that determines if two items (one item in the database, and the query) have the same meaning. This is easy to see if the isomorphism between the representation and the meaning is simple and compositional, but it is very difficult if there are many possible isomorphisms, all very hard to compute, and none of them is compositional.

How can we make searches in a database if we cannot match meanings? We are not the first in history looking of this answer. Many simple animals, who don't have a nervous system extended enough to sustain complex perception, faced the same problem a few hundred millions years ago. The way they solve the problem is simple: instead of extracting and matching meanings, they look for generic perceptual *similarities* in the images [16].

Our image database should do the same. Rather than trying to give all possible meanings to an image[2], databases should rely on simple perceptual cues, and on a reasonable similarity measure. They should not try to recognize objects in the image, or even attempt object segmentation, but should rely on the naïve and acritical observation of the patterns of color and intensity in the image.

This kind of similarity is common in animals (especially animals without a sophisticated central nervous system), and has proven surprisingly effective for many necessities of their life. It corresponds roughly to what in humans is known as *preattentive similarity* [4, 28, 47, 48]. So, our claim could be rephrased as follows: *image database should use preattentive similarity as much as possible.*

Preattentive similarity is based on different features than recognition and categorization processes. Preattentive similarity processes are responsible for perceptual grouping, and so the study of perceptual grouping can give us valuable information about them. Olson and Attneave [34] showed their subjects a series of displays like those in figure 1 asking them to identify the "odd" quadrant. The ease with which people do that can be taken as a measure of the dissimilarity between the stimuli in the "normal" quadrant and those in the "odd". This turns out to be quite different from the judgment we do when we look attentively at something and try to identify it. For instance, the stimuli L and ∨ are judged more similar than the stimuli L and T, yet they produce a much stronger discrimination in the experiment of Olson and Attneave: preattentively, L and T are more similar than L and ∨ .

The case for preattentive similarity seems to lose some of its strength in restricted databases. In this case, in fact, our own similarity judgment can be the result of a priori knowledge and, therefore, of attentive activity. The problem, however, disappears if we consider that the preattentiveness of similarity depends on the relation between the observer and its environment [3, 7, 13]. The perception of stimuli depends on their ecological importance and, in general, animals evolve preattentive mechanisms to deal with stimuli of great ecological significance and that require quick action [17, 25]. The environment of a

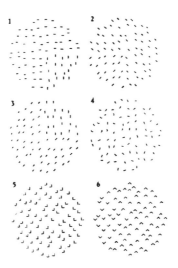

Figure 1. Displays used by Olson and Attneave for the study of perceptual grouping.

database engine is radically different from that of a human being and so are its goals (or, we might say, its evolutive pressure). Because of this, stimuli that are artificial for humans, and recognized only through reasoning and training, can be as natural and preattentive in the database environment as, say, a color. Human perception evolved in an environment in which certain natural stimuli were connected to proximal stimuli of great ecological validity or, in other terms, important natural stimuli are connected to our perceptual system through strong ecological cues. If we can create, in the artificial world of a database similarly strong ecological cues for the stimuli we have to recognize, these will become just as preattentive as common natural stimuli are for us.

In other words: if we determine the relevant ecological cues (e.g., deriving them from similarity experiments through multidimensional scaling [8, 11, 43, 44, 46]) and use them as part of the database environment, the same mechanisms that we use for preattentive similarity in unrestricted databases can be used in the restricted case.

2. Measuring similarity

The first thing we have to think about in a similarity database is how to measure similarity. We obviously want a similarity measure to which the user sitting in front of the computer can relate, but there are limits to what we can and want to do [39]. The first limit comes from the assumption we make (that, admittedly, can be relaxed in real world applications) that there are no annotations, and there is no information except from the information provided by the images. But, what information do images exactly provide? Consider the two persons of figure 2 representing Bill Clinton and a man called Oscar Luigi Scalfaro. There isn't much apparent similarity between the two, but it just so happens that Oscar Luigi Scalfaro is

Figure 2.   Bill Clinton and Oscar Luigi Scalfaro: why are they similar?

the president of Italy and, therefore, the two have a similar role in their respective countries. This is a perfectly good example of similarity, and a query based on this kind of similarity can be useful in many occasions, but is it a query our similarity database is expected to answer?

The similarity between the two is cultural: we would not expect a three years old, or our cat, to recognize it[3]. In a sense, the similarity *is* in the images (since it is the sight of the images that elicits our judgment) but, in an equally real sense, the similarity *is not* in the images. We could just as easily have mentioned the names "Clinton" and "Scalfaro" and somebody would have recognized the similarity anyway. The image, in this case, is just a *trigger* used to fire two concepts we have acquired, and it is the similarity between these two concepts that we recognize.

Should we try to answer these queries in a perceptual database? This question takes us back to the problem of information encoding. In a very broad sense, similarity depends on the information contained in the image and the context in which the image is interpreted [36]. Let us put this straight: *there is no information in the image independent of the context in which the image is seen.* So, if we say that we refuse the Clinton/Scalfaro similarity because is based on information that is not in the image, and want to restrict it to similarity that can be decided based *only* on the image data, we are building on empty. There is no similarity based purely on the image data. Interpretation and similarity arise only in a certain context that transforms the meaningless pixel matrix of an image into a meaningful set of perceptual impressions. Just to give an example: an image is produced by some part of the environment reflecting electro-magnetic radiation. It is part of the context that only the radiation with wavelength between 400 nm and 700 nm should be used to measure similarity[4].

Since we can't get rid of the context, we might wonder what kind of context should we use. In nature, the minimal context necessary for similarity assessment is established by the environment in which an animal lives [7, 13]. Different environments, and different evolutive pressures, will generate different types of similarity.

The database "lives" in an environment radically different from that of a human being: human perception uses motion, depth cues and, more importantly, human beings interact with the world and use similarity to recognize situations they already met in the past. There is nothing like this in a database. The world of an image database is composed of a discontinuous series of images, which make no sense when placed one beside the other. The database cannot move around to get a glimpse of the same scene from a different point of view, and its goal is not to look for things to hunt or to mate.

We can have a clue on what type of construct to use in a perceptually database looking at animals. Some animals live in perceptual environments that are at least as alien as that of a perceptual database [6]. If we can determine that some processes and some features are shared by a number of different species, then the same processes will probably be useful in our databases as well.

We have argued that the only constructs that can at least approximately translate to the database domains are *preattentive* and therefore that the similarity concept to be used in an image database should be preattentive. Preattentive similarity judgment is done without focusing attention on any part of the image. It is probably done in relatively low-level processing areas of the brain in time lapses too short to allow multiple foveations to take place. The higher processes responsible for recognition also cannot operate and therefore preattentive similarity is based on different features than attentive perception. Our theory is built on the assumption that the relevant features for preattentive similarity perception can be derived from a multi-resolution analysis of the image. Multi-resolution analysis is probably connected to what early areas in the human visual system, like the Lateral Geniculate Nuclei and the Striate Cortex do [31, 42, 51, 53], and is a type of processing that depends only on the image data, without any reference to models of the world or to stored knowledge.

2.1. *Psychological models of similarity*

Similarity has been the subject of many psychological studies for many years. There are a number of "black box" theories of similarity perception, which make different assumptions about the similarity mechanism, and explain different aspects of experimental findings. We gave a quite detailed review of these models in [39], to which the reader is referred. In this section we will briefly cover the major points of debate and the most successful theories to give the reader the background necessary to follow the rest of the paper.

One natural assumption, and the easiest we can make, is that similarity depends on a distance in some suitable perceptual space [1, 19, 50]. Stimuli are translated into features in this space, which has a metric structure that depends on the nature of the stimulus (visual, aural, etc.) and a function is applied to this distance to yield the similarity [44]. That is, similarity is something like

$$s(S_a, S_b) = g[d(S_a, S_b)] \tag{3}$$

where d is a distance and, as such, satisfies the distance axioms:

$$d(S_a, S_a) \leq d(S_a, S_b) \tag{4}$$
$$d(S_a, S_b) = d(S_b, S_a) \tag{5}$$
$$d(S_a, S_b) \leq d(S_a, S_c) + d(S_c, S_b) \tag{6}$$

Using this model, Shepard [44] showed that the function g is universal. That is, all the experimental data from different types of stimuli (not necessarily visuals) could be explained assuming that g has an exponential behavior and d is a suitable metric.

The fact that the function d is a distance, and satisfies the metric axioms, allows the theory to make some predictions about the outcome of the similarity experiment. For instance, the metric theory predicts that the similarity is symmetric and that self-similarity (the similarity of a stimulus with itself) is constant across the stimuli, and minimal. There is quite convincing empirical evidence that this is *not* the case: experimental data reveal that human similarity assessment is not symmetric and that self similarity is neither constant nor (under special circumstances) minimal. This finding inspired a number of "æmendaments" to the raw distance model. Krumhansl [24], for instance, assumed that similarity is based on a "pseudo distance function" given by:

$$d(S_a, S_b) = \phi(S_a, S_b) + \alpha h(S_a) + \beta h(S_b) \tag{7}$$

where ϕ is a distance function, and $h(S)$ is the density of stimuli around S. This model allows violation of the distance axioms. For instance, symmetry is violated if $\alpha \neq \beta$, and the self-similarity is not constant, being given by

$$d(S_a, S_a) = (\alpha + \beta)h(S_a) \tag{8}$$

A completely different approach was taken by Tversky [49] in his famous *Feature Contrast Model*. Tversky assumes that a stimulus S_a is described by a set of binary features, A. The features are binary in the sense that a given feature either is or is not in A, but it doesn't assume any value. These features can also be seen as the set of predicates that are true on S_a. For instance, a typical Tversky feature would be "to have rounded corners," and it can be seen as the truth of the predicate "the figure has rounded corners." If two stimuli S_a and S_b are characterized by the feature sets A and B, then Tversky proved that a wide class of similarity measures can be reduced to the form

$$S(S_a, S_b) = \theta f(A \cap B) - \alpha f(A - B) - \beta f(B - A) \tag{9}$$

that is, the similarity is the difference (contrast) between a function of the features the two stimuli have in common and of the features that distinguish them. The function f is called the *saliency function* and is usually a monotonically increasing function of the size of its argument:

$$f(A) = f(|A|). \tag{10}$$

This model has been very successful in explaining the different aspects of human similarity, and is the basis in which we will build our similarity theory.

2.2. Extending the feature contrast model

From our point of view, Tversky model has one fatal drawback: it requires binary features. This is fatal both to our endeavor to use preattentive similarity and to the practical feasibility of the system that will result. Binary features, as we have seen, are the truth of predicates about the stimulus. It is quite unlikely that at the level of preattentive similarity humans and animals have available the machinery necessary to express such predicates. During the early stages of vision, the visual system does *measurements* on the image, and it is likely that preattentive similarity is based more directly on these measurements. From a more practical point of view, in artificial systems we start with measurements on the image. Predicates like those necessary to express Tversky binary features are very hard to extract: they are computationally expensive, unstable, and extremely context sensitive.

In [39] we extended Tversky's theory to deal more directly with measurements on the image rather than on predicates. We did this by borrowing some ideas from fuzzy logic. A predicate like "this area is green" is based on measuring the hue of a given area in the scene. We can model this as a fuzzy predicate whose truth is based on the measurement of the hue of that particular area.

More in general, suppose we have n measurements on the image

$$s = \{s^1, \ldots, s^n\}. \tag{11}$$

We can use these measurements to compute the truth value of m fuzzy predicates and collect them into a vector:

$$\mu(s) = \{\mu^1(s), \ldots, \mu^m(s)\}. \tag{12}$$

We call $\mu(s)$ the (fuzzy) set of the true predicates. In order to apply the Tversky model, we choose the saliency function to be the cardinality of the fuzzy set:

$$f(\mu) = \sum_{\lambda=1}^{m} \mu^\lambda \tag{13}$$

and define the intersection of two fuzzy sets, based on the measurements s_1, s_2 as:

$$\mu_\cap(s_1, s_2) = \{\min\{\mu^1(s_1), \mu^1(s_2)\}, \ldots, \min\{\mu^m(s_1), \mu^m(s_2)\}\}. \tag{14}$$

The difference of two fuzzy sets is defined as:

$$\mu_-(s_1, s_2) = \{\max\{\mu^1(s_1) - \mu^1(s_2), 0\}, \ldots, \max\{\mu^m(s_1) - \mu^m(s_2), 0\}\}. \tag{15}$$

with these definitions, the Tversky similarity becomes:

$$S(s_1, s_2) = \theta \sum_{\lambda=1}^{m} \min\{\mu^\lambda(s_1), \mu^\lambda(s_2)\} - \alpha \sum_{\lambda=1}^{m} \max\{\mu^\lambda(s_1) - \mu^\lambda(s_2), 0\}$$

$$- \beta \sum_{\lambda=1}^{m} \max\{\mu^\lambda(s_2) - \mu^\lambda(s_1), 0\} \tag{16}$$

More often, we will be interested in the dissimilarity between two stimuli, which can be expressed simply as minus the similarity:

$$D(s_1, s_2) = \alpha \sum_{\lambda=1}^{m} \max\{\mu^\lambda(s_1) - \mu^\lambda(s_2), 0\} + \beta \sum_{\lambda=1}^{m} \max\{\mu^\lambda(s_2) - \mu^\lambda(s_1), 0\}$$

$$- \theta \sum_{\lambda=1}^{m} \min\{\mu^\lambda(s_1), \mu^\lambda(s_2)\}. \tag{17}$$

3. Geometric feature contrast

The majority of similarity models proposed by psychologists assume that similarity is a function of a distance in some suitable metric space. These models are appealing for preattentive similarity because are directly based on *measurements* on the stimuli rather than on *predicates* like the Tversky model. On the other hand, metric models have problems in explaining some characteristics of human similarity perception which are explained well by Tversky's model.

In this section we show that it is not necessary to give up the power of set-theoretic models if we want to have the advantages of geometric models. All we have to do is to give up the requirement that the perceptual space should be a simple one in which the metric is Minkowski. In order to retain the advantages of set-theoretic models, we will have to use geometries in more general Riemann spaces [5, 27, 33, 52]. We do this by deriving the geometry of a Riemann space in which (17) is the distance function.

Let two stimuli be given characterized by measurements $s, r \in \mathcal{F} \subset \mathbb{R}^n$, where s^i is the ith measurement of the set s. The similarity between the two stimuli is based on the truth value of m predicates, which are contained in a suitable predicate space. The truth value of the λth predicate[5] based on the measurements s is:

$$\eta^\lambda = \mu^\lambda(s) = \mu\left(A_i^\lambda s^i\right) \tag{18}$$

while the truth value of the predicates based on the measurements r is

$$\pi^\lambda = \mu^\lambda(r) = \mu\left(A_i^\lambda r^i\right) \tag{19}$$

Given the truth values $\mu^\lambda(s)$ and $\mu^\lambda(r)$, the truth value of the predicate: "predicate λ is true for both s and r" is a suitable function of the truth values of the two predicates:

$$\cap^\lambda(s, r) = \cap(\mu^\lambda(s), \mu^\lambda(r)) \tag{20}$$

while the truth value of the predicate "predicate λ is true for s but not for r" is:

$$\ominus^\lambda(s, r) = \ominus(\mu^\lambda(s), \mu^\lambda(r)) \tag{21}$$

Finally, given a set of truth values η^λ of predicates referred to a given stimulus, the *saliency* of the set is

$$f(\eta^\lambda) = \sum_\lambda \eta^\lambda \tag{22}$$

Definition 3.1. The Tversky distance between stimuli $s, r \in \mathcal{F}$ is

$$T(s, r) = \alpha f(\ominus^\lambda(s, r)) + \beta f(\ominus^\lambda(r, s)) - \theta f(\cap^\lambda(s, r)) \tag{23}$$

Fuzzy logic uses operators like max and min applied to truth values. Since our goal is the derivation of a geometric theory of similarity, the discontinuity in the derivatives of min and max is a problem. The following definitions provide two alternative operators with the required continuity:

Definition 3.2. Let μ and τ be the truth values of two fuzzy predicates Λ and T, respectively. Then the truth of the fuzzy predicate $\Lambda \wedge T$ is:

$$\cap(\lambda, \mu) = \mu\sigma(\omega(\tau - \mu)) + \tau\sigma(\omega(\mu - \tau)) \tag{24}$$

and the truth of the fuzzy predicate $\Lambda \wedge \neg T$ is

$$\ominus(\lambda, \mu) = (\mu - \tau)\sigma(\omega(\mu - \tau)) \tag{25}$$

where

$$\sigma(x) = \frac{1}{1 + e^{-x}} \tag{26}$$

and ω is a positive constant.

If μ^λ and τ^λ are the truth of a fuzzy predicate Λ applied to two measurements s and r, respectively, then we will stretch the notation a little bit and write indifferently $\cap(\mu^\lambda, \tau^\lambda)$ or $\cap(s, r)$. Similarly, we will write $\ominus(\mu^\lambda, \tau^\lambda)$ or $\ominus(s, r)$.

The measurements s belong to the feature space $\mathcal{F}$. It will be convenient for a while to work on a different space: the *predicate space* $\mathcal{M}$. The predicate space is an m-dimensional manifold (where m is the number of predicates) which is a subset of $\mathbb{R}^m$. It is related to $\mathcal{F}$ by the relation:

$$\Xi : \mathcal{F} \to \mathcal{M} : s^i \mapsto \mu(A_i^\lambda s^i) \tag{27}$$

With the membership function

$$\mu(x) = \sigma(x) \tag{28}$$

$\mathcal{M}$ is an open subset of $\mathbb{R}^m$ whose closure is the unit cube $[0, 1]^m$. Moreover, $\mathcal{M}$ is diffeomorphic to $\mathcal{F}$, and hence it is an m-dimensional submanifold of $\mathbb{R}^n$.

Consider two measurements $s, r \in \mathcal{F}$, and the truth values of the predicates based on those measurements: $\pi = \Xi s$ and $\eta = \Xi r$. Then, in $\mathcal{M}$, the Tversky distance between π and η is given by:

$$T(\eta, \pi) = \alpha f(\ominus(\eta^\lambda, \pi^\lambda)) + \beta f(\ominus(\pi^\lambda, \eta^\lambda)) - \theta f(\cap(\eta^\lambda, \pi^\lambda))$$
$$= \alpha \sum_\lambda \ominus(\eta^\lambda, \pi^\lambda) + \beta \sum_\lambda \ominus(\pi^\lambda, \eta^\lambda) - \theta \sum_\lambda \cap(\eta^\lambda, \pi^\lambda) \qquad (29)$$

that is:

$$T(\eta, \pi) = \alpha \sum_\lambda (\eta^\lambda - \pi^\lambda)\sigma(\omega(\eta^\lambda - \pi^\lambda)) + \beta \sum_\lambda (\pi^\lambda - \eta^\lambda)\sigma(\omega(\pi^\lambda - \eta^\lambda))$$
$$- \theta \sum_\lambda [\eta^\lambda \sigma(\omega(\pi^\lambda - \eta^\lambda)) + \pi^\lambda \sigma(\omega(\eta^\lambda - \pi^\lambda))] \qquad (30)$$

Let us consider the last term. Since $\sigma(x) = 1 - \sigma(-x)$, we have:

$$\sum_\lambda [\eta^\lambda \sigma(\omega(\pi^\lambda - \eta^\lambda)) + \pi^\lambda \sigma(\omega(\eta^\lambda - \pi^\lambda))]$$
$$= \sum_\lambda [\eta^\lambda - \eta^\lambda \sigma(\omega(\eta^\lambda - \pi^\lambda)) + \pi^\lambda \sigma(\omega(\eta^\lambda - \pi^\lambda))]$$
$$= \sum_\lambda \eta^\lambda - \sum_\lambda (\eta^\lambda - \pi^\lambda)\sigma(\omega(\eta^\lambda - \pi^\lambda)) \qquad (31)$$

So that the distance becomes:

$$T(\eta, \pi) = \theta \sum_\lambda \eta^\lambda + \gamma \sum_\lambda (\eta^\lambda - \pi^\lambda)\sigma(\omega(\eta^\lambda - \pi^\lambda))$$
$$+ \beta \sum_\lambda (\pi^\lambda - \eta^\lambda)\sigma(\omega(\pi^\lambda - \eta^\lambda))$$
$$= -P(\eta; \theta) + M(\eta, \pi; \gamma, \beta) \qquad (32)$$

with $\gamma = \alpha + \beta$.

The term P will be called the *saliency* of the reference stimulus η, and the term M the *distance* between η and π.

The term P depends on the reference stimulus only. We have already noted that in many psychological experiment there is an asymmetry in the roles of the two stimuli that the subject must compare. The typical experimental question is "how similar is s to r?" Where $\Xi r = \eta$ and $\Xi s = \pi$. This term is absent when the request does not emphasize any stimulus. Requests like "how similar are s and r?" have $P = 0$.

The term P is interesting from a psychophysical point of view [49], but does not influence the relative judgment ("what is more similar to r, s or t?") and therefore is not very interesting in the context of perceptual databases based on similarity.

M is the distance in the *predicate space* $\mathcal{M}$. The distance M induces a geometric structure in $\mathcal{M}$. To determine the structure of this space, write M as:

$$M(\eta, \pi; \gamma, \beta) = \sum_\lambda [(\gamma + \beta)\sigma(\omega(\pi^\lambda - \eta^\lambda)) - \gamma](\pi^\lambda - \eta^\lambda) \qquad (33)$$

we can write down the derivatives

$$
\begin{aligned}
M_\lambda &= \frac{\partial M}{\partial \pi^\lambda} \\
&= (\gamma + \beta)[\sigma(\omega(\pi^\lambda - \eta^\lambda)) + \omega(\pi^\lambda - \eta^\lambda)\sigma'(\omega(\pi^\lambda - \eta^\lambda))] - \gamma \\
&= m_{\gamma,\beta}(\omega(\pi^\lambda - \eta^\lambda))
\end{aligned}
\tag{34}
$$

where we have defined the *space density function*

$$
m_{\gamma,\beta}(x) = (\gamma + \beta)[\sigma(x) + x\sigma'(x)] - \gamma.
\tag{35}
$$

With the derivatives of M, we can write the distance as:

$$
M(\eta, \pi; \gamma, \beta) = \sum_\lambda \int_{\pi^\lambda}^{\eta^\lambda} m_{\gamma,\beta}(\omega(\tau^\lambda - \pi^\lambda)) \, d\tau^\lambda.
\tag{36}
$$

This equation defines the length of the geodesic curve joining the point π and the point λ. We can build a geometry of a space once we can measure the length of a curve with an expression of the type

$$
L(C) = \int_{t_1}^{t_2} F(x, \dot{x}) \, dt
\tag{37}
$$

We can study the geometry induced in the space by the Tversky distance if we can cast the integral (36) that determines the length of a curve in this space into the form (37). The form of Eq. (37) is not evident at first because of the particular parameterization of the curve (it corresponds to the case in which $\dot{x} = 1$ along the whole curve). In order to see the structure of the distance function more clearly, it is convenient to re-parameterize (37) in a more general way. Let us define

$$
\zeta^\lambda = \zeta_0 + \zeta_1 \frac{\tau^\lambda - \pi^\lambda}{\eta^\lambda - \pi^\lambda}
\tag{38}
$$

with this re-parameterization we have:

$$
d\tau^\lambda = \frac{\eta^\lambda - \pi^\lambda}{\zeta_1} d\zeta^\lambda
\tag{39}
$$

and

$$
\tau^\lambda = \pi^\lambda + \frac{\eta^\lambda - \pi^\lambda}{\zeta_1}(\zeta^\lambda - \zeta_0).
\tag{40}
$$

The distance integral can then be written:

$$
M(\eta, \pi; \gamma, \beta) = \sum_\lambda \int_{\zeta_0}^{\zeta_1} m_{\gamma,\beta}\left(\omega(\eta^\lambda - \pi^\lambda)\frac{\zeta^\lambda - \zeta_0}{\zeta_1}\right) \frac{\pi^\lambda - \eta^\lambda}{\zeta_1} d\zeta^\lambda
\tag{41}
$$

Note, however, that the ζ^λ are actually the same variable, so we can write:

$$M(\eta, \pi; \gamma, \beta) = \int_{\zeta_0}^{\zeta_1} \left[\sum_\lambda m_{\gamma,\beta}\left(\omega(\eta^\lambda - \pi^\lambda)\frac{\zeta - \zeta_0}{\zeta_1} \right) \frac{\pi^\lambda - \eta^\lambda}{\zeta_1} \right] d\zeta \tag{42}$$

This is the integral of the function

$$\Phi(\tau, \dot{\tau}) = \sum_\lambda m_{\gamma,\beta}(\omega\tau^\lambda)\dot{\tau}^\lambda \tag{43}$$

over the curve joining ζ_0 and ζ_1. This expression holds if we assume that the curve is traced in the positive direction of the parameter. This expression doesn't give us a distance, yet. We have considered going through the geodesic in one direction only and, as a result, we have obtained a function whose integral along a closed curve is zero. We can correct this by postulating the behavior of the distance function on curves other than the geodesic. We do this in such a way that:

$$\Phi(\tau, \lambda\xi) = |\lambda| F(\tau, \xi) \tag{44}$$

holds. We can do this by defining:

$$\Phi(\tau, \dot{\tau}) = \sum_\lambda |m_{\gamma,\beta}(\omega\tau^\lambda)\dot{\tau}^\lambda|. \tag{45}$$

This will not change our distance function along a geodesic, but will make Φ comply with the requirements for a metric.

Note, however, that we have obtained a C^1 function, which is not continuous enough to provide a metric. For the moment, however, let us ignore this problem (we will return on this point in a while), and try to derive an expression for the metric tensor $g_{\nu\kappa}$. This is given by:

$$g_{\nu\kappa} = \frac{1}{2} \frac{\partial}{\partial\xi^\nu \partial\xi^\kappa} \Phi(\tau, \xi) \tag{46}$$

With the function

$$sgn(x) = \begin{cases} 1 & \text{if } x > 0 \\ 0 & \text{otherwise} \end{cases} \tag{47}$$

we can write

$$\frac{1}{2}\frac{\partial}{\partial\xi^\nu} \Phi(\tau, \xi) = \sum_\lambda |m_{\gamma,\beta}(\omega\tau^\lambda)||\xi^\lambda| \cdot |m_{\gamma,\beta}(\omega\tau^\nu)| \, sgn(\xi^\nu) \tag{48}$$

and

$$g_{\nu\kappa} = |m_{\gamma,\beta}(\omega\tau^\nu)m_{\gamma,\beta}(\omega\tau^\kappa)| \, sgn(\xi^\nu\xi^\kappa) \tag{49}$$

As we mentioned before, this expression is not continuous enough to be a proper distance function. We can however derive an approximation that is analytic (C^ω).

Let us remember that the Tversky model is empirical and, as such, it has been created only to explain some empirical data. Its only claim of validity rests in the interpretation it gives of empirical data. So, as long as the approximation is close enough to leave intact the peculiar characteristics of the model, the approximations we are making are epistemologically correct. We will use again the function σ. Remember that it is:

$$|x| = \max(x, -x) \tag{50}$$

so, with the function σ, we can substitute $|x|$ with

$$x\sigma(\omega x) - x\sigma(-\omega x) = x \cdot (2\sigma(\omega x) - 1). \tag{51}$$

Our metric then becomes:

$$\Phi(x, \dot{x}) = \sum_\lambda m_{\gamma,\beta}(\omega x^\lambda)(2\sigma(\omega \dot{x}^\lambda) - 1)\dot{x}^\lambda \tag{52}$$

For the sake of brevity, let us define yet another function:

$$p(x) = (2\sigma(\omega x) - 1)x \tag{53}$$

its derivatives (that we will use in the following) are given by:

$$
\begin{aligned}
p'(x) &= \frac{dp}{dx} \\
&= 2\sigma(\omega x) - 1 + 2\omega x\sigma'(\omega x) \\
&= 2(1 + \omega x - \omega x\sigma(\omega x))\sigma(\omega x) - 1
\end{aligned}
\tag{54}
$$

and

$$
\begin{aligned}
p''(x) &= \frac{d^2 p}{dx^2} \\
&= 2\omega[(2 + \omega x)(1 - \sigma(\omega x))\sigma(\omega x) + 2\omega x\sigma^3(\omega x)(1 - \sigma(\omega x))]
\end{aligned}
\tag{55}
$$

We define the metric tensor of the space as:

$$\tilde{g}_{\nu,\kappa} = \frac{1}{2}\frac{\partial^2}{\partial\xi^\nu\partial\xi^\kappa}\Phi^2(x, \xi) \tag{56}$$

computing the derivatives of Φ^2, we have

$$g_{\nu\kappa}(x, \xi) = m_{\beta,\gamma}(\omega x^\nu)p'(\xi^\nu)m_{\beta,\gamma}(\omega x^\kappa)p'(\xi^\kappa) + F(x, \xi)m_{\beta,\gamma}(\omega x^\nu)p''(\xi^\nu)\delta_{\nu\kappa}$$

This expression is quite complicated and, as mentioned before, can be made as close as we want to (49). Therefore, once we have proved that the definition of a suitable metric tensor is possible, we will revert to the use of (49) for the rest of the section.

The space $\mathcal{M}$ is not very interesting. We are much more interested in discovering how similarity is obtained based on the features of the image, that is, we are interested in the geometry of the perceptual space $\mathcal{F}$. The spaces $\mathcal{F}$ and $\mathcal{M}$ are related via the diffeomorphism Ξ and, through Ξ, the metric in $\mathcal{M}$ induces a metric in $\mathcal{F}$.

Remember that, in our case, Ξ is defined as

$$\Xi s^i = \eta^\lambda = \sigma\left(A^\lambda_j s^j\right) \tag{57}$$

This relation between $\mathcal{F}$ and $\mathcal{M}$ induces two relations between the tangent spaces at s and $\psi = \Xi s$: the *differential*

$$\Xi_* : T_s\mathcal{F} \to T_\psi\mathcal{M} \tag{58}$$

and the *pull-back*:

$$\Xi^* : T^*_\phi\mathcal{M} \to T^*_s\mathcal{F} \tag{59}$$

The differential is defined as follows: let $X \in T_s\mathcal{F}$, and $f : \mathcal{M} \to \mathbb{R}$. Then

$$\Xi_*X = \Psi \in T_\psi\mathcal{M} \tag{60}$$

is defined as

$$\Psi f = (\Xi_*X)f = X(f \circ \Xi) = XF \tag{61}$$

where $F = f \circ \Xi$. This can be described in terms of local coordinates as follows: let s^i be the coordinate functions of $\mathcal{F}$ and η^λ the coordinate functions of $\mathcal{M}$. Then the map Ξ has a local representation $\eta^\lambda = \eta^\lambda(s^i)$, and $F = f \circ \Xi$ can be written as $F(s^i) = f(\eta^\lambda(s^i))$. Then, for $X = X^i\partial_i$ and $\Psi = \Xi_*X = \Psi^\lambda\partial_\lambda$ we have:

$$XF = X^i\frac{\partial F}{\partial s^i} = X^i\frac{\partial f}{\partial \eta^\lambda}\frac{\partial \eta^\lambda}{\partial s^i} = \Psi^\lambda\frac{\partial f}{\partial \eta^\lambda} = \Psi f \tag{62}$$

which implies that the components of X and Ψ are related by

$$(\Xi_*X)^\lambda = \Psi^\lambda = X^i\frac{\partial \eta^\lambda}{\partial s^i} \tag{63}$$

The pull-back is defined as follows: let $\omega \in T^*_\psi\mathcal{M}$. The image of ω under Ξ^* is $\epsilon \in T^*_s\mathcal{F}$[6] such that, for all $X \in T_s\mathcal{F}$ it is

$$\epsilon X = (\Xi^*\omega)X = \omega(\Xi_*X) \tag{64}$$

In local coordinates, if $\omega = \omega_\lambda d\eta^\lambda$ and $\epsilon = \epsilon_i ds^i$, we have

$$\epsilon(X) = \epsilon_i X^i = \omega(\Xi_* X) = \omega_\lambda \Psi^\lambda = \omega_\lambda \frac{\partial \eta^\lambda}{\partial s^i} X^i \tag{65}$$

so

$$\epsilon_i = (\Xi_* \omega)_i = \omega_\lambda \frac{\partial \eta^\lambda}{\partial s^i} \tag{66}$$

The pull-back transforms a 1-form ω defined on T^*_ψ into a 1-form ϵ defined on T^*_s. The tensor product of two pull-backs will similarly transform the doubly covariant metric tensor $\tilde{g}$ of $\mathcal{M}$ into the doubly covariant metric tensor g of $\mathcal{F}$. The components of g are:

$$g^{(s)}_{ij} = \tilde{g}^{(\eta)}_{\zeta\xi} \frac{\partial \eta^\zeta}{\partial s^i} \frac{\partial \eta^\xi}{\partial s^j} \tag{67}$$

from $\eta^\zeta = \mu(A^\zeta_i s^i)$ it follows

$$\frac{\partial \eta^\zeta}{\partial s^i} = \mu'\left(A^\zeta_k s^k\right) A^\zeta_i \tag{68}$$

The ξ^λs are contravariant vectors, and are transformed according to the rule

$$\xi^\lambda = \frac{\partial \eta^\lambda}{\partial x^i} s^i \tag{69}$$

into the contravariant vector s^i into the perceptual space. The metric Φ is pulled back to $F(z, s)$, with

$$F_y(z, s) = \sum_\lambda \left| m_{\gamma,\beta}\left(\mu\left(A^\lambda_i z^i\right) - \mu\left(A^\lambda_i y^i\right)\right) \mu'\left(A^\lambda_i z^i\right) A^\lambda_i s^i \right| \tag{70}$$

where y is the reference stimulus, z the stimulus we are comparing to y, and s the tangent to the geodesic joining them. Note that the function Φ in the predicate space was a function of the *difference* between the coordinate of the stimulus and those of the reference (namely, it was a function of $\pi^\lambda - \eta^\lambda$). In this case the functional dependence on the reference y is more complicated. So much, in fact, that we can say that F is a function of the absolute coordinates of the stimulus z parameterized by the reference y.

This fact has a very interesting and intriguing interpretation: *the perceptual space is deformed by the presence of the reference y.*

Similarity measurement can be explained as a distance function, but we have to admit that the presence of a reference influences the geometry of the perceptual space. The effects of this assumption are easily seen in similarity experiments. When in an experiment we ask a subject "how similar is A to B?" the subject tends to concentrate more on the features of B than on those of A. It is this concentration on the features of B that determined the shape of the perceptual space. It is significant that certain effects, like the asymmetry of the similarity, are much less pronounced when subjects do not focus on any of the two stimuli

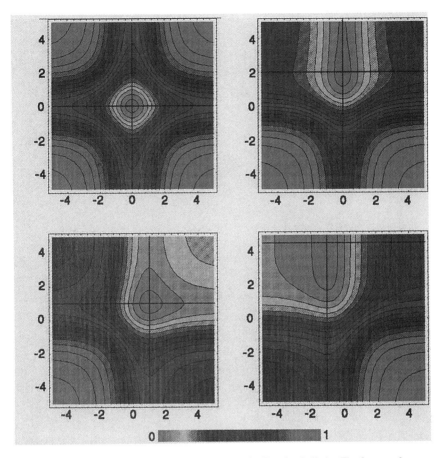

Figure 3. Graphs of the distance function obtained from the Tversky similarity. The figures refer to a two-dimensional measurement space and two-dimensional predicate space. The matrix A is the 2×2 identity matrix. The four figures are distances with respect to the references $r = [0, 0]^T$, $r = [0, 2]^T$, $r = [1, 1]^T$, and $r = [-1, 4.5]^T$, respectively.

(that is, when there is no reference), as is the case when the question is phrased: "how similar are A and B?"

Figure 3 shows the distance function obtained from the Tversky dissimilarity. Both the measurements space and the predicate space are two dimensional for the sake of representation. The matrix A would only cause a rotation and skew in the coordinate system. For the sake of simplicity, we have assumed that the matrix A is the 2×2 identity (in fuzzy-set theoretic terms: each predicate is build on one of the two measurements alone). The four graphs show the distance from four different references, with coordinates:

$$ r = \begin{bmatrix} 0 \\ 0 \end{bmatrix}, \ r = \begin{bmatrix} 0 \\ 2 \end{bmatrix}, \ r = \begin{bmatrix} 1 \\ 1 \end{bmatrix}, \ \text{and } r = \begin{bmatrix} -1 \\ 4.5 \end{bmatrix}, \tag{71} $$

respectively.

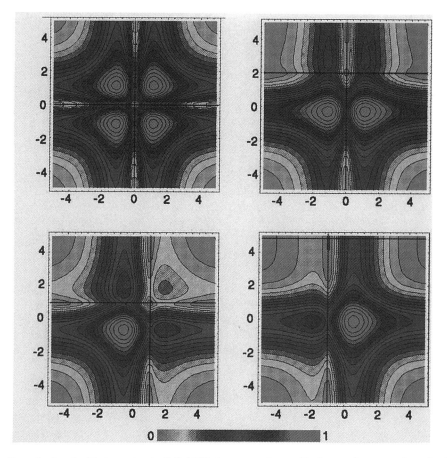

Figure 4. Length of the tangent vector [1/2, 1/2] in the perceptual space. The figures refer to a two-dimensional measurement space and two-dimensional predicate space. The matrix A is the 2×2 identity matrix. The four figures are distances with respect to the references $r = [0, 0]^T$, $r = [0, 2]^T$, $r = [1, 1]^T$, and $r = [-1, 4.5]^T$, respectively.

The function F can be used to look at the differential structure of the space. It gives information about the local behavior of the metric. In short, if we are at the point of coordinates x^1, x^2, and move of an amount $X_1 dx^1 + X_2 dx^2$, how does our distance from the reference change? Figure 4 shows this. It represents the length of the tangent vector

$$X = \begin{bmatrix} \frac{1}{\sqrt{2}} \\ \frac{1}{\sqrt{2}} \end{bmatrix} \tag{72}$$

at the different points of the perceptual space for the same reference stimuli of figure 3. If we set a point in the space and change the vector X, its length varies as in figure 5.

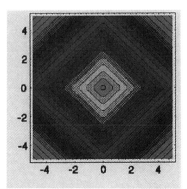

Figure 5. Length of a tangent vector at a given point in the perceptual space as a function of the vector coordinates. The shape of the graph is the same at all points in the perceptual space. Its values are scaled so that the vector $[1/2, 1/2]$ has the length in figure XX.

4. Unification of similarity theories

The Riemann space formalism has allowed us to give a purely geometrical formulation of Tversky's similarity theory. The same formalism, however, is an extremely flexible tool, and can provide us with a much more flexible and comprehensive similarity theory. To do this, we will couple the Riemann space formulation with *multi-resolution analysis* of the images.

4.1. Multi-resolution similarity

Not all similarity judgments are the same, nor are they based on the same image data [1, 49]. You look at the image of a twilight at sea, and look for something similar. The most relevant features you want to consider for this search are the orange-red of the sky in the upper part of the picture, and the deep blue of the sea in the lower part. There is no much need for a more detailed analysis of the image. Quite the contrary, in fact. The dark speckle of a boat sailing the sea can be a distraction for the search, and does not provide much useful information.

Now you look at the image of a human face, and want to retrieve other faces. The most important "facehood" information is contained in the edges [14, 18, 30]. So, at least, you want to look for images with lots of edges in the right places. This *edge density* type of search is mainly based on high frequency components of the image. The color of the skin (which is a typical low frequency information) is not relevant to determine the "facehood". This remark is confirmed by psychological findings. Similarity judgment depends on the nature of the stimuli being compared. Stimuli that psychologists define "global" (and that we could call "low frequency"), like color, are judged according to a simpler similarity metric than "composite" stimuli [1].

Let us first try to see intuitively how we can incorporate these observations into the Riemann space theory of similarity. In the last section we assumed the existence of one *perceptual space* in which the features were mapped. It is the geometry of this perceptual space that determines the similarity measure. Let us now assume that the perceptual space is the product of a number of perceptual spaces, one for each resolution of the image[7]. The metric tensor g is defined on the Cartesian product of the spaces.

This way, we can adapt the metric of the composite perceptual space to the characteristics of the similarity measure. A query like the one about the twilight at sea will have a nonzero tensor g only in those areas corresponding to low frequency components of the image, and will have zeroes in areas corresponding to high frequency components. Where the metric tensor is zero, the perceptual space is completely wrapped around itself, and all the stimuli are identical. This means that, in this example, the high frequency components are irrelevant.

4.2. Multi-resolution analysis

Let consider things from a more general point of view. Let (X, m) be a measured space, and $\mathfrak{G}$ a group acting on X. We require that m be quasi-invariant with respect to the action of $\mathfrak{G}$, i.e., that the transformed measure $dm(\mathfrak{z} \cdot x)$ be absolutely continuous with respect to $dm(x)$ for all $\mathfrak{z} \in \mathfrak{G}$. We want to construct representations of functions in $L^2(X, m)$ which are covariant with respect to $\mathfrak{G}$.

There is a canonical unitary representation of $\mathfrak{G}$ on $L^2(X, m)$ given by:

$$\pi(\mathfrak{z}) \cdot f(x) = \sqrt{\frac{dm(\mathfrak{z}^{-1} \cdot x)}{dm(x)}} f(\mathfrak{z}^{-1} \cdot x) \tag{73}$$

Given this representation and a *mother wavelet* $\psi \in L^2(X, m)$, there is a natural candidate for the associated wavelet transform, that is, the map

$$\mathfrak{T}_f : L^2(X, m) \to L^2(\mathfrak{G}, \mathfrak{m}) : f \mapsto \mathfrak{T}_f \tag{74}$$

where

$$\mathfrak{T}_f(\mathfrak{z}) = \langle f, \pi(\mathfrak{z}) \cdot \psi \rangle \tag{75}$$

The elementary wavelets are given by

$$\psi_{(\mathfrak{z})}(x) = \sqrt{\frac{dm(\mathfrak{z}^{-1} \cdot x)}{dm(x)}} \psi(\mathfrak{z}^{-1} \cdot x) \tag{76}$$

Since the representation is unitary, the covariance of the representation naturally follows:

$$\mathfrak{T}_{\pi(\mathfrak{h}) \cdot f}(\mathfrak{z}) = \mathfrak{T}_f(\mathfrak{h}^{-1} \cdot \mathfrak{z}) \tag{77}$$

One problem that arises with many significant groups is that the transformation is not invertible because the inversion operator is unbounded. The inversion operator is defined as:

$$A : L^2(X, m) \to L^2(X, m) : f \mapsto A \cdot f \tag{78}$$

$$A \cdot f = \int_G \mathfrak{T}_f(\mathfrak{z}) \psi_{(\mathfrak{z})}(x) \, d\mu(\mathfrak{z}) \tag{79}$$

In this situation, many times is convenient to consider, instead of the group $\mathfrak{G}$, a suitable quotient space $\mathfrak{P} = \mathfrak{G}/\mathfrak{H}$. A natural candidate in this case is the *phase space*, defined as follows.

Differentiating π around the identity of $\mathfrak{G}$, we obtain a representation $d\pi$ of the Lie algebra $\mathfrak{g}$ of $\mathfrak{G}$. For a large class of groups, the representation $d\pi$ can be constructed from a linear form on $\mathfrak{g}$, i.e., an element $F_\pi \in \mathfrak{g}^*$, the dual space of $\mathfrak{g}$. This element F_π can be associated with a family of vectors $F_\pi^{\mathfrak{h}} \in \mathfrak{g}$, defined as

$$F_\pi^{\mathfrak{h}}(X) = F_\pi(\mathfrak{h}X\mathfrak{h}^{-1}) \tag{80}$$

By definition, the *coadjoint orbit* $\mathcal{O}_\pi$ associated with the representation π is the set of such $F_\pi^{\mathfrak{h}}$ vectors or, in other words, the quotient of $\mathfrak{G}$ by the subgroup $\mathfrak{G}_\pi$ of elements that leave F_π invariant:

$$\mathfrak{O}_\pi \approx \mathfrak{G}/\mathfrak{G}_\pi \tag{81}$$

$$\mathfrak{G}_\pi = \left\{ \mathfrak{h} \in \mathfrak{G} : F_\pi^{\mathfrak{h}} = F_\pi \right\} \tag{82}$$

$\mathfrak{O}_\pi$ is called the *phase space* associated with $\mathfrak{G}$.

With this decomposition, we consider a *section* $\sigma : \mathfrak{O}_\pi \to \mathfrak{G}$. Then we can introduce the generalized coherent state (wavelet). If $\psi \in L^2(X, m)$, then

$$\psi_{(\mathfrak{p})} = \pi \circ \sigma(\mathfrak{p}) \circ \psi \tag{83}$$

and the operator

$$A_\sigma : L^2(X, m) \to L^2(X, m) : f \mapsto A_\sigma \cdot f \tag{84}$$

$$A_\sigma \cdot f = \int_{\mathfrak{O}_\pi} \langle f, \psi_{(\mathfrak{p})} \rangle \psi_{(\mathfrak{p})} \, d\mu(\mathfrak{z}) \tag{85}$$

For our purposes, we need a decomposition that allows us to control both the frequency and the direction of the analysis. To generate this decomposition, we use an extension of the two-dimensional inhomogeneous Weyl-Heisenberg group, which we call the *Scaled Heisenberg* group $\mathfrak{H}$ which, in matrix form, is the subgroup of $GL(4)$ composed of matrices of the form:

$$\begin{bmatrix} 1 & \mathfrak{x}^T & \mathfrak{z} \\ 0 & \mathfrak{S} & \mathfrak{y} \\ 0 & 0 & 1 \end{bmatrix} \tag{86}$$

where $\mathfrak{x}, \mathfrak{y} \in \mathbb{R}^2$, $\mathfrak{z} \in [0, 2\pi)$ and $\mathfrak{S}$ is a 2×2 diagonal *scaling* matrix. The multiplication law for the group $\mathfrak{H}$ is:

$$\begin{aligned} \mathfrak{h}(\mathfrak{x}, \mathfrak{y}, \mathfrak{S}, \mathfrak{z}) \cdot \mathfrak{h}(\mathfrak{x}', \mathfrak{y}', \mathfrak{S}', \mathfrak{z}') \\ = \mathfrak{h}(\mathfrak{x}' + \mathfrak{S}'\mathfrak{x}, \mathfrak{y} + \mathfrak{S}\mathfrak{y}', \mathfrak{S}\mathfrak{S}', \mathfrak{z} + \mathfrak{z}' + \langle \mathfrak{x}, \mathfrak{y}' \rangle \bmod 2\pi) \end{aligned} \tag{87}$$

The representation of $\mathfrak{H}$ in $L^2(\mathbb{R}^2)$ is:

$$\pi(\mathfrak{x}, \mathfrak{y}, \mathfrak{S}, \mathfrak{z}) \cdot \psi(x) = \mathfrak{S}^{-\frac{1}{2}} \exp(2\pi i \lambda(\langle \mathfrak{y}, \mathfrak{x} \rangle + \mathfrak{z})) \psi(\mathfrak{S}^{-1}x + \mathfrak{x}) \tag{88}$$

These functions analyze the image at the different frequencies and along different directions. If ψ is a Gaussian function, the representation of $\mathfrak{G}$ generates the family of *Gabor functions*.

The representation π induces a transform:

$$\mathfrak{T}_f : L^2(\mathbb{R}^2) \to L^2(\mathfrak{H}) \tag{89}$$

with

$$\mathfrak{T}_f(\mathfrak{h}) = \langle f, \pi(\mathfrak{h}) \cdot \psi \rangle \tag{90}$$

This transform associates a real number to every element $\mathfrak{h} \in \mathfrak{H}$, that is, it can be seen as an element in $\mathfrak{H} \times \mathbb{R}$. We make the hypothesis that *this space is the perceptual space on which distances are computed.*

A stimulus is a closed submanifold (a hyper-surface, in fact) in this space. The perceptual space can also be seen as a fiber bundle generated by the action of the additive group $\mathbb{R}$ on the group $\mathfrak{H}$. Geometric similarity in this space can be defined by integrating over the fibers. Suppose we have two images I_1 and I_2 that we need to compare. The two are transformed, and the results are two elements in $\mathfrak{H} \times \mathbb{R}$, that is $I_i : \mathfrak{H} \to \mathbb{R}$. The metric tensor of the space is

$$g \in T^*_{\mathfrak{H} \times \mathbb{R}} \times T^*_{\mathfrak{H} \times \mathbb{R}} \tag{91}$$

with components $g_{ij}(\mathfrak{h}, u)$, $\mathfrak{h} \in \mathfrak{H}$, $u \in \mathbb{R}$. The dissimilarity between the two images is given by:

$$D(I_1, I_2) = \int_{\mathfrak{H}} d\mathfrak{h} \int_{I_1(\mathfrak{h})}^{I_2(\mathfrak{h})} du \, g_{ij}(\mathfrak{h}, u) \dot{x}^i(u) \dot{x}^j(u) \tag{92}$$

One problem here is that the inhomogeneous Weyl-Heisenberg group, as well as the scaled Heisenberg group, generate an unbounded operator $\mathcal{A}$. This is not necessarily a problem for us, since in a database application the decomposition is used only for indexing, and it is not necessary to reconstruct the image. Nevertheless, it is useful to consider subgroups of the general group $\mathfrak{H}$ which lead to transforms with a smaller number of parameters than the whole group.

We have a number of choices for the group $\mathfrak{O}_\pi$. One is the subgroup

$$\mathfrak{W} = \{\mathfrak{h}(\mathfrak{x}, 0, \mathfrak{S}, 0)\} \tag{93}$$

which is isomorphic to the affine group, and generates the multi scale Wavelet transform of $L^2(\mathbb{R}^2)$.

Another possible choice is to connect the modulation frequency $\mathfrak{y}$ to the scaling parameter $\mathfrak{S}$, so as to end up with four parameters representing position, frequency (or scale of the representation), and direction. This is done defining

$$\sigma : \mathfrak{O} \to \mathfrak{G} : \mathfrak{o}(\mathfrak{x}, \theta, \lambda) \mapsto \mathfrak{h}(\mathfrak{x}, \mathfrak{y}(\theta, \lambda), \mathfrak{S}(\theta, \lambda)) \tag{94}$$

where

$$\mathfrak{y}(\theta, \lambda) = (\lambda \cos \theta, \lambda \sin \theta) \tag{95}$$

and

$$\mathfrak{S}(\theta, \lambda) = \begin{bmatrix} \lambda \cos \theta & 0 \\ 0 & \lambda \sin \theta \end{bmatrix} \tag{96}$$

which generates something similar to the Gabor analysis of the image.

The analysis carried out for the whole group is still valid in this case, and the dissimilarity is given by:

$$D(I_1, I_2) = \int_{\mathfrak{O}} d\mathfrak{o} \int_{I_1(\sigma(\mathfrak{0}))}^{I_2(\sigma(\mathfrak{0}))} du \, g_{ij}(\sigma(\mathfrak{o}), u)\dot{x}^i(u)\dot{x}^j(u) \tag{97}$$

5. Some examples

In this section we present a few examples of similarity searches which use a demo we are developing[8] at the Visual Computing Lab at UCSD.

The similarity model presented in the previous section is very general and subsumes—at a preattentive level—many behaviors observed in human beings. First of all, for color images we can replicate the measure for the three color channels, or for some other decomposition. We use the HSI decomposition for a number of reasons: first, the separation of the Intensity channel makes easier to replicate similarity behaviors of humans, since in the human visual system intensity and color follow separate pathways from the very early stages. Second, the presence of the H channel allows us to make more intuitive queries, since "hue" and "saturation" are more intuitive for the person making the query that, say, the "U" and "V" components.

The examples we present here are based on three different similarities. *Similarity in color* considers the overall color in the image, with some weight given to the overall color distribution. *Similarity in color distribution* considers the distribution of colors in the image. *Similarity in image structure* considers the places in the image where "things happen." This means basically that we look at the areas of the images with a high density of edges. We are also working on more complex similarities that can be useful in specific contexts. One example is *color harmony*, which has been defined in a subject-independent manner in [22], and which has application for art databases.

The database on which we are experimenting contains about 2,000 color images, represented in the HSI color system. Each of the three channels has been decomposed independently.

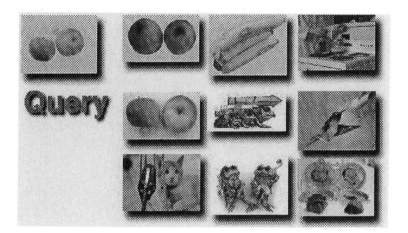

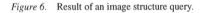

Figure 6. Result of an image structure query.

Figure 7. Result of a color distribution query.

Figure 6 shows the result of an "image structure" query. While figure 7 shows the result of a "color distribution" query.

Figure 7 gives only the first images retrieved, but gives no indication about the perceived similarity between them and the query. Figure 8 shows some of the results superimposed to a graph of the perceived distance between the samples and the query.

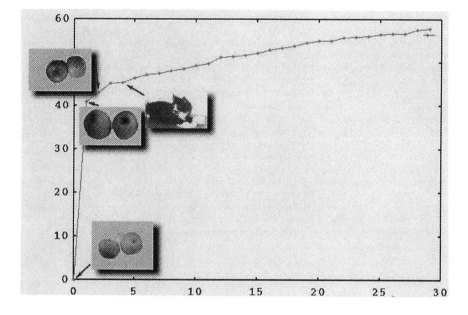

Figure 8.

6. Conclusions

Multimedia databases (in particular image databases) are different from traditional system since they cannot ignore the perceptual substratum on which the data come. There are several consequences of this fact. The most relevant for our purposes is that it is no longer possible to identify a well defined *meaning* of an image and, therefore, matching based on meaning is impossible. Matching should be replaced by similarity assessment and, in particular, by something close to human *preattentive* similarity.

This conclusion led us to study perceptual models of similarity. We have seen that many characteristics of human similarity, which are desirable in the context of a database, could be successfully explained only by models based on set-theoretic considerations while others can be explained by simple geometric models.

In this paper we have unified these models by providing a geometric framework that subsumes both geometric and set-theoretic models, and we have studied its application to preattentive search in image databases.

The unification of all the different similarity measures in a single geometric framework is important also for practical purposes. For starter, it makes indexing independent of the particular type of similarity that is being employed. Once one has an indexing system that works well in the framework, she can use the same indexing mechanism for a wide variety of different similarity searches with equal efficiency.

Notes

1. Images are static, discontinuous, have the same resolution at all coordinates, and do not have any temporal coherence when placed one after the other.
2. Which is impossible even for humans. I have vivid in my mind a picture of Stalin in the 1920's on a podium which would probably mean very little to most people. That happens to be one of the pictured in which Trotsky was with Stalin, but had been later "removed" for propaganda reasons. Sometimes the information is not in what's in the picture, but in what *isn't* in the picture.
3. Therefore it violates the cat's principle, with the possible exception of Clinton's cat Socks.
4. Don't be fooled by things like infrared images: perceptually there is no such a thing as an infrared image. There is some machine that captures infrared radiation and uses it to produce a regular, good ol' visible light image, and only the latter is perceived. The fact that this image can be used to infer some properties of the infrared emission, and that two of such images will appear similar if the infrared emissions are similar is a fact that belongs to the realm of physics, and not to that of perception.
5. In this section, all Latin symbols refer to quantities defined in the perceptual space, and all Latin indices span $1, \ldots, n$. All Greek symbols refer to quantities defined in the *predicate space*, and Greek indices span $1, \ldots, m$. Moreover, we will use Einstein's summation convention: when an index is repeated twice in a monomial expression, a summation over the range of that index is implied, so:

$$x_i y^i = \sum_{i=1}^{n} x_i y^i.$$

6. This notation is an exception to the convention of using Latin letter to indicate quantities defined in $\mathcal{F}$ and Greek letters to indicate quantities defined in $\mathcal{M}$: the 1-form ϵ is indicated by a Greek letter in spite of its being defined in a space derived from $\mathcal{F}$. We made this exception to the convention because it is customary in differential geometry to indicate all 1-forms with lower case Greek letters.
7. Actually we can assume, as we will do in a while, that there is a *continuum* of perceptual spaces, corresponding to an infinite number of resolutions. In practice, of course, we will have a finite number of resolutions.
8. The demo is available on-line at the home page of one of the authors at http://vision.ucsd.edu/$\bar{s}$santini. The demo requires a Java compliant browser.

References

1. F. Gregory Ashby and Nancy A. Perrin, "Toward a unified theory of similarity and recognition," Psychological Review, Vol. 95, No. 1, pp. 124–150, 1988.
2. J.R. Bach, S. Paul, and R. Jain, "A visual information management system for the interactive retrieval of faces," IEEE Transactions on Knowledge and Data Engineering, Vol. 5, No. 4, pp. 619–628, 1993.
3. Roger G. Barker, "On the nature of the environment," in The Psychology of Egon Brunswik, Kenneth R. Hammond (Ed.), Holt, Reinheart and Winston, 1966.
4. J. Beck, "Textural segmentation," in Organization and Representation in Perception, J. Beck (Ed.), Erlbaum, 1982.
5. William M. Boothby, "An introduction to differentiable manifolds and Riemannian geometry," Pure and Applied Mathematics, Academic Press, 1975.
6. Vicki Bruce and Patrick Green, "Visual perception: Physiology, psychology, and ecology," Lawrence Erlbaum Associates, 1985.
7. Egon Brunswik, "Perception and the representative design of psychological experiments," University of California Press, 1956.
8. J. Douglas Carroll and Phipps Arabie, "Multidimensional scaling," Annual Review of Psychology, Vol. 31, pp. 607–649, 1980.
9. Shih Fu Chang and John R. Smith, "Extracting multi-dimensional signal features for content-based visual query," in SPIE Symposium on Communications and Signal Processing, 1995.

10. H. Chen, B. Schatz, T. Ng, J. Martinez, A. Kirchoff, and C. Lin, "A parallel computing approach to creating engineering concept spaces for semantic retrieval: The illinois digital library initiative project," IEEE Transactions on Pattern Analysis and Machine Intelligence, Vol. 18, No. 8, Aug. 1996.

11. Daniel M. Ennis, Joseph J. Palen, and Kenneth Mullen, "A multidimensional stochastic theory of similarity," Journal of Mathematical Psychology, Vol. 32, pp. 449–465, 1988.

12. Myron Flickner, Harpreet Sawhney, Wayne Niblack, Jonathan Ashley, Qian Huang, Byron Dom, Monika Gorkani, Jim Hafner, Denis Lee, Dragutin Petkovic, David Steele, and Peter Yanker, "Query by image and video content: The QBIC system," IEEE Computer, 1995.

13. J.J. Gibson, The Ecological Approach to Visual Perception, Houghton Mifflin, 1979.

14. Alvin G. Goldstein and June Chance, "Measuring psychological similarity of faces," Bulletin of the Psychonomic Society, Vol. 7, No. 4, pp. 407–408, 1976.

15. Armanath Gupta, "Visual information retrieval technology: A virage perspective," Technical report, Virage, Inc., 1995.

16. J.P. Hailman, Optical Signals: Animal Communication and Light, Indiana University Press, 1977.

17. Kenneth R. Hammond, "Probabilistic functionalism: Egon brunswik's integration of the history, theory, and method of psychology," in The Psychology of Egon Brunswik, Kenneth R. Hammond (Ed.), Holt, Reinheart and Winston, 1966, pp. 15–80.

18. Ronald Henss, "Dimensionen der ahnlichkeit von gesichtern-eine kreuzvalidierung (dimensions of similarity of faces: A cross-validation study)," Zeitschrift fur Experimentelle und Angewandte Psychologie, Vol. 41, No. 3, pp. 398–414, 1994.

19. Alston S. Householder and Herbert D. Landahl, Mathematical Biophysics of the Central Nervous System, Principia Press: Bloomington, Ind., 1945.

20. Chih-Cheng Hsu, Wesley W. Chu, and Ricky K. Taira, "A knowledge-based approach for retrieving images by content," IEEE Transactions on Pattern Analysis and Machine Imtelligence, Vol. 8, No. 4, pp. 522–532, Aug. 1996.

21. F. Idris and S. Panchanathan, "Image indexing using wavelet vector quantization," in Proceedings of the SPIE, Vol. 2606—Digital Image Storage and Archiving Systems, Philadelphia, PA, USA, 25–26 Oct., 1995, pp. 269–275.

22. Johannes Itten, The Art of Color, Reinhold Pub. Corp: New York, 1961.

23. Charles E. Jacobs, Adam Finkelstein, and Savid H. Salesin, "Fast multiresolution image querying," in Proceedings of SIGGRAPH 95, Los Angeles, CA. ACM SIGGRAPH, New York, 1995.

24. Carol L. Krumhansl, "Concerning the applicability of geometric models to similarity data: The interrelationship between similarity and spatial density," Psychological Review, Vol. 85, pp. 445–463, 1978.

25. Robert W. Leeper, "A critical consideration of Egon Brunswik's probabilistic functionalism," in The Psychology of Egon Brunswik, Kenneth R. Hammond (Ed.), Holt, Reinheart and Winston, 1966.

26. Barry Loewer and Georges Rey, Meaning in Mind: Fodor and his Critics, Blackwell, 1991.

27. D. Lovelock and H. Rund, Tensors, Differential Forms, and Variational Principles, Dover Books on Advanced Mathematics, 63. Dover Publications, Inc.: New York, 1975, 1989.

28. Jitendra Malik and Pietro Perona, "Preattentive texture discrimination with early vision mechanisms," Journal of the Optical Society of America A, Vol. 7, No. 5, 1990.

29. B.S. Manjunath and W.Y. Ma, "Texture features for browsing and retrieval of image data," IEEE Transactions on Pattern Analysis and Machine Intelligence, Vol. 18, No. 8, pp. 837–842, 1996.

30. Kinya Maruyama, Shusei Minakawa, and Hitoshi Okada, "Face similarity and its effect on length discrimination about eyebrows," Tohoku Psychologica Folia, Vol. 48, No. 1–4, pp. 107–113, 1989.

31. Carol Mason and Eric R. Kandel, "Central visual pathways," in Principles of Neural Science, Eric R. Kandel, James H. Schwartz, and Thomas M. Jessell (Eds.), Appleton & Lange, 1991, Chapt. 30, pp. 420–439.

32. Mohammad Nabil, Anne H.H. Ngu, and John Sheperd, "Picture similarity retrieval using the 2D projection interval representation," IEEE Transaction on Knowledge and Data Engineering, Vol. 8, No. 4, pp. 533–539, Aug. 1996.

33. T. Okubo, Differential Geometry, Monographs and Textbooks in Pure and Applied Mathematics," Marcel Dekker, Inc.: 270 Madison Ave, New York 10016, 1987.

34. R.R. Olson and F. Attneave, "What variables produce similarity grouping?" Americal Journal of Psychology, Vol. 83, pp. 1–21, 1970.

35. A. Pentland, R.W. Picard, and S. Sclaroff, "Photobook: Tools for content-based manipulation of image databases," in SPIE Conference on Storage and Retrieval of Images and Video Databases II, San Jose, CA, Feb. 1994, Vol. 2185.

36. Lewis Petrinovich, "Probabilistic functionalism: A concept of research method," American Psychologist, Vol. 34, No. 5, pp. 373–390, May 1979.

37. N.K. Ratha, K. Karu, Shaoyun Chen, and A.K. Jain, "A real-time matching system for large fingerprint databases," IEEE Transactions on Pattern Analysis and Machine Intelligence, Vol. 18, No. 8, pp. 799–813, 1996.

38. H. Samet and A. Soffer, "MARCO: MAp retrieval by content," IEEE Transactions on Pattern Analysis and Machine Intelligence, Vol. 18, No. 8, pp. 783–798, 1996.

39. Simone Santini and Ramesh Jain, "Similarity matching," IEEE Transactions on Pattern Analysis and Machine Intelligence, 1995 (submitted).

40. Simone Santini and Ramesh Jain, "Similarity queries in image databases," in Proceedings of CVPR '96, International IEEE Computer Vision and Pattern Recognition Conference, 1996.

41. H. Sawhney and S. Ayer, "Compact representation of videos through dominant and multiple motion estimation," IEEE Transactions on Pattern Analysis and Machine Intelligence, Vol. 18, No. 8, Aug. 1996.

42. Robert Shapley, Terrence Caelli, Stephen Grossberg, Michael Morgan, and Ingo Rentschler, "Computational theories of visual perception," in Visual Perception: The Neurophysiological Foundation, Lothar Spillman and John S. Werner (Eds.), Academic Press, 1990, pp. 417–448.

43. Roger N. Shepard, "The analysis of proximities: Multidimensional scaling with unknown distance function," Part I, Psychometrika, Vol. 27, pp. 125–140, 1962.

44. Roger N. Shepard, "Toward a universal law of generalization for physical science," Science, Vol. 237, pp. 1317–1323, 1987.

45. Hans-Georg Stark and Gernod P. Laufkötter, "Image indexing and content based access to databases of medical images with wavelets," in Proceedings of the SPIE, Vol. 2569—Wavelet Applications in Signal and Image Processing III, San Diego, CA, USA, 12–14 July, 1995, pp. 790–800.

46. Warren S. Torgerson, "Multidimensional scaling of similarity," Psychometrika, Vol. 30, pp. 379–393, 1965.

47. A. Treisman, "Features and objects in visual processing," Scientific American, Vol. 255, pp. 114B–125, 1986.

48. A. Treisman, "Properties, parts, and objects," in Handbook of Perception and Human Performance, K.R. Boff, L. Kaufman, and J.P. Thomas (Eds.), Wiley, 1987.

49. Amos Tversky, "Features of similarity," Psychological Review, Vol. 84, No. 4, pp. 327–352, July 1977.

50. Amos Tversky and David H. Krantz, "The dimensional representation and the metric structure of similarity data," Journal of Mathematical Psychology, Vol. 7, pp. 572–597, 1970.

51. David C. Van Essen, H.R. Newsome, T. William, and Maunsell, "The visual field representation in striate cortex of the macaque monkey: Asymmetries, anisotropies, and individual variability," Vision Research, Vol. 24, No. 5, pp. 429–448, 1984.

52. Frank W. Warner, "Foundations of differentiable manifolds and lie groups," Graduate Texts in Mathematics, 94. Springer-Verlag, 1983.

53. Hugh R. Wilson, Dennis Levi, Lamberto Maffei, Jyrki Rovamo, and Russel DeValois, "The perception of form, retina to striate cortex," in Visual Perception: The Neurophysiological Foundation, Lothar Spillman and John S. Werner (Eds.), Academic Press, 1990.

PART IV

MULTIMEDIA NETWORKS

9

Concepts for Resource Reservation in Advance

LARS C. WOLF   Lars.Wolf@kom.th-darmstadt.de
RALF STEINMETZ   Ralf.Steinmetz@kom.th-darmstadt.de
Industrial Process and System Communications, Department of Electrical Engineering and Information Technology, Technical University of Darmstadt, Merckstr. 25, D-64283 Darmstadt, Germany

Abstract. Resource management offers Quality-of-Service reliability for time-critical continuous-media applications. Currently, existing resource management systems in the Internet and ATM domain only provide means to reserve resources starting with the reservation attempt and lasting for an unspecified duration. However, for several applications such as video conferencing, the ability to reserve the required resources in advance is of great advantage. This paper outlines a new model for resource reservation in advance. We identify and discuss issues to be resolved for allowing resource reservation in advance. We show how the resource reservation in advance scheme can be embedded in a general architecture and describe the design and implementation of a resource management system providing reservation in advance functionality.

Keywords: multimedia, quality of service, resource management, resource reservation, advance reservation, ReRA

1. Introduction

Computer systems used for continuous media processing must cope with streams having data rates of several Mbits/s and must provide timely processing guarantees. For instance, an endsystem shall synchronize audio and video streams up to a granularity of about 80 ms [16]. Since available system resources are not abundant, applications have to be 'protected' such that they have access to the required resources in time. Otherwise the user will notice a glitch or drop in the presentation quality. Hence, means to manage the available system resources are necessary.

Resource management provides a way to offer applications reliability with respect to *Quality-of-Service* (QoS) [21]. A resource management system controls the access to scarce system resources needed for audio and video data processing. It checks whether additional service requests can be satisfied, and if yes, the required resources are reserved for that application, else, the request is rejected. Sophisticated systems will allow for a negotiation according to the available capacities and constraints (e.g., by tariffs).

1.1. Requirements of application scenarios

Today existing resource management systems, for instance, HeiRAT [18, 19], QoS Broker [12], Tenet [1, 7], offer functions which only allow to reserve resources for a time interval which starts with the reservation attempt and which lasts for an unspecified time.

For several application scenarios this model of immediate reservations is not appropriate. Consider, for instance, a virtual meeting room (conferencing) scenario supported by multimedia systems. Traditionally, a meeting will be scheduled for a specific time at a well defined location (room). To be sure that the respective room will be available at the scheduled time, a reservation entry, in some form of a meeting room calendar, is written *before* the meeting starts. The time between the reservation and the meeting itself can vary from short intervals, e.g., half an hour or a few hours, to very long periods, e.g., months. In addition to 'one time events', meetings such as project meetings occur periodically. To support these 'virtual meeting room' scenarios the resource reservation system must offer mechanisms to reserve in advance the resources needed for the conference, i.e., certain capacities of networks, routers, and end-system resources.

Resource Reservation in Advance (ReRA) is not only needed for conferencing but for other scenarios such as video-on-demand as well. This resembles a video rental scenario where a user 'orders' a video for a specific time: for the video-on-demand system it means that the resources necessary to retrieve, transfer and present the video have to be reserved in advance, i.e., video server, network, router, and end-system resources. Further application areas can also be found outside of typical multimedia applications, e.g., within manufacturing process control systems (where time-critical data must be processed and transmitted) or any kind of remote surgery in medicine. The need for ReRA has also been expressed by Degermark, et al., in [5, page 4] as:

> "Where resources are plentiful, not even immediate reservations may be necessary, but where resources are scarce enough to justify reservations at all, it makes sense to be able to make them in advance."

1.2.   Contents of this paper

We discuss a model for ReRA, identify the issues to be resolved and describe the design and implementation of a resource management system offering ReRA functionality. The paper is organized as follows: Section 2 provides a description of a common resource management scheme and an according architecture. Section 3 introduces the notion of ReRA, the used model, and characteristics of ReRA. Section 4 presents the architecture of a ReRA system and some aspects of the prototype implementation. Related work is discussed in Section 5 before we conclude the paper.

2.   Resource management

In the following we describe the main issues of resource management relevant to the ReRA scheme. For a more detailed view please refer to, for instance, [12, 19, and 21].

Any resource management component on each system which is part of an application must provide certain functionality for each "active" resource (i.e., CPU, network adapter):

- *Interpretation and translation* of the application specified QoS in metrics applicable to the affected resources.
- *Capacity test* to check whether the available resource capacity (taking the existing reservations into account) is sufficient to handle the new request.

- *QoS computation* to calculate the possible performance the resource can provide for the new stream.
- *Resource reservation* to reserve the required resource capacities.
- *Resource scheduling* to perform the scheduling of the resource during data processing such that the QoS guarantees are satisfied.

Figure 1 illustrates how this functionality interact at two resource management phases. In the set-up phase (also called 'QoS negotiation') applications specify their QoS requirements (e.g., throughput and delay). These parameters are used for capacity test and QoS computation which finally results either in resource reservation or in rejection of the reservation attempt if the QoS cannot be met due to a lack of resources. After the negotiation phase has been successfully completed, in the data transmission phase, the resources used to process the user data are scheduled with respect to the reserved resources (also called 'QoS enforcement').

In a ReRA system, the negotiation phase is not in close vicinity to the enforcement phase and the resources are not reserved for immediate but for delayed use.

The resulting states for a stream are idle, negotiate, established and active (see figure 2). During the set up of a stream, it changes due to a request from idle to negotiate. If the set up was successful (accepted by the resource management system)

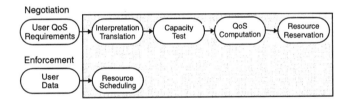

Figure 1.   Resource management phases.

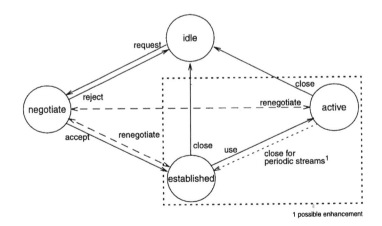

Figure 2.   States of a stream.

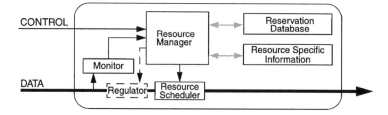

Figure 3. Components of a resource management system.

the stream is `established` which is in a non-ReRA system identically with `active` (dashed box). In a ReRA System, both states must be distinguished since negotiation and usage can be potentially very distant.

To achieve QoS provision for a distributed multimedia application, resource management is applied to all resources on the transmission and processing path, from the sending host via gateways or any other computers and networks to the receiving host. Resource reservation protocols such as ST-II [17] and its more recent version ST2+ [6], and RSVP [22] offer the functionality for QoS provision in distributed systems.

The local resource management system contains among others components for QoS interpretation and translation, schedulability tests and the according scheduling mechanisms, databases for available and reserved resources, monitor and regulator mechanisms to detect and potentially enforce the characteristics of data streams. A simplified architecture is shown in figure 3.

3. Resource reservation in advance model and issues

This section introduces the notion of ReRA, presents its basic ReRA model, and discusses issues to be addresses by ReRA systems.

3.1. Classification of reservation types

To distinguish ReRA schemes from other reservation schemes, e.g., existing reservation techniques, we classify reservations based on two key factors:

- whether the resources are exploited at reservation time, and
- whether the reservation duration is known at reservation time.

The most stringent use of resource management is in the domain of process and control systems including embedded real-time systems. There, resources are reserved for the whole active phase of such systems, i.e., for the lifetime. Changes can only be done at the initialization phase (and not at the actual run-time phase). Therefore we characterize such approaches as "static" (see figure 4) opposed to the dynamic approaches discussed in the remaining of this paper.

Traditional resource management systems (non-ReRA) assume that the resources are immediately used after they have been successfully reserved and no assumptions are made

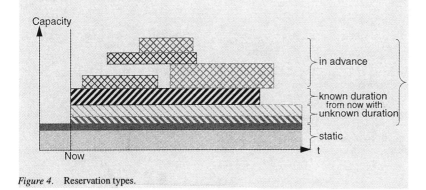

Figure 4. Reservation types.

on the duration of the reservations. A ReRA scheme, on the contrary, is characterized by deferred resource usage and reservations of known duration (which might possibly be enlarged).

In case of immediate usage and known duration, both schemes can be realized. We clarify this point at the end of this section, after introducing the ReRA model.

This leads to the simple matrix presented in Table 1.

Table 1. Classification of reservation schemes.

		Duration of reservation	
		Known	Unknown
Dynamic usage	Deferred	ReRA	
	Immediate		Traditional approaches
Static usage		Unlimited duration	

3.2. Basic model

To provide an appropriate model for ReRA, we start from the common reservation scenarios of everyday life. In such scenarios, appropriate actions are required as part of the reservation, e.g., we have to specify at what time and for how many persons we intend to reserve. Here, we introduce a simple model to define these actions and regulate the interaction between the reservation requestor (i.e., the client application itself or a ReRA agent acting on behalf of the application, cf. Section 4) and the service provider (e.g., network and server applications). The model is shown in figure 5.

The ReRa scheme consists of two parts:

- resource reservation in advance;
- usage of reserved resources.

In the first part of the ReRA scheme, the client issues a REQUEST and it specifies the nature of its request by indicating how much of the resource capacities will have to be reserved

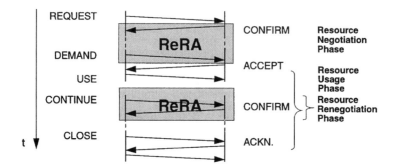

Figure 5. Reservation in advance primitives.

for its application, i.e., it gives a *workload specification*. It also specifies the points in time that define *beginning* and *duration* of the reservation. The service provider may then CONFIRM the reservation. As part of this confirmation, it possibly provides the client with a *reservation identifier* for later client identification. This terminates the first part of the ReRA scheme.

The second phase begins shortly before the client intends to exploit its reservation. The client contacts the service provider to DEMAND the previously reserved resources. It may be requested to show some form of identification, which the service provider will ACCEPT. After receiving this acceptation, the client eventually exploits its reservation by making USE of the reserved resources.

While a session is established, the participants may like to either finish earlier (than previously reserved) or they may like to extend the time. The drop of the session before the actual reservation time expires is what usually will happen, it is shown by the close primitives in figure 5. The extension request is shown as a continue primitive which again must be confirmed by the whole set of involved resources.

It is possible to further simplify this scheme by eliminating DEMAND and ACCEPT. In this case, the client attempts directly to make use of the allocated resources and client identification can be associated with USE. However, we feel that the scheme described in figure 5 is more convenient because it provides for the management system the ability to prepare the resource usage phase and generally allows for higher flexibility. For instance, it is often necessary to change reservations at the very last moment. A common example is a couple of unexpected guests for dinner making a larger table necessary. With the DEMAND and ACCEPT scheme, DEMAND can be used to adjust reservations appropriately when possible. Also, an explicit ACCEPT from the service provider is desirable because it informs the client that everything is set so that its requirements can be met.

3.3. Timing

In order to appropriately define a ReRA system, it is important to analyze the temporal relationships among the events. Consider the events in figure 6.

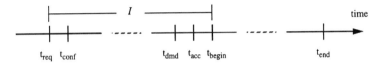

Figure 6.   ReRA model temporal sequence.

In our view of a ReRA system, we assume that the distance between t_{req} and t_{conf} is short, about the order of delay tolerated by Remote Procedure Calls (RPC). The same holds for t_{dmd}, t_{acc} and t_{begin}. On the contrary, t_{req} and t_{begin} are possibly very distant, possibly in the order of weeks or months. Let us call I the time interval between resource reservation and exploitation:

$$I = t_{begin} - t_{req}$$

When I is too small, making a ReRA reservation is pointless and a normal reservation scheme can be adopted. A ReRA system may define a value for I, say I_{min}, such that requests with:

$$t_{begin} - t_{req} < I_{min}$$

are rejected because the overhead induced by the management of resources might otherwise be too large. In the same way, an I_{max} value for I can be defined to prevent applications to request their reservation long ahead of time, e.g., to prevent storing too much reservation state. These definitions help clarify Table 1 when both non-ReRA and ReRA are possible, the I_{min} value can be used to decide which of the two schemes to adopt. However, if limits for I are defined it must be considered that in the 'real' world we have the possibility to specify exceptions, e.g., if hotel rooms for a large event can be reserved long time in advance, similarly, it might be necessary to be able to reserve network and other system resources for large events already long time in advance.

Instead of using single values for the events, the use of intervals and a target value within this interval is more general. For instance, instead of the single value t_{req}, the interval $[t_{req,earliest}, t_{req,latest}]$ and the according target value $t_{req,target}$ might be used. If a certain application will be run periodically, e.g., the video conference of the weekly project meeting, it is useful to specify the reservation already as periodically.

All specified time values must be unambiguous within all components participating in the provision of a distributed and ReRA supported application. Hence, absolute time values, based on synchronized and coordinated clocks must be used. The granularity of specified times might be system dependent and influence the overhead incurred by the ReRA system. As for 'real-world' reservations, we believe that introducing a certain granularity, e.g., a virtual conferencing room is only reservable for one or several slices of 15 minutes, would be acceptable to users. If necessary, a distinction among 'close' and 'far away' events may be added, e.g., for events starting soon the granularity might be set to one minute, for events far in future it might be 30 minutes.

3.4. Reservation duration

ReRA schemes require that the applications reserve resources over a certain time interval. The problem is, it is difficult to predict in advance how long some applications may need their reservations. In a video-on-demand system, it is usually possible to foresee the duration of a movie. Still, the user may increase this duration by pausing playout or even by stopping and rewinding to watch his favorite sequence a second time. In the same way, meetings take often longer than expected. Note that also shorter durations may be induced, e.g., by skipping through movie sequences or by rapidly adjourning a meeting.

When the actual duration does not correspond to the reservation, several issues arise:

- if the *duration is shorter*, exceeding resources should be freed and made available for other applications. In this case, resources are more likely to be made available for immediate use and for traditional reservation requests than for new ReRA requests, because of the short notice (which is likely $<I_{min}$).
- if the *duration is longer*, the system may or may not have a sufficient amount of resources to serve the application with its needed QoS. If enough resources are available, one possibility is not to interrupt the service and to provide the application with the means to extend its previous reservation. If insufficient resources are available, the system may still attempt to serve the application on a best-effort basis with a degradation in the QoS.

Means to extend a previous reservation are desirable for a ReRA system, i.e., in addition to the primitives discussed in Section 3.2 a CONTINUE primitive to enlarge an already established reservation is necessary.

Sometimes, the delay can be foreseen, e.g., it becomes clear that the meeting will take longer than expected. In such cases, it may be possible to extend in advance, i.e., before it expires, a previous reservation. This will only be successful if sufficient resources are available, e.g., if no other reservation overlaps with the extended reservation. For the prolongation of the reservation, we differentiate two alternatives, (i) the management system informs the application/user that the reservation will expire and queries whether the reservation should be extended or (ii) the application has complete responsibility about the reservation state and must take appropriate action to lengthen the reservation.

The ability to extent reservations encourages applications not to book resources over too long time intervals in order to be guaranteed against unpredicted longer durations. In a cost-based ReRA system, this can also be imposed by adequate payment policies of the associated reservation costs.

If it is known before the beginning of usage that the needed reservation duration is different to the originally specified length, the DEMAND mechanism can be used to adapt the reservation to the required duration. If the duration shall be shortened, the reservation requestor might be charged for preventing other reservations. For prolongation, the necessary resources might be unavailable, however, due to the earlier request, the risk is lower than during the usage phase of a reservation.

3.5. States

The state diagram for non-ReRA streams as shown in figure 2 must be extended to allow for the reservation of resources in advance. That figure distinguishes already between

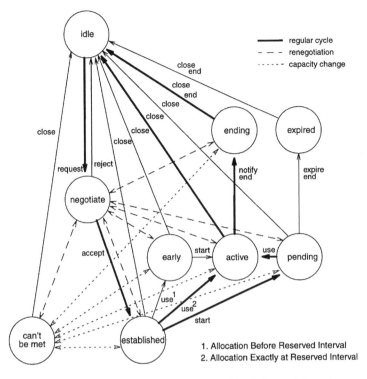

Figure 7.   Extended state diagram for advance reservation with additional characteristics and error conditions.

established and active which are identical in a non-ReRA system. Yet, this simple
extension falls short, e.g., it does not provide the ability to handle failure situations which
can occur between the reservation and the use of the resources which can be very distant
in a ReRA system. Yet, in the time between reservation and use, resource characteristics
and availability might change. Therefore, additional states must be introduced as shown in
figure 7.

The regular 'state cycle' consisting of idle, negotiate, established, active,
and ending is basically identically with the one described above. However, between
established and active time can pass and, hence, resource capacities might change
in such a way that the negotiated QoS can no longer be guaranteed. In that case, the stream
is still established but moved into the can't be met state; if later the capacity becomes
sufficient again its state is changed back to established. Otherwise, the application may
renegotiate its resource requirements or close the stream. Serving an 'established' stream
with insufficient resources is not considered as useful because then a stream without any
resource reservation can be used.

The timely distinction between the reservation and the use of resources implies that the
begin of the usage phase (marked by the use primitive) can occur before, at or after the
scheduled begin date. Therefore, three cases have to be distinguished:

- The use request is given too early. The stream is marked as 'in-use' and put into the state early but not yet scheduled with real-time priority. Hence, it is served in a best-effort mode without any QoS guarantee. When the reserved time is reached (start) the stream changes into the active state and it is scheduled with real-time priority in order to achieve the negotiated QoS.
- The use request occurs exactly at the specified time. Then the stream changes directly to the active state and is scheduled with real-time priority. This case is, depending on the granularity of time measurement, the exception and not the regular case.
- The use request comes within the reserved time interval. From the beginning of the reserved interval until the use request the stream is in the pending state from where it changes to the active state. If the use never occurs (or occurs very late, i.e., after a specified 'reservation holding time') the reservation expires and the stream goes via expired into the final idle state.

A certain time before the reservation ends the application can be notified by the system about this coming event (and changes into the ending state). Hence, the application can prolong and renegotiate the reservation.

3.6. Distribution of announcement information

In addition to the information about stream characteristics which are exchanged via resource reservation protocols such as RSVP and ST-II, information about the date of the stream and even basically the knowledge about its existence time must be distributed as well. Such information is today usually distributed via other means than the one later used for the application, e.g., the invitation to join a multi-user phone conference is given to the potential participants by contacting each person independently via a point-to-point phone call.

Considering distributed multimedia applications, two different scenarios can be distinguished:

- the sender of the data stream has complete knowledge about the set of receivers, i.e., their identities,
- the sender has no knowledge about the set of receivers, i.e., the sender knows neither identity of receivers nor even whether anyone is listening.

The former scenario occurs in point-to-point communication or in multicast communication using a sender oriented communication setup, this is the case, for instance, in ST-II. The latter scenario is used in multicast communication where the receivers are not specified by the sender and is typical for IP multicast communication.

In both cases, the human users who will consume the presentation of the transmitted data must be informed about the intended transmission of the multimedia data and accept or reject the stream. While it would be possible, in the first scenario, to perform the announcement phase together with the reservation attempt, it should be avoided. The reason is the severe drawback that until the user decided about the delivery of the stream, the resources on the complete path from the sender to the receiver must be set aside (for the future time frame) for the case that the receiver accepts the stream. However, the reaction of the user might be delayed for an unknown amount of time—the user might even not be at the computer for days or weeks, e.g., during business trips or vacations. Keeping resources reserved for such a long time can lead to rejected reservation attempts for other applications even if finally the user decides not to receive the stream and, therefore, available resources at the time the other applications intended to run. Additionally, it complicates the implementation of the ReRA components and the recovery from system failures. Altogether, it becomes clear that a distinction into the *announcement* of the data stream and ReRA for that stream is necessary.

The information about these announcements can be handled by a 'user agent' which is similar to the user agent of a mail system. It provides the interface for the user to handle resource reservations in advance. An incoming invitation to a multimedia application (to be started sometime in the future) is presented to the user who can acknowledge or reject the invitation. Using this agent, users can also start reservation attempts themselves. The user agent should provide the ability to start automatically the application at the time the data stream has been scheduled, i.e., just before the conference begins.

3.7. Failure situations

For the handling of failures, we must distinguish when the failure occurs:

- during the negotiation and reservation,
- after the reservation, but before the usage (between REQUEST and USE), or
- during the usage phase.

The first and the last case is not different from failures within traditional reservation-based systems. The second case, however, requires special attention since it was not present in non-ReRA systems.

The reservation state information stored at nodes might be needed for long lasting time periods. State information must be stored in stable storage not only to protect against failures, but also since any node may be restarted between REQUEST and USE also regularly, e.g., for maintenance.

In opposite to failures occurring during data transmission, no client is running when a node notices a failure. The failure itself might, however, not be detected at the failing node but only at a neighbor which has only partial information about the reservation state stored at the node. Means to inform the clients explicitly about the failure situation and whether it can be resolved in time must be provided, respectively the application must be able to query the correctness and availability of the reservation before it starts its usage phase.

Applications which have been written for a scenario where resource reservation is done but which are not aware that they are running within a ReRA system might encounter during their resource reservation usage phase the additional problem that the resources are not available as expected. This can occur if the application is early and wants to use resources before the reserved time interval or if the reservation interval ends and the application continues to use the resources, e.g., if a video conference lasts longer than originally scheduled. In the first case, the application is served on a best-effort basis until the begin time of its reservation, hence, the perceived QoS might be low. In our system, the application is informed about this situation by an according flag in the acknowledgment of the allocation. In the second case, the resource reservation ends and the application is served from that time with a best-effort mode only. Yet, the system offers the ability to inform the application *before* the reservation ends (state notify in figure 7). Then the application can extend the reservation if necessary. This functionality will lead to optimistic reservations, i.e., an application will usually reserve for tight bounds and not necessarily reserve for a surplus of time. Service provider can even foster such a reservation behavior (which is desirable for them) by offering better rates for such reservations.

If an application which reserved resources in advance fails to start and hence does not use the reservation, the service provider will probably nevertheless charge the application (resp. its user) somehow because the resources have not been available for other applications whose reservation attempts might have been rejected. This is similar to reserved but not used hotel rooms, etc. In order to reduce the effect, a time after which reserved resources are made available to other applications is defined. The state expired is introduced for this purpose.

3.8. Management of the resource pool

It is not possible for all applications to know in advance their duration, e.g., video conferences. For other applications, it is not possible to determine (long enough in advance) when they will run. Therefore, advance reservations and immediate reservations must coexist.

Advance reservations may block immediate reservations if both are served from the same pool of resources (see figure 8). This blocking can occur if at a later time all resources are reserved by advance reservations. The reason is that since the duration of an immediate reservation is unknown, it must not overlap with any existing advance reservation. Hence, the reservation is rejected despite all needed resources may be available. The same applies to advance reservations. They are rejected if existing reservations (immediate and advance) use all resources, since immediate reservations can last for undefined time.

This blocking problem can only be solved by splitting the available resources among the two reservation styles. A simple scheme would be to use fixed-sized partitions—one part

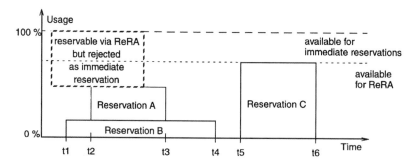

Figure 8.   Partitioning of resources.

is used for immediate, the other for advance reservations. However, it is nearly impossible to find partition sizes which satisfy the reservation needs over a longer interval for varying requirements. Thus, partitions with floating boundaries must be used, to avoid that one partition becomes empty (and the other contains all resources) water marks for minimum values are needed.

In figure 8, an example for the use of resources is illustrated. For the intervals t_1–t_4 and t_5–t_6 advance reservations have been set. As can be seen, advance and immediate reservations block each other. The dashed part could be reserved as advance reservation but it cannot be reserved as immediate reservation because its duration is unknown.

Instead of using only two partitions, one for immediate and one for advance reservations, more partitions for advance reservations can be used to distinguish among short and long-term reservations.

4. Architecture for resource reservation in advance

Now we describe the architecture of our ReRA system and some aspects of its prototypical implementation.

4.1. Management of reservations

To allow for reservations in advance, the time axis is divided into slices. Within each slice a certain set of reservations exists and there is no change of this set or of the QoS parameters of these reservations, i.e., the reservation state is stable within each slice and changes only at the boundaries (as described in [9]). Thus, the resource management system has a similar view as before: at a certain point in time (in a time slice) a fixed set of reservations with fixed QoS exist corresponding to a fixed resource utilization and free resource capacity. This view changes only if new reservations are established or existing ones end. Therefore, the following components of the resource management system need modification:

- The interface of the resource management system needs in addition to the QoS parameters now also specifications of the time parameters (begin and duration).
- These time values must also be contained in the flow specification distributed via the resource reservation protocols to all affected network nodes.
- The database of existing reservations must represent the time slices. For each time the set of existing resp. reserved streams with their QoS parameters and the free resources must be known.
- The resource management algorithms must take the time parameters into account.
- Additional failure handling mechanisms and means to save state information in permanent storage are necessary.

Furthermore, the reservation protocols must be enhanced. New PDU types to support the additional states and transitions (e.g., USE explained in Section 3.2) and to handle failure situations and notify neighbor nodes about such are needed.

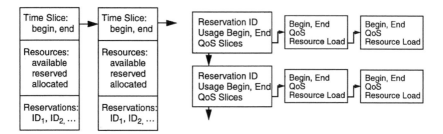

Figure 9.   Data structures for management of time slices (left) and reservations (right).

Figure 9 illustrates the data structures for the management of time slices (left side) and for reservations (right side). Information for all slices is kept in a list so that splitting a slice or joining adjacent slices is simple. For each slice the information about its beginning and its end, the amount of resources (available, reserved, and allocated) and the identifiers of set reservations are stored. Binding available resources to time slices allows the change of resource capacities over time. By keeping separately track about reserved and allocated resources provides the possibility to distinguish between established, active and not serviceable reservations (cf. state diagram in Section 3.5).

The list for all reservations contains one entry per reservation where a list of times, the (potentially varying) QoS within this time, and the corresponding resource load is stored.

The data structures for the management of the resources hold information about the used scheduling algorithm, the amount of resources to be managed and further parameters affecting the schedulability test (e.g., the maximum packet size for a transport system). This provides for the check whether sufficient resources are available for a new stream.

4.2.   Management of resources characteristics

The usable capacity of a resource can vary within a long time interval, for instance, due to necessary maintenance work only parts of the full capacity, e.g., in a network, might be available. Therefore, a system component independent of the reservation management should exist which keeps track of the capacities and characteristics of the managed resources.

The time of the reservation of resources does not necessarily coincide with the beginning of the usage phase, hence, the reserving application is in the mean time usually not active and reachable. Thus, in case of changes, another instance must be available which can implement corresponding reactions. This part can be taken over by the reservation management—it is informed about resource capacity changes and checks then whether all active and reserved streams can still be served. If the available resources are not sufficient to serve all these streams, some of the streams must be modified. For active streams, the application can be informed, whereas for reserved but not yet active streams, the application might not be reachable now. It will be informed about the changed situation when it contacts the reservation management, i.e., when it wants to use the reserved resources.

The introduction of components for resource dependent functions, i.e., for capacity determination and for mapping between QoS and resource load, generally provides for independence of the reservation management from the actual resources and the usage scenario of the reservation system. Complete independence is not possible, since several policy decisions implied by the usage scenario must be taken by the reservation management, e.g., the decision which reservations are marked as can't be met in case of resource capacity reduction. Further, the workload model has impact on the behavior of the resource and the used scheduling algorithm influences the maximum resource utilization (cf. [11]) and hence the amount of available resources.

4.3. Notification component

The reservation management should be designed as general as possible and independent of resource and application specific details. In the last subsection this led already to the distinction between management of reservations and resources. To allow for independence from applications and reservation protocols, an additional component is introduced. This notification component accepts 'sign in' and 'sign out' of an application and hence knows whether the initiator of a reservation can be reached. Further, it informs an application in case that the state of one of its reserved streams changes, e.g., time controlled or due to resource changes. Whether this notification of the application by the notification component occurs immediately or delayed depends on the reachability of the application which is known by the notification component due to the 'sign in' and 'sign out' operations.

Some applications might not be aware of the notification mechanism, hence, it cannot be mandatory. Applications can specify that they want to be informed about state changes and which state changes should be traced.

4.4. User agent

A user agent is introduced to allow the user to coordinate its work flow with the use of certain applications. The user agent, similar to a calendar and comparable to a mail user agent, provides the ability for a user to make reservations for a specified time interval and to visualize statistical information about the reservations stored within the resource management system, for example to find out the best time interval for a new reservation.

Another task of the user agent is to control the state of existing reservations: Can a reservation still be served? Till when will the failure be repaired? Could the stream be served with lower QoS? Another useful feature is the detection of the start time of the usage duration and the automatic start of the application which serves also as reminder.

The user agent is additionally the component which receives announcements about events such as conferences from other users. It notifies the user about that event who can then decide to accept the invitation and participate in the event. From the information given inside the announcement, the user agent should be able to deduce an according reservation.

4.5. Announcement system

The user agent integrates the announcement service into the reservation system. The characteristics of the event such as date, duration, required QoS and additional information such

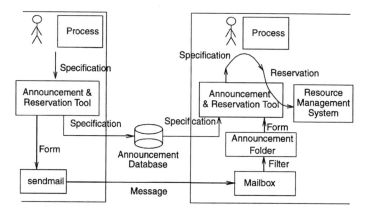

Figure 10.   Architecture of the announcement system.

as agenda, contact person, participants, etc., are specified via the reservation tool and made available with its help to the other users, e.g., the participants of a conference call or all interested persons in case of public events.

Using their user agents, other users can search in public databases containing event announcements and perform reservations with database provided information for the events which are of interest to them. Such databases can be compared to magazines or announcement boards.

For private events, the number of interested persons is usually limited (confidential information) or the interest is geographically concentrated (local announcements). Therefore, the announcement can be sent to each interested party personally via email.

The architecture of the announcement system is illustrated in figure 10. The 'announcement & reservation tool' is used to specify the event characteristics. Then the event is either announced in a publically available database or the announcement is packaged into a form and send via email to the participants.

Users search for public events in the databases. Private announcements are taken and filtered from their incoming mailbox and put into a separate box which is checked periodically by the reservation tool. Then the user only has to accept or reject the invitation to join the announced event. In future, the announcement generation and processing might be integrated into calendar and groupware applications.

4.6.   Overall architecture

The described components interact as illustrated in figure 11. The central part is the reservation management which uses the databases holding the information about the resource characteristics and the usage of resources over time intervals. The resource database keeps information about the resource capacities for every point in time. The reservation database stores for every time interval the information about existing streams and their resource

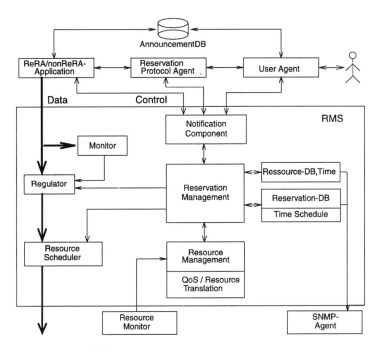

Figure 11.   Architecture of a ReRA resource management system.

load and also about the available resources in that interval. With this information, the schedulability test can decide whether a new request can be satisfied.

In case of a change of a time interval (a new time slice starts), the resource scheduler gets information about all active streams and their priorities. Based on this, it enforces the QoS by appropriate dispatching.

The mapping between QoS parameters and resource requirements must be done before the schedulability test can decide whether to accept or reject a request. This mapping is done within a resource-specific component which also keeps track about changes of resource capacity and characteristics.

The notification component offers the interface to the using system by accepting the service requests from applications. Resource requests and also requests for statistical information (e.g., state of a reserved stream, available resource capacity within a certain time interval) are forwarded to the reservation management. The resource reservation requests come from a local application, from the protocol engine of a resource reservation protocol, e.g., RSVP or ST-II, or from the user agent.

The user agent is only a ReRA application, reservations performed via the agent cannot be distinguished from applications made by other applications. The difference is outside of the RMS. A 'normal' application reserves resources for a particular work effort and duration, the user reserves in order to have needed resources available *at a certain time* for his task (then means to hand over the reservation to an application are needed).

The user agent offers an interface to the announcement database. It can be used to announce own events and perform queries of announced events. If a user schedules an event such as a conference call, he must inform the other participants about the beginning and duration of the event and must also provide information about the required QoS parameters. Additional information such as topic/agenda, participants, etc., is useful. Some events such as conferences or lectures will be public, others such as conference calls are private. The announcements of public events are stored in public databases where the users can perform the above mentioned queries.

For system administration purposes, a SNMP (or CMIP) agent should be attached to the RMS as indicated by the dashed lines and box on the right side of figure 11. Administration would also be possible via the regular interface through the notification component, however, because of standardization and security reasons a separate interface is preferable. For instance, any user should only be able to retrieve information about his/her personal reservations and anonymous information about the rest. However, system administrators need access to all reservation information.

4.7. Implementation decisions

We decided to place no limit on the period of time for reservations in advance and that no minimum interval between reservation and usage is necessary.

At stream establishment time only one QoS which is valid for the whole interval can be given; however, during renegotiations the interval boundaries can be changed and parts of the reserved interval can get a different QoS. Additionally, time intervals directly following the current reservation can be reserved to extend the overall stream duration. This both allows for the adaptation to changing requirements and considers the dynamic character of future applications. Alternatively, it could have been implemented that at set-up time several intervals with varying QoS might be specified, yet, we felt that such a feature would be seldomly used and hence did not justify the induced overhead.

We support only two partitions, one for immediate reservations, the other for advance reservations. The boundary between them can be changed. The watermarks of the partitions are fixed inside the reservation management.

The state of the RMS about reservations, etc., must be saved in permanent storage to provide means for failure recovery and for shutdowns before maintenance operations. In our prototype, its state is only saved either as part of its shutdown or on request via an API call provided for that purpose. This must be enhanced for a production system so that the state is either saved periodically or in case of state changes.

If a capacity reduction occurs so that not all established reservations can be served anymore then the reservations which are farest in the future are marked as can't be met first. If later the resources are again sufficient to serve reservations which have been marked as can't be met then the reservations which are closed to their start will be reactivated first. This straight-forward approach tries to keep the currently active streams serviceable and to move the resource allocation for not active streams so far that they might become serviceable due to release of resources by currently active streams. Priorities might be added as further decision criterion in the future.

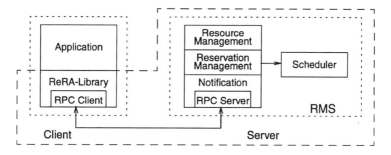

Figure 12. Module structure.

4.8. Module structure

The ReRA RMS prototype is implemented as a server (figure 12). The server stub calls functions of the notification component which communicates with the reservation management. The latter uses the services of the resource management component and loads the information about streams and their priorities into the scheduler when a new time slice begins.

The ReRA library on the client side offers APIs to set-up, to allocate, or to free reservations, to renegotiate QoS or reservation duration, to retrieve state and also statistical information, and to register for and perform functions of the notification service.

4.9. Prototype

Figure 13 shows a screen shot of the user agent as user interface to the management component. The vertical axis is divided into areas for announcements, for reservations, and for statistical information about the resource usage. Additionally, menus for the announcements and reservations (generation, query, control, . . .) are present on the screen.

Private and public announcement are kept separately and are not displayed at the same time, yet, the user can toggle between them. Own, new announcements are generated by filling in a form.

The list of reservations contains two immediate and one advance reservation. The statistics area illustrates the corresponding resource utilization. The immediate reservations occurred within a short time interval leading to the first two steps on the left side. The time of the release of the resources is unknown, hence, the utilization does not drop below that value. The advance reservation increases the resource utilization after several time ticks. Its duration is known in advance (leading to the displayed 'drop' after some time).

5. Related work

In the last few years, several publications detailed the need for ReRA and discussed some ideas on appropriate mechanisms: the necessity for ReRA has become evident. However, to our knowledge only little work has been performed on that subject yet.

Roberts and Liao present in [15] a mathematical model for a reservation process and calculate the capacity requirements of video-conference networks in order to avoid bottlenecks

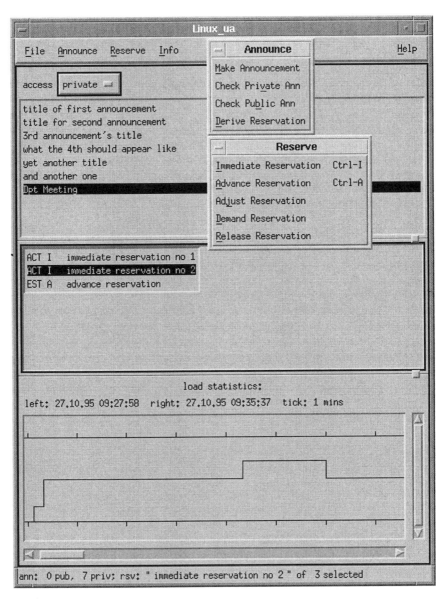

Figure 13.   Initial version of the user agent.

and severe resource contention. This work is directed towards the (at the time of that article) upcoming ISDN networks. Hence, its applicability to computer-based multimedia
systems is somewhat limited due to the different application and usage characteristics and
the restricted system environment.

Ferrari et al., are among the pioneers who notice in [8] that ReRA is a useful concept. They describe the parameters for the start and duration of a reservation. They also discuss that the resource management system (only considering the network but not any other resources such as crucial resources involved in the processing within a video-on-demand server) must verify that a client does not exceed the time interval granted to him. Neither further requirements of ReRA nor design aspects are described in more detail.

Campbell et al., describe in [2] their Quality of Service Architecture and specify start and end time parameters for 'forward reservations', however, they also state that these parameters have been omitted and remain for further study.

Chang presents in [3] a scheduling service based on the telephone system as basic model: Conferences are set up via a special service offered by a (phone system) service provider. The work describes a programming interface which offers functions for the creation and deletion of conferences (`conference_schedule()` resp. `conference_cancel()`) as well as for announcement of new conferences (`conference_announcement()`) and for searching (`conference_search()`) of created conferences. It is proposed to use X.500 for the provision of this function. Chang identifies (1) that the scheduler components of a resource management system can be kept unchanged and (2) that the reservation database and the schedulability test algorithms must be changed in order to take the time parameters into account. However, it is not discussed how this can be done. In Chang's work, all reservation requests must contain information about begin and duration of the reservation, yet it is not described what happens if a conference lasts longer than specified.

Reinhardt gives in [13] a straight-forward extension of the resource reservation protocol ST-II [17] to exchange (within the flow specification) the necessary information about start and end time of a reservation in advance and describes some problems to be solved within ReRA. In [14], he discusses application classes which can make use of ReRA and evaluates the resource reservation protocols ST-II and RSVP with respect to their suitability to reserve resources in advance. However, no general model is presented.

The NOSSDAV 1995 workshop contained three papers about ReRA [5, 9, 20]. Ferrari et al., from the Tenet group at the University of Berkeley describe in [9] a scheme for advance reservations of real-time connections without a general architecture. They present methods for connection establishment where the usage duration must only be stated by advance reservations; 'immediate channels' are established for an undetermined amount of time. To avoid conflicts with advance reservations (resources already reserved for the latter cannot be used for reservations of unknown duration since then no guarantee about the availability of these resources can be given) the resources are partitioned into separate areas for immediate and for advance reservations. The boundary between the areas can be varied within certain constraints (watermarks). The authors developed also a mechanism to manage effectively the table of all set advance reservations by dividing the time into intervals which describe regions of constant resource availability.

Degermark et al., show in [5] an extension of the admission control algorithm for predicted service suggested by Jamin et al. [10] and Clark et al. [4]. Furthermore, they discuss briefly how such a service can be implemented using RSVP [22] by periodically repeating RSVPs PATH and RESERVATION messages (already in advance to set up and keep the reservation state) and adding time parameters to the flow specification. A general model or architecture is not presented in their work.

Wolf et al., present in [20] a model for resource reservation in advance. In that paper, the issues to be resolved in resource reservation in advance systems have been discussed and it has been shown how the resource reservation in advance scheme can be embedded in a general architecture. This was the initial work which has been enhanced since then to serve as a basis for this publication. Many of these initial ideas have been refined during the design and implementation of the architecture with its prototype presented in Section 4.

6. Conclusions

While current resource management systems provide mechanisms which offer reliability with respect to QoS, this is not sufficient since many well established application scenarios, e.g., from the cooperative work area, are not well supported. Only with the advent of ReRA mechanisms several cooperative work applications will be accepted in our daily life.

ReRA is more than a simple extension of current resource reservation systems. As part of the development of ReRA systems, several issues must be attacked: The integration of current reservation schemes with ReRA requires resource partitioning methods. Applications must be offered a variety of mechanisms to prolong and adapt reservations. Failure handling raises difficult questions and must be carefully integrated into the system architecture. The provision of reservation mechanisms remains to be only one issue of a complete ReRA system. Agents to interact with the user, for reservation request generation as well as for the presentation and handling of incoming invitations, are necessary.

We presented an architecture which addresses such issues and offers suitable ReRA functionality. Our implementation shows that it is possible to provide ReRA capabilities to time constrained multimedia applications.

Acknowledgments

The practical work performed by Gerhard Sittig on ReRA provides the base of the architecture and implementation. His contributions together with fruitful discussions with Winfried Kalfa are gratefully acknowledged. Further thanks are due to our former colleagues Luca Delgrossi, Sibylle Schaller and Hartmut Wittig who participated actively in the early discussions and a preliminary report about ReRA.

Part of this work was done while the authors were with IBM's European Networking Center, Germany. This work is sponsored in part by: Volkswagen-Stiftung, D-30519 Hannover, Germany.

References

1. A. Banerjea, D. Ferrari, B.A. Mark, and M. Moran, "The Tenet Real-Time Protocol Suite: Design, Implementation, and Experiences," Technical Report TR-94-059, International Computer Science Institute, Berkeley, CA, USA, Nov. 1994.
2. A. Campbell, G. Coulson, and D. Hutchinson, "A quality of service architecture," ACM Computer Communication Review, Vol. 24, No. 2, pp. 6–27, April 1994.
3. Y.-H. Chang, "Network support for a multimedia conference scheduling service," Proceedings of SPIE, 1994, Vol. 2188, pp. 109–119.
4. D. Clark, S. Shenker, and L. Zhang, "Supporting real-time applications in an integrated packet services network: Architecture and mechanisms," SIGCOMM 1992.

5. M. Degermark, T. Köhler, S. Pink, and O. Schelén, "Advance reservation for predicted service," Fifth International Workshop on Network and Operating System Support for Digital Audio and Video, Durham, NH, USA, April 19–21, 1995.

6. L. Delgrossi and L. Berger (Eds.), "Internet STream protocol version 2 (ST2)—Protocol specification—Version ST2+," Internet RFC 1819, Aug. 1995.

7. D. Ferrari, A. Banerjea, and H. Zhang, "Network Support for Multimedia: A Discussion of the Tenet Approach," Technical Report TR-92-072, International Computer Science Institute, Berkeley, CA, USA, Oct. 1992.

8. D. Ferrari, J. Ramaekers, and G. Ventre: "Client-network interactions in quality of service communication environments," Proceedings of the Fourth IFIP Conference on High Performance Networking, University Liege, Belgium, Dec. 1992, pp. E1-1–E1-14.

9. D. Ferrari, A. Gupta, and G. Ventre, "Distributed advance reservation of real-time connections," Fifth International Workshop on Network and Operating System Support for Digital Audio and Video, Durham, NH, USA, April 19–21, 1995.

10. S. Jamin, D. Clark, S. Shenker, and L. Zhang, "Admission control algorithm for predictive real-time service," Third International Workshop on Network and Operating System Support for Digital Audio and Video, San Diego, CA, USA, Nov. 1992.

11. C.L. Liu and J.W. Layland: "Scheduling algorithms for multiprogramming in a hard real-time environment," Journal of the ACM, Vol. 20, No. 1, pp. 47–61, Jan. 1973.

12. K. Nahrstedt and R. Steinmetz: "Resource management in networked multimedia systems," IEEE Computer, Vol. 28, No. 4, April 1995.

13. W. Reinhardt, "Advance reservation of network resources for multimedia applications," Proceedings of the Second International Workshop on Advanced Teleservices and High-Speed Communication Architectures, Heidelberg, Germany, Sept. 26–28, 1994.

14. W. Reinhardt, "Advance resource reservation and its impact on reservation protocols," Proceedings of Broadband Island'95, Dublin, Ireland, Sept. 1995.

15. J.W. Roberts and K. Liao: "Traffic models for telecommunication services with advance capacity reservation," Computer Networks and ISDN Systems, No. 10, pp. 221–229, 1985.

16. R. Steinmetz, "Human perception of jitter and media synchronisation," IEEE Journal on Selected Areas in Communications, Vol. 14, No. 1, pp. 61–72, Jan. 1996.

17. C. Topolcic, "Experimental internet stream protocol, version 2 (ST-II)," Internet RFC 1190, Oct. 1990.

18. C. Vogt, R.G. Herrtwich, and R. Nagarajan, "HeiRAT: The Heidelberg resource administration technique—design philosophy and goals," Kommunikation in Verteilten Systemen, Munich, Germany, Mar. 3–5, 1993.

19. C. Vogt, L.C. Wolf, R.G. Herrtwich, and H. Wittig: "HeiRAT—quality-of-service management for distributed multimedia systems," to appear in ACM Multimedia Systems Journal—Special Issue on QoS Systems.

20. L.C. Wolf, L. Delgrossi, R. Steinmetz, S. Schaller, and H. Wittig: "Issues of reserving resources in advance," Fifth International Workshop on Network and Operating System Support for Digital Audio and Video, Durham, NH, USA, April 19–21, 1995.

21. L.C. Wolf, Resource Management for Distributed Distributed Multimedia Systems, Kluwer, 1996.

22. L. Zhang, S. Deering, D. Estrin, S. Shenker, and D. Zappala, "RSVP: A new resource reservation protocol," IEEE Network, pp. 8–18, Sept. 1993.

10

Improving End System Performance for Multimedia Applications over High Bandwidth Networks

S. ZEADALLY, G. GHEORGHIU AND A.F.J. LEVI
Department of Electrical Engineering, University of Southern California, University Park, DRB 116, Los Angeles, CA 90089-1111

Abstract. Digital video services, scientific visualization and other multimedia applications require delivery of high network throughput to end user applications. In this paper we identify bottlenecks in the data path between high-speed networks and applications. Using performance of multimedia applications as a metric, the effectiveness of solutions to reduce network, operating system, and user bottlenecks is explored experimentally.

Keywords: multimedia, networking, operating systems, performance, TCP/IP

1. Introduction

The past few years have seen development of applications with high bandwidth requirements such as medical image transfer, video conferencing, scientific process simulation, and visualization. Popular local area networks such as Ethernet and Token Ring (4 Mbit/s and 16 Mbit/s) are incapable of providing the bandwidth needed by these multimedia applications. New network technologies such as Fiber Distributed Data Interface (FDDI), Fast Ethernet (100BASE-T), and Asynchronous Transfer Mode (ATM) have emerged and are capable of providing high bandwidth to users' desktops. However, the challenge remains for operating system designers and application developers to deliver the bandwidth of these networks to end user applications. In order for applications to reap the benefits of high-speed networks, the entire path from network to application must be optimized. This involves removing bottlenecks introduced both at the operating system and application levels as depicted in figure 1.

This paper describes our experiences delivering multimedia services over high-speed networks and our attempts to optimize application performance. We deal with *real-life multimedia applications* as opposed to using *raw data*. The use of raw data in performance tests provides an upper bound on achievable performance that can be delivered by the underlying software and hardware. However, raw data does not identify other bottlenecks that are normally associated with actual applications such as the presentation of information (e.g., video display in a window) or the effect of running multiple applications concurrently.

Related work undertaken by other researchers in similar areas include: Keller et al. [14] showed the effectiveness of shared memory in the delivery of digital video to user applications. However, no optimization was attempted at either operating system or network layers, which led to poor overall application performance due to various protocol and system overheads (e.g., data copying). In [23], Yau and Lam proposed an architecture which provides

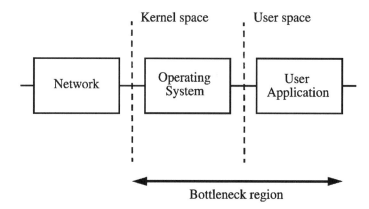

Figure 1. Illustration of bottlenecks in typical multimedia network-application data path for conventional end systems considered in this study.

operating system support for multimedia networking. Their work focused on optimizing efficient data transfers between user and kernel, and exploit independently scheduled kernel threads for control transfer between user and kernel in order to minimize system calls. Although simulation experiments were used for demonstrating the effectiveness of the architecture, issues related to multimedia data presentation and real-life multimedia application performance were not discussed. Saha et al. [20] improved network-application data path at the operating system level using kernel data paths between network adapters and CODEC adapter. Similarly, they did not discuss network-application performance.

This paper differs from these efforts in that we apply optimizations wherever possible to the *entire* data path between network and applications as opposed to focusing on just one stage in the transfer whereby later stages introduce other overheads which degrade the overall application throughput. For instance, no matter how fast the network delivers data to the host, if the operating system itself cannot transfer the data to the application at a high enough sustained rate, then there will be a bottleneck introduced in the network-application data path.

The structure of this paper is organized as follows. In Section 2, we discuss techniques that we applied to increase application-application throughput. Section 3 describes the experimental setup we have used for our multimedia applications. Section 4 presents an analysis of in-host data movement for our scientific graphics visualization application and digital video playback. Section 5 discusses the results obtained by implementing the various optimization techniques given in Section 2. In Section 6, we analyze the overall performance when multiple applications are running. Finally, Section 7 makes some concluding remarks and presents future work.

2. Improving application-application throughput

To achieve high application-application throughput in a network environment, it is essential that high sustained throughput be delivered by the network, operating system, and application.

Recent advances in the performance of network physical layers have essentially solved the network bandwidth problem. As a result, it is now feasible to deliver large volumes of data at high rates with minimal loss. In this work, we have used a conventional Ethernet network, a higher speed FDDI network, and an experimental network called Jetstream [21] (Section 3) in order to study their impact on application performance. The basic physical layer characteristics of these networks include: Manchester code Ethernet signalling at 20 Mbit/s giving a maximum data rate of 10 Mbit/s, 4b/5b coding on FDDI signalling at 125 Mbit/s delivering a maximum data rate of 100 Mbit/s, and 16b/20b coding for Jetstream signalling at 1 Gbit/s giving a maximum data rate of 800 Mbit/s. These maximum data rates are reduced by media access control, network subsystem, application, and of course, limitations imposed by the host architecture.

The last few years have witnessed significant hardware improvements that have led to the development of powerful computers. Some of these improvements include: increased CPU performance, high bus bandwidth, large memories, and fast disk systems. However, there has been little change in the structure of conventional operating systems such as UNIX, consequently the availability of new hardware technologies has not been exploited to the fullest. This has made existing operating systems become a bottleneck in end systems. Well-known overheads include data copying, network protocol processing, context switches, and interrupts [13, 16, 18]. Several techniques have been proposed and implemented to avoid these overheads [6, 7, 10, 19]. In this work, we minimized data copying by using a UNIX kernel which supports "single-copy" TCP/IP, a modified version of TCP/IP. Throughout this paper, we refer to "two-copy" TCP/IP as the standard version that normally comes with UNIX operating systems. In this case, data transfer between network and application normally involves two copies: the first copy is between a network buffer and kernel buffer followed by a copy from the kernel buffer to a user application (for an incoming packet). The reverse takes place for an outgoing packet. However, in the case of a single-copy TCP/IP implementation we use for our experiments in this paper, there is only one data copy between network and application thereby eliminating the copy to kernel buffer. Moreover, the single-copy implementation of TCP also supports RFC 1323 window scaling [11], and is capable of calculating checksum during data movement.

It is not easy to come up with general techniques to increase throughput at the application level. The main reason is that different applications have different requirements and each is implemented in its own way. However, it is true that multimedia applications have a common element: they all present information (e.g., video display) to the end user. Most desktop applications running on UNIX platforms are built on standard X window systems to increase their ease of use, and offer a common look and feel to users. The X window system has become the de facto standard graphical user interface for UNIX systems. We argue that there is scope for improving application performance in the X environment in the area of data presentation. In this context, we note that without careful tuning, data display by the X server can degrade performance in the final delivery of information to the user. Our choice was to use the X shared memory extensions [3] in order to speed up image display.

The usual way to display an image is to use the X11 library call **XPutImage**() on an application's data. The call to **XPutImage**() moves data from the application's buffer via Inter-Process Communication (IPC) to a private buffer of the X server (using UNIX domain sockets when the X client and the X server are on the same machine). The data is then moved by the X server to the frame buffer. With X shared memory extensions support, there is no data movement involved between the application and the X server. Instead the image data is placed into a memory segment that is shared between the application and the X server. In this case, a call to **XShmPutImage**() allows the X server to move data directly from the shared memory segment containing the application image data to the frame buffer.

3. Experimental arrangement for multimedia applications

The experiments described in this section have been carried out between two HP 9000 Series 700 workstations (99 MHz PA-RISC) which reside on the Jetstream network. Jetstream is a Gbit/s token-ring network which uses copper coaxial or fiber optic cable for the physical link. The network adapter for the HP 9000 Series 700 workstations is made up of two cards—one is called Afterburner which is equipped with 1 MByte of video random access memory used in a dual ported configuration. Afterburner is the host interface; the other card, Jetstream, is the link adapter. The shared memory present on the Afterburner board enables the support of *single-copy* implementations of network protocols such as TCP/IP and UDP/IP. Further details of Afterburner and Jetstream are given in [21] and [4].

The hardware architecture of the host is illustrated in figure 2. The Standard Graphics Connector (SGC) [5] is the system bus used on the HP 9000 Series 700 workstation and has a maximum data transfer rate of a Gbit/s. However, it is only possible to achieve a maximum of 400 Mbit/s transfer rate by the CPU between memory and input/output (I/O) space (e.g.,

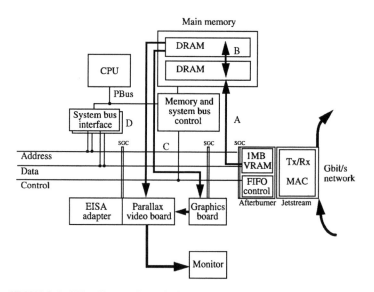

Figure 2. HP 9000 Series 700 architecture data paths for application displaying network data and video playback. A network adapter connects the workstation to the Jetstream network. A Parallax video board performs video decompression and drives the monitor. Graphics data is passed from main memory to the graphics board and overlayed on the monitor by the Parallax video board. A: Network—Application (main memory), B: Application— X server, C: X server—Framebuffer, D: Main memory—Parallax board.

graphics devices or network interface) [8]. A principal feature of the hardware architecture is the memory and system bus controller chip which connects the CPU to memory and the I/O system components. The system bus controller chip communicates to the SGC bus via two system bus interface chips. The workstations used in our experiments have 128 MByte of main memory and two GByte of hard disk. The operating system used was HP-UX 9.01 with single-copy TCP/IP support.

We have used two different applications in our experiments: one is a scientific visualization application and the other is digital video playback.

The visualization application uses a series of gray scale images (8 bit/pixel) of a volume rendered CAT-scan medical image of a child's head. The head can be rotated and viewed at different angles. In our experiment, the images are stored on a remote server and sent over the network to the client machine which displays the images. The image set consists of 20 image frames each of size 512×512 pixels (almost 2.1 Mbit per frame) and stored in pixmap format. This makes direct display by the X server possible without requiring any further manipulation. The user interface to the visualization application supports simple operations such as play, stop, and rewind.

The video application uses the PowerVideo700 hardware video codec (compression/decompression) from Parallax [17] which supports Motion-JPEG. Motion-JPEG applies JPEG (Joint Photographic Experts Group, a standardized image compression technique for still images) to individual frames of a video sequence. The video board is capable of handling high quality video at 30 frames per second in real-time during either recording or playback sessions. The PowerVideo700 is an overlay card which resides in one of the EISA slots of the EISA interface attached to the SGC bus as shown in figure 2. We have used the MovieTool software from Parallax for recording and playing digital video stored as Motion-JPEG files.

For our experiments, the files used during video playback were stored on the hard disk of a remote machine. This disk was mounted on the host machine using NFS via the Jetstream interface (details are given in Section 4). In a typical video playback session, the use of NFS enables the host machine to receive compressed video clips over the Jetstream network. The video board decompresses the incoming compressed video stream. The analog signals originating from the graphics card are digitized and the result is overlaid with the uncompressed video image. After the overlay is completed, the entire frame is converted back to analog and sent to the monitor (figure 2).

In all measurement tests for both the video and scientific visualization applications, we use average playback frame rate as our quantitative metric to characterize application performance. Moreover, in all experiments, these applications were run as normal user processes, along with the usual system processes and daemons in the background. Furthermore, all our tests were conducted using *unloaded* networks, which carried no other traffic but the one from the applications under investigation.

4. Analysis of in-host data movement

In this section, we identify the data paths used when running the video and visualization applications based on the architecture presented in figure 2.

To understand the impact of the underlying architecture on application performance, we measured the throughput at different stages when moving data from the network to the

X window display for the visualization application. The major aim of performing such analysis is to identify areas where performance can be improved, and at the same time assess the suitability of the HP 9000 Series 700 workstation architecture in supporting high-speed network applications. Our observations are applicable to other similar networked multimedia applications (e.g., medical imaging, video conferencing).

Equation (1) summarizes the inverse of total throughput R for typical applications that read data from the network and use the X window system for display.

$$\frac{1}{R} = \frac{1}{Z_{\text{Network-Application}}} + \frac{1}{Z_{\text{Application-X server}}} + \frac{1}{Z_{\text{X server-Frame buffer}}} \tag{1}$$

where Z represents the throughput at different key stages of the data path from network to frame buffer as depicted in figure 2. Furthermore, Eq. (1) applies to conventional bus-based systems of the type used in our experiments.

To understand the impact of running multiple network applications on the performance of the end system, we have chosen to simultaneously run both the video and the visualization applications over Jetstream. For this to be possible in the case of the video application, we used NFS over the Jetstream network interface as shown in figure 3. This enables playback

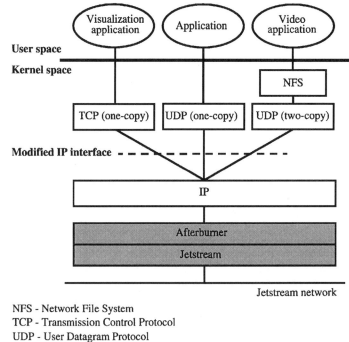

NFS - Network File System
TCP - Transmission Control Protocol
UDP - User Datagram Protocol
IP   - Internet Protocol

Figure 3. Protocol stacks with one-copy and two-copy support. IP layer has been modified to allow NFS support (which uses two-copy UDP/IP) to co-exist with applications using single-copy UDP/IP.

of digital video clips stored on a remote disk which has been mounted on the host machine (used as an NFS client). Our UNIX kernel supports NFS 2.0 which uses UDP.

Although the UNIX kernel we have used does support both single-copy TCP/IP and single-copy UDP/IP stacks, it was not possible for NFS to use the single-copy UDP/IP stack. This is because NFS does not understand the buffer structures used in the single-copy implementation of UDP/IP. We did not consider it worth modifying NFS to allow it to support our single-copy protocol stacks. The justification was that we do not see significant throughput improvement with a version of NFS that allows single-copy protocols since the disk (at the NFS server) will still be the bottleneck (although latency would be slightly better). For our experiments, it would have been sufficient to use a single-copy TCP/IP stack (for the visualization application) and a two-copy UDP/IP stack (for video application over NFS) by simply disabling single-copy support for UDP/IP in the UNIX kernel. However, the disadvantage of this approach is that it prevents other applications from using single-copy UDP/IP. Our solution was to modify the IP layer in order to distinguish packets destined for NFS which will use two-copy UDP/IP from all other incoming network packets which will use single-copy UDP/IP or single-copy TCP/IP (figure 3).

5. Network measurements and results

Initial experiments were conducted using *raw data* to investigate how much of the available network bandwidth can actually be delivered to the application. Figure 4 presents the

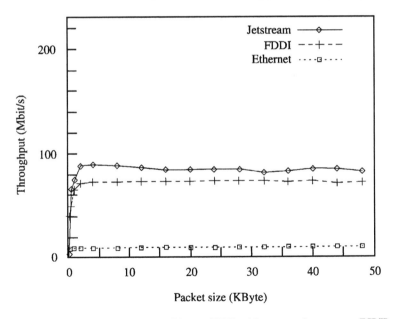

Figure 4. Measured raw data throughput over Ethernet, FDDI and Jetstream using two-copy TCP/IP and 32 KByte socket buffer size.

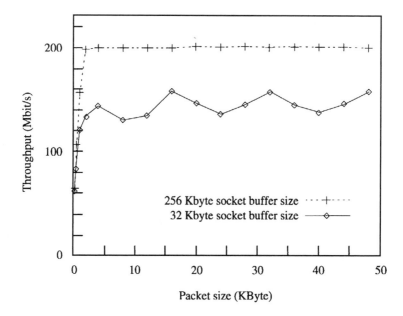

Figure 5.   Measured raw data throughput over Jetstream using single-copy TCP/IP and socket buffer sizes of
32 KByte and 256 KByte.

observed throughput using a two-copy TCP/IP stack over Ethernet, FDDI and Jetstream.
The laboratory Ethernet has been used for Ethernet tests. In the case of FDDI, an EISA
FDDI adapter designed for HP 9000/700 EISA systems was used to attach to an FDDI
network. Performance measurements were made with a tool called ***netperf*** [12] which
measures the transfer of data from a producer process (generating the data) to a consumer
(receiving data) running on a remote machine. The maximum network data bandwidths
for Ethernet, FDDI, and Jetstream are 10 Mbit/s, 100 Mbit/s, and 800 Mbit/s respectively.
However, the maximum raw data throughput values obtained using two-copy TCP/IP in
our experiments were around 9.6 Mbit/s, 74 Mbit/s and 90 Mbit/s for Ethernet, FDDI, and
Jetstream respectively. These results confirm our initial assumption that the end system has
become the bottleneck in a high-speed network environment.

Figure 5 shows raw data application throughput using single-copy TCP/IP over the Jetstream network. The use of a single-copy kernel increases throughput by almost 56% using
32 KByte socket buffer size. Increasing the socket buffer size, if the kernel allows it, results
in higher throughput values. For instance, the single-copy kernel enabled us to specify a
socket buffer size of 256 KByte. In this case the maximum throughput achieved was around
200 Mbit/s.

Having established the achievable throughput possible using raw data, we then ran the
visualization application to measure the maximum throughput for a real application running
over various networks, using a two-copy TCP/IP kernel and 32 KByte socket buffer size. In
contrast to raw data throughput results, we obtained frame rates and corresponding throughput values given in Table 1. Two important observations can be made: first, performance

Table 1. Measured graphics visualization application frame rate and the equivalent throughput using two-copy TCP/IP and 32 Kbyte socket buffer size over Ehternet, FDDI and Jetstream.

Network type	Ethernet	FDDI	Jetstream
Frame rate (frames/s)	4	11	22
Throughput (Mbit/s)	8.4	23.1	46.2

based on raw data is not enough to characterize application throughput; second, in the case of slow networks like Ethernet, software (e.g., operating system) on end systems is able to deliver most of the available network bandwidth to the application. However, as network speed increases, the discrepancy between network bandwidth and actual application throughput is increasing.

Next, we ran the graphics visualization application over Jetstream using single-copy TCP/IP with a large socket buffer size of 256 KByte and obtained a frame rate of 33 frames/second. This corresponds to a throughput of 69.3 Mbit/s (33 frames per second multiplied by 2.1 Mbit per frame). To verify the correctness of Eq. (1), we measured the throughput values corresponding to the three stages of the network-application data path as follows:

- The application reads data from a socket into its buffer. The fact that we are using a single-copy TCP/IP stack allows direct data transfer from a network interface buffer to the application's buffer (avoiding the additional copy to a kernel buffer). The throughput obtained was 200 Mbit/s ($Z_{\text{Network-Application}}$).
- The application acting as an X client sends the data to the X server using inter-process communication. The rate of data movement is 240 Mbit/s ($Z_{\text{Application-X server}}$).
- The X server then moves the data to the frame buffer. The transfer rate obtained along this path is 230 Mbit/s ($Z_{\text{X server-Frame buffer}}$).

Using the measured throughput values, we calculated the total throughput R from Eq. (1) and obtained 74 Mbit/s. This value is slightly higher than the observed Jetstream throughput of 69.3 Mbit/s. The difference of 4.7 Mbit/s is due to the fact that we did not take into account various overheads such as system calls, context switches, interrupts and memory allocation by the X server during data copying.

We now discuss how the various optimizations mentioned in previous sections can be applied to the data path described by the three terms of Eq. (1).

- *Network*: We use the Jetstream Gbit/s network capable of supporting high bandwidth applications. It is worthwhile noting that an individual application will benefit from an increase in network bandwidth, but this is not necessarily true when multiple traffic streams are competing for the available bandwidth. In this case, bandwidth allocation schemes [1, 22] are required for guaranteed performance. We do not discuss these issues here, however, since this is not the topic of this paper.

- *Operating system*: A UNIX kernel that supports single-copy TCP/IP has been used. This allows direct data copy from the network to the application. As a result, data movement, considered to be the major bottleneck in current operating systems, is minimized. Moreover, network protocol overheads such as checksum calculations have also been significantly reduced. We have therefore optimized the first term of Eq. (1) with $Z_{\text{Network-Application}}$ being 200 Mbit/s. This value is the maximum throughput obtained when using raw data as illustrated in figure 5.
- *Application*: We have used the X shared memory extensions to eliminate data movement from the application to the X server. This optimizes the overall throughput by eliminating the second term $Z_{\text{Application-X server}}$ of Eq. (1). It is also worth noting that applications should exploit the capability of using large socket buffer size whenever the kernel allows it. Although this is done at application level, it influences the throughput between network and application at the operating system level.

Figure 6 summarizes the effects of the various optimization approaches on the performance of the visualization application. It is interesting to note from the graph that for socket buffer sizes up to 48 KByte (the maximum allowable by standard UNIX kernels), the application performs better using a two-copy TCP/IP and X shared memory extensions than using a single-copy TCP/IP without X shared memory extensions.

The underlying architecture did not allow further optimization of the last term of Eq. (1). This is because the system and memory bus controller shown in figure 2 becomes the

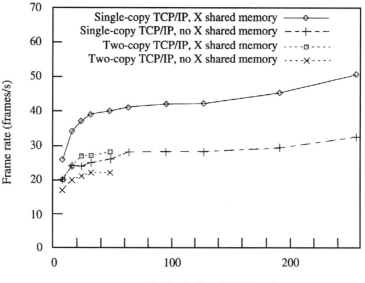

Figure 6. Measured effect of single-copy TCP/IP, X shared memory extensions, and socket buffer size on final throughput for the graphics visualization application.

bottleneck when subjected to intensive data traffic to and from main memory and system bus. This is not a problem for one way traffic between main memory and a peripheral device or vice-versa. However, it becomes a limitation in the case of networked multimedia applications where data flows in continuously from network to main memory and back out from main memory to graphics display. A possible solution is to transfer data directly from a network device to the frame buffer over the system bus, a mechanism commonly referred as *kernel-level streaming* [15]. Unfortunately, the SGC bus implementation in the machines used for our experiments does not allow the needed slave-slave bus transactions.

After applying all the above optimizations, Eq. (1) becomes:

$$\frac{1}{R} = \frac{1}{Z_{\text{Network-Application}}} + \frac{1}{Z_{\text{X server-Frame buffer}}} \tag{2}$$

Calculating the value of R from Eq. (2), using 200 Mbit/s for $Z_{\text{Network-Application}}$, and 230 Mbit/s for $Z_{\text{X server-Frame buffer}}$, we obtain an overall expected throughput of 107 Mbit/s. To verify the correctness of Eq. (2), we measured the average frame rate for the visualization application after we implemented all the above optimizations. The value obtained was 50 frames/second, which translates to a throughput of 105 Mbit/s. The difference between the measured and the expected values is smaller (2 Mbit/s) than that obtained in Section 4 (i.e., 4.7 Mbit/s). This is because of the elimination of the second term of Eq. (1) has also reduced overheads such as memory allocation by the X server.

6.   Overall performance for multiple applications

To quantify the impact of running *both* video and visualization applications on overall performance, we used the following metrics: CPU usage, frame rate (visualization application), and percentage of frames dropped (video application). CPU usage was measured using *Glance* [9], a performance monitor tool that comes with standard HP-UX operating system. Table 2 summarizes the results obtained using the Jetstream network. All tests have been performed on a kernel that supports single-copy TCP/IP. For the visualization application, we used a socket buffer size of 256 KByte. Digital video playback was via NFS at 30 frames/second, the size of each frame being 512×380 pixels and 24 bit color per pixel.

To better understand the degradation in performance when both applications are running concurrently, we first make some observations on their performance when executed on their own. When the video application is running by itself, there are no video frames dropped. For the visualization application, the frame rate without using X shared memory is 33 frames/second. However, when running both applications, there was a 39% drop of frames displayed with video and the frame rate observed for visualization decreased to 26 frames/second as shown in the Table 2. The degradation of video performance is due to the high percentage of CPU time (56%) spent in system mode. This is because the visualization application uses IPC to move data to the X server which involves multiple kernel-user interactions. The 34% of CPU cycles left for user mode are not sufficient for the demands of video, which requires 42% user-mode CPU time. On the other hand,

Table 2.   Measurement of impact of CPU utilization on video and graphics visualization applications performance.

	VIDEO	GRAPHICS	VIDEO and GRAPHICS	GRAPHICS-SHARED-M	VIDEO and GRAPHICS-SHARED-M
% CPU in user mode	42	27	34	40	41
% CPU in system mode	48	66	56	54	50
GRAPHICS frame rate (frames/s)	—	33	26	50	35
% frames dropped for VIDEO	0	—	39	—	10

VIDEO	video playback application.
GRAPHICS	visualization application without X shared memory extensions.
GRAPHICS-SHARED-M	visualization application with X shared memory extensions.

56% of CPU time spent in system mode is not sufficient for the needs of the visualization application which requires the CPU to spend 66% of its time in system mode. Thus, it is evident that the conflicting requirements of the two applications affect their overall performance.

From Table 2, we note that with X shared memory extension support, not only the visualization application has a higher frame rate on its own, but there is also an improvement in overall performance when both applications run. That is, only 10% of frames are dropped by the video application and the frame rate increased from 26 to 35 frames per second for the visualization application. The use of shared memory significantly reduces kernel-user interactions by eliminating data movement by IPC. As a result, less time is spent in system mode (50%) thereby increasing the availability of CPU for user mode (41%). This obviously benefits the video application. Also, the frame rate increase for the visualization application can be explained by the fact that with shared memory it requires 54% of CPU in system mode as opposed to 66% when not using X shared memory.

7.   Conclusions and future work

In this paper, we demonstrate that to achieve high application-application throughput in a high-speed network environment, we need to solve bottlenecks at all levels: network, operating system, and application. We have shown how using various optimization techniques, it is possible to increase network-application performance. These techniques include the use of a Gbit/s network, single-copy schemes (including improved protocol processing), and X shared memory extensions. Figure 7 summarizes the throughput optimizations for the visualization application. At each level of the data path between network and application, we apply the optimizations from the previous level. Thus, the final throughput of 105 Mbit/s for Jetstream is the result obtained after applying optimizations at all levels. Compare this to the results shown in Table 1, where without any optimization, the throughput was 8.4 Mbit/s for Ethernet, 23.1 Mbit/s for FDDI, and 46.2 Mbit/s for Jetstream.

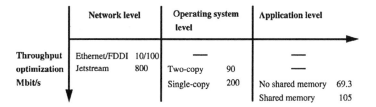

	Network level		Operating system level		Application level	
Throughput optimization Mbit/s	Ethernet/FDDI Jetstream	10/100 800	— Two-copy Single-copy	90 200	— No shared memory Shared memory	69.3 105

Figure 7. Summary of all applied optimizations. Each level includes the optimizations from the previous level.

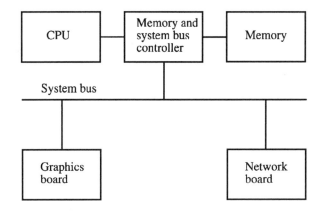

Figure 8. Simplified HP 9000 Series 700 architecture.

As pointed out in Section 4, the hardware architecture prevents the set up of a direct data path between network adapter and display for those network applications that require minimal or no data processing. Furthermore, as depicted in figure 8, the system and memory bus controller interconnects CPU, memory, and the I/O subsystem, thereby typically becoming the bottleneck during concurrent access or transfer of data between these components. This can limit the performance of network multimedia applications which involve *simultaneous* data transfer from network to main memory, and from memory to display device.

We are investigating new architectures which will better cope with the demands of multimedia applications in the context of high-speed networks. We anticipate that new switch-based bus architectures will allow greater flexibility in setting up different data paths between components of the system. Historically, switching logic and interconnect components were expensive thereby limiting their use in systems. However, progress in silicon and packaging technology has changed the relative cost of interconnections and now it is possible to build general purpose computer systems based on switched bus architectures [2]. In this context, the data path used to derive Eq. (1) no longer holds since in the case of these architectures, many paths can be used simultaneously to improve performance.

We believe that the next generation of networked multimedia applications will require more than just network displays: in addition, it should be possible to *manipulate* the multimedia data before storing, displaying or transmitting over the network. In this context, we are exploring a design space that will provide the user with the capability of setting up data paths between devices and also the flexibility of selecting portions of multimedia data in transit (e.g., from network card to display) and performing any manipulation required.

Acknowledgments

The authors wish to thank the many employees of Hewlett-Packard laboratories, Bristol, UK for their support and encouragement during the course of this project, in particular we are grateful to Aled Edwards for his valuable discussions on many aspects of this work. We thank Dr. Ulrich Neumann for his help in developing the visualization application. We also thank Kaleb Keithley of The X Consortium for his explanations on the X shared memory extensions. This work was supported by the Integrated Media System Center NSF grant EEC-9529-152 and the DARPA POLO consortium agreement MDA972-94-3-0038.

References

1. A. Banerjea, D. Ferrari, B.A. Mah, M. Moran, D.C. Venna, and H. Zhang, "The tenet real-time protocol suite: Design, implementation, and experiences," IEEE/ACM Transactions on Networking, Vol. 4, No. 1, Feb. 1996.
2. A. Boxer, "Where buses cannot go," IEEE Spectrum, pp. 41–45, Feb. 1995.
3. J. Corbet and K. Packard, "The MIT shared memory extension," MIT Consortium, 1991.
4. C. Dalton, G. Watson, D. Banks, C. Calamvokis, A. Edwards, and J. Lumley, "Afterburner," IEEE Network, Vol. 7, No. 4, pp. 36–43, July 1993.
5. A. DeBaets and K. Wheeler, "Midrange PA-RISC workstations with price/performance leadership," Hewlett-Packard Journal, pp. 6–11, Aug. 1992.
6. Z. Dittia, J. Cox, Jr., and G. Parulkar, "Design of the APIC: A high performance ATM host-network interface chip," in Proc. of IEEE INFOCOM 95.
7. P. Druschel and L. Peterson, "Fbufs: A high-bandwidth cross-domain transfer facility," in Proc. of Fourteenth Symposium on Operating System Principles 1993, pp. 189–202.
8. C. Frink, R. Hammond, J. Dykstal, and D. Soltis, "High-performance designs for the low-cost PA-RISC desktop," Hewlett-Packard Journal, pp. 55–63, Aug. 1992.
9. Hewlett-Packard, HP Visual User Environment 3.0 User's Guide, Hewlett-Packard Company, 1992.
10. V. Jacobson, "Efficient protocol implementation," ACM SIGCOMM Tutorial, Sept. 1990.
11. V. Jacobson, R. Braden, and D. Borman, "TCP extensions for high performance," RFC 1323, May 1992.
12. R. Jones, "Netperf: A network performance benchmark," Revision 1.7 Information Networks Division, Hewlett Packard, March 1993.
13. H. Kanakia and D. Cheriton, "The VMP network adapter board (NAB): High- performance network communications for multiprocessors," in Proc. ACM SIGCOMM 1988, Symposium on Communication Architectures and Protocols, pp. 175–187.
14. R. Keller, W. Effelsberg, and B. Lamparter, "Performance bottlenecks in digital movie systems," in Proc. of the 4th International Workshop on Network and Operating System Support for Digital Audio and Video, Lancaster House, Lancaster, UK, 1993, pp. 163–174.
15. B.J. Murphy, S. Zeadally, and C.J. Adams, "An analysis of process and memory models to support high-speed networking in a UNIX environment," in Proc. of Usenix Winter Technical Conference 1996.
16. J.K. Ousterhout, "Why aren't operating systems getting faster as fast as hardware?," in Proc. of Usenix Summer Conference 1990, pp. 247–256.
17. Parallax Hardware Guide, "XVideo700, MultiVideo700, and PowerVideo700," Parallax Graphics Inc., Santa Clara, CA.

18. J. Pasquale, G. Polyzos, E. Anderson, and V. Kompella, "A digital video-conferencing experiment using DECstation 5000 workstation and an FDDI network," Internal Report, Department of Computer Science and Engineering, University of California, San Diego, CA, 1992.

19. J. Pasquale, E. Anderson, and P.K. Muller, "Container shipping—Operating system support for I/O intensive applications," IEEE Computer, Vol. 27, No. 3, pp. 84–93, March 1994.

20. D. Saha, D. Kandlur, T. Barzilai, Z. Shae, and M. Willebeek-LeMair, "A video conferencing testbed over ATM: Design, implementation and optimizations," in Proc. of the International Conference on Multimedia Computing and Systems, Washington, DC, May 1995, pp. 23–31.

21. G. Watson, D. Banks, C. Calamvokis, C. Dalton, A. Edwards, and J. Lumley, "AAL5 at a gigabit for a kilobuck," Journal of High Speed Networks, Vol. 3, No. 2, pp. 127–145, 1994.

22. C.L. Williamson, "Dynamic bandwidth allocation using loss-load curves," IEEE/ACM Transactions on Networking, Vol. 4, No. 6, Dec. 1996.

23. D.K.Y. Yau and S.S. Lam, "An architecture towards efficient OS support for distributed multimedia," in Proc. of Multimedia Computing and Networking, San Jose, CA, Jan. 1996.

PART V

MULTIMEDIA APPLICATIONS

11

Multimedia Applications Development: Experiences

NICOLAS D. GEORGANAS   georgana@mcrlab.uottawa.ca
Multimedia Communications Research Laboratory (MCRLab), Dept. of Electrical and Computer Engineering, University of Ottawa, Ottawa, Ontario, Canada K1N 6N5, http://www.mcrlab.uottawa.ca/

Abstract. The multimedia applications developer is often presented with challenges that at times go beyond informatics technologies. In this paper, the MCRLab experiences in various multimedia applications development are described. Applications developed include tele-medicine, tele-conferencing with joint text editing, multimedia mail, multimedia fax, multimedia news-on-demand and shared multimedia workspaces in distance learning.

Keywords: multimedia, applications

1. Introduction

The term "multimedia" is used very frequently these days but there is no standard definition of it yet. "Media" refers to a form of human interaction that is amenable to computer capture and processing, such as video, audio, text, graphics, images, ..., whereas "multi" signifies that several of those "media" are present in the same application. We like the definition given by some authors that an application will be considered as "multimedia", if it involves at least one time-continuous medium, such as video and audio, and at least one discrete one, such as text, image or graphics [22].

A universal multimedia application is viewed in [5] as the one manipulating data types that can be combined in a document, displayed on a screen, or printed, with no special manipulations that the user needs to perform. The media composing the document may be obtained from distributed sources or servers in a corporate network, and will have to be synchronized before delivered to the user. In general, multimedia synchronization denotes a temporal, spatial or even logical relationship between objects, data entities or media streams [22]. In the context of multimedia computing and communications, however, it has become common sense to address by synchronization the temporal relationship only. This notion is still very broad and it captures a large variety of issues, including inter-process communication mechanisms. The universal multimedia application includes multimedia desktop conferencing capabilities, where users can see and talk to each other, as also view multimedia documents and performed collaborative work in shared visual/audio workspaces.

Since the early 80's many prototype multimedia applications and products have been reported in the literature. They involve enabling technologies such as image/video processing and coding, other DSP, networking, databases, operating systems, computer hardware and software architectures.

In this paper, we give a brief presentation of our experiences and lessons learned in multimedia applications development in a university laboratory. Section 2 presents the development of IRIS, a multimedia medical application. In Section 3, the development of a collaborative system with joint text editing is highlighted. Section 4 describes the multimedia mail project, while Section 5 deals with multimedia fax. In Section 6, multimedia synchronization work for a news-on-demand prototype is described. Section 7 presents the development of a multimedia whiteboard for a distance learning application. In Section 8, JETS, a Java-Enabled TeleCollaboration System is described.

2.   IRIS: Multimedia in medicine

In 1984, the Multimedia Communications Research Laboratory (MCRLab) at the University of Ottawa was established, and the first major project was to develop a multimedia communications system for medical applications [10–13, 17]. The research efforts focused on the development of a multimedia system for facilitating the communications between radiologists and physicians. The system was to enable radiologists to have instant access and examine digital radiograms, as also radiologists and physicians to engage into a multimedia real-time conference for consultation purposes, thus improving the response time required for the analysis of patients' cases.

Before we discuss our experiences with this development, let us have a quick look at a typical radiological examination procedure. Figure 1 depicts such a procedure in a typical Canadian hospital. When a physician in a hospital ward requires a patient to have a radiological examination, an examination request form is filled and the patient is sent to the department of radiology, where x-rays (or other imaging forms) are taken. In the Civic Hospital, 10 x-rays per patient case are typically taken and only one copy of each is produced and kept in the film library. (The hospital produces 150,000 such x-ray films

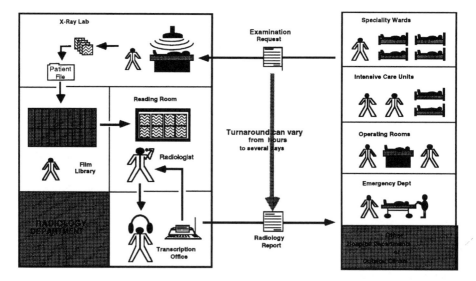

Figure 1.   Radiological examination process in a hospital.

per year. For legal purposes, these films have to be kept for 10 years). A radiologist picks from the film library and examines the x-rays, by placing several of them at a time in a light box, and dictates remarks in a portable dictaphone. A transcription service will later type a written report from the audio tape and send it back to the radiologist for corrections. Finally, the written report is sent back to the attending physician. This process may take from a few hours to several days. If the physician wants to see the x-ray films, the single copies have to be brought over from the film library. If files are lost during transit or misplaced, and that often happens, the whole process has to be repeated and that prolongs the patient's stay in the hospital. Should the attending physician wish to discuss a film with the radiologist, they have to arrange a meeting. This is rarely done, however, because of time constraints on both groups of very busy practitioners.

A large University-industry-medical team was formed with funding from industry, government and the Telecommunications Research Institute of Ontario (TRIO). From the very beginning, the users of the system, namely radiologists and physicians at the Ottawa Civic Hospital, became close partners, defined the system requirements and evaluated the prototypes. Following the understanding and assessment of user needs, a multimedia radiological communications system had to be designed and implemented. Patient records that would contain text (exam requests), radiological images and voice annotations, should be stored in a multimedia database. Access through a well designed and friendly human interface should be fast. The system should permit multimedia conferencing with a shared visual workspace for image sharing among workstations. Video communications were not considered absolutely essential at that time, but audio was very important.

An early decision was made to use PCs, with off-the-shelf imaging cards, monitors and other components, as the basic system platform. In those early days (1984–88), Intel Intellec-MDS and then 286 and 386 machines were first used. Because of DOS limitations, it was also decided to use Xenix, with later introduction of Unix System V. High resolution image monitors are essential to radiology applications, but the cost of 2000×2000 lines monitors was then prohibitive. Instead 1280×1024 lines monitors ($\times$ 10 bits per pixel) were adopted. A laser film scanner that could digitize up to a large $14'' \times 11''$ radiological film was acquired. It had the ability to produce both 2000×2400 and, by sub-sampling, 1000×1000 resolution images at 10 bits per pixel. It was crucial to find whether the image quality produced by this system would be acceptable to radiologists.

A prototype of the system, called IRIS (Interactive Radiological Information System), was developed and underwent trials first at the Ottawa Civic Hospital (1989–90) (figure 2) and then between the Civic and the General Hospitals linking the cancer clinics (1990–91) (figure 3). This prototype consisted of multimedia workstations, a multimedia database server and an image acquisition workstation. The workstations were linked together at the Civic Hospital by the Sytek 6000 LAN, then used for supporting all non-voice communications (i.e., text, and image data). On the other hand, voice communications were supported by a separate telephone network (a PBX with an attached voice mail server that could store 24h of voice annotations).

Digital image storage in a large hospital was an issue in the late '80s. There was no system available that could store the large amounts of radiological images, mentioned above. For our emergency-radiology trials, however, images taken at the emergency department had only to be kept digitally for a day or two, as patients are not kept in emergency for a long

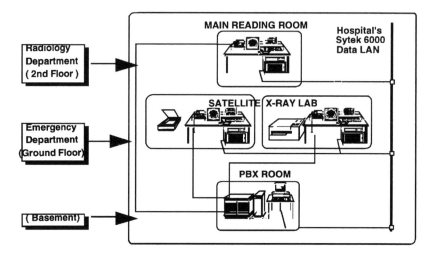

Figure 2. IRIS emergency-radiology trial at the Ottawa Civic Hospital.

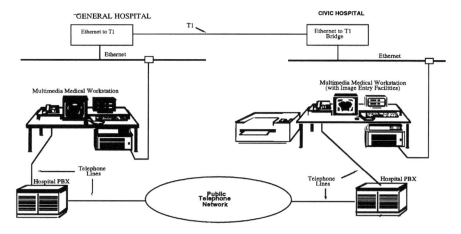

Figure 3. IRIS cancer clinics trial between two hospitals.

time. With a few very large disks in our IRIS workstations, we were able to store all needed images. Of course, we always had the analog films as back -up!

The major challenges in the IRIS design were the human/computer interface, that had to be really simple, the image manipulations and enhancements and the simultaneous viewing of image files (with all such transformations) during a telephone conference. Psychologists in the team participated in the design and evaluated the user acceptance of this technology. Radiologists were able to do correct diagnosis from the digital system, but they would have liked to browse through many images quickly. The system did not have enough fast video memory for that. The image resolution of 1280 × 1024 was far off the 5000 × 5000 resolution of the analog x-ray film, and it was hard for us to convince some older radiologists of the merits of the digital technology. Nonetheless, we did a study at the Civic Hospital and found that the decision curves of right and wrong diagnosis using the analog and digital technologies were parallel and close to each other. In addition, the image enhancements and transformations that we had built into the IRIS prototype made the system very attractive to radiologists [12]. MDs that were not very computer-literate learned how to use the system in less than 15 min. The shared visual workspace features of the CONSULT function among medical workstations, though not used very frequently during the trials, were found to be very useful in tele-consultations. Faster network response was desirable, but the existing Sytek LAN at the Civic Hospital and its LAN interfaces were slow. Images had to be downloaded to local disks before the tele-consultation. Similarly, the inter-hospital cancer-clinics trial used 10 Mbps Ethernet connections, but the two hospitals were linked by only a T1-capacity line (figure 3) [17]. We should not forget to mention that there were also legal issues that had to be resolved before the clinical trials, pertaining to liability when doing diagnosis from the IRIS prototype. These issues were resolved by the Solomonian decision to have both the traditional radiological film and the IRIS system in parallel operation during the trials!

The radiologists at the Civic Hospital really loved the system and, should the hospital had the money required at the time, they would have bought the system. The main lesson that we learned from this development experience is that applications must be designed from the beginning with the help of the users and that social scientists, like the psychologists in our team, are most valuable in user acceptance studies.

3. Multimedia collaborative work: Real-time conferencing with joint text editing

A multimedia conferencing system should provide most of the standard communication modes for a face-to-face meeting. Furthermore, in order to handle rapid group decisions, real-time conferencing is required. However we distinguish between those providing a simulation of face-to-face meetings, providing for instance audio discussion over a displayed document, and those which extend this possibility, supporting collaborative work during the conference.

The multimedia conference is normally provided with a shared workspace [1]. In most systems, the concept of shared visual workspace is used to describe the part of the display screen which is replicated on every workstation. In the case of multimedia workstations, there should also be a shared voice communication channel.

Early prototype systems reported in the literature include Diamond [23], MMConf [9] running in Diamond, the systems in [2, 19, 20] and Rapport [3, 4].

In 1990, we initiated the development of a multimedia collaborative application, over conferencing, namely joint text editing [14], with the support of the Canadian Institute for Telecommunications Research (CITR). We first designed a general purpose real-time conferencing architecture (figure 4). It allowed establishing, joining, conducting, leaving and closing a conference among participants across LANs interconnected by Wide Area Networking. Conference agents (CA), conference managers (CM) and directory servers (DS),

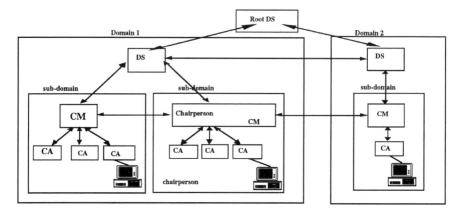

Figure 4. Functional model of conferencing architecture.

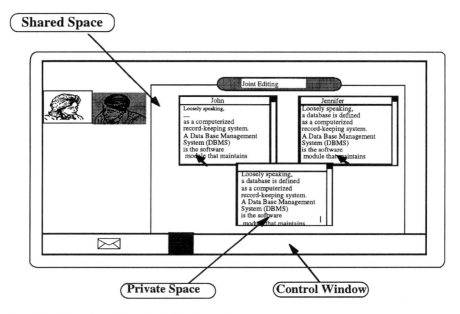

Figure 5. Conferencing windows in collaborative work.

were the essence of the architecture. Four functional windows were included in the model: conference window, group window, user window and private window (figure 5). The conference window conveys general information about the conference and provides conference control. The group window provides the shared visual workspace for collaborative work. The user window provides a working space specific to a participant, but accessible to other conference participants. Finally, the private window provides a space in which personal documents may be loaded and edited without other participants having access to them. A conference chairperson could select one or more of these windows for inclusion in a conference and permit participants a tightly-or loosely-coupled view of the shared document. The ability to specify the number of windows and type of participant interaction allows our architecture to easily support diverse applications such as distance learning, joint text editing, concurrent software engineering, remote medical diagnosis and other. The windows used in our prototype were developed using an object-oriented multimedia user interface development system, the Andrew User Interface System (AUIS), previously known as the Andrew Toolkit [7], jointly developed by Carnegie Mellon U. and IBM.

In a joint-editing application, a group of users can manipulate a shared document but coordination and concurrency control is required. Most of the time coordination is reduced to floor-control mechanisms. Other systems used token or floor passing mechanisms to prevent concurrency problems. The shared document could only be accessed by the participant that had the token. To avoid conflicts occurring in concurrent access, we developed a system with concurrency control. Modifications to the shared document were performed by reserving a portion of the document in the group window. Our method of working in the group window was different than techniques used by other researchers. The users would see the portion of the document that was reserved and the name of the person that reserved it. Although other participants would not be able to edit the reserved portion, they could still work on other portions of the document. A built-in algorithm allowed for the detection of collisions (two or more participants trying to reserve the same portion of the document). If a lock is granted by the conferencing system (i.e., no collisions occur), the locked portion of the document can be modified in a user window. Reservation collisions were resolved by our concurrency control algorithm.

The development platform consisted of 386 PCs running SCO UNIX. Video-conferencing was provided by analog video cards! This constituted a limitation in presenting an integrated digital application, but that was the best that we could find for that platform in 1990.

Following the development and demonstration of our prototype in 1993, user experience was limited and research in that area was abandoned, as our sponsor (CITR) decided to direct us in other applications. The main reason was that many commercial desktop video-conferencing systems were coming to the market, though we did not find one that could then provide the collaborative work features that we had built into ours. To us, it was at least a learning experience, and good training for students, to built such an application from ground zero.

4. Multimedia mail over X.400: A pragmatic approach

The X.400 electronic messaging standard was initially published in 1984, with updates in 1988 and 1992 by the CCITT (now ITU-T). The equivalent of X.400 in the ISO realm is the Message Oriented Text Interchange System (MOTIS, ISO 10021). It is interesting to note that X.400 has included the ability to transmit multiple media in electronic mail since its inception in 1984. Unfortunately, while this capability has been refined over the past twelve years, wide-spread use of X.400-based multimedia mail has been limited. This is largely due to the fact that very little in the way of content type encoding is defined in the standard, although the X.400 standard defines many body parts. Even with the recent revisions to X.400, this issue remains largely unresolved. In the 1988 standard, the following body parts were defined: ia5-text, voice, g3-facsimile, g4-class 1, teletex, videotex, encrypted, message, mixed-mode, bilaterally-defined, nationally-defined and externally-defined. Multimedia E-Mail, using the 1988 standard was impossible, since there were no body parts for video, images and music. The voice body part was not of much use since it did not describe how the voice would be encoded. In 1988 also, the telex (TLX) and simple formattable document (SFD) body parts were dropped and new ones added. The new ones were bilaterally-defined and externally-defined (body part types 14 and 15). In 1992, the voice basic body part was dropped but still no video, images and music body parts were adopted. Additional body parts and explicit content type encoding are required before X.400 can carry multimedia mail messages.

While the advantages and disadvantages of X.400-based messaging are still being debated on a daily basis in various forums such as the Internet, many government organizations have implemented or are in the process of implementing X.400-based messaging systems. X.400 is providing important features such as delivery and non-delivery notifications, better audit traces, guaranteed delivery and built-in support for encryption. Those features are necessary for organizations that require electronic mail accountability. The Canadian Government is quite committed to X.400 but so are many other nations. For example, Canada has now in operation at least three X.400 networks: at the Department of National Defence (DND), Canada Post, the Department of Foreign Affairs and International Trade (DFAIT) and at the Government Telecommunications Agency (GTIS). Some of those networks (DFAIT and DND) are currently being upgraded with security mechanisms hat, in the near future, will allow the elimination of older "narrative" message services that are quite manpower intensive. The DND 120 million dollar project (Defence Message Handling System) is in its early stage but it is an approved and funded project.

As X.400 is now the protocol of choice between major government departments, the exchange of multimedia content will become an issue. The exchange of simple file attachments between LANs is sometimes problematic; the exchange of multimedia files has a lot to gain from a standard approach such as the one reported here.

In 1992, the Telecommunications Research Institute of Ontario (TRIO) asked us to implement a multimedia mail system. The goal of the MCRLab effort was to develop and demonstrate an X.400-based multimedia E-Mail prototype [8] that will have a maximum functionality and interoperability with existing systems. It was intended to use an existing X.400 commercial software with minimal modifications to make it multimedia ready. That ought to be done without making the software incompatible and with minimal change to the way the software was used for text only messages. This goal was very similar to what has been done by MIME (Multipurpose Internet Mail Extensions) for the Internet. That was done with a practical approach that is maximizing the use of defined conversion rules and existing presentation applications.

We decided to use MIME for Multimedia Mail and map its body parts into X.400 body parts. Under the mapping approach, the various MIME content-types are mapped into equivalent X.400 EBPs according to RFC 1495. The MIME content-types for which no equivalent X.400 EBPs have been done are created by following the methodology described in RFC-1494.

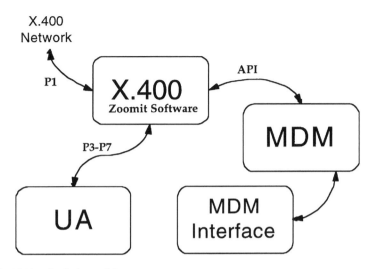

Figure 6. Multimedia display module.

A Multimedia Display Module (MDM) was added to the X.400 software as shown in figure 6. The MDM was added in a way as to become the interface between the multimedia body parts and the user. Normal text messages are still handled by the usual UA (User Agent) in the usual fashion. The X.400 software however has to detect the presence of the MDM and pass multimedia body parts to it if they can be displayed. The actual display of multimedia information will follow the concept of the recommendations made in RFC 1524 by using the WIN.INI file under Windows (figure 7). The MDM was developed on a standard Windows-based 386 PC with a Visual C++ compiler.

The creation of the Multimedia Display Module (MDM) that would become the core element of the prototype posed a few development problems. The MDM as the interface between an X.400 MTA/MS and a standard X.400 UA was an ideal candidate for a Dynamic Link Library (DLL) under Microsoft Windows 3.1. However, the MDM was no ordinary DLL, as it required a main window with an independent user interface, its own variables and memory space. The proper operation of such a DLL could not be done in Microsoft C++. Other options were to have the MDM as a separate executable with a DLL as the interface with the MTA/MS, use Dynamic Data Exchange (DDE), or have the MDM as a separate executable but using Windows messages to communicate with the MTA/MS. MS-Windows messages was the technique selected for its simplicity and it proved to be quite effective. Expert Windows programmers could implement the concept using more advanced techniques such as DDE or even Object Linking and Embedding (OLE) but most of this would be transparent to the user and would not change the concept proposed.

The implementation undertaken by the MCRLab was split in two parts: the lab took care of the multimedia element while the required modification to a standard X.400 MTA/MS was left to a private partner. Figure 7 shows the client interface. Text is displayed in the usual X.400 UA, whereas video, audio, . . . icons are added by the MDM and played by standard MIME media players.

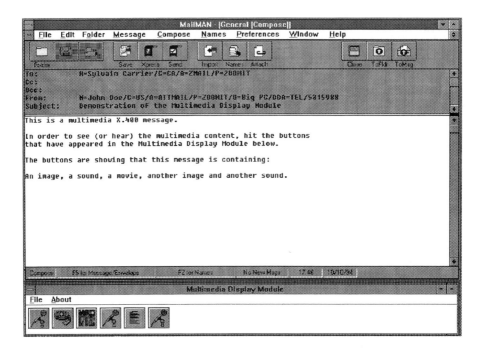

Figure 7. Multimedia mail client interface.

Buttons in the MDM will only appear when multimedia body parts are present. For example, if there is only one image there will be only one button with the image icon. The MDM will not appear at all if there are no multimedia body parts (or if they cannot be handled by the user's workstation). That ensures minimal change to what the user is used to for ordinary messaging. If there are many images or a mix of multimedia body parts, many buttons with the image icon will appear or a mix of image, sound or other icon/buttons corresponding to the body parts present in the message. The user does not have to know where the body parts are as each multimedia body part is identified, sent to the MDM and a corresponding button is automatically shown.

We did not develop a storage concept in this project. The complete message is always sent with all the parts to each user. Other projects such as the BERKOM one did look into this and can send only the references to "big" body parts. The down side could be that user agents can no longer be fully X.400 compliant as they probably have to be modified to handle this reference mechanism. As many implementations are client-server with the standard X.400 interface only between MTAs, that may not be a big problem (as long as the standard MTA to MTA protocol, P1, is standard).

The major challenge in this development was message passing in the Windows operating system. Like most of the University research teams, we had some experience in UNIX development but had difficulty in some Windows tasks. We searched in vain on the Internet and asked for help in many news groups. Our industrial partner could not help in this problem. Eventually, we found a solution from a Windows developer in a major telecommunications industry. Apart from needs of a project with an industrial partner, a University team should stick to the OS that it knows best!

5. Multimedia fax gateway

The term *multimedia fax* appears to be an oxymoron, as it is well known that normal fax refers to transmission of text and images only. However, the worlds of fax and Email are changing and in fact converging. By the year 2000, 70% of the world fax machines will be PC based.

In 1993, inspired by a presentation in an industrial workshop and by [6], we looked closer at the worlds of fax and Internet and initiated a project on the development of a multimedia Fax-MIME gateway. At that time, the Internet Remote Printing Experiment (IRPE) had been announced [16]. Internet Email messages could be routed to remote printer servers, or *cells*. These cells then automatically transmit the Email as local facsimile to the recipient. At that time, many people did not have Internet access for Email, but only fax. We decided to build a gateway that could extend IRPE and not only allow Internet Email (text, TIFF images, Postscript) to Fax users but also allow those users to access Internet services, such as messaging, ftp and Internet news. Moreover, we wanted to carry multimedia files to/ from PC-based fax users. In addition to the IRPE development, ITU-TS had recently developed an extension protocol for Group 3 facsimile, called *Binary File Transfer* (CCITT, Rec. T.434, 1992). BFT-enabled fax boards can be used to transfer multimedia documents in binary form through high-speed modems.

We first developed at the MCRLab the first IRPE server for Canada (now managed by IEEE Canada). We then developed a Fax-MIME gateway (figure 8) [18] that permitted MIME Internet messages to a remote printer service, which in turn did the required BFT transformations and faxed them to a BFT enabled fax machine (PC). Should the gateway detect that the destination fax machine is an ordinary one (non-BFT), it would use Group 3 protocols and only transfer text, TIFF and Postscript parts of the message, with a note

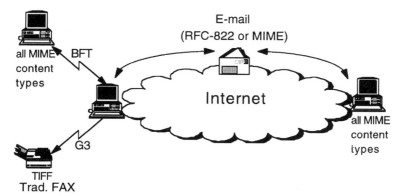

Figure 8. Multimedia fax-MIME gateway.

indicating that other multimedia parts had to be retrieved by a BFT-enabled Fax machine. In the reverse direction, a home user with a BFT-enabled fax machine could route a MIME message to an Internet address through our gateway. The gateway translates from BFT to MIME. Our gateway could provide several advantages over IRPE, for both the Internet and fax communities, including: multimedia message services in a uniform manner (MIME); bi-directional messaging, as opposed to the IRPE unidirectional capability; access to Internet resources for multimedia fax; and a simplified connection/ set-up model, as compared to SLIP/PPP connections.

During the development process a proprietary toolkit made available with the Kalman Technologies fax card was used to implement the inbound gateway on a PC. Also for the Internet interface of the gateway on the PC, a shareware toolkit was used.

The prototype gateway constructed consisted of two PCs, one implementing the inbound communication and one the outbound one. The inbound (PSTN $\rightarrow$ Internet) gateway that we implemented was fully functional. The multimedia message would be transmitted as a BFT transmission to the inbound server, which would e-mail it (MIME) to the destination Internet address. This server was implemented on a PC rather than a UNIX machine. The reason here was that the BFT fax cards that we had (Kalman Technologies and Delrina) were both for the PC environment only. The outbound (Internet $\rightarrow$ PSTN) gateway was the IRPE server that we set up at MCRLab. This gateway only supported G3 fax. The reason for it not being multimedia were: (i) Implementing the BFT protocol in software was too big a project for the given time (tasks required embedding MIME documents in BFT format and a BFT interface for PSTN) and (ii) the BFT software also needed to be integrated into the IRPE software.

User experience for the inbound communications was limited to the development team only. On the other hand, however, the outbound (IRPE) server was very heavily used (70–80% load) but proved to be very reliable.

6. Multimedia synchronization for a news-on-demand application

The Canadian Institute for Telecommunications Research (CITR) has sponsored five Canadian Universities to take part into a major project called "Broadband Services". The target application was a multimedia News-on-Demand (NoD) service over ATM networking. The constituent projects were designed such that they are complementary and that the results can be integrated into a working prototype. The projects include Multimedia Data Management (Univ. of Alberta), Quality of Service Negotiation and Adaptation (Univ. of Montreal), Synchronization of Multimedia Data (Univ. of Ottawa), a Distributed Continuous-Media File System (Univ. of British Columbia) and Project Integration (Univ. of Waterloo). The MCRLab at the University of Ottawa has been responsible for studying and implementing the synchronization of the multimedia data (figure 9) [15].

The initial overall system architecture is shown in figure 10. The servers are divided in Continuous Media File Servers (CMFS) (audio, video) and Non-Continuous Media File Servers (text, images, graphics). When a user wants to retrieve a NoD article composed of multiple media, the following actions are initiated. The user GUI activates the QoS negotiation module and the DBMS Client Interface. QoS negotiations among the client,

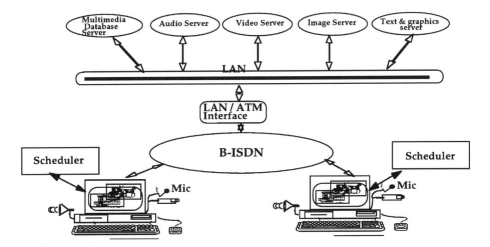

Figure 9. Media scheduler for broadband services NoD application.

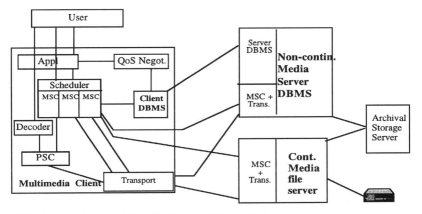

Figure 10. System architecture for broadband services NoD application.

the servers and the network produce QoS parameters that are needed by the synchronization algorithms, namely: delay, jitter and throughput. These parameters are sent to the synchronization scheduler at the client. When a multimedia NoD document is selected at the Client DBMS interface, the DBMS returns to the client the document's media synchronization scenario and the IDs and locations of the media files. The scenario describes the media temporal synchronization relationships.

Our synchronization algorithms are executed in two levels and involve the following modules. At the first level, the "Scheduler" receives the synchronization scenario and negotiated QoS parameters, as also estimates of decoding delays, and uses our Time Flow

Graph (TFG) method in order to schedule the presentation times of the media, i.e., the times that the servers should start transmitting their media. In this way, minimal buffering will be required at the client. "Media Synchronization Controllers (MSCs)" at both the client and the servers are activated. These modules are responsible for opening and controlling ATM connections, plus some other functions to be described later. The Client MSCs are also implementing the second level of synchronization, the so called Stream Synchronization Protocol (SSP) and deliver the media to the various players for screen display. SSP involves co-ordination among client MSCs in sending data to the display devices. Synchronization "fine-tuning" is provided in this way. The XTP 4.0 protocol, ported to AIX by the UBC team, was first used over ATM for data transport. It was later replaced by a Multimedia Transport Protocol (MTP), a variant of UDP, since XTP was taking too much CPU power. Coded media (MJPEG, MPEG) are first received at the "Pre-decoder Synchronization Controller" (PSC) of the client. The PSC control of MJPEG streams uses buffer occupancy as a control parameter. Upper and Lower thresholds for this parameter have been defined. If the buffer hits the lower threshold, i.e., threat of starvation, a time expanding policy is used. Namely, a unit is sent twice to the decoder instead of once. If the buffer hits the upper threshold, i.e., threat of overflow, a time compression policy is used. Namely, units are discarded in an alternate way in order to speed up the buffer freeing process. The CMFS could not provide QoS guarantees, but only an admission control procedure.

A prototype centralized synchronization scheduler was designed, implemented and demonstrated at the MCRLab first over Token Ring, then Ethernet, connecting two IBM RS-6000 workstations (server and client). It was then tested over ATM in early 1995, when the MCRLab obtained a Newbridge VIVID ATM switch. The prototype presented a Graphical User Interface (GUI), designed using the IBM AIX Interface Composer software and a sample news article (coding: Audio: digital mu-law, 176 kbps (22 kHz, 8 bits/sample); compressed video: initially Berkeley MPEG-1 (software), 15 frames/s, 160×112 pixels, then Motion JPEG using the IBM Ultimedia Services MotionJPEG card). The Audio and Video streams of the news article were synchronized (Lip-Synchronization). Text Captions (translation of audio) were synchronized with the audio stream (this is an attractive feature when news captions are required in another language, or for audio-impaired people). The design of the Scheduler and the MSCs was modified several times, in order to facilitate integration with the other teams. ATM trials of the centralized synchronization prototype on OCRInet, the ATM research network in Ottawa, were performed. User experience indicated that the two-level synchronization algorithms were robust enough to recover from synchronization errors introduced by the ATM network (eight ATM switches in the path). The latest prototype (summer 1996) uses UBC's Real-Time Threads (RTT) from the client scheduler to the CMFS. ATM trials from the Ottawa synchronization client to the Vancouver CMFS will be performed over the 5,000 km CANARIE National ATM Test Network.

This NoD collaborative application development was a true challenge, since it involved software integration of distant University teams. Tight project management and coordination, of which we take only partial credit, resulted in a successful NoD prototype. The prototype is currently extended to include a distributed synchronization scheduler and a QoS monitoring function.

7. Multimedia whiteboard for distance learning applications

Multimedia Distance Learning is a key multimedia application, of importance to academic institutions, industry and government laboratories, since (a) education and training are of major significance to all of them, (b) it costs a lot to send people physically to training courses and (c) Internet, in its current or future broadband versions, will permit opening up the world knowledge base from a desktop! Our view of a Distance Learning Application or system is that it should permit not only the retrieval of multimedia documents from distant databases or digital libraries but <u>also</u> allow opening up real-time conferencing connections and tele-consultation or collaborative work among participants, with shared multimedia applications whiteboards. We may note at this point that these objectives are also common in other multimedia applications: Tele-medicine, Banking Kiosks, Insurance Claims, Investment Counseling, etc.

Since 1994, the "Multimedia Communications" project, sponsored by the Telecommunications Research Institute of Ontario (TRIO), the Knowledge Connection Co., and the NSERC Industrial Oriented Research program, is aimed at the development of a multimedia distance learning application and testing and performance evaluation of it over the ATM testbed OCRInet.

We have completed (1996) a prototype of a simple multimedia whiteboard (MMwb) using the InSoft Co. OpenDVE Multimedia Applications Development Environment over a conferencing engine (*Communique!*, a multi-platform conferencing product of InSoft Co., which was developed on OpenDVE). During a *Communique!* videoconference over ATM, and upon command of a participant, a multimedia server multicasts a Distance Learning document onto the Shared Whiteboard (MMwb) of all conference participants, which is brought at the desktop as a "plugin" of *Communique!* (figure 11).

Retrieved continuous media (video, audio) are played on all workstations' MMwb simultaneously. For media synchronization purposes, we did not use the algorithms reported

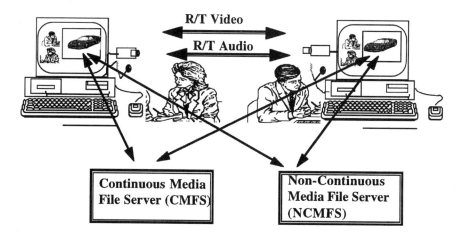

Figure 11.   Multimedia whiteboard (MMwb) in a distance learning session.

in the previous section. Each conference member keeps a dynamically updated table which translates other conference members' local time to its own. Commands are time stamped locally before being distributed along with the current whiteboard status. Each computer plays its media with reference to its own clock. Commands involving scheduling, like the *play* instruction, are slightly delayed and take effect simultaneously on all the workstations involved. Other control events take effect immediately and the status variables are used to ensure consistent results for all the conference participants.

The Multimedia Whiteboard brings recorded audio and video to the virtual conference room of a Communique! session and lets the participants share synchronized video/audio. Each conference member can play, stop, rewind, or otherwise control a motion JPEG movie with text captions. The Multimedia Whiteboard offers a work frame for the possible insertion of other media, like VRML and hypertext documents.

User experience indicated that MMwb played during a live videoconference, required a lot of CPU power to maintain both the live conferencing windows and a large shared MJPEG file. Even our SPARC 20s running Solaris 2.3, 2.4 and 2.5, had difficulty in that task. Current efforts on this prototype focus on multimedia server multicasting aspects.

8.   JETS: Java-Enabled TeleCollaboration System

The objective of this project, sponsored by the TeleLearning Network of Centres of Excellence and initiated in 1995, was to design, implement and test over ATM, a telelearning system offering, among other things, the ability to view, manipulate and share 3-D objects.

Our Machine Intelligence Research Laboratory (MIRLab) developed the following procedure for capturing 3-D objects. The 3-D model of an object can be determined from a camera and a structured light, by matching the view from the camera with the projected pattern. The structured light is a grid of color-coded vertical and horizontal lines. This color coding eliminates errors in finding the correspondence between the image from the camera and the structured light. This matching yields points in 3-D. Typically one view of the object yields 1000 and more 3-D points. Since multi-views of the object are required to fully represent it, there is a need for a method which models the projected points and interpolates between the grid lines to simplify the 3-D representation. The modeling is done with Non-Uniform Rational B-Splines (NURBS). NURBS are the only type of curves which can be used to model any type of shapes (e.g., planes, circles and hyperboloids). NURBS make the process of interpolation more accurate since they are of a higher degree than a simple linear interpolation.

In the context of telelearning, the 3-D model has to be represented in a common format. VRML has been chosen, since it is widely accepted as the Internet standard for 3-D representation of objects. A VRML object can be generated from its NURBS representation with varying accuracy. This is particularly useful, when objects are grouped together. The smaller ones having less details than the bigger ones.

Using Java, we then developed JETS (Java-Enabled TeleCollaboration System) that permits collaborative work, including 3-D object manipulation. In this system (figure 12), users in conferencing mode on their Java-enabled browsers have four separate "windows" (frames), realized by four Java applets, for sharing a) VRML objects , b) HTML documents,

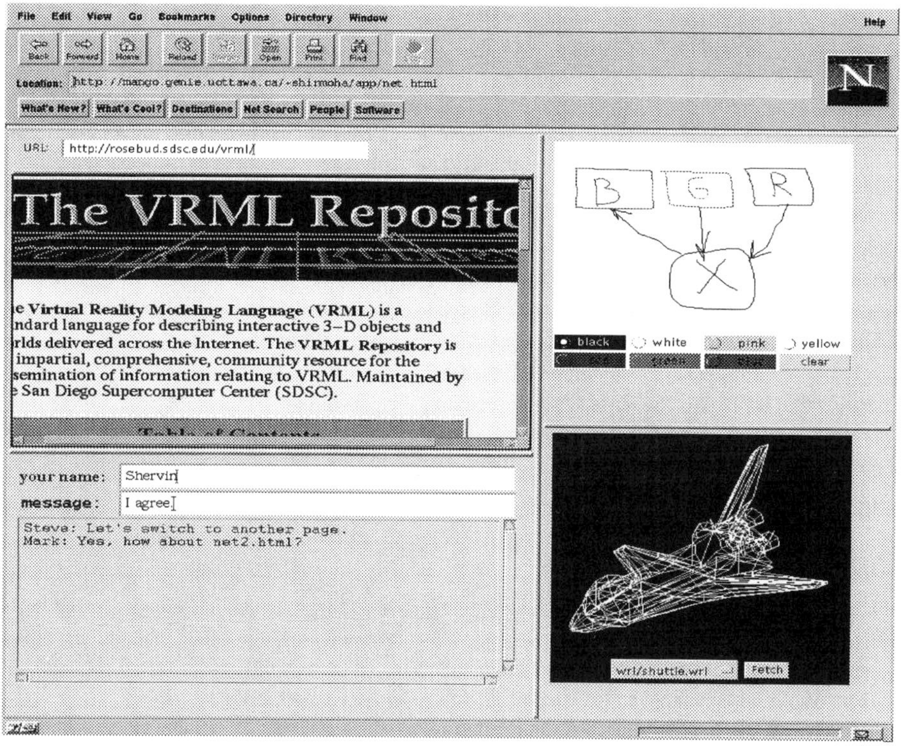

Figure 12. Screen of JETS applets.

as also c) a "chat" window for passing to each other text messages and d) a shared whiteboard. Sharing all this information in real-time is the main contribution of this research. JETS uses a client-server model for multi-participant applications, using multimedia windows. The main advantage of this system remains in its ease of use. Since the application on the client side is a Java applet, it can run on any platform, any operating system and any Java-enabled web browser. Any required downloading or installation is handled by Java. Thus, the users only have to make sure that they are calling the URL of our server.

The server was implemented using the Java language for the prototype, although any language could have been used. Writing it in C++, instead of Java, would have made its response faster. Its responsibility lies in asynchronous message passing among clients, as well as the handling of special requests from clients, such as access to a shared object. The server also provides consistency for applications that require consistency, such as VRML-Browsers, and it monitors the state of every individual client during the session.

Generic client and server objects are available to provide the above mentioned functionalities as BASIC functionalities. They can easily be extended to support additional specific tasks since they are coded in Java, which is a true object-oriented language. We must also note that both the client and the server are multi-threaded to provide high performance.

Performance tests of the JETS application over the regional ATM network (OCRInet) were done between the MCRLab and the NORTEL COBRAnet laboratory in Ottawa. Details on JETS are given in [21].

User experience with this prototype indicates wide acceptance. Response times on Solaris and Windows95 platforms were quite fast, but running under Netscape on the PowerMacs was rather slow. Just-In-Time compilers (JITS) can certainly increase the speed.

9. Conclusions

This paper described the development of multimedia applications prototypes, and experiences gained therefrom, at the Multimedia Communications Research Lab (MCRLab), University of Ottawa. Applications developed in medicine, collaborative work, multimedia mail, multimedia fax, news-on-demand and multimedia distance learning were described. One important lesson learned was that applications should be designed from the very beginning to fit user needs.

Acknowledgments

Applications development is a team effort and I want to thank the many MCRLab students, researchers and collaborators at other institutions that participated in the above described work. Particular recognition should be given to Morris Goldberg, Jim Mastronardi, John Robertson, Gary Belanger (for the IRIS project), Louise Lamont, Grant Henderson, Jeff Brinskelle, Renaud Brimont, Jerzy Jarmasz, Mourad Daami (for the synchronization NoD project), Sylvain Carrier (for multimedia mail), Sanjiv Patel (for multimedia fax), Steve Caron, Susanna Yi Zheng (for the multimedia whiteboard) and Shervin Shirmohammadi (for the JETS prototype). The financial and in kind support of this research by the Centres of Excellence (Telecomunications Research Institute of Ontario, Canadian Institute for Telecommunications Research, TeleLearning Research Network), industry (NORTEL, Bell Canada, Telesat Canada, Zoomit Co., Kalman Technologies, Delrina, InSoft Co. (now Netscape)) and government agencies (NSERC, URIF) are also gratefully acknowledged.

References

1. H.M. Abdel-Wahab, S.U. Guan, and J. Nievergelt, "Shared workspaces for group collaboration: An experiment using internet and UNIX interprocess communications," IEEE Communications Magazine, Vol. 26, No. 11, pp. 10–16, Nov. 1988.
2. L. Aguilar and J.J. Garcia Luna Aceves, "Architecture for a multimedia teleconferencing system," Proc. ACM SIGCOMM'86 Symposium, Aug. 1986, pp. 126–136.
3. S.R. Ahuja, J.R. Ensor, and D.N. Horn, "The rapport multimedia conferencing system," Conf. on Office Information Systems, Palo Alto, CA., March 1988, pp. 1–8.
4. S.R. Ahuja, J.R. Ensor, D.N. Horn, and D.D. Seligmann, "Conducting multimedia conferences with rapport," Proc. IEEE Multimedia'89, Montebello, Canada, paper 1.1, April 1989.
5. P.K. Andleigh and K. Thakrar, Multimedia Systems Design, Prentice Hall, 1996.
6. B.St. Arnaud, "Multimedia fax," Proc. ICCC Multimedia Communications'93, Banff, Canada, April 1993.

7. N.S. Borenstein, Multimedia Applications Development with the Andrew Toolkit, Prentice Hall: Englewood Cliffs, NJ, 1990.
8. S. Carrier and N.D. Georganas, "Practical multimedia electronic mail on X.400," IEEE Multimedia, Vol. 2, No. 4, pp. 12–22, Dec. 1995.
9. H. Forsdick, "Explorations into real-time multimedia conferencing," Computer Messaging Systems, R. Uhlig (Ed.), IFIP, North Holland, pp. 331–347, 1986.
10. N.D. Georganas, M. Goldberg, L. Orozco-Barbosa, and J. Mastronardi, "A multimedia communications system for medical applications," Proc. IEEE Intern. Communications Conf. (ICC'89), Boston, June 1989, pp. 49.2.1–49.2.5.
11. M. Goldberg, J. Robertson, G. Bélanger, N.D. Georganas, J. Mastronardi, S. Cohn-Sfetcu, R. Dillon, and J. Tombaugh, "A multimedia medical communication link between a radiology department and an emergency department," J. of Digital Imaging, Vol. 2, No. 2, pp. 92–98, May 1989.
12. A. Karmouch, L. Orozco-Barbosa, N.D. Georganas, and M. Goldberg, "A multimedia medical communications system," IEEE J. Selected Areas in Communications, Vol. 8, No. 3, pp. 325–339, April 1990.
13. R. Kositpaiboon, P. Tsingotjidis, L. Orozco, and N.D. Georganas, "Packetized radiographic image transfer over local area networks for diagnosis and conferencing," IEEE J. Selected Areas in Communications, Vol. 7, No. 5, pp. 842–856, June 1989.
14. L. Lamont, G. Henderson, and N.D. Georganas, "A multimedia real-time conferencing system: Architecture and implementation," Proc. IBM CASCON'93, Toronto, Oct. 1993.
15. L. Lamont, L. Li, R. Brimont, and N.D. Georganas, "Synchronization of multimedia data for a multimedia news-on-demand application," IEEE J. Selected Areas in Communications: Synchronization Issues in Multimedia Communications, Vol. 14, No. 1, Jan. 1996.
16. C. Malamud and M.T. Rose, "Principles of operation for the TPC.INT subdomain: Remote printing-technical procedures," RFC 1528, RFC 1529, RFC 1530, Oct. 1993.
17. L. Orozco-Barbosa, A. Karmouch, N.D. Georganas, and M. Goldberg, "A multimedia inter-hospital communications system for medical consultations," IEEE J. Selected Areas in Communications, Vol. 10, No. 7, pp. 1145–1157, Sep. 1992.
18. S. Patel, G. Henderson, and N.D. Georganas, "Multimedia fax-MIME interworking," IEEE Multimedia, Vol. 1, No. 4, pp. 64–70, Winter 1994.
19. S. Sakata, "Development and evaluation of an in-house multimedia desktop conference system," IEEE J. Selected Areas in Communications, Vol. 8, No. 3, pp. 340–347, April 1990.
20. S. Sarin and I. Greif, "Computer-based real-time conferencing system," IEEE Computer, Vol. 18, No. 10, pp. 33–45, Oct. 1985.
21. S. Shirmohammadi and N.D. Georganas, "JETS: A java enabled telecollaboration system," In process. IEEE Multimedia Systems'97 , Ottawa, June 1997.
22. R. Steinmetz and K. Nahrstedt, Multimedia: Computing, Communications and Applications, Prentice Hall, 1995.
23. R.H. Thomas, H.C. Forsdick, T.R. Crowley, R.W. Schaaf, R.S. Tomlinson, V.M. Travers, and G.G. Robertson, "Diamond: A multimedia message system built on a distributed architecture," IEEE Computer, Vol. 18, No. 12, pp. 65–78, Dec. 1985.

12

Multimedia Meets the Internet: Present and Future

MICHAEL WYNBLATT wynblatt@scr.siemens.com
DAN BENSON dbenson@scr.siemens.com
ARDING HSU ahsu@scr.siemens.com
Siemens Corporate Research Princeton, New Jersey
http://www.scr.siemens.com/mt.htm

FELIX BRETSHNEIDER felix.bretshneider@internet.siemens.com
LARRY SCHESSEL larry.schessel@internet.siemens.com
GRAHAM HOWARD graham.howard@internet.siemens.com
Siemens Public Communications Networks, Internet Solutions, Boca Raton, Florida
http://www.internet.siemens.com

Abstract. Recently maturing technologies for digital multimedia and the Internet exhibit a powerful synergy with the potential to provide a whole range of new applications and tools. Not only do multimedia and Internet technologies offer enhancements to one another, but their combination suggests entirely new communication paradigms. This paper reviews the state of the art in Internet multimedia from the perspectives of the developer, the network administrator, the content provider and the user, and then investigates some of the up-and-coming application areas: participatory publishing, enriched multimedia databases, integration of the WWW with broadcast media, and universal messaging systems. Remaining challenges, such as missing authoring features, multimedia information management, network latency, and browsing issues, are then discussed.

Keywords: multimedia information systems, online information services, comunications applications, computers and society, computers in publishing

1. Introduction

Among the most exciting technological developments in the past few years are the maturation of digital multimedia and of the Internet's World Wide Web into consumer-ready technologies. Digital multimedia, the ability to create and include images, audio, and animated content, along with text, in digital compositions, promises to fundamentally change the way in which people communicate and chronicle their lives. The World Wide Web offers the most powerful and wide reaching new publishing medium since television, and may well surpass all previous media in its scope and importance.

One of the most interesting aspects of these two technologies is that they are complementary. The Internet promises to enhance multimedia by making it more widely available and practical, while multimedia is what has brought the Internet into the mainstream. Moreover, the synergy between the two technologies promises entirely new metaphors in publishing, communication and commerce.

The Internet promises to impact multimedia computing in three important ways. The first is that it allows content vendors virtually unlimited storage capability for their applications and data. Traditional software distribution on floppy disks or CD-ROMs is quite restrictive to multimedia developers, due to the high storage demands of digital audio and video. The Digital Versatile Disc (DVD) [1] offers an improvement, but still bounds the quantity of media which can be included. The Internet gives the user direct access to the vendor's possibly vast storage facilities, albeit with a restricted transfer rate. In this way, the quantity and quality of the audio, video and image data that a developer may include within a multimedia presentation is significantly increased. It also allows for more interactive and customizable applications, since large amounts of media make it possible to offer the user more choices.

The second major impact of the Internet on multimedia is the addition of an important new multimedia application domain: communication. Without networks, multimedia is generally limited to prefab presentations of one author's ideas, with user interaction mostly limited to navigating through the presentation. Once attached to a network, especially the Internet, multimedia can be used for real multi-way applications, unlocking the great power of audio and video for transferring live data. The promise of truly interactive television and radio is one of the more exciting prospects of the near future. Multimedia collaboration tools have already found application in a few specialized fields, such as medicine and academics, and we expect to see such tools used for a wider variety of applications in the future.

A final important impact of the Internet is that it gives the general public broad access to sources of digital audio, video and images. If digital multimedia is to become commonplace in everyday communication, everyday people must have access to digital content. The Internet not only provides vast collections of free media, but also allows users access to the collections provided by commercial content developers. In a sense, the Internet acts as a huge shared database of content. With such a database, it is no longer necessary to have expensive digitizing hardware and software in order to include non-text media in a document.

Multimedia's impact on the Internet is clear: without multimedia, the World Wide Web [52] would not exist as it does today. The text-only WWW, and its pre-cursor, gopher, predated NCSA's graphical Mosaic browser [31] by several years, but it wasn't until Mosaic added images and graphics that the Web really took off. Today, the Web is adorned with visual media of all kinds, including animated graphics and images, and a large amount of audio content is also available. It's fair to say that a great deal of the Web's popularity has stemmed from these compelling visual and audio presentations.

One important example of this is the integration of the mainstream mass media into the Web. Traditional mass media channels, like television networks and magazines, have always used non-text media extensively, especially in their advertisements. Before such services were available on the Web, there was very little mainstream media presence on the Web. With the addition of images, graphics, audio, and video and other types of animation, we have seen nearly all major national magazines, newspapers, and television networks create a significant presence on the Web. Their presence has, in turn, improved the breadth and timeliness, and thus the utility, of the Web's information content.

The impact of multimedia on the Internet is not entirely positive. One problem is that non-text data is much more resource intensive than text, especially in terms of bandwidth requirements. On the WWW, load-time latency is significantly increased due to the much larger size of individual pages. On the USENET, groups for distributing binary images account for a large percentage of the total bandwidth used, despite producing a comparably small number of articles. Moreover, the Internet has long suffered from the problem of information overload, that is, there is so much information present that it can be difficult to find exactly what you want, even if it is available. Non-text data tends to exacerbate this problem, since such data is particularly difficult to index or search. Overall, providing content in non-text formats makes finding it more difficult and retrieving it slower.

Thus far we have discussed how both multimedia and the Internet are affected by their combination. Section 2 of this paper describes the current state of the art, the technologies which make this combination possible. But the convergence of the Internet and multimedia yields more than just the sum of the two parts; there is a synergy between the two that opens up a wide range of new applications and entirely new paradigms of communication and information management. Section 3 of this paper discusses some of these potentially exciting new uses for multimedia. Section 4 looks at what challenges await the designers of these applications, how these challenges might be met, and the future of multimedia on the Internet.

2. The state of the art

In this section we present the current state of the art of multimedia on the Internet, at the time of our writing. This technology is evolving so quickly that some of our discussion may have become dated just in the time it took to publish this paper, but hopefully not too much of it. After a brief overview of architecture of the Internet, the discussion is divided into sections by task, featuring the tales of the developer, the content provider, the network, and the user.

2.1. General architecture of the Internet

Figure 1 shows a representation of the Internet from the perspective of a corporate user. The user is part of a proprietary network of computers called an *Intranet*, which may consist of one or more LANs or WANs. Access to the Intranet from the outside is restricted to a few local gateways, which support communications services but otherwise provide a *firewall* against unauthorized use. A *proxy* machine allows the Intranet user to take part in two-way protocols, by providing a trusted host outside the firewall. Beyond the firewall, hundreds of other LANs and WANs are connected by the Internet backbone, as well as millions of single users connecting through Internet Service Providers. The user may access information or run programs stored on remote servers, and communicate with remote users, using dozens of protocols for data transfer.

2.2. The developer's tale

From the perspective of the multimedia developer, the important questions regarding the state of multimedia on the Internet, are "What kinds of multimedia can I author for the Internet", and "How good are the authoring tools I can use to develop them?". Since the major forum for publishing on the Internet, multimedia or otherwise, is now the World Wide Web, the questions may be best answered in that context. As we consider the different tools for preparing WWW multimedia, we'll try to stress three particular issues that differentiate

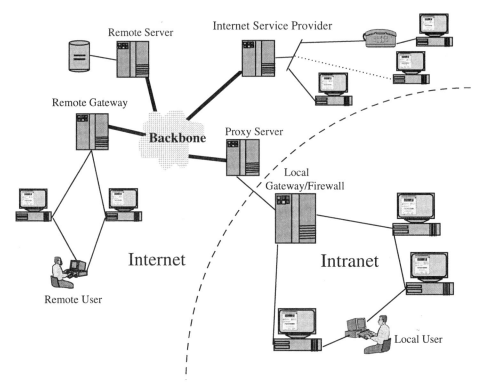

Figure 1.   An individual's perspective of the Internet.

them: how well they support dynamic media, how much interactivity they allow, and what limitations they suffer from.

The primary language for authoring on the Web is HTML [53]. As the 'T' implies, HTML is a text oriented language, and most of the features it provides are for representing text. Additionally, HTML offers support for two-dimensional layout specifications, including the layout of still images. Most WWW browsers support several image formats, notably GIF and JPEG. Support for images includes "image maps" defined at either the client or server side, which allow the designation of hot spots within an image. HTML also allows access to some HTTP commands, such as automatic timed refreshes, which can be used to do simple animation. Further, the GIF89a image format allows "flip book" style animations to be encoded, and several major WWW browsers support presentation of this feature, often called "animated GIF".

Many software companies seem to be betting that WWW page design programs, which output HTML code, are the next "killer app", and dozens are hitting the marketplace. Many such programs feature graphical layout spaces and generate the HTML code automatically. These tools save a lot of time, and allow less technically inclined developers to get involved with the web design process. Fine tuning of truly custom pages, however, is still in the domain of the text editor.

As a multimedia specification language, HTML is somewhat limited. Except for the features mentioned above, it generally does not support dynamic presentations, nor does it offer much support for audio. Moreover, since HTML does not describe how to render any given data format, each individual browser must be equipped to handle each data format which it encounters, or fail to render its content. Finally, although HTML does support form-based interaction, more sophisticated types of direct manipulation are not supported. As a result, support for several technologies which help to fill these needs have been provided by many WWW browsers, the most notable being applets, plugins, helper applications and scripting languages.

Applets are small programs written in a platform independent bytecode, which can be referenced by a WWW page. The client-side browser downloads and executes the applet upon accessing the page. An applet occupies a fixed rectangle of space on the web page, and can render output to that space and accept mouse and keyboard input focused within it. Since applets are arbitrarily complex programs, they can generate sophisticated output including all manner of multimedia. Indeed, the term "applet" seems to have become synonymous with the small animations which adorn many web pages. The major limitation of this complexity is that the playback environment varies widely from user to user, and as is discussed in Section 4, more demanding applets may have to be scaled back to allow access to a broad base of users. Applets can also access local resources like audio speakers, although security concerns limit the generality of the access.

Currently, the most popular and widely supported language for building applets is *Java* [20]. A wide range of Java classes are available to support animation and audio output, both of digital waveforms and MIDI data, but are conspicuously absent for audio input. One can work around this shortcoming using Java's native code interface, but at the cost of platform independence and security.

From the developer's perspective, the major drawback of Java is that it is a programmer's language, rather than a multimedia developer's language. Java programming, only a few skips away from C++ programming, is very unlike the drag-drop-and-script multimedia specification systems found with most modern authoring tools. But developers who would prefer visual and 4GL environments to hard core programming have an excellent alternative: content developed from such programs may be accessible using plugins.

Plugins are code libraries, dynamically linked to a WWW browser at runtime. The plugin API, developed by Netscape and also supported by several other browsers, is intended to allow a WWW browser to support a new data format without requiring a modification or re-release of the browser itself. The browser recognizes a particular data format by its filename extension, and then passes the data along to the plugin module for rendering. The plugin may be assigned a rectangle on the page in which to draw, or may be given the entire page. Plugins can be built for any data type, making browsers extremely extensible in the data that they can represent, and in turn allowing developers a great flexibility in the types and formats of media they can employ. *A helper application* is an alternative to a plugin, in which the browser invokes an independent application to render an unknown data format. In the case of helper applications, the rendering is always separate from the browser window, and thus is not integrated into the presentation of the rest of the web page.

The rendering process used by a plugin can be much more sophisticated than simply drawing a bitmap on the screen. The plugin can capture user events, create separate threads, and generally act as an independent program from the browser. This flexibility allows very complex data formats to be rendered faithfully. Notably, the *Shockwave* [24] plugin can render output files from Macromedia's popular multimedia authoring tools, Director and Authorware. Multimedia developers can therefore build presentations using these high level tools, and have the results be immediately accessible on the Internet.

Another data format for which plugins are available is *VRML* [4]. VRML allows the description of three dimensional regions, and VRML plugins like *Cosmo* [43] and *Live3D* [35] allow the user to navigate within these regions. Three dimensional environments, as discussed in Section 5, are a promising area for new kinds of information representation and human-computer interfaces on the Net. Thanks to these plugins, VRML can be incorporated directly on any web page.

Other popular data formats for which plugins have already been built include: MPEG, AVI, MIDI, WAV, AU, AIFF, AutoCAD, Corel, TIFF, PDF, OLE/ActiveX, Astound and PowerPoint.

One of the major limitations of plugins is that the API does not allow much interaction between the plugin and the browser itself. The original concept for a plugin was that it would receive its data from the browser, but otherwise work independently. The API therefore does not allow the browser and plugin to share events or pass much information back and forth. This limits the degree to which the presentation made by the plugin can be integrated with other presentations on a Web page. The limitation is mitigated somewhat by the new *LiveConnect* [39] technology which allows communication between applets and plugins.

An authoring technology which is widely available on the WWW is *scripting*. Scripts are programs which are distributed on web pages as source code and interpreted by the client side browser. The term "scripts" might suggest a higher level language than traditional programming languages, but this is somewhat misleading. The two most popular WWW scripting languages, *JavaScript* [36] and *VBScript* [28], aren't particularly approachable for non-programmers, but rather are subsets of popular programming languages, Java and Visual Basic.

Although they may seem similar, there are several practical differences between precompiled WWW applets and uncompiled WWW scripts. One is that the scripting languages have been designed to integrate easily with HTML forms, and so most client-side form-based processing is done with scripts. A second difference is that while applets are generally self-contained within a web page, WWW scripts can actually generate new HTML code on the fly, and thus can have significant impact on their environment. Similarly, since scripts are included directly in a web page, they can be created or changed dynamically whenever HTML can be generated, such as by other scripts, or by CGI programs. Finally, applets are written in complete programming languages while scripts are written in language subsets. As a result, the scripts do not have the entire functionality of applets; for example, although Java offers a wide variety of classes to support animation, JavaScript does not include those classes.

Overall, the technologies for authoring multimedia on the Web are maturing, and are nearing the level of authoring multimedia for CD-ROMs. Table 1 gives a summary of the

Table 1. A comparison of WWW authoring technologies.

Feature	HTML	Applets	Scripts	Plugins
Dynamic Media	launch only	arbitrary control	launch only	arbitrary control
Interactivity with user	forms with server support	flexible within regions	forms on client side, with some event handling	flexible within regions
Generate HTML on the fly	no	no	yes	no
Complexity	moderate	as traditional programming	moderate	building a plugin is quite complex, authoring plugin data can be done at a high level
Tools	many available, improving quality	first generation IDEs	primitive stage	none for building plugin, many for authoring plugin data

relative capabilities of the different technologies. Some of the difficulties still encountered are described in Section 4.

2.3. The content provider's tale

Once a multimedia presentation has been authored, the next question is how can it be organized and made available to Internet users. Once again, the emphasis of this section will be on the WWW.

One simple way to provide multimedia content on the Internet is through a remote access file system like *WebNFS* [46]. WebNFS allows traditional file sharing, in the UNIX style, across the Internet. The World Wide Web has instead been built around a browsing- oriented model in which accesses are by *document* rather than by file, and accessing a document is equivalent to rendering it. To this end, WWW servers have been developed which deliver a single document at a time, where a document may consist of several files. Making use of both the HTTP and FTP transfer protocols, WWW servers can transfer all of the data types described in the developer's tale: HTML, applets, WWW scripts, and plugin data. WWW servers make use of Universal Resource Locators (URLs) to index files of various types. The URL identifies a server, a file within that server's filesystem, and possibly a marker within the file (for HTML files).

The major limitation of URL-based indexing is that it requires a filesystem-like storage model, and does not allow the structured organization and query-style access of a more traditional database. This restriction quickly led to the development of the *CGI* [30], which allows web clients to launch independent programs on the server side. These programs can be used for any purpose, but are often query engines for server-side databases. The CGI protocol allows the programs to accept text parameters, and to return HTML files, which may include references to non-text, applet, and plugin data, as well as WWW scripts. Thus, interactive multimedia presentations are possible in which content is generated on-the-fly from database stores as a result of user actions. The CGI paradigm is extended in the *BGI* [44] protocol which allows the client to send binary data through the interface as well as text, but BGI is not widely supported at this writing.

CGI-based multimedia applications are limited primarily in the granularity of interactivity which they allow. Since a full web page is transmitted as the result of each CGI request, and the latency of a client-server communication must be endured, very fine grained interactivity is not possible. Another limitation of CGI is that a separate process is generated by each client request. This overhead is not reasonable if a server is expected to handle large numbers of simultaneous requests. This drawback is addressed in BGI, as well as in several built-in web-server APIs like *ISAPI* [27], *NSAPI* [38], and *Apache* [47], which only use a light-weight thread for each request.

Another limitation of CGI applications is that they are completely transaction based, and do not maintain state information about clients. This limitation has been remedied to some extent with recent support in WWW browsers of *cookies*. Cookies are data blobs stored on a clients machine, which are sent and retrieved by the server side. They allow the server to note the previous transactions of the client and use this information during current transactions, in effect maintaining some state information.

Given these technologies, the major problem for accessing multimedia content over the Internet is not retrieving known content but finding the content to begin with. In this regard, Internet multimedia is limited by the more general problem of indexing non-text media. The primary indexing schemes used on the Web today are variations of the *Wide Area Information System (WAIS)* protocol [45], which allows keyword indices of a site's contents to be queried remotely, and third party search engines. The latter use a number of indexing techniques to build proprietary databases of WWW URLs, also indexed by keyword. These techniques are optimized for text based information and usually involve such measures as the number of occurrences of a keyword on a page, or the relative position of several keywords on a page. None of these systems are particularly effective at recovering non-text objects, as they are successful only when those objects appear with extensive text information which categorize them.

One alternative to keyword search which has some prominence on the Web is search by progressive refinement. Some third party ventures have built hierarchical catalogs of WWW pages which are organized by category [58]. A user may navigate down through the hierarchy by choosing progressively more refined categories until eventually a leaf category is reached. The leaves are URLs, which may then be loaded. This kind of catalog can be equally useful for finding text or non-text information. Unfortunately, such catalogs must be built manually so they do not offer an improvement over keyword searches in terms of the effort required to index non-text information.

2.4.   *Delivery techniques and protocols: The network's tale*

Between the server and the client, a protocol is needed to transfer data across the network. The *MIME* [7] format was developed so that Internet e-mail messages could include an arbitrary variety of data formats. Foreshadowing the emergence of plugins on the WWW, MIME could transfer any data format but left the responsibility of rendering the data to the receiver's local software. MIME was the first widely used multimedia transfer mechanism on the Internet.

The development of the WWW was encouraged by the wide acceptance of the HTTP protocol [5], which optimizes the transfer of text, and also can communicate with servers of other protocols including FTP, SMTP, WAIS, and gopher. This was the first step in supporting on-demand multimedia transport over the WWW. Since WWW documents are expected to be reaccessed by the same user, HTTP also includes facilities determining the last modified date of a document, so that caching schemes can be used.

Although HTTP allows on-demand access to arbitrary data formats, early browsers had the limitation that an entire file must be downloaded before it could be rendered. This led to a very long latency period for storage-intensive media like audio and video. For dynamic media, this latency was unwarranted: since the medium's samples are typically sent in chronological order, the client could begin playback immediately upon receiving the first few samples. Playback of this kind requires a moderately consistent delivery rate and a buffering scheme, otherwise quality of service is unacceptable; these features are not present in HTTP.

To meet this challenge, several continuous stream delivery protocols have been developed, such as *RealAudio* [41]. On the client-side, RealAudio works in conjunction with a WWW browser as a helper application (see Section 2.2), so that hyperlinks to audio files can be provided within WWW pages. RealAudio works by bypassing the HTTP server, and connecting directly to a dedicated server. Since individual packets are not critical in audio, UDP is used as the underlying transport protocol, which improves the transfer rate at the risk of lost packets. RealAudio also uses a custom compression format to help reconstruct lost data, filling in the gaps due to lost packets.

While RealAudio is designed for client-initiated audio-on-demand, the *Internet Multicast Backbone* (*MBONE*) [40] is a set of protocols designed for server-initiated multicasting. The MBONE is used for audio or video presentations, sometimes live, which are sent to a large number of clients at the same time. Like RealAudio, the MBONE uses unreliable service in order to gain a performance benefit, providing a UDP-like protocol built on top of IP-multicast.

RealAudio and the MBONE are *best effort* protocols, in the sense that the quality of the output may vary widely as a result of the current network traffic. For higher quality presentations, it would be desirable to reserve network bandwidth to guarantee a certain quality of service. The *Resource Reservation Protocol* (*RSVP*) [8] is designed to allow applications to request a certain amount of dedicated bandwidth between the client and server. This protocol is obviously useful for stream oriented multimedia presentations and one of its first applications will be in the MBONE.

The *Real-time Transport Protocol* (*RTP*) [19] is a proposed standard for Internet transport suitable for audio or video over either UDP or IP-multicast. Netscape's announced *LiveMedia* [37] system is based on RTP, but as of this writing, LiveMedia is not yet available. Other notable streaming protocols for the WWW include *ActiveMovie* [26] and *VDO* [48].

2.5. *The user's tale*

From the user's perspective, there are basically two ways in which to use multimedia over the Internet today. The first is to use a WWW browser to view, and possibly interact with, the multimedia content. The second is to use a multimedia communications tool to interact directly with other people.

At a minimum, WWW browsers are expected to support the standard WWW browsing environment, first introduced with NCSA's *Mosaic* [31]. This environment provides a two-dimensional rendering of structured text and graphics, which the user manipulates through a windows/menus/pushbuttons GUI. It is desirable that browsers support all of the specification methods described in Section 2.2: HTML, animated GIF, applets, WWW scripting, and plugins. Several commercial browsers do. Additionally, many browsers can play audio files which are attached by links, and the *background audio* tag specifies an audio file to be played automatically while the page is being viewed. The *Lynx* browser [6] is still maintained as the standard bearer for text-only browsers.

In the constantly changing WWW, browsers are expected to be extensible to new data types, and plugins provide this extensibility. HTML is also constantly being extended with new custom tags, which eventually become official or *de facto* standards. Since the extension of HTML is driven by competition among the browser companies themselves, the latest browsers support a wide variety of the latest tags.

Several techniques have been developed for browsing the Web based around the idea of using audio for input or output. Work at Texas Instruments has investigated applying speech recognition technology to a browser interface so that a user can follow WWW links simply by speaking the text of the link anchor [13]. This work also offers an alternative to graphical forms, by allowing web pages to offer a set of speech-based inputs. Systems like *WebOnCall* [33] from NetPhonic, give access to participating Web sites over a normal telephone. In WebOnCall, a user browses the web using touch tone keys to select from lists of links, and listens to audio versions of a page's content provided by text-to-speech conversion or pre-recorded narration. A fax-back service is provided so that purely visual information can still be made available if necessary, or to obviate the need for an extended phone call in order to browse long documents.

WebTV [51] technology, licensed recently by several hardware manufacturers, allows users to browse the WWW using their television sets. The system renders HTML and image formats for the low resolution of television and provides a custom input device used like a remote control. Although WebTV does not itself offer new multimedia features, it does hint at a future direction for Internet multimedia: integration with traditional television.

Multimedia has been important in the communication side of the Internet as well. In the asynchronous world, the MIME protocol has been very successful in allowing the transmission of non-text data. The idea behind MIME is that each message only has the responsibility of identifying the boundaries and types of its content. The receiving system is responsible for understanding how to render any particular content "part". In a heterogeneous environment like the Internet, with dozens of data formats, this approach was critical to encourage widespread use of the protocol. Many e-mail programs also allow the inclusion of formatting instructions for text, so that text fonts, styles, and colors may be rendered in a message.

Since these instructions are contained in a separate MIME part, mail readers which only handle ASCII text are not inconvenienced.

Multimedia has also been useful in the new "near synchronous" communications methods offered on the WWW. Web servers equipped with appropriate CGI programs have been turned into IRC-like chat-servers, in which a user reads other people's comments on a "chat page", enters their own comments using a form, and a CGI program recreates the chat page with the new comments appended at the bottom. The new twist here is that the posted comments can include any HTML instructions which the browser understands. Not only can text be formatted, but non-text media can be included directly into the posted message.

But multimedia's most prominent impact on Internet communications has been in synchronous communications. Internet conferencing tools like Insoft's *CoolTalk* [34] rely heavily on audio channels and graphical whiteboards for information transfer. Some, like Vocaltec's *Internet Conference* [50], actually include a shared WWW browser. Video conferencing tools, like Connectix's *VideoPhone* [10], can also run across the Internet, although their frame rate over Internet is reduced compared to their LAN performance. Internet telephone applications, which allow users to make phone calls without paying long distance charges, have been immediate hits, and one list notes 27 different vendors providing this service already [29]. Since 8 KHz, 16-bit playback is well within the capability of modern PCs, telephone quality audio can be realized.

3.   Future multimedia applications for the internet

The synergy between the Internet and multimedia promises to bring about a tremendous explosion in application possibilities. Over the years we've seen how technologies such as graphical user interfaces, the mouse, and plug-and-play devices made computers easier to use and resulted in greatly increasing the number and variety of people who use computers. And these new groups of users in turn created new demands on the technology as well as added new creative input to applications. With the tremendous growth of the Internet we expect a similar burst of creativity and technological demands for multimedia applications. The most important trend will probably be toward more personalized and interactive applications, through which the user can make their use of the Internet more productive. In this section we give just a few examples of the direction where things are heading and the kinds of things we might expect to see.

3.1.   Participatory publishing

Web pages are currently the most common form of publishing on the Internet. When compared with other traditional forms of mass media, from print to electronic broadcasts, Internet publishing has the unique abilities of interactivity and data sharing. With this in mind, we envision a new form of publishing that we call "participatory publishing" in which readers are able to contribute to and influence the content along with authors. This might range from individual requests for specific topics to personalized novels to live commentaries on top of web pages. With more direct reader participation, writers and editors of multimedia publications will begin to create and deliver documents that can be customized and modified according to individual readers. We envision several potential applications illustrated below.

One of the early services promoted with video-on-demand, and now with Internet services, is personalized news. The general notion of the major news services is that they provide all worthy news and subscribers merely have to decide which stories they are most interested in, the format and degree of detail they desire, and when they want to receive the stories. With participatory publishing, one can imagine subscribers taking a more active role such as making requests for specific stories they would like to have covered or investigative inquiry into topics that may otherwise go unnoticed. This would be a major step toward providing news that people really want.

Another form of participatory publishing involves advertisers. We will undoubtedly see more and more innovative ways of introducing advertising on the WWW, as it seems to be one of the easiest ways of producing revenue on the Internet. One of the best forms of advertising is word-of-mouth, in the sense of having others do your advertising for you. We already see this in many ways, such as conspicuous labels on clothing or brand names on T-shirts where, in effect, people actually pay money to advertise for companies! Now imagine companies on the web that offer not T-shirts, but multimedia messages or presentations that are very entertaining and compelling—e.g., a video of a TV commercial or a cartoon animation. Furthermore, these multimedia presentations are customizable and can be personalized. For example, you might send in a picture of your face and get back an animation in which you star as an avatar which just happens to be drinking a can of a well-known soft drink. You could place this animation on your own home page or send it to others as a sort of web-postcard.

A third form of participatory publishing is adding dynamic annotations to web pages. Other than email links and input forms, current web pages are essentially one-way communication from publisher to reader. One of the major functionalities missing in current web browsers is the ability to capture comments and discussions related to the contents of web pages, store these comments, and share them with others. There have been some attempts of adding text or links as annotations to web pages [12, 31] but our notion of web page annotation goes well beyond these approaches. Next generation multimedia web browsers, like one under development at Siemens Corporate Research, will be capable of capturing free-form dynamic annotations on top of web pages. Recorded annotations can be made accessible to others through the WWW, or sent directly as messages. We believe this form of participatory publishing will greatly enhance information exchange through the web.

3.2. Enriched multimedia databases

Databases already play a significant role on the web, but we believe the uses and demands of databases on the Internet and Intranet will increase dramatically, particularly when it comes to managing multimedia. If we consider the WWW as an enormous collection of loosely organized multimedia, one of the most fundamental and difficult problems is finding what you want. It is no surprise that some of the first Internet applications to become so popular are the myriad of search services available on the web. But these initial search engines are vastly limited when it comes to multimedia, particularly content-based searching.

Suppose you would like to find a sound bite of a dog barking. Certainly, with all the multimedia that people have made available on the web there must be an audio clip of a dog barking somewhere. Better yet, what about a video clip or even an animation of a barking dog? The future "web multimedia search service" will be able to find all relevant sources containing desired media types given a description of specific content. Choices will range from search services based on pre-defined, hierarchical categories to more free-form searches with natural-language front-ends. Going beyond the use of text to formulate queries, advanced media search engines will be capable of accepting various types of media as input to do similarity searches, e.g., "Find pictures that look like this picture," [2, 15, 17] or "Find audio clips of music where the melody goes like this. . ." [11].

Databases will deliver everything from straight HTML text documents to full-blown multimedia presentations. Users browsing the web will not know or care about the actual source of the information. In fact, some queries will be invisibly dispatched across the web to multiple databases, merging the results from each database to form a coherent result. Future Internet multimedia databases will be capable of *constructing* multimedia to match the query request. A simple example of this is an animation database that returns an animated GIF file consisting of several small pictures that are selected according to the query criteria. Imagine a weather report web page that constructs dynamic icons on-the-fly based on current forecast models, traffic report web sites, or other sites offering animated rendering of dynamic data. A more complex database might construct a video sequence by mixing together certain actors, backgrounds, or sound tracks. Negroponte has suggested entire television programs based on objects and scripts rather than raster images [32].

Given the cost and effort it often takes to create significant multimedia compositions, many authors will want to reuse data whenever possible. Besides the data itself, whether it's a picture, video, or composition, there may be links to associated information that goes along with the data. Internet multimedia databases will store *wrapped media* that encapsulate multimedia objects to include additional inherent information about that object such as alternative renderings, URLs, or other related documents. In this way, a wrapped media object inserted in any web document automatically inherits its own *content-links* (see Section 4.2). For example, a picture of the Mona Lisa might be wrapped along with a URL pointing to a page about Leonardo Di Vinci, or text giving a brief history of the painting. Any web document that includes the wrapped picture also gets the link and history text. In a sense, the wrapped media becomes an independent document or composition in and of itself.

3.3. Integration of the WWW with traditional broadcast media

One of the first metaphors to catch hold on the WWW was publishing. The Web was seen as an alternative to printed material, not only for companies to distribute product information and colleges to post their course guides, but for mass-market magazines and technical journals as well. Not only have dozens of "webzines" been created, available only on the Internet, but nearly all major American print magazines and newspapers have a significant web presence as well.

As non-text media becomes more integrated into the WWW, the Internet will begin to receive similar attention from the non-print mass media. Already, several radio stations have begun making their live feed available over the WWW (e.g., [21, 22, 56]), using protocols like RealAudio. No doubt, with the maturation of protocols like RTP, television stations will follow suit. In fact, a few stations already offer freeze-frame access to their live feeds [9, 55]. Since broadcast media stations earn money almost exclusively from advertising, unlike the more subscription-oriented print media, the WWW is an even more natural fit. With the emergence of technologies like WebTV (see Section 2.5) the distinction between WWW content and broadcast content will become even more blurred in the mind of the user.

As WWW and broadcast media become more coupled, they will likely become more integrated. WWW URLs will appear regularly on TV feeds and both TV and computer interfaces will allow users to follow them immediately with their integrated browsers. Broadcast media will absorb some of the interactivity of the WWW, sending multiple simultaneous streams which the user can navigate between, depending on their personal interests. Advertisers will welcome the chance to market toward more specific audiences. Moreover, just as Web pages today choose their advertisements based on a user's profile and history, so will broadcast stream commercials attempt to target the most likely customers.

Perhaps the biggest change in mass media will come from the explosion of small audience, WWW-based audio and video "stations". The capital required to start a true broadcast station, or even a cable TV station, puts it out of the range of the small businesses or hobbyists. But to start a WWW-based station will require more modest costs. Just as broadcast stations can attach their feed to the Internet, so eventually will small business ventures and even amateurs. These endeavors, using either advertising or subscription fees to cover their costs, will produce a huge variety of radio- and TV-like programs for both broad and narrow audiences. The world-wide reach of the WWW offers to provide a reasonable audience base for even the most esoteric subjects. Some programs will support active user feedback or even participation, and in some cases the line between video-conferencing and television programming may itself become blurred.

3.4.   Webspace in three dimensions

The current metaphor for the content of the WWW is "documents". When users access a remote site, they view the content much like they would read a magazine. Unlike a magazine, WWW documents may be created on the fly, customized to a particular user, and can include time-based or interactive content. Like a magazine however, the Web has adopted a metaphor of viewing "pages", which is both a familiar and a useful concept for structuring information.

An alternative metaphor which has begun to appear [54] is that WWW content represents "spaces". Support for the *Virtual Reality Modeling Language* (*VRML*) in WWW browsers, through the use of plugins like *Cosmo* [43] and *Live3D* [35], is beginning to allow developers to present their content as places rather than documents. Rather than flipping through the pages of a document, users "fly" through the virtual space, exploring it as they might explore a real room or building. "Doors" encountered in these spaces may serve as hyperlinks, allowing access to new spaces. More than ever, WWW sites could become "places you go" rather than just information you download.

Whether or not the "spaces" metaphor gains as much acceptance as the document metaphor, or even replaces it, depends mainly on what additional utility it can provide. The challenge for user-interface designers, information managers, and artists, is to take advantage of the rich metaphor of "space" to help organize WWW content and make it more easily accessible.

3.5. Universal messaging systems

One by-product of the recent advances in telecommunications is that electronic messages now take many different forms. Many professionals are accustomed to sending and receiving FAXes, voicemail, and e-mail containing a variety of document types and media. As FAX and voice services become more common over the Internet, it will be natural to move toward a *universal mailbox*, a single repository for voice, image, and text data, and whatever other media become popular. Such a mailbox will not only offer the convenience of centralized message retrieval, it will also allow retrieval of messages from many different types of access stations. Text-to-speech synthesis will allow telephone access to text e-mail, and FAX-back interfaces will allow access to image data in the absence of a monitor. At Siemens Corporate Research we have developed a prototype system which allows this functionality, as well as a novel phone/FAX interface for browsing long documents, and even video messages, without the use of a computer monitor. This type of functionality will lead to a more complete blending of media and merging of information devices.

Another form of messaging which multimedia and the Internet allow is the *replayable workspace* [16, 25], in which a user records a session in their workspace, including voice and mouse gestures. Once recorded, the session becomes an animated presentation which can be delivered asynchronously via e-mail or the WWW. Such presentations are particularly useful for tutorials and online help systems, where a demonstration can be significantly more descriptive than a series of instructions.

4. Challenges and visions

Before the applications described in Section 3 can be realized there are a number of challenges which must be addressed. In this section we present some of the issues which we think are more unique to multimedia applications on the Internet, rather than to Internet applications as a whole. For some of these challenges we present our vision of how they may be overcome in the future.

4.1. The developer's tale: Missing authoring features

The tools available for authoring multimedia on the Internet are primarily the same tools available for authoring multimedia CD-ROMs. This arrangement has the advantage of jump-starting Internet multimedia with the richness of these existing tools, but it also means that some features which are desirable in Internet environments may not be well supported.

4.1.1. Hypermedia support. Hypertext is one of the central ideas underlying the WWW. The generalization of hypertext to hypermedia requires that non-text media can both anchor hyperlinks and also be the target of hyperlinks. In HTML, links can be anchored on any size unit of text and can be targeted on a label at any arbitrary location within a passage. Hypermedia should allow non-text media the same flexibility. In the image domain, current support for hyperlinks is fairly good. Image-maps allow hyperlinks to be anchored over arbitrary parts of an image, and entire images may be the target of hyperlinks. The ability to target a part of an image with a hyperlink is missing, and that could be increasingly useful as increasing transmission speeds encourages the use of larger and larger images.

Current support for hyperlinks in dynamic media is not as good. It is not possible, for example, to specify that a link anchor is available during a particular interval of a video or animation. It is not possible to target a link so that it starts a video or animation from some point in the middle. It is not possible to have different hyperlinks cause different directions of playback of the same animation file. Audio has even less support; there has yet to be consensus of what it means to have an anchor in an audio presentation, or how to activate it.

The lack of these features limits the richness of the hypermedia that can be represented on the WWW. Video, animation, and audio are only available as results of navigation, and cannot be part of the navigation itself. Truly interactive hypermedia will allow first-class treatment of all of these kinds of media, so that for example, a menu may be presented as a dynamic video rather than as a static image or list.

Another problem which the Internet brings to hypermedia is what might be called *authoring in the large*. Without the size restrictions which are required in CD-ROM based multimedia, Internet authors can now tackle problems of multimedia presentations involving very large collections of documents or objects. Typically, large databases or collections of existing documents should be structured, linked, and made available on the WWW. If the collections are large enough, automated tools are required, both to make the project feasible and to maintain its consistency.

At Siemens Corporate Research, several tools have been developed to help in this process. Given a database of objects and documents, our *Automated Document Composition Tool* [23] automatically extracts the relevant content, generates a web of hyperlinks within it, and builds a consistent structured multimedia presentation suitable for WWW distribution. For managing video data, our *Video Logging and Archiving Tool* facilitates the segmenting, logging, archiving and efficient retrieval of large quantities of video data, and makes it available from a central server.

4.1.2. Content-based links. Hypermedia on the WWW differs from multimedia on CD-ROMs in that there is much more reuse of media objects. Multimedia CD-ROMs typically carry stand-alone presentations which are not meant to be reconfigured. WWW hypermedia, on the other hand, consists of a huge collection of media objects which can be reused many times in many different presentations. Such reuse is much less common in pure hypertext, since the semantics of a text passage is much less context-sensitive.

The potential for media reuse in hypermedia emphasizes the distinction between *structural hyperlinks* and *content-based hyperlinks* [57]. The links supported in HTML are structural links; an HTML document describes a presentation of several media objects, and the links are specific to the particular document. Content-based links are links which are specific to a particular media object rather than to a particular document. For example, an image of a famous personality might be linked to a text biography, other images, or an audio clip of a famous statement. Such links might be useful in many presentations of the original image. To properly support content-based links, links such as these should be "attached" to the object rather than the document. Any document which included the object would inherit its content-based links. We might call a link which travels with a media object a *sticky link*.

Content-based links represent knowledge about an object; they show context-independent relationships that are known about the object. Since information management of multimedia data is one of the difficult problems on the Internet, the omission of sticky links seems to be a significant loss. Not only would sticky links allow the knowledge inherent in content-based links to be shared widely but following content-based links would yield a much more productive path for automated search engine robots.

4.1.3. Degradation of service.

Another flexibility missing from Internet multimedia authoring systems is a way to specify how a presentation should degrade when degradation is necessary. When bandwidth is insufficient, most available streaming protocols make a best effort attempt to meet the need anyway. Often, however, the semantics of the presentation dictate that some information is critical in delivery while other is less important [42]. Faced with insufficient bandwidth, it makes more sense to drop or degrade the less significant data and try to maintain the critical data. Moreover, the way in which a stream should be degraded also depends on the specifics of the presentation. A video stream might be degraded by dropping frames, losing resolution, or reducing the frame rate. Each of those techniques may be appropriate to different types of presentation.

Since the semantics of the presentation are completely unknown to the underlying protocol, that protocol cannot make appropriate decisions about how degradation should take place. The content developer, whose message is to be delivered by the presentation, can best describe the relative importance of the parts of the message, and how they can best be rendered in sub-optimal conditions. Thus the developer should have the opportunity to specify these concerns.

The emerging MPEG-4 standard for audio and video data [18] offers support for user/decoder control of presentation quality. The implication is that the developer may have some choice over which degradation techniques might be available to the user/decoder, but the developers' role in this process is not discussed specifically.

4.1.4. Varied playback environments.

Another challenge which faces Internet multimedia developers is that the environment in which different users view a presentation is extremely varied. Even among typical PC-based systems, variation is found in the processor speed, available memory, display size, color capability, audio capability, and network connection speed. Even different browsers offer support for different data formats, or render them somewhat differently. Users with (currently) non-standard environments, such as TV based browsers, or telephone or other audio based browsers, provide even more extreme variation. More than most computing applications, multimedia presentations tend to be system-dependent, and so this variation presents particular problems for multimedia developers.

The simplest variation is in the power of the target machine. Multimedia playback is taxing on a system's processing and memory capabilities; a 15 MB Shockwave presentation with video clips and tightly synchronized animations performs differently on a 386-based machine with 8 MB RAM than on a Pentium Pro with 64 MB. This problem will always exist, as use of resources in multimedia presentations grows to fill the capabilities of the newest high-end systems.

More fundamental problems arise if a system lacks an entire service, for example a system with no audio card or a text-only terminal. At first glance we may be tempted to dismiss such problems; after all, in a few years will we not be rid of such anachronisms? It's possible however, that lack-of-service problems will not disappear so easily. As Internet access becomes more and more significant in people's lives, we can expect an increase in the number of places and times when people will require access. They will require access stations in more varied locations. If only for reasons of cost, many of these ubiquitous access stations will provide stripped down services. In some environments it may be *desirable* to leave out some services, such as audio playback in public areas. Access stations for the disabled may present similar restrictions.

CD-ROM based multimedia typically comes with a recommended minimum configuration, and WWW based multimedia developers may adopt a similar policy as they build more demanding presentations. In this way, WWW multimedia may differ from the mainly text-based WWW information found so far, which, with some exceptions, has generally been available to any user who could manage an Internet connection. To a certain extent this is unavoidable: a user without audio capability is simply not going to be able to hear audio playback.

Another option would be to allow developers to specify alternative presentations for clients that are unable to render certain media or certain combinations of media. HTML's *image* tag already allows an alternative text description to be specified, for use by clients which cannot render images. This arrangement puts the burden of choice on the browser, freeing the developer from specifying the conditions under which to show one alternative or the other. A more general way of specifying alternatives may go a long way to mitigating the problem of varied playback environments.

4.2. The content provider's tale: Multimedia information management on the Web

One of the most challenging problems in traditional multimedia is information management. Non-text information is decidedly difficult to index in any automated manner, and manual indexing is not only time consuming, it is often incomplete. On the Internet this problem is compounded by the sheer volume of media available, and by the heterogeneous organization which makes many conventional search strategies useless.

The spectacular amount of image and audio data available on the Internet is a gold mine for multimedia developers, especially for those who do not have the facilities to digitize their own content. More importantly, if the use of raster images, audio, and video is ever to become commonplace in the communications of ordinary people, they will first require a vast source of such material to draw upon. The Internet promises to be such a source. In order for the Internet to serve this purpose, however, there must be some way to access all of this content, to find an appropriate media object somewhere on the Web.

Right now that is problematic. Most commercial WWW search engines are keyed entirely by keywords, and thus there is no possibility to query by likeness, or by sketch, or by some other form of example. Moreover, the techniques used in building these databases are keyed around the textual information on the page. Even non-text objects which might be well identified by keyword tags cannot be discovered using these systems.

Several groups are working to bring Query-by-Example-like interfaces to the Web for image data [17, 49]. Related techniques have even been developed for audio data [11]. More research in these areas is needed, however, in both indexing and interface techniques. Even if effective indexing techniques can be developed, tools will be needed either to do automated indexing across the vastness of the Web, or to help WWW authors index their own content.

In the state of the art, searching for information on the Web is difficult for two reasons. The first is that information is distributed fairly randomly around the thousands of web servers. The second is that the information itself is unstructured and can generally only be indexed using free-text indexing techniques. A separate problem is that non-text media on the Web is not indexed at all, forcing a reliance on indexes of nearby text.

One remedy to these problems is to build structure into the Web itself. This cannot be achieved very easily by attempting to organize existing information in a top down manner. A better approach is to have WWW authors build the necessary structure directly into their content. Such an approach may be acceptable to WWW authors whose main motivation of putting content on the WWW is to make it available to the widest possible audience. As authors generally want people to find their content as easily as possible, they may be willing to invest some effort in generating the information needed to allow some indexing of the WWW.

But in order for author generated information to be useful, there must be a standard way of describing the contents of a page or site. The standard must be sufficiently easy to generate so that authors will follow it, and rich enough to allow an improvement in the quality of searches which can be made on the Web. Moreover, it should provide help in finding non-text information as well as text.

One way to provide structured information is to assign scores to each page in a set of different categories. A set of scores forms a *description vector* for each page which can support many search styles and activities. Searches can be declared over a subset of the available categories, or which assign weights to the different categories. Results of searches, including traditional keyword searches, can be presented visually by using pages' score profile to generate icons or relative positions in a result map.

An information management problem closely related to access and retrieval is how to protect intellectual property. The personal computer revolution of the seventies and eighties created all manner of new questions regarding intellectual property, but most of these involved the new medium of software. The proliferation of multimedia on to the Internet has brought a whole new round of questions, but perhaps surprisingly, these questions center on very traditional media like images and audio.

Although it can be a difficult question just to determine exactly what types of media should be copyrightable [14], perhaps the most important question is, how can we protect copyrights that exist in the instant access / instant duplication world of the Internet. If one considers that the purpose of copyrights is not to prevent access, but to recover royalties from use, it seems clear that some pay-per-use model must be developed for digital media. Until such a system is in place, artists will be loathe to make their work too widely available.

4.3.   The network's tale: Network delay

One difficulty with transferring multimedia over the Internet is the large amount of delay experienced. This causes two problems, the infamous "World Wide Wait" experienced by users waiting for their non-text media to load, and latency in client-server interaction which make some applications impractical.

The first problem is that it simply takes a long time to download large files over the Internet. For an extreme example, consider a typical user who connects to the net over a 28.8 Kbps line. A multimedia presentation distributed on CD-ROM can be as large as 660 MB. If the user was to download this presentation in one chunk, it would take about 51 hours! This problem will ease somewhat in the future, but not entirely. If the user upgrades their service to a 128 Kbps ISDN line, the transmission would still require more than eleven hours at sustained peak throughput. Available bandwidth continues to improve; the transmission described would take only about 9 minutes on a 10 Mbps ATM line. Unfortunately, the bandwidth requirement of content tends to increase along with bandwidth available. As ATM or cable modems become more commonplace, content developers will increase the size of their creations.

The above example is extreme because a multimedia presentation can often be downloaded piecemeal, with each media object being fetched on demand. HTML documents, for example, are downloaded one file at a time, allowing the document to be rendered incrementally. HTML is not sufficient, however, for highly dynamic or interactive presentations, and the piecemeal approach is not available with all types of presentation. Applets, for example, are downloaded completely before they are available for use. Similarly, the Shockwave plugin for WWW browsers allows streaming of a presentation's audio track, but otherwise requires that the entire presentation be downloaded before playback can commence. Thus a multimedia presentation designed as an applet or Shockwave file could require a significant loading time. As multimedia developers attempt to provide CD-ROM quality multimedia on the Web, either some piecemeal scheme must be developed for non-HTML presentations, or extreme downloading times must be endured.

The ultimate form of piecemeal downloading is streaming, in which the server sends data continuously and only slightly before it is needed by the client. Streaming makes sense for continuous media such as audio or video in which one can usually predict which units the client will need next. Streaming is not particularly useful for highly interactive presentations, however, since the server will not know which unit to send until the user's input is recorded.

This broaches the second delay problem, which arises in interactive applications. The problem is that there is a delay between the time the user issues a command, and the time which the client receives a response from the server. This delay is *latency* in the traditional sense, and is basically independent of transfer rate; faster modems will not improve the performance much. In an application like a video game, where fine-grained interactivity is critical, such latency is unacceptable. The current solution to the problem of highly interactive presentations is to download the entire presentation initially, but this leads back to the problem described above. Moreover it eliminates the chance to interact with a server-side database when deciding the result of the user's action.

4.4. The user's tale: Multimedia browsing

The browsing metaphor used on the WWW of jumping from page to page is fine for text, but begins to break down somewhat with other media. Two particular problems are with dynamic media, like video, or in very large images, like schematic drawings. In media such as these, browsing is possible *within an object*, as well from object to object, due in one case to the temporal dimension and in the other case to the extended spatial dimension of the media. Similarly, hyperlinks may be targeted to (or from) particular places within these media.

At Siemens Corporate Research, several tools have been developed to help address these problems. Our *Video Browser* automatically breaks a long video sequence up into meaningful segments based on scene changes and represented by key frames. Browsing through the video is facilitated by direct and hierarchical access to the content. Our *Content-Based Video Player* allows video segments to be played back *intelligently*, with variable speed depending on the context of the events within the video. Browsing is facilitated by providing a more efficient scanning mode [3]. Our *Schematic Viewer* facilitates browsing of large images by providing automatic feature location, and supporting hyperlinks to (as well as from) particular regions of an image [23].

5. Conclusions and the role of ISPs

The complexity and rapid change of Internet technology, resulting at least partially from the rapid advancement of Internet multimedia technology, has expanded the role of the *Internet Service Provider* (*ISP*). Where ISPs were once mainly concerned with physical network connections, they are now driven by fierce competition to provide a wide range of server and client-side services. The ISP has become the channel through which the state-of-the-art in Internet technology is constantly provided to businesses and consumers. For example, an ISP outfitted by Siemens might offer services from all four parts of our tale:

Developers: Web-site authoring software, content tailoring for specific browsers or customers, live data feeds, database access tools.
Content Providers: Access control, billing services, content indexing, session management, access statistics, advertising support.

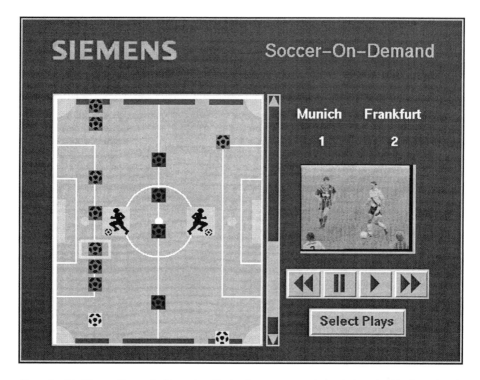

Figure 2. The Siemens *Soccer-On-Demand* application demonstrates modern techniques in video browsing. A user can quickly browse to any part of the match that they want to see.

Networks: Access through analog, ISDN, and high-speed leased lines.
Users: Library and information-base access, video conferencing, media broadcasts, message boards, voice services, "edutainment", surveys and polling, mailing lists.

The synergy between new digital multimedia technologies and the Internet's World Wide Web is undeniable. Not only are both individually enhanced by the presence of the other, but entirely new modes of communication, new delivery mechanisms, and new types of applications are developing from their union.

The first wave of research and application development has been focused on the more technical challenges, and we are still faced with perhaps the harder problem of how best to use our new tools. What new metaphors for publishing and mass media can better reach and involve their audiences? What new information structures can allow users better access to the Web's wealth of multimedia information? What new communication paradigms can add efficiency to our ever more distributed businesses? Our vision of a more deeply structured World Wide Web, and of a close integration between the Web and mass media, hints at answers to these questions, but the door is wide open for investigation and experimentation.

The technologies and standards which are developed in the next few years will have a profound impact on everyday habits of many people for a long time to come.

References

1. R.L. Aas, DVD; http://www.unik.no/~robert/hifi/dvd/
2. G. Ahanger, D. Benson, and T.D.C. Little, "Video query formulation," Proceedings of the SPIE, Vol. 2420; Storage and Retrieval for Image and Video Databases III, pp. 280–291, 1995; http://www.scr.siemens.com/ pubpprs mtpubs/spie95_1.ps
3. F. Arman, R. Depommier, A. Hsu, and M.-Y. Chiu, "Content-based browsing of video sequences," Proceedings of the 1994 ACM Multimedia Conference, ACM, New York, pp. 97–103; http://www.scr.siemens.com/ acmcp.htm
4. G. Bell, A. Parisi, and M. Pesce, The Virtual Reality Modeling Language v1.0 Specification, May 1995; http://vag.vrml.org/ www-vrml/
5. T. Berners-Lee, R. Fielding, and H. Frystyk, Hypertext Transfer Protocol—HTTP/1.0; http://www.ics.uci.edu/ pub/ietf/http/draft-ietf-http-v10-spec-03.html
6. G. Blythe, About Lynx; http://www.phys.nthu.edu.tw/lynxhome/about_lynx/about_lynx.html
7. N. Borenstein and N. Freed, MIME (Multipurpose Internet Mail Extensions), Network Working Group RFC 1521-2; http://www.oac.uci.edu/indiv/ehood/MIME/MIME.html
8. B. Braden and D. Erstin, RSVP—ReSerVation Protocol; http://www.isi.edu/div7/rsvp/rsvp.html
9. Comedy Central Cable Television Station; http://www.comcentral.com/CC/livetv.htm
10. Connectix Corporation, Connectix Videophone for Windows; http://www.connectix.com/connect/VPW.html
11. A. Ghias, J. Logan, D. Chamberlin, and B. Smith, "Query by humming—Large musical information retrieval in an audio database," Proceedings of the 1995 ACM International Conference on Multimedia, pp. 231–236; http://cs.cornell.edu/Info/Faculty/bsmith/query-by-humming.html
12. W. Gramlich, Public Annotation Systems; http://playground.sun.com/~gramlich/1994/annote/index.html
13. C. Hemphill and P. Thrift, "Surfing the Web by voice," Proceedings of the 1995 ACM Multimedia Conference, pp. 215–222.
14. S. Higgs, "MIDI files and copyrights," International MIDI Association Bulletin, Spring 1993; http:// www.higgs.org/MIDI/IMA-Copyright.html
15. T.Y. Hou et al., "A content-based indexing technique using relative geometry features," Proceedings of SPIE/IS&T Symposium on Electronic Imaging Science and Technology, San Jose, 1992, pp. 59–68.
16. T.Y. Hou, A. Hsu, and M.Y. Chiu, "An active multimedia system for delayed conferencing," SPIE Proceedings on High-Speed Networking and Multimedia Computing, pp. 97–104, Feb. 1994; http://www.scr.siemens.com/ pubpprs/mtpubs/spie94_1.ps
17. IBM Corporation, QBIC project; http://wwwqbic.almaden.ibm.com/
18. International Organization for Standardization, ISO/IEC JTC1/SC29/WG11 Coding of Moving Pictures and Audio; http://drogo.cselt.stet.it/mpeg/mpeg-4_requirements.htm
19. Internet Engineering Task Force, RTP: A Transport Protocol for Real-time Applications (RFC 1889); http:// ds.internc.net/rfc/rfc1889.txt
20. Java Soft, The Java Platform; http://www.javasoft.com/aboutJava/index.html
21. KNRK, Portland, Oregon; http://www.teleport.com/~knrk
22. KPLX, Dallas, Texas; http://www.kplx.com
23. P. Liu, K. Hampel, and A. Hsu, "Towards automating the creation of hypermedia service manuals by compiling specifications," Proceedings of the International Conference on Multimedia Computing and Systems, pp. 203–12, 1994; http://www.scr.siemens.com/pubpprs/mtpubs/ieee94_2.ps
24. Macromedia Corporation, Shockwave Center; http://www.macromedia.com/shockwave/
25. N.R. Manohar and A. Prakash, "A flexible architecture for heterogeneous replayable workspaces," Proceedings of the Third IEEE International Conference on Multimedia Computing and Systems, pp. 274–278, June 1996; http://www.eecs.umich.edu/ nelsonr/online-docs/ieeemm96/all.html
26. Microsoft Corporation, ActiveMovie; http://www.microsoft.com/imedia/activemovie/activem.htm

27. Microsoft Corporation, The Microsoft Internet Application Programming Interface; http://www.microsoft.com/msdn/sdk/platforms/doc/sdk/internet/src/isapimrg.htm
28. Microsoft Corporation, VBScript: Working Description; http://www.microsoft.com/intdev/vbs/vbscript-f.htm
29. MIT Research Program on Communications Policy, Internet Telephony Resource List; http://rpcp.mit.edu/~itel/resource.html
30. National Center for Supercomputing Applications at the University of Illinois at Urbana-Champaign, Common Gateway Interface; http://hoohoo.ncsa.uiuc.edu/cgi/intro.html
31. NCSA at University of Illinois in Urbana-Champaign, NCSA Mosaic; http://www.ncsa.uiuc.edu/SDG/Software/Mosaic
32. N. Negroponte, Object Oriented Television, Wired, p. 188, July 1996.
33. NetPhonic Communications Inc., WebOnCall Product Info; http://www.netphonic.com/infopage.htm
34. Netscape Communications Corporation, CoolTalk; http://home.netscape.com/comprod/products/navigator/version_3.0/communication/cooltalk/index.html
35. Netscape Communications Corporation, Introducing Live3D; http://home.netscape.com/misc/developer/conference/proceedings/v1/index.html
36. Netscape Communications Corporation, JavaScript Authoring Guide; http://home.netscape.com/eng/mozilla/Gold/handbook/javascript/index.html
37. Netscape Communications Corporation, Netscape Announces New Real-Time Audio and Video Framework for Internet Applications; http://home.netscape.com/newsref/pr/newsrelease81.html
38. Netscape Communications Corporation, The Netscape Server API; http://home.netscape.com/newsref/std/server_api.html
39. Netscape Communications Corporation, Using LiveConnect; http://home.netscape.com/comprod/products/navigator/version_3.0/building_blocks/liveconnect/how.html
40. B. O'Sullivan, The Internet Multicast Backbone; http://ganges.cs.tcd.ie/4ba2/multicast/bryan/index.html
41. Progressive Networks, Real Audio Product Information; http://www.prognet.com/products/index.html
42. G. Schloss and M. Wynblatt, "Presentation layer primitives for the layered multimedia data model," Proceedings of the IEEE International Conference on Multimedia Communications and Systems, May 1995; http://www.cs.sunysb.edu/ wynblatt/icmcs95.ps
43. Silicon Graphics Incorporated, The Cosmo Player VRML 2.0 Browser; http://vrml.sgi.com/cosmoplayer/specification.html
44. S. Spero, Binary Gateway Interface—An API for Dynamically Extensible HTTP Servers; http://sunsite.unc.edu/mdma-release/BGI-spec.txt
45. A. Steegstra, WAIS and WWW pointers; http://www.cs.vu.nl/~anne007/waissearch/pointers.html#WWWandWAISreading
46. Sun Microsystems, WebNFS: The Filesystem for the World Wide Web; http://www.sun.com/960710/feature2/index.html
47. R. Thau, "Design Considerations for the Apache Server API," Fifth International World Wide Web Conference, Paris, May 1996; http://www5conf.inria.fr/fich_html/papers/P20/Overview.html
48. VDOnet Corporation, VDOnet: Real-Time Video & Audio Over the Internet; http://www.vdo.net
49. Virage Information Retrieval; http://www.virage.com/online/
50. VocalTec, Internet Conference; http://www.vocaltec.com/conference/iconf2.htm
51. WebTV Networks Inc., About WebTV; http://www.webtv.net/HTML/home.about.html
52. World Wide Web Consortium, "About the World Wide Web and the Web Community; http://www.w3.org/pub/WWW/WWW
53. World Wide Web Consortium, HyperText Markup Language (HTML); http://www.w3.org/pub/WWW/MarkUp/
54. Worlds Inc.; http://www.worlds.net
55. WRAL Channel 5, Raleigh, North Carolina; http://www.wral-tv.com/whatson/
56. WRRK, Pittsburgh, Pennsylvania; http://www.rrk.com
57. M. Wynblatt and G. Schloss, "Control layer primitives for the layered multimedia data model," Proceedings of 1995 ACM Multimedia Conference, pp. 167–178; http://www.cs.sunysb.edu/ wynblatt/acm95.ps
58. Yahoo!; http://www.yahoo.com

13

Virtual Sample Processing: Extending the Reach of Multimedia

VANU G. BOSE
ANDREW G. CHIU
DAVID L. TENNENHOUSE

vanu@lcs.mit.edu
agchiu@lcs.mit.edu
dlt@lcs.mit.edu

Software Devices and Systems Group, Laboratory for Computer Science, Massachusetts Institute of Technology,
545 Technology Sq., Cambridge, MA 02139. http://www.sds.lcs.mit.edu/

Abstract. Traditional multimedia systems deal with only a few basic media: text, graphics, audio and video. However, many other types of media, such as ultrasound, infrared and RF signals, can be represented by streams of data samples and processed within multimedia applications. In this paper, we introduce some of these new media domains and identify interesting opportunities enabled by their software-based processing. We also describe our SpectrumWare testbed for experimenting with these new media types and report on our experience to date.

We believe that the time has come to broaden the scope of 'multimedia' to include any form of sampled information. Advances in processor and analog-to-digital conversion technology have brought raw sample streams within the grasp of desktop computers and media processing systems. Coupling these new media types with software-based processing allows the construction of virtual devices that can handle different sample sources, modify their behavior based on information extracted from the media, and transform information between media domains.

Keywords: multimedia, virtual devices, digital signal processing, wireless communication, media transformation

1. Introduction

Today's multimedia systems greatly enhance the user's ability to interact with the environment and with other users at remote locations. Furthermore, as processing power has increased, many media-specific functions are now realized in software. For example, software codecs [12] and image compressors [1] perform signal processing that has traditionally been implemented in custom hardware. This software-based media processing allows applications to make decisions based on the content of the media and to alter their behavior appropriately, thereby enhancing the functionality and flexibility of the overall system.

However, there are many other sources of information, such as ultrasound, instrumentation, infrared and radio frequency (RF) signals which, if captured, could add new dimensions to desktop computing. Until recently, these types of media were inaccessible to multimedia systems, but recent advances in processors, memory subsystems and analog-to-digital conversion have made it possible to extend multimedia into these new realms. For example, figure 1 illustrates the GUI of our virtual oscilloscope.

Our approach to these new media types is to minimize the amount of analog hardware required, and to perform as much of the processing as feasible in application level software. This is accomplished by moving the analog-to-digital (A/D) converter close to the raw

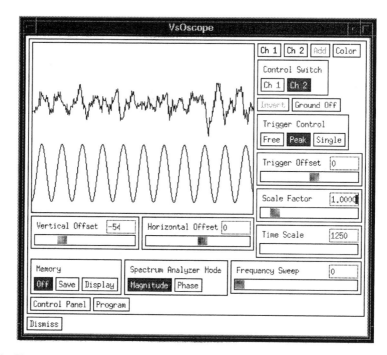

Figure 1. The virtual oscilloscope application.

information source and streaming the data samples into memory that is directly accessible to the application. In most cases, the only hardware involved is a media specific transducer, a pre-amplifier and an anti-aliasing filter. None of this hardware extracts information of interest from the signal, but simply prepares it for digital conversion and software processing. Similar techniques are used to generate outgoing sample streams and, leveraging advanced D/A, convert them to signals.

Once the media signal can been converted from or to a stream of samples, multimedia processing techniques can be leveraged and adapted to construct virtual devices with a range of processing capabilities. However, this in turn introduces some challenges to the design of media-processing systems. These challenges result from the new types of information and control which accompany each media type and the increased bandwidth and processing requirements placed on the system.

This paper describes our experience in building such virtual devices. In the next section we introduce some of the novel application domains that are now within the reach of multimedia processing, and in Section 3 we consider the trends in hardware components that make our approach timely. Section 4 presents the SpectrumWare testbed for wideband sample processing [10] and the adaptation of an earlier multimedia programming environment [6] for use with a number of types of sampled information. We conclude with a discussion of the opportunities and challenges that these new media types present to the multimedia community.

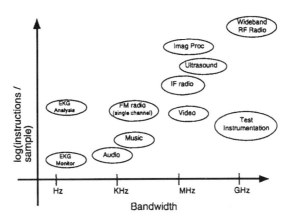

Figure 2. Media application phase space.

2. Application domains

Virtual devices encompass a wide range of potential applications. Only the transducer and the software differ between applications, the network, host and operating system can be shared by all of the devices.

Nonetheless, media types and applications have varying bandwidth and computational requirements and figure 2 shows where various applications lie in this phase space. The bandwidth is the rate at which the information must be digitized, and the instructions per sample is a metric that indicates the amount of processing that the particular media requires. The product of the required bandwidth and the instructions per sample is a rough measure of the average number of instructions per second required to process the media.

Some interesting, non-traditional applications lie towards the edges of the space. For example, many medical devices, such as EKG monitors, only require low bandwidths (typically a few hundred Hz). However applications such as the identification of irregular heartbeats require significant computation on the data. Test instrumentation, such as oscilloscopes, lie in the high-bandwidth, low-computation portion of the space. These devices generally capture data at very high rates but perform little sample processing.

Wideband software radios occupy a demanding portion of the space. High bandwidth is required to digitize a wideband of RF or down-converted portion of the spectrum, and partitioning and demodulation of the individual channels within such bands is computationally intensive. While extremely demanding in terms of computational resources, these radios are very flexible, as all aspects of the communication system, including modulation, coding, and channel assignment, are realized in software. Some wideband applications, such as the AM receiver described in Section 4.2, are feasible on currently available platforms. Other types of radios, such as single channel IF receivers, trade some flexibility for reduced resource requirements and are also realizable today.

The following subsections introduce some specific examples of application domains in which virtual devices can significantly enhance the functionality and utility of the desktop environment.

2.1. Medical instruments

Virtual devices provide an opportunity to create dynamically retargetable medical monitors. One monitor differs from the next only in the type of transducer used and the specific software being executed. With the appropriate transducer, virtual medical monitors such as EKG, EEG, pulse oximetry, temperature and ultrasound can be created. In environments where mobility is essential and weight is at a premium, a single portable device could emulate many different monitors by simply snapping the right transducer into place and running the appropriate software.

Using network-based virtual medical monitors, real-time medical data can be accessed and processed remotely. Coupled with a wireless network link, this greatly enhances a doctor's ability to perform remote diagnosis and consultations. The raw data generated by the transducers could be multicast to multiple locations, such as a local display, a permanent storage site and a remote display. Furthermore, data from multiple transducers can be combined, as described in Section 5.4, to improve the quality of the information extracted from the signals.

2.2. Test instrumentation

Virtual test instruments can save prototyping time and costs. Rather than design a custom test setup for a new analog component or hybrid chip, the input and output can be handled by D/A and A/D converters, and the calibration and characterization of analog components can be performed entirely in software. This reduces the design of test equipment to the construction of the appropriate transducer(s) and the development of test and analysis software.

The software intensive approach also increases the flexibility of test instruments. They can modify their functions, based either on user input or information extracted from the data stream itself, and allow the user to reprogram the instrument dynamically. Section 4.1 describes the implementation of one such test instrument, an oscilloscope, which demonstrates some of this flexibility.

2.3. Radio frequency signals

A tremendous amount of information is available via radio frequency signals: broadcast information, such as radio and television, point to point communications like cellular telephony, and position information from the GPS and Loran systems [2]. As processor speeds continue to increase, wider bands of RF and more sophisticated modulation and coding schemes will come within the grasp of desktop computers, enabling them to incorporate these rich sources of information. A virtual radio, coupled with a true multiband front end [5], would allow emulation of many different radios without any dedicated hardware.

Many wireless networks, such as WaveLAN [11] utilize the 900 MHz ISM band. With a 900 MHz wideband receiver, or a multiband front end, a virtual radio would be capable of interacting with many different wireless networks. This is because all of the processing, right down to coding, modulation and channel assignment are controlled in software. A virtual wireless RF adapter would allow a mobile user access to different wireless networks without having to carry around multiple network adapters.

Finally, we note that in many cases, what is desired is a relatively short burst of information, such as the latest stock quotes or sports scores or, in the case of GPS, an occasional position update. In such instances, the virtual radio could occasionally transform itself into the desired receiver, possibly during a period of inactivity, and receive the update, without the user having to change any hardware.

3. Feasibility

A/D conversion defines the boundary between the analog and digital signal processing domains, but for our purposes, it also defines the boundary between hardware and software-based processing. Eliminating dedicated hardware, either analog or digital, increases the flexibility of the media processing system. This section reviews current A/D conversion technology and the ability of commercially available platforms to handle the data streams produced by these devices.

A/D conversion technology

For the purposes of comparison, we distinguish between three levels of commercially available A/D conversion devices:

- *Narrowband* devices, quantizing at 16 or more bits, have an input bandwidth up to 1 MHz.
- *Wideband* devices, quantizing at 10–14 bits, have an input bandwidth of up to 20 MHz.
- *Broadband* devices, quantizing at 8 bits, have an input bandwidth up to 250 MHz.

Table 1 shows the current capabilities of commercial and research grade analog to digital converters[1].

Processor technology

The important observation that makes the use of general purpose processors feasible is that processor clock rates are increasing at a faster pace than the sampling rates of A/D

Table 1. Comparison of current commercial and research grade A/D converters.

	Sampling rate	
Resolution	Commercial	Research
16 bits	2 MSPS (Analog Devices)	5 MSPS (Hewlett-Packard)
10–14 bits	40 MSPS (Analog Devices)	60 MSPS (Hughes Aircraft)
8 bits	500 MSPS (Harris)	1 GSPS (Hewlett-Packard)

converters. This trend means that more instructions per sample will be available with each new generation of processors, enabling software implementation of more demanding tasks.

The current commercially available DEC Axp chip (21164) issues instructions 500 million times per second, and is capable of issuing four instructions per cycle. At a *wideband* sampling rate of 20 MSPS (i.e., a 10 MHz input bandwidth) this corresponds to an upper bound on the processing budget of 100 instructions per sample.

DSP chips pay careful attention to the synchronization and time management of I/O and computation, keeping interrupt latencies low and avoiding the use of caches, since some DSP applications (e.g., the Fast Fourier Transform) do not display locality of reference. However, these features are not fundamental barriers to signal processing in a workstation environment [9]. The key observation is that *unpredictable* timing events, such as interrupts and cache misses are not specified in units of time, but in units of clock cycles. As processor speeds increase, the absolute amount of time required to service these events decreases, making real-time processing more tractable. Furthermore, commercial processor technology, driven by the workstation market, is improving at a much faster pace than digital signal processor (DSP) technology.

Memory and I/O

Recent improvements in memory, I/O and network technologies have made the acquisition of many wideband signals feasible. The memory interface of new DEC Axp chips (21164) has a maximum pin bandwidth of 1.6 GB/sec [7]. The I/O system of a standard PCI-based workstation supports a transfer rate over 1 Gbps, with planned extension up to 4 Gbps. Finally, commercially available ATM networks run at an OC-12 rate of 622 Mbps.

Putting it all together, we observe that it is feasible for a PCI-based host connected to an ATM network to handle commercial wideband A/D data rates (e.g., 40 MSPS at 12 bits or a 480 Mbps data rate). Furthermore, the sample streams produced by narrowband converters can be easily handled by all of the aforementioned sub-systems.

4. Implementation and experience

We have implemented several virtual devices in the SpectrumWare testbed, as illustrated in figure 3. This section describes the testbed and some of the prototype applications that have been constructed.

The backbone of our prototyping environment for virtual devices is the VuNet [3], an ATM desk area network. Data is captured using network-based appliances, with transducers for RF signals (e.g., AM radio and cellular telephony) as well as conventional baseband audio and video. These signals are processed on hosts (DEC workstations) distributed around the network. We have also developed a PCI bus [4] adapter that allows the same appliances to be directly connected to a PCI-based host and take advantage of the 1 Gbps data transfer rate directly into application accessible memory.

The network appliances, shown in figure 4, have two components: a generic network adaptor and an application-specific daughter card. The network interface is common to

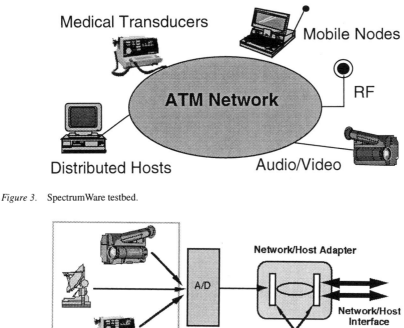

Figure 3. SpectrumWare testbed.

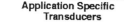

Figure 4. Generic network-based transducer.

all appliances and is implemented on the appliance base while the transducer filtering and A/D conversion are resident on the daughter card. This approach allows specific devices to be rapidly prototyped for very low cost, since the only application-specific daughter card needs to be customized.

The programming environment is based on the VuSystem [6], which has demonstrated the feasibility of a software-based approach to conventional media, including audio, video, text and graphics. The VuSystem implements a two level strategy in which programs are partitioned along an *in-band* axis that supports the flow of temporally sensitive information, and an *out-of-band* axis that supports event driven program components such as the user interface and the configuration of the in-band processing pipeline. The in band processing components are arranged into modules that exchange data in dynamically typed and time-stamped *payloads* through input and output ports.

The VuSystem has been extended to support a variety of new media types. In particular, payload types have been added to handle sampled and complex valued data streams, as well as framed bytes and generic bit streams. Sampled data payloads support a broad range of media. Each payload represents a fragment of a sequence of samples with no inherent framing. Complex data payloads are used to represent the Fourier transforms of sampled data. These payloads have a natural framing that is determined by the windowing function used prior to computing the FFT.

The infrastructure described above is being used to prototype a range of distributed virtual devices, such as test and measurement equipment, a diagnostic ultrasound system and radio receivers for broadcast, cellular telephony and wireless LAN applications. The following sections detail the implementation of these prototype systems.

4.1.   Test instrumentation

This section describes a prototype instrumentation application, a virtual oscilloscope and spectrum analyzer. The network appliance for the oscilloscope consists of an analog sensor, an anti-aliasing filter and an A/D converter. The data stream from the converter is segmented into ATM cells which are then transmitted over the network to the memory of a host machine. The application obtains the data from the network via a socket interface, and a VuSystem source module assembles the incoming data into time stamped payloads that are then passed to processing modules within the application.

In addition to the real signal source, a simulated source has been created. This source is useful not only for testing and debugging processing modules, but as a known reference for comparison purposes. The source is also used as a signal generator, whose output stream can be directed to the D/A converter. Figure 1 is a screen shot of a virtual oscilloscope application which is simultaneously displaying data from a network appliance and a simulated source. The controls on the user interface allow the user to modify oscilloscope parameters, much like on a hardware oscilloscope.

The flexibility of the software implementation allows the oscilloscope to be reprogrammed in ways that are not possible in hardware based oscilloscopes. The trigger function can be any algorithm that can be expressed as a C++ program, involving current, past and future samples, as well as pattern matching algorithms and information derived from computation on the sample stream.

The software implementation also takes advantage of the large amounts of storage available in the desktop environment to save multiple waveforms in memory or to disk for permanent storage. Once multiple waveforms have been stored in memory, the oscilloscope can manipulate and combine them to derive new signals for display, storage, or use in the triggering function.

The input to the oscilloscope is a stream of samples and its output is a sequence of pixel maps with 320×240 resolution, displayed through an X-windows application. In effect, the application is performing a mapping between the instrumentation and video media domains.

An output rate of 30 video frames per second corresponds to a data rate of 18.4 Mbps. While running at this output rate, the oscilloscope can sink data streams in excess of 3.6 Mbps on both DEC 3000 model 400 and Sun UltraSparc1 workstations and streams of 1.8 Mbps on a 120 MHz Intel Pentium system. The oscilloscope actually outputs data at a higher rate than it takes in, since video frames contain significantly more data than the serial input stream. Since all of the processing is in application software, any resources saved by reducing the output frame rate could be applied to additional processing of the data, or to the support of higher input data rates. For example, if the output frame rate on

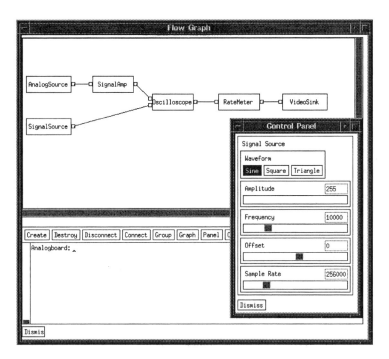

Figure 5.   Visual programming interface.

the Pentium system is reduced to 20 frames per second, the applications is then capable of sinking input data rates of 2.4 Mbps.

The oscilloscope can be dynamically reconfigured, while running, via the visual programming interface shown in figure 5. Modules can be modified, created, or destroyed through this interface, dynamically altering the functionality of the application. Each of the modules shown in the flow graph has an associated control panel, through which parameters specific to that module can be modified. For example, the control panel for the simulated source allows the user to change the waveform, frequency, DC offset and sampling rate of the generated signal.

Spectrum analysis

In figure 6, an FFT module has been inserted into the processing stream while the application is running. The FFT takes in payloads of the type *SampleData* and outputs payloads of the type *ComplexData* containing the Fourier transform of a windowed section of the incoming data. The number of payloads coming in to the module is not necessarily equal to the number leaving, as the windowing function determines the size of the outgoing payloads. The oscilloscope module, noticing that the type of payloads it is being passed has changed, automatically transforms itself into a spectrum analyzer and displays the frequency data. A screen shot of the spectrum analyzer is shown in figure 7. In this example, the signal source

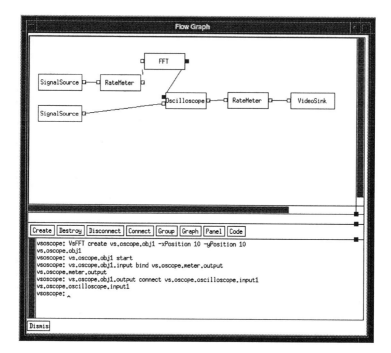

Figure 6. Dynamic incorporation of FFT module.

is generating a square wave, and the spectrum analyzer shows the associated harmonic components.

The oscilloscope program takes direction both from the user, via the graphical interface, and from the information stream itself by analyzing the media coming in. The application can make decisions based on the content of the media and modify itself, launch new applications and provide information that might otherwise be inaccessible to the user.

4.2. AM radio

There is a tremendous amount of information available through conventional broadcast media such as radio and television. The information present in these media signals can be incorporated into user applications once it has been extracted from the media stream. This section describes a system where broadcast radio media is transformed into audio streams.

An entire AM radio transmission and reception demonstration has been implemented in the testbed. The *Source* module takes an input from a file containing μlaw-compressed audio, which is then converted to 16-bit linear audio by the *AudioConverter* module. This signal is then modulated onto an AM carrier and passed to the *AmDemodulator*, which performs asynchronous AM detection. The resulting audio signal is then μlaw compressed

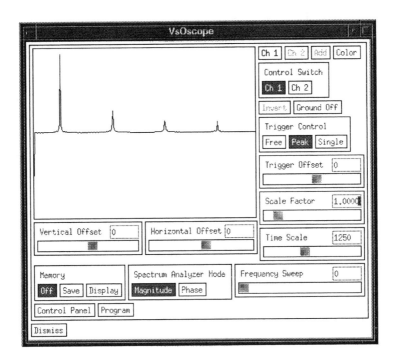

Figure 7. Spectrum analyzer.

back to its original form. The system has been run in real time handling a 64 kbps audio input, modulating this onto an AM carrier sampled at 4 MHz and then demodulating to produce a 64 kbps output stream.

Although this example emulates a traditional AM receiver, the software implementation lends itself to much more flexible designs. Multiple channels can be simultaneously demodulated and information from different channels can be combined. While this may not be particularly useful for conventional broadcast applications, it can add new capabilities to point-to-point services such as wireless networking. Multiple disjoint sections of spectrum can be treated as one logical higher bandwidth channel, allowing bandwidth to be dynamically assigned to different users as needed.

Since the AM modulator produces samples of an actual RF signal, simulations of wireless channels can be performed by simply connecting a channel simulation module to the output of the modulator. To this end, an additive white Gaussian noise channel module has been implemented for the purpose of evaluating the performance of different demodulation algorithms in the presence of noise.

4.3. IP software radio

An IP software radio integrates the notion of a software radio with the IP networking layer. Without changing any hardware, this radio could interoperate with IP networks employing

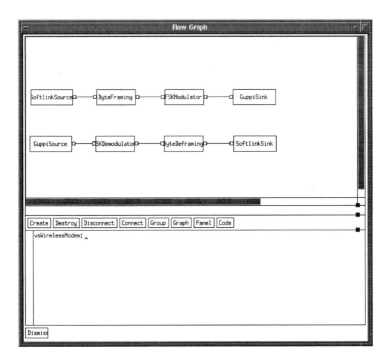

Figure 8.   IP software radio.

different air standards, such as CDMA, CDPD and FDMA. To demonstrate some of this flexibility, we have prototyped an IP software radio, as illustrated in figure 8.

This system is different from the previous examples as it has two separate processing streams running simultaneously, one for receiving data, and the other for transmitting. The SoftLink Source is a user-level interface to the IP layer, which allows the *radio* to forward IP packets to and from the network. The example illustrated applies simple byte level and packet level framing schemes to the IP packets and then FSK modulates the framed data. The resulting RF data is then transmitted to a General Purpose PCI Interface (GuPPI) [4] which transfers the data to a D/A converter connected to an antenna. On the receive side, the digitized RF signal is demodulated and de-framed, resulting in IP packets which are then passed down to the IP layer for further processing or routing. Modules for performing CDMA transmission and reception have been created, and can be dropped in as replacements for the FSK modules. This allows interoperation with two different kinds of networks, without any additional hardware.

Table 2 indicates the number of processor cycles required to perform the different tasks[2]. The units for each measurement differ, since the modules operate on different media types. For example, the FSK modulator outputs IF samples at a 4 MHz sampling rate, but 10 of these samples correspond to one framed byte. The relevant metric for the modulator is the number of processor clock cycles required to produce each output sample. Similarly, the demodulator is evaluated in terms of the number of cycles required per input sample.

Table 2. Average number of cycles required to perform the signal processing tasks associated with the IP software radio.

Function	Avg. cycles	Unit
FSK modulation	12	Output sample
FSK demod.	75	Input sample
De-framing	23	Output bit

The de-framing actually consists of two operations, locking on to the framed IP packets, and de-framing and parity checking each byte to produce a stream of bits which represents the transmitted IP packet.

These metrics allow us to assess how well the modules perform relative to real time. For example, the 12 cycles required to produce an output sample corresponds to 0.06 μsec of actual time. The samples are being output every 0.25 μsec (the period of the 4 MHz clock), so this module not only runs in real time, but leaves plenty of cycles available for other processing. However, the current implementation of the demodulator requires 0.375 μsec to process each input sample, so it can only maintain real-time throughput for input sampling rates of 2.6 MHz or less. For sampling rates less than 2 MHz, the entire system system currently runs in real time on a Pentium Pro-200 under the Linux operating system. With improvements in the demodulation algorithms and use of parallelism such as Intel's MMX instruction set, we expect to significantly reduce the number of cycles required by each processing module, thus increasing the data rates that can be handled in real-time. Continuing improvements in processors will also facilitate the processing of wider bandwidth signals, or provide more free cycles which could be applied to applications running simultaneously.

5. Opportunities

This section discusses the opportunities that arise from both the dynamic reconfigurability of a software-based approach, as well as those presented by the set of tools provided by a general purpose media processing environment.

5.1. Media transformations

The software intensive approach of virtual devices allows media to be dynamically transformed between domains. A simple example of media transformation is used commonly in closed captioning for television. The captions are encoded on the video stream in the VBI lines, and at the receiver, the video lines are converted back to text. In this case, the original text information was transformed into a video representation to facilitate transmission over existing channels. At the receiver, this information is then transformed back to its symbolic form to allow for additional processing.

Ultrasound signals provide a more sophisticated example. The waveform from the ultrasound probe can be digitized and represented as a stream of sampled data. This media stream is often transformed to a sequence of images for display. Once this information is in the image media domain and accessible to software processing, the power of computer vision and pattern recognition algorithms can be brought to bear on the problem. These tools allow more detailed information to be extracted from the media stream.

Media transformation is a very powerful operation that allows the tools from one domain to be applied to another. The transformation decisions can be based on information extracted from the stream itself, as the software has access to the media as well as the ability to convert payloads from one media type to another as required.

5.2. *Leveraging memory*

Networks, operating systems and applications each manipulate data in discrete units of different size, and none of them are designed to deal with continuous streams of data. Networks segment data into units such as IP packets or ATM cells, operating systems handle incoming data in memory pages and buffers, and applications deal with data in larger units such as video frames. In order to process continuous streams of data, the stream must be *temporally decoupled*, i.e., the incoming stream is segmented and each segment is time-stamped. Instead of preserving exact timing throughout the system, we need only observe relatively coarse timing constraints, provided the timestamps are later used to reconstruct the signal timing near the edge of the system, i.e., at the display, speaker or D/A converter.

Temporal decoupling frees algorithms from tight synchronous processing restraints and opens up opportunities for new algorithms for data processing. Samples can be processed out of temporal order, delaying the processing of some samples until certain other information has been received. In cases where, the processing requirements of sample payloads vary with time, it may be possible to *time-shift* processing resources from one payload to another. For example, the reception of a wireless signal that is subject to bursty noise may require little processing when the noise is not present, but may require a more computationally intensive algorithm when the data is corrupted by a noise burst. The amount of processing can be varied dynamically and the resources saved can also be applied to other applications.

5.3. *Leveraging computation*

Even within the same media type, computational requirements can vary depending upon the application. Image processing applications work with the same media sources (e.g., a camera) as video player applications, and thus the bandwidth requirements are similar. However, image processing applications such as face finding [8] require significantly more computation than simply capturing the data and assembling it into video frames.

Desktop processors can exploit parallelism by using their 64 and 128 bit wide buses, pipelining and multiple instruction paths to increase the available computational power per sample. Multimedia extensions to processor instruction sets allow algorithms to take advantage of parallelism at the register level. These instruction sets, offered by both Sun (VIS) and Intel (MMX), perform parallel operations by packing multiple samples into one longer word. For example, by packing four 16 bit words into one 64-bit register, one MMX instruction can perform four simultaneous 16-bit adds. These enhancements, coupled with parallel processor configurations, will enable fairly extensive processing of wideband signal streams.

As the available computation power has increased, signal processing applications such as codecs and modems have followed a migration path from analog hardware, through dedicated digital hardware, to programmable digital hardware, and finally to software. Each step along the path introduces more flexibility into the signal processing system. This flexibility brings with it many opportunities to leverage computation in support of: new algorithms, new applications, and multi-modal combinations of media types.

5.4.   Leveraging networks

A network of workstations provides a natural distributed environment for virtual devices. In such an environment, the sensors or actuators can be located remotely from the processing sites, since state of the art networks are capable of handling the required data rates. This allows workstations to have access to multiple remote sensors, or to take advantage of distributed parallel processing to process sample streams from the sensors.

A network-based sensor is a relatively simple device since it does not have to process the signal it captures. Figure 9 illustrates the network-based transducer concept. The device, consists of an application-specific transducer, minimal amplification and filtering, an A/D converter, FIFO, and a PLA-based network interface.

Network-based appliances extend the reach of multimedia systems to remote sensing and control. For example, several different types of medical sensors could be connected via a network to the same computer. Information derived from one signal could be utilized in the processing of another. If a sensor detecting the patients respiration pattern were connected, then this information could be used to remove respiration induced baseline drift from the EKG signal.

For radio applications, multiple network-based RF antennas could be used to form small cells for wireless communications systems, or to achieve antenna diversity so that signals from multiple antennas can be used to reduce multipath interference.

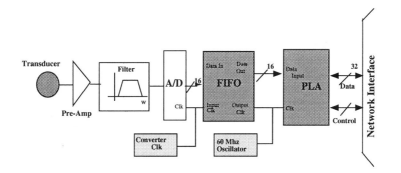

Figure 9.   Network-based appliances.

6. Conclusion

We believe that the time has come to broaden the domain of multimedia systems to encompass any type of information that can be digitally sampled and processed. This approach makes new types of media accessible to the desktop environment, extending the capabilities of media processing systems in several dimensions:

- The transformation of information between media domains creates new opportunities for the extraction of signal features and for the storage and display of information streams.
- There is an opportunity to develop new software-based, temporally decoupled signal processing algorithms that take advantage of the instructions set extensions and large amounts of memory available on commercial platforms.
- Communications ability is enhanced by providing direct access to signals in the RF and infrared domains. These media bring a wide range of broadcast and point-to-point communications methods under the control of desktop applications.
- The network-based approach facilitates distributed computing by permitting access to remote sensing and control devices and by providing access to clustered hosts for parallel processing of sample streams.

Moving the A/D boundary as close to the raw information source as possible, and moving the software boundary right up to the A/D conversion increases the flexibility and adaptability of multimedia systems. This approach, coupled with the use of mainstream platforms, allows virtual devices to ride the processor technology curve. Each new generation of technology will bring new media types and new applications within our grasp.

Acknowledgments

The authors would like to thank the many individuals who have influenced and contributed to the development of our testbed: Mike Ismert and Brett Vasconcellos for their work on some of the testbed components; the original developers of the VuSystem; and in particular Bill Stasior for his helpful advice and guidance. This research was supported by the Advanced Research Projects Agency under contract No. DABT-6395-C-0060 (monitored by US Army, Fort Huachuca) and by equipment grants from Sun Microsystems and Intel Corporation.

Notes

1. For the remainder of the discussion, we restrict ourselves to the commercially available converters, as we will be evaluating them with respect to commercially available processors and networking technology.
2. Measurements were made using the cycle counter on a Pentium Pro-200 processor.

References

1. E. Amir, S. McCanne, and M. Vetterli, "A layered DCT coder for internet video," in International Conference on Image Processing, 1996.
2. Ivan A. Getting, "The global positioning system," IEEE Spectrum, pp. 36–47, Dec. 1993.
3. Henry H. Houh, Joel F. Adam, Michael Ismert, Christopher J. Lindblad, and David L. Tennenhouse, "The VuNet desk area network: architecture, implementation, and experience," IEEE J-SAC, Vol. 13, No. 4, pp. 710–721, May 1995.
4. Mike Ismert, General Purpose PCI I/O Specification. http://www.tns.lcs.mit.edu/izzy/gppi.ps.
5. Raymond J. Lackey and Donal W. Upmal, "Speakeasy: The military software radio," IEEE Communications Magazine, Vol. 33, No. 5, pp. 56–61, May 1995.
6. Christopher J. Lindblad and David L. Tennenhouse, "The VuSystem: A programming system for compute-intensive multimedia," Journal on Selected Areas of Communication, 1996 (to appear).
7. Sharon E. Perl and Richard L. Sites, "Studies of Windows NT performance using dynamic execution traces," in Second Symposium on Operating Systems Design and Implementation, pp. 169–183, Oct. 1996.
8. Henry A. Rowley, Shumeet Baluja, and Takeo Kanade, "Human face detection in visual scenes," Technical Report CMU-CS-95-158R, School of Computer Science, Carnegie Mellon University, 1995.
9. Lawrence C. Stewart, Andrew C. Payne, and Thomas M. Levergood, "Are DSP chips obsolete?" Technical Report CRL 92/10, Cambridge Research Laboratory, Cambridge, MA, 1992.
10. David L. Tennenhouse and Vanu G. Bose, "The SpectrumWare approach to wireless signal processing," Wireless Networks, Vol. 2, pp. 1–12, 1996.
11. Bruce Tuch, "Development of WaveLAN, an ISM band wireless LAN," AT&T Technical Journal, pp. 27–37, July 1993.
12. T. Turletti, "H.261 software codec for videoconferencing over the internet," Technical Report 1834, INRIA, Jan. 1993.

INDEX